PRAISE FOR *Lincoln*

"Reshaped my view of our most rever... biographies of both Lincoln and Ada..., tells this story with precision and eloquence."
—Mary Ann Gwinn, *Seattle Times*

"What we have is a complicated tale that, thanks to this book, can be more clearly understood, and its similarities with today's imbroglio will fascinate the reader."
—*Washington Times*

"Anyone who wants to understand the United States' racial divisions will learn a lot from reading Kaplan's richly researched account of one of the worst periods in American history and its chilling effects today in our cities, legislative bodies, schools, and houses of worship."
—*St. Louis Post-Dispatch*

"*Lincoln and the Abolitionists* is a nuanced study of Presidents Abraham Lincoln and Quincy Adams. With his unmatchable credentials as a historian, Kaplan demystifies President Lincoln's role as a great emancipator of black slaves. . . . A necessary and very important book on President Abraham Lincoln."
—*Washington Book Review*

"Kaplan successfully unearths another president, John Quincy Adams, as the real force behind the movement that would end in Northern victory. . . . But by contrasting the Great Emancipator with his fervent abolitionist predecessor, Kaplan shows Lincoln for what he was: complicated, calculating, accommodationist."
—Vulture

"This is a must for readers looking for an insightful look at two American presidents."
—Bookish

"In this insightful, often disturbing dual biography, [Kaplan] makes a convincing case that Adams, working decades before Lincoln, was the real hero. . . . An eye-opening biography from a trusted source on the topic." —*Kirkus Reviews* (starred review)

"Kaplan has published acclaimed biographies of both Lincoln and John Quincy Adams, and his knowledge of both frees him to tell their intertwining stories with clarity and concision. . . . Kaplan does not build up one man at the expense of the other, but shows how both helped liberate our country from a horrifying institution." —*Booklist*

"Elegantly written and thoroughly researched." —*Publishers Weekly*

"[Kaplan's] arguments about Adams's foresight into slavery's violent end will find many takers. Kaplan effectively demonstrates how moral courage must be the true measure of leadership." —*Library Journal*

ALSO BY FRED KAPLAN

John Quincy Adams: American Visionary

Lincoln: The Biography of a Writer

The Singular Mark Twain: A Biography

Coffee with Mark Twain

Gore Vidal: A Biography

Henry James: The Imagination of Genius

Charles Dickens: A Biography

Thomas Carlyle: A Biography

Sacred Tears: Sentimentality in Victorian Literature

Dickens and Mesmerism: The Hidden Springs of Fiction

Miracles of Rare Device: The Poet's Sense of Self in Nineteenth-Century Poetry

LINCOLN *and the* ABOLITIONISTS

John Quincy Adams, Slavery, and the Civil War

FRED KAPLAN

NEW YORK • LONDON • TORONTO • SYDNEY • NEW DELHI • AUCKLAND

HARPER PERENNIAL

A hardcover edition of this book was published in 2017 by HarperCollins Publishers.

FIRST HARPER PERENNIAL EDITION PUBLISHED 2018.

Designed by Bonni Leon-Berman

Library of Congress Cataloging-in-Publication Data has been applied for.

ISBN 978-0-06-244002-0 (pbk.)

HB 12.12.2019

TO FRIENDS LONG ENOUGH TO BE LIFELONG

Leslie Epstein, Edward Geffner, David Kleinbard,

Carol Molesworth, and Charles Molesworth

CONTENTS

PREFACE

Our sixteenth president is often either vilified or deified, his great strengths exaggerated, his flaws minimized or disregarded. Since the assassination that transformed him into a martyr, it has been nearly impossible to see Lincoln plain, almost as difficult as Robert Browning remarked it was to see "Shelley plain," the Romantic poet whose early death had made him a legend rather than a man.

Lincoln was of course born into a world that shaped him. He was not originally a mythologized face on Mount Rushmore, the perfect president who freed the slaves and saved the Union. He was in no rush to free any slaves at all. He believed the slave problem would best be solved by voluntary deportation, known as colonization. One of the legacies of emancipation would, he feared, be a hundred years or more of volatile racism. As a minority president, he found himself backed into a corner by secession, a corner from which he reluctantly took the Union to war to save it. The South started the war to save slavery. The North fought it to keep the Union intact. Like many Americans, Lincoln believed the war would be short. He never imagined it would be as devastatingly long as it turned out to be. The South would, he hoped, relent, or its armies be defeated quickly. Slow to realize no peaceful solution or wartime compromise possible, he stumbled in his choice of strategies, mostly because he misjudged the South, partly because of his ameliorative personality.

Lincoln had no specific plan for postwar reconstruction and national reunification. Whatever he may have attempted if he had lived was likely to have been no more successful, however, than what followed his death.

Southern racism was too deeply entrenched ever to have acquiesced in civil rights for blacks without bitter resistance. It's unlikely that if Lincoln had not been assassinated, America's racial history would have been a better one. The conflict between state sovereignty and federal authority, differing interpretations of the Constitution, and the belief, deeply embedded in white America's psyche and laws, that the United States was exclusively a white man's country would have persisted, regardless of Lincoln's longevity.

Early in the nineteenth century, John Quincy Adams, our sixth president, had become convinced that slavery would destroy the Union. Slavery would be ended, he came to believe, only through a civil war. The emancipation schemes his contemporaries proposed, including voluntary immigration of free blacks and emancipated slaves to a nation of their own, seemed to him impractical and unjust. He refused to support the American Colonization Society. Lincoln, who also abhorred slavery as a moral crime, put all his hopes in the Colonization Society. Adams thought it absurd to suppose that free blacks would immigrate voluntarily to Africa or that slave owners would ever cooperate in emancipation. Convinced that slavery would not be the rock against which the nation split, Lincoln believed the South would not succumb to the folly of secession. Adams knew the Southern mind better, having observed its uncompromising, quasi-violent character day after day in Congress from 1833 to 1848. By temperament and willful self-delusion, Lincoln hoped (until the reality was forced upon him) that good sense and the "better angels of our nature" would prevail. Over time, slavery would be eliminated peacefully. Adams never believed that possible. There were no "better angels."

As political philosophers, these two presidents, our most literate, forward-looking statesmen of the nineteenth century, held similar views about how to guide America toward a prosperous future. Both belonged to the Whig Party that existed from 1832 to 1856. At first a Federalist, then a National Republican, Adams, after 1832, aligned himself with the segment of the National Republicans that morphed into the Whig Party. Yet he always kept his distance from whatever party he had an association with. At heart, he detested parties and party politics. Lincoln was always a party man, at first a Whig and then one of the Republican Party's leading founding members. Adams worked mostly from the outside, by personality outspoken and a radical; Lincoln from inside, a consensus politician who met his destiny when conciliation was no longer possible. On matters of policy (a national bank, paper money, trade, education, infrastructure, manufacturing, and the proper balance between federal and state power), they were, with the exception of how to deal with slavery, entirely in agreement.

That exception is the focus of this book. Its why and how illuminate much about Lincoln and the crosscurrents of his life and times. Both Adams and Lincoln were antislavery moralists. Lincoln, unlike Adams, never became an antislavery activist, even when a brutal civil war forced him to take action against slavery. Adams envisioned a multiracial America as inevitable. Long before his death he became deeply sympathetic to abolitionists and abolitionism. Lincoln distrusted abolitionism. Though he believed slavery a moral abomination incompatible with American principles, and looked toward its eventual elimination, he desired that all blacks residing in the United States immigrate to a land of their own. He worried that the attempt of the two races to occupy the same country would lead to a century or more of racial conflict.

Different as they were by background and temperament, Lincoln and Adams had much in common. Both were masters of English prose, Adams in the classical style of the late eighteenth century into which he had been born, Lincoln in the colloquial style of common speech that became the hallmark of modern American prose. Though they diverged on the issue of antislavery activism, both had an abiding commitment to the dynamic interaction among literature, character formation, and public life. Lincoln and his favorite newspaper, his hometown *Sangamo Journal*, admired everything about Adams except his outspoken antislavery activism. Abolition and abolitionists were the third rail of national politics for Whig newspapers and politicians. As a personality and writer, Adams had one foot in the eighteenth century; Lincoln, one foot in the twenty-first. In their own time and on slavery and racism, they meet, diverge, and illuminate each other. Surprisingly, on these issues, Adams is more a citizen of the twenty-first century than Lincoln. Their lives also overlapped. Congressman Lincoln was in the hall of the House of Representatives when, in February 1848, Congressman Adams suffered a fatal stroke. Interweaving their direct and indirect relationship, especially on the most controversial issue of the first half of the nineteenth century, reveals a dynamic relevant to our past and present. Mutually complementary, Adams and Lincoln, in their differences and similarities, represent the richness of the American experience and the complicated challenge of leading a divided country. They also, together, testify to the long-standing and complicated historical relationship between leadership and moral self-definition.

This book approaches these two extraordinary leaders through numbers of overlapping emphases. It opens with Adams in 1837 and Lincoln in 1841: how they experienced slavery and race. It highlights the murder of Elijah Lovejoy, the "first American martyr," and Lincoln's and Adams' reactions to it. The story dramatizes Adams' radicalization and Lincoln's moderation about slavery; Lincoln's coolness towards abolition and abolitionists; and why Adams rejected and Lincoln embraced colonization. It dips back into their origins of parentage and place: the New Englander and the border state Southerner; then into the challenge of Louisiana and Haiti in 1790, 1804, and 1828. Its supporting cast of characters is colorful, from the obscure to the famous: Dorcas Allen, Moses Parsons, Violet Parsons, Theophilus Parsons, Phoebe Adams, John King, Charles

Fenton Mercer, Philip Doddridge, David Walker, Usher F. Linder, and H. Ford Douglas have little modern presence; Elijah Lovejoy, Francis Scott Key, William Channing, Wendell Phillips, Rufus King, Hannibal Hamlin (Lincoln's first vice president), and even James Buchanan and Andrew Johnson, the two presidents on either side of Lincoln, rise to the level of being somewhat better known; in contrast, Abigail Adams, John Adams, Henry Clay, Stephen A. Douglas, and Frederick Douglass hold honored places in the American historical memory. The subject of this book is, of course, slavery and racism, Lincoln as an antislavery moralist who believed in an exclusively white America, and Adams as an antislavery activist who had no doubt that the United States would become a multiracial nation. Its narrative includes Texas and the Mexican War; Adams and Lincoln as colleagues in the House of Representatives; Adams' death in Lincoln's presence; the slavery extension controversy and "popular sovereignty"; the dramatic Democratic convention in Charleston in 1860; the nomination of Andrew Johnson in 1864; and Lincoln, slavery, emancipation, black soldiers, and the Civil War.

This is a book in praise of Adams and Lincoln. Their achievements were immense. Yet the praise is better highlighted if the reality is honored. It demeans the man and his situation to simplify Lincoln. He was "the Great Emancipator" in a limited sense only. And by using a historically inaccurate wish fulfillment version of Lincoln, we make the burden heavier on other presidents, including candidates for the presidency in our own time. The mythologized, ahistorical Lincoln is an impossible standard. No one can measure up to it, not even Lincoln. He was a great president, despite his limited vision and his conciliatory politics; despite his inability to embrace some version of abolitionism; despite his fixation on colonization; despite his belief, almost to the end of his life, that America should remain a white man's country; despite his mistakes as commander in chief, especially his attempt to bribe the South back into the Union and his counterproductive efforts to keep the border states from breaking away; and, most of all, despite his willingness to buy union at the cost of perpetuating slavery indefinitely.

Circumstances beyond Lincoln's control determined a series of momentous events for him and the nation. They also determined the degree to which he could become an active agent of change. To his immense credit, when faced with disunion, he drew a number of practical and moral lines in the interest of which he was willing to take great risks. The first was the nonextension of slavery into the territories. Abolitionists could, understandably, think this so little as to be almost contemptible. But given who Lincoln was and what he faced politically, it was important enough to have significant consequences. The second was that military force was required to keep the Union intact. Faced with secession, he decided to resupply Fort Sumter, though there was reason to believe the Confederacy would respond with force, initiating armed conflict. And faced with the likelihood that the war would be prolonged excruciatingly or even lost, he at last, in 1863, decided on partial emancipation. And when he finally found the right generals and gave up his efforts to bribe the border states, he also discovered the courage, born of desperation, to commit himself to black manpower to strengthen his army and weaken the Confederacy.

For John Quincy Adams, all this would have seemed a recognition of the inevitable. For abolitionists such as Wendell Phillips, William Lloyd Garrison, Frederick Douglass, and H. Ford Douglas, Lincoln's journey toward the place they had long occupied seemed painfully slow. That he would not have arrived there had he not been forced by circumstances beyond his control to confront the abyss does not, however, detract from the courage it took to do it. White America had no desire to shed blood or pay money to emancipate slaves. Lincoln had to find ways, halting, difficult, and indirect as they were, to take white America down the road of what became total war and, eventually, total emancipation. At the end, he well knew that this extraordinary accomplishment had left the country with a damaging reality, an almost fatal wound: the difficulty of reconciliation between North and South, between anti-black racism and white America. Eight million bitterly resentful white Southerners would be forced to co-exist with four million ex-slaves whose freedom they deplored and whose liberators they detested.

> *Three hundred thousand Yankees is stiff in Southern Dust.*
> *We got three hundred thousand before they conquered us.*
> *They died of Southern fever and Southern steel and shot.*
> *I wish they was three million instead of what we got.*
>
> *I can't take up my musket and fight them now no more,*
> *But I ain't gonna love them, now that is certain sure.*
> *And I don't want no pardon for what I was and am.*
> *I won't be reconstructed, and I don't care a dam.*

The result: the failure of reconstruction; the virtual re-enslavement of most Southern blacks; Jim Crow; the civil rights movement; and the still existing post–Civil War hangover of widespread racial prejudice. In April 1865, in Ford's Theatre, Lincoln knew that he had saved the Union and ended slavery, but also that the racism underlying slavery was widespread and powerful. When he died, he had no solution for this reality, and he knew that his beloved country had entered into a century and more of racial misery. The racism that he feared would dominate black-white relations, white America's unwillingness to share power with what it believed to be an inferior race, would have characterized the United States even if he had remained president until March 1869: Jim Crow would still have become the new Southern reality; the North would eventually have looked the other way; the white knights of the Ku Klux Klan would have raised their torches as they rode, burning and lynching in the night; the march across the bridge at Selma would have been in America's future; Ferguson and Dallas still would have happened. The racist alt-right and white nationalist movements would have arisen. I don't think that this hypothetical Lincoln, melancholy and pessimistic by nature, leaving office after eight wearying years, would have been a happy man. Of course, happiness was not in his nature, but it was not in the historical reality, either.

ONE

A Continual Torment

On a blessedly cool early morning in late October 1837, after what had seemed an endless Washington summer, seventy-year-old congressman and ex-president John Quincy Adams, having recently returned to the nation's capital from his Massachusetts home, opened his morning newspaper. The advertisement he read in the *National Intelligencer* startled him. It was headed "Sale of Slaves": a mother and two of her children, the property of James H. Birch, a well-known slave dealer, were to be auctioned at four o'clock that afternoon by Edward Dyer, auctioneer and corn merchant. It riveted his attention.

A man named Rezin Orme had incorrectly certified that five slaves he had sold to James Birch in August were "sound in body, and in mind." Soon after Birch purchased Dorcas Allen and her four children, the mother had murdered the two youngest "in a fit of insanity, as found by the jury who consequently acquitted her." Birch now requested that Orme repay the $700 he had paid him for Allen, her four-month-old, seven-year-old, and nine-year-old girls, and a four-year-old boy. If Orme refused to repurchase the slaves, including the value of the two dead children, the mother and her two surviving girls would be offered to the public.

Immediately putting down his newspaper, Adams went to see his brother-in-law and neighbor, Nathaniel Frye. "I asked Mr. Frye what this advertisement meant. He seemed not to like to speak of it, but said the woman had been sold with her children, to be sent to the South and separated from her husband; that she had killed two . . . by cutting their throats, and cut her own to kill herself, but in that had failed; that she had been tried at Alexandria for the murder of her children, and acquitted on the ground of insanity; and that this sale now was by the purchaser at the expense of the seller, upon the warranty that she was sound in body and mind." The seller was a local resident, Frye explained. His net worth had been badly reduced by the depression ravaging the country. Desperate to turn his assets into cash, he had sold Allen and her children to Birch.

Dorcas Allen's trial and acquittal in early October had made national news. Preoccupied with his attempt to prevent the House of Representatives from excluding antislavery petitions and with the politics of the financial crisis, Adams missed the story. He soon learned more of the gruesome details. "HORRIBLE BARBARITY," the *Alexandria Gazette* had announced on August 24, 1837. "On Tuesday night last, a black woman . . . committed a most barbarous and unnatural murder, by seizing and strangling her two infant children, one about four, the other about two years of age. She also attempted to murder her other two children, who are much older and stouter than the two killed, by beating them in the face and on the head with brick bats . . . by which they were horribly mangled . . . the dress and person of the unnatural mother herself clotted with gore, and the walls and floor of the room covered here and there with the blood of her innocent offspring."

At her trial, Allen had claimed that she was not a slave. Was there any truth to that? Adams wondered. And how was it possible that the mother and her children were being resold when her acquittal on the grounds of insanity made her valueless as a slave? Was there some way to prevent the sale from occurring? Could the disagreement between Orme, who refused to return the $700, and Birch, who wanted his money back, be straightened out in a way that redeemed Birch's investment without a sale, perhaps by a subscription that raised money to free Allen and her children? Were there any legal complications? What was the woman's status now? Probably, Adams thought, she was still a slave, but who would buy her after the acts she had committed? What potential purchaser would not worry that she might become violent again?

John Quincy Adams had lived on and off in the nation's capital for much of the second half of his life, a U.S. senator from 1803 to 1808, secretary of state from 1817 to 1825, the sixth president of the United States from 1825 to 1829, and now a member of the House of Representatives. For six months of the year he lived in slave-free Massachusetts; the rest, in the northernmost large slave city in the country. Everyday life in Washington had an overwhelming black presence. Adams had witnessed, during his father's presidency, slaves build the White House. Four of the first five presidents—Washington, Madison, Jefferson, and Monroe—had brought slaves with them to staff it. Slaves attended Southerners living in or visiting Washington. In most middle-class and elite homes, in hotels and restaurants, in the streets, wherever a building was being erected or any physical work being done, a black population did all the backbreaking and some of the skilled labor.

Deeply hostile to slavery, Adams found its presence painful. He struggled to contain his anguish. Slave auctions were held almost daily close to where he lived. Traders imprisoned slaves in hotel rooms or local jails, paying a daily fee, or in privately owned holding pens. When a slave lot was large enough to make transport profitable, it would be shipped south, usually from Alexandria, the seaport hub for slave activity. Since 1832, Adams' harangues and maneuvers in Congress against the gag rule, which forbade any discussion of slavery, had outraged his Southern colleagues. There was a price to be paid for attacking the slavery establishment. Yet slavery was, he believed, a national wound and a catastrophe waiting to happen. The nation's capital, he observed, was where the nation's fault lines met. He could hardly walk or ride on its streets without being aware of the mistreatment of Negroes. And he had already had, over the years, numbers of encounters with the nastiness of slavery. His New England conscience had been put to the test. In Philadelphia, he had recently had "long conversations" with Benjamin Lundy, the Quaker abolitionist. "He and the abolitionists generally are constantly urging me to indiscreet movements," Adams wrote in his diary, "which would ruin me and weaken and not strengthen their cause."

When Adams was born in 1767 there were a small number of black slaves in Quincy and Boston. By 1803, when the young U.S. senator came to Washington, slavery had been abolished in Massachusetts. Free blacks, in modest numbers, formed a small part of the Boston community. In vision-searing contrast, the nation's capital depended for its daily bread on slave labor. It also had a sizable population of free blacks. When Adams, returning in 1817 from eight years of diplomatic service in Europe, took up his duties as James Monroe's secretary of state, he became inextricably a part of a slave society. Dissent was unavailing; protest counterproductive. The governing class accepted that slaves cooked its meals, washed its clothes, cleaned its homes, drove its carriages, and existed according to the codes and regulations that kept them without legal or civil rights. Like his parents before him, John Quincy refused to keep slaves, though slaves indirectly provided services to his household. In Washington, he himself employed only free blacks, as did a small number of Washington residents, mostly New Englanders and Quakers.

On an evening in late October 1820, the chargé d'affaires of the French embassy appeared at the secretary of state's F Street home. His black cook had been imprisoned, accused of having two checks that a shopkeeper had dropped in the street. They had been found by "a mulatto boy of fourteen." Unable to read, the boy took the checks to a shop to find out what they were. "Tortured, thumb screwed, and hung by the neck . . . to extort confession from him," he implicated the father of the chargé d'affaires' cook. The chargé d'affaires claimed that diplomatic privilege protected his cook. When Adams consulted "the list of persons attached to the French legation furnished, according to the law of Congress, to the Department of State," her name did not appear on it. "This is a sample," Adams wrote in his diary, "of the treatment of colored people under criminal charges or suspicions here." He ordered his State Department clerk to inform the magistrate "that this woman was in the service of the French legation" and for that reason should be released immediately. He could do nothing for the mulatto boy.

In early April 1824, a year before he became president, a friend came to him "about a negro woman" named Jenny, who belonged to Adams' sister-in-law Nancy Hellen. The daughter of a Maryland slave-owning family, Nancy wished to sell Jenny to Kentucky-born Ninian Edwards. A slave owner from Illinois, Edwards, the former governor of the territory, had just resigned his seat in the Senate to become the first American minister to Mexico. A border state Southerner, Edwards embraced his Kentucky roots and the legitimacy of slavery. His eldest son was to marry Mary Todd Lincoln's sister, another son to serve in the Lincoln administration. Jenny "has several Children," Adams wrote, "one an infant of about 6 Months, and another two years old. This last Mr. Edwards would not take [to Mexico]; and they were about separating her from that and all her other Children except the infant. . . . Mrs. Hellen was determined to sell them all, and to save [Jenny] from being separated from her Children." Adams "interposed to prevent" the sale, promising "to make good what they should sell for less than 200 dollars, the condition of Sale being that they should not be sold out of the District. Mr. Cook however now informed me that this stipulation though often made is easily, and frequently evaded."

NOW, AS he left home on the morning of October 23, 1837, Adams was preoccupied with Dorcas Allen's situation, as if he were in some way responsible, though he had no connection to it. He assumed that the sale that afternoon would resolve the matter. "It is a case of conscience with me whether my duty requires or forbids me to pursue the inquiry in this case—to ascertain all the facts and expose them all in their turpitude to the world." He felt uncertain, but it was his duty, he had decided, to oppose slavery, an injustice that, he believed, was a threat to the existence of the Union, to whose continuation he gave the highest priority. In Congress, the Southern representatives, certain that they and the Constitution were being betrayed, had made their position clear: no slavery, no Union. Adams believed that "the prohibition of the internal slave-trade is within the constitutional power of Congress, and, in my opinion, is among their incumbent duties." He had gone further: "I have gone as far upon this article, the abolition of slavery, as the public opinion of the free portion of the Union will bear, and so far that scarcely a slave-holding member of the House dares to vote with me upon any question." Early in the year, he had almost been censured by his colleagues for his introduction of antislavery petitions in defiance of the gag rule.

Before he took action in the Dorcas Allen case, he needed to obtain the available facts. Walking to the office of the *National Intelligencer*, he called on one of its editor-owners, his friend William Seaton, but he learned nothing more than what Nathaniel Frye had told him, and Seaton responded reluctantly. Probably Seaton had little desire to have the former president involve himself, even if only in a personal capacity. He added to Frye's account "that there was something very bad about it, but without telling me what it was." Adams went about his usual business, including a visit to an old friend, the recently widowed Dolley Madison, who had resumed her residence in Washington. Having assumed that the contesting parties would have settled the matter, he was startled the next morning to see an advertisement for the sale of Allen and her children. At Dyer's auction house, he found them "weeping and wailing most piteously." They had not been sold, the auctioneer told him. Actually, he explained, they had been sold to Dorcas' husband, Nathaniel Allen, a free

Negro who worked as a waiter at Gadsby's Tavern and who had "bought them in" for $450. But since Nathaniel Allen had been unable to raise the money, they were up for sale again. What could Dyer tell him, Adams asked, about Dorcas Allen's history and the facts of her crime and trial?

She was indeed a slave, Dyer assured him. She had been owned by Mrs. Anna Davis of Georgetown. Davis' husband, when she was dying, promised to free Allen. He did so in practice but not in law. Dorcas Allen had assumed she was legally free. Another interested party, whom Adams knew, joined the conversation: Francis Scott Key, the U.S. district attorney for the District of Columbia, an Andrew Jackson partisan, a fervent Democrat, a political appointee, and a slave owner. A longtime Washington operative, Key—the brother-in-law of Roger Taney, Chief Justice of the United States—had prospered as a lawyer, real estate magnate, and Jackson administration beneficiary. He had been one of the founders of the American Colonization Society. A proponent of selective manumission and an opponent of abolition, he believed voluntary deportation the solution to the slave problem. In the nation's capital, where his patriotic poem from the War of 1812 was widely sung along with "Hail, Columbia," Key was defined by his politics, his views on slavery, and his career as a defense lawyer and district attorney.

The Allen case caused Key almost as much concern as it did Adams. He wanted it to go away, and the best way to get it out of the popular press would be for Dorcas and her children to be released from the cycle of slavery. But how would Nathaniel Allen get the money needed to purchase her? There was an additional complication: who actually owned Dorcas Allen was still in question. Anna Davis' widower, Gideon Davis, had, in 1821, married again. His widow, Maria, in 1836, had married Rezin Orme, who then sold Dorcas through Dyer's auction house to James Birch. From Rezin Orme's point of view, his wife had owned Dorcas Allen. With his wife's permission, he had had the right to sell her. But Adams and Key now discovered that Gideon Davis had in fact died insolvent. So, his creditors had had first call on his estate. Allen and her children were part of that estate, not the property of Maria Davis, now Mrs. Rezin Orme. Consequently, Rezin Orme had had no right to sell Allen and her children to Birch, who consequently had had no right to sell them at auction. When Adams asked Dyer by what authority he had sold Allen and her children, the story further unraveled. Dyer had done so exclusively by Birch's authority, trusting "to his word." Since Orme had disappeared, could Birch prove that he had legally bought the Negroes, and could Orme, if he could be found, prove that he had had the right to sell them? Adams and Key worried that they could not. "Here, then, is another danger to which these unhappy beings are subjected," Adams wrote in his diary. Even if Nathaniel Allen could raise the money to purchase their freedom, they could still be "reclaimed" into slavery by Davis' creditors.

It seemed unlikely to Key and Adams that the claimants would ever materialize. So, if Rezin Orme were to repay Birch $700, which seemed unlikely, or Nathaniel Allen pay Birch $450, all the parties could, with different degrees of satisfaction, go about their business without further troubling themselves. And the abolitionists, who would otherwise make hay with the case, would be held at bay. Birch would lose $250, not his entire $700. Having fled to Maryland to take refuge from the claim against him, Orme would keep his money. Key could continue his colonization enthusiasm. Adams could feel he had accomplished something. Dorcas Allen could resume her life as if she were a free person. And there would be no further publicity about a series of legal and moral crimes.

That afternoon, at City Hall, Adams consulted his cousin William Cranch, the chief justice of the District of Columbia District Court, who read his trial notes to Adams. "The evidence of [Allen's] killing" the two children was incontrovertible. The defence was insanity. But there was "not the slightest evidence of insanity at the time, except the mere fact of her killing the children. There was evidence of her being subject to fits . . .

that she is passionate and violent, and sometimes violent in her talk. The jury acquitted her as insane. . . . Upon being asked why she had killed her children, she had said they were in heaven; that if they had lived she did not know what had become of them; that her mistress," whom she held responsible for her not being manumitted, "had been wrong" not to make sure that it had been done. "Her mistress was a Methodist; and so she was herself." Rezin Orme was also a Methodist. So were all the white people in the chain of Allen's slave provenance. Since the Methodist Church condemned slavery and slave ownership, Dorcas Allen had believed that her religion and the promises made to her would give her and her children safe haven in this world and in the hereafter.

The next week, a distraught Nathaniel Allen appeared at Adams' doorstep. He was finding it difficult to raise the $450. Adams offered a $50 contribution to the subscription fund, "to be paid if the sum be made up to complete the purchase." Though he wanted Dorcas and her children freed, he had reason to worry about their uncertain legal status, even if they were liberated from Birch. And it seemed unlikely that Allen could raise the additional money. "It is very doubtful," he wrote in his diary, "whether I have not imprudently engaged myself in this matter." But there was not much time to lose. Dyer was again advertising that Allen and her children were for sale. Nathaniel Allen "came again about the contribution to purchase his wife and children, which he finds it very difficult to accomplish," though he was getting closer. General William Smith, a well-known resident of Georgetown, "had agreed to endorse the balance of the sum . . . but the doubt remains whether they will be emancipated." Adams held back his $50.

Two days later, Allen once again came to Adams' door, this time with his wife. Having agreed to take the $450 as payment in full, Birch had remitted Dorcas to her husband's custody. He had, though, kept two of the girls to ensure that the full sum would be paid. "I told him that whenever the bill of sale should be ready I would give the check for fifty dollars which I had promised." When Allen returned later in the day with the assurance that General Smith was "entirely satisfied with the validity of Birch's title, and that he had the right to make the sale," Adams "gave him the check . . . payable . . . to Walter Smith, Esq., or his order, and told him when the affair should be completed to bring me the bill of sale, that I may see it. I could pursue the question of Birch's title no further," Adams concluded, "without becoming liable to the imputation of shrinking from my own promise and prevaricating upon the performance of my engagement." He still doubted "the legality of the sale to Birch." If "Birch's title should be disproved, they would still be slaves. . . . Such is the condition of things in these shambles of human flesh that I could not now expose this whole horrible transaction but at the hazard of my life. Any attempt to set aside the purchase for illegality would be stigmatized as mean and dishonorable. Iniquity must have its whole range." The law and the Constitution were hostile to the suffering of almost four million people.

A year later, Adams rose to his feet in the House of Representatives to respond to an anti-abolition speech. He had not forgotten James Birch. Perhaps the member of the House from South Carolina, Adams told the nation, does indeed believe that slavery is beneficent.

> *But he does not know the cruel, the tyrannical, the hard-hearted master. He does not know the profligate villain who procreates children from his slaves, and then sells his own children as slaves. He does not know the crushing and destruction of all the tenderest and holiest ties of nature which that system produces, but which I have seen, with my own eyes, in this city of Washington. Twelve months have not passed since a woman, in this District, was taken with her four infant children, and separated from her husband, who was a free man, to be sent away, I know not where. That woman . . . killed with her own hand two of her children, and attempted to kill the others. . . . The woman was asked how she could perpetrate such an act, for she had been a woman of unblemished character and of pious*

> *sentiments. She replied, that wrong had been done to her and to them; that she was entitled to her freedom, though she had been sold to go to Georgia; and that she had sent her children to a better world. . . . I was a witness to it.*

Personal witness had deepened and enriched moral conviction and republican principle. Yes, "I am well aware," he told his colleagues, "of the change which is taking place in the moral and political philosophy of the South. I know well that the doctrine of the Declaration of Independence, that 'all men are born free and equal,' is there held as incendiary doctrine, and deserves Lynching; that the Declaration itself is a farrago of abstractions. I know all this perfectly; and that is the very reason that I want to put my foot upon such doctrine; that I want to drive it back to its fountain—its corrupt fountain—and pursue it till it is made to disappear from this land, and from the world."

SIX YEARS before joining Adams in the House of Representatives, thirty-two-year-old Abraham Lincoln stepped aboard the steamboat *Lebanon* to begin his return trip from Lexington, Kentucky, to his home in Springfield, Illinois. It was Tuesday, September 7, 1841. His height and dark complexion, and the prominent lines on his slanted, beardless face, made him rivetingly noticeable. Accompanied by his closest friend, Joshua Speed, he had been visiting the Speed family plantation, Farmington, near Lexington. Lincoln and Speed had become friends four years earlier. Lincoln had accepted Speed's invitation that he share Speed's bedroom above the Springfield general store, which Speed half-owned. Good-looking, well-groomed, well-dressed, and well-educated, Joshua was the son of a wealthy slave-owning family who adored him and whom he adored. Lucy Speed, Joshua's recently widowed mother, had welcomed Lincoln at the family's 550-acre hemp plantation. Any friend of her son's was a friend of the family. Every comfort or luxury that sixty slaves and extensive gardens could offer was at his disposal. A domestic slave was assigned exclusively to attend to the guest from Illinois, and Lincoln ate Southern-style meals in a bountiful summer, including "delicious dishes of peaches and cream" he long remembered. He enjoyed the company of Joshua's half-sister, Mary. Noticing that the gaunt man from Springfield seemed depressed, Lucy gave him a Bible, "the best cure for the 'Blues,'" if only he could benefit from it. The agnostic Lincoln could not.

He spent some of his time in the Lexington law office of Joshua's older brother James, with whom he talked at length "about his life, his reading, his studies, his aspirations. . . . He was earnest, frank, manly, and sincere in every thought and expression," James later wrote. They talked about slavery, an obsessive topic for James. An active state legislator, he was traveling the difficult road of a pro-union, antislavery Southerner who struggled for much of his life with the reality that most of his fellow Kentuckians feared and, like Lincoln, opposed abolition. And with the problem that much of the Speed family wealth resided in those 550 acres and the sixty slaves, each worth on average about $800, about $1.5 million in today's money. The brothers probably knew that, in 1837, Lincoln had coauthored a resolution in the Illinois legislature stating that the "institution of slavery is founded on both injustice and bad policy." Congress had the power, the resolution maintained, to abolish it in the District of Columbia, though abolitionism, the authors concluded, was as great an evil as slavery.

At James Speed's office, Lincoln was in sight of the largest, most active slave market in Kentucky. On court days, crowds gathered in front of the Fayette County Courthouse, where traders sold their wares at the "Cheapside Auction Block." Jails and holding pens were close by. This was not a new sight to Lincoln. He had seen slavery in one of the country's most vivid cities when, in the spring of 1831, at the age of twenty-two, he had been in New Orleans and "saw Negroes Chained—maltreated—

whipt and scourged," though what he exactly saw and felt in New Orleans comes through testimony many decades later, from an often unreliable witness. Yet he indeed also saw slavery in Springfield, Illinois, where it was legal until 1848, though in semi-disguised forms and in small numbers. Lincoln was a regular visitor in the few Springfield homes where there were slaves.

No record exists of what mental stratagems Lincoln employed during the month in which he lived on a slave plantation, attended to around the clock by household slaves. Field hands toiled long hours in easy sight. An amiable man, Lincoln had a talent for accommodation. He did not criticize the Speeds for owning slaves. He never argued about slavery with them or with any individual slave owners. The mind-set that dominated his approach to slavery in the next two decades seeps through his Lexington experience: the South was as much a victim of history as the North; the institution was to be tolerated, with emancipation a distant goal, as long as slavery remained sanctioned by the Constitution and restricted to the South. Speed and his parents were "not enemies, but friends."

Leaving Farmington, Lincoln boarded the aptly named *Lebanon*. On board were twelve slaves, "chained six and six together . . . like so many fish upon a trot-line," he later wrote to Mary Speed. Shipped by a slave trader to be sold in Natchez or New Orleans, or already purchased by one or more plantation owners, they would be put to work in the expanded cotton fields of the Deep South, where slaves were in greater demand than in Kentucky. They were "being separated forever," Lincoln wrote, "from the scenes of their childhood, their friends, their fathers and mothers, and brothers and sisters, and many of them, from their wives and children, and going into perpetual slavery where the lash of the master is proverbially more ruthless and unrelenting."

In 1841, Lincoln seems to have made the distinction between slaves who were treated humanely and slavery as dehumanizing bondage. How long these slaves had been in Kentucky, whether they were local or imports from Maryland or Virginia, he could not know. He may not have had any thoughts at all about their origin. But he was not ignorant of the geographic, economic, and moral complications of the slave trade. And he would know that the Speeds bought and sold slaves. Writing to Mary Speed, he began his account of what he had seen with a comment about human nature, as if it were important to stress a philosophic overview. In the Deep South, he acknowledged, "the master is *proverbially* more ruthless" than masters in Kentucky and in the border states, but "a fine example was presented on board the boat for contemplating the effect of *condition* upon human happiness." As the *Lebanon* made its way down the Ohio River, one of the slaves, Lincoln reported, "played the fiddle almost continually; and the others danced, sung, cracked jokes, and played various games with cards from day to day. How true it is that 'God tempers the wind to the shorn lamb,' or in other words, that He renders the worst of human conditions tolerable, while He permits the best, to be nothing better than tolerable."

Fulfilling the conditions of his generalization, Lincoln was tempering his own response, making "the worst of human conditions tolerable." He may have been unaware that "some traders tried to lift the spirits of their bondservants, and thus reduce the risk of resistance, by forcing them to sing, dance, or listen to an instrument," and that slaves in chain gangs had ample motivation to pretend to be happy. They would want to make their guards less wary about plans to escape or at least avoid the punishment that recalcitrant slaves provoked. Were there women and children in this slave caravan? Lincoln does not reveal what he saw in full or fully felt, nor what he saw but declined to mention to Mary Speed, nor what he chose not to see. The philosophic tone and overview are characteristic. So, too, is the artful language.

Fourteen years later, in 1855, Lincoln could not afford to look the other way to the extent that he did in 1841. His political needs and the politics of slavery had changed considerably. Yes, he admitted in a letter to Joshua Speed, he would, like most of his antislavery contemporaries, tolerate slavery in the South until some long-term solution could be found. The Constitution required that. The preservation of the Union depended on it. But he and other Northerners would not allow, if it could be prevented, the spread of slavery to the Western territories and the new states, from Kansas and Nebraska to California; and they would oppose the reinstitution of slavery in the territories obtained from Mexico. In order to keep peace between the South and North, they would, with reluctance, enforce the Fugitive Slave Law of 1850, though "I hate to see the poor creatures hunted down, and caught, and carried back to their stripes, and unrewarded toils; but I bite my lip and keep quiet." In response, Speed granted that slavery was wrong in the abstract. But he would rather have the South leave the Union than give up its right to own slaves. No one is asking you to give that up, Lincoln countered. The only line drawn in the sand was that slavery must not be extended to the territories.

How sharply was Lincoln biting his lip on the trip from Louisville to St. Louis in 1841? "You may remember," he wrote in 1855, that "there were, on board, ten or a dozen slaves, shackled together with irons. That sight was a continual torment to me; and I see something like it every time I touch the Ohio, or any other slave-border. It is hardly fair for you to assume, that I have no interest in a thing which has, and continually exercises, the power of making me miserable. You ought rather to appreciate how much the great body of the Northern people do crucify their feelings, in order to maintain their loyalty to the constitution and the Union." Much had happened to Lincoln and in his world since 1841. He was to continue to hope until 1861 that the South would maintain its "loyalty to the constitution and the Union." And in his inaugural address, he appealed to "the better angels of our nature," though there were no "better angels" to hear him. Joshua and James Speed, in border state

Kentucky, retained their commitment to the Union. But much of the South was not listening, and it had decided not to bite its lip but to fight.

FOR THREE months, from December 1847 to late February 1848, a young congressman and an old congressman—one a novice from Illinois, the other an ex-president; one a self-educated Midwesterner, the other a Harvard graduate; both brilliant masters of the English language—voted in each other's presence in the House of Representatives. They voted against a war they hated and an institution they detested: the Mexican War and slavery. Abraham Lincoln was thirty-nine years old; John Quincy Adams was eighty. It's not possible to know whether, in the three months during which they sat in the same large hall, they spoke to each other. Adams stood close by when Lincoln and other newly elected congressmen were sworn in by the Speaker of the House. Moments before, Adams, famous and venerated, had been given the honor of swearing in the Speaker. No one in that room could escape Adams' presence and voice. In the drawing for seats, Lincoln, unluckily, drew number 191, which earned him a seat far at the rear of the chamber. Adams' "name was early drawn, and I took the same seat which I have occupied for the last ten years," he later wrote. "No other member having manifested the disposition ever to take it, though certainly one of the best seats in the House."

What degree of awareness Adams had of the freshman congressman is unknown, but he was likely to have taken notice of the resolutions Lincoln introduced on December 22, 1847, soon after arriving in Washington for the opening of the Thirtieth Congress. Lincoln called on Congress to require that President James Polk answer a series of questions, referred to as "spot resolutions," about the origin of the Mexican War. Had the Mexicans or the Americans initiated hostilities? Both Adams and Lincoln believed that the United States had been the aggressor. The rules of the House required that resolutions be "laid over." This meant that they could be called up on another day, when someone chose to do so. No one did. A self-confident, self-righteous, and aggressive slave owner from Tennessee, Polk may not have been aware of Lincoln's resolutions. He had moved up the ladder of party politics to find himself the last-ditch compromise candidate of the Democrats in 1844. He had barely beaten the Whig candidate, Henry Clay, whom Lincoln venerated and campaigned for. On every vote of significance, Adams and Lincoln voted the same way: against Polk's Mexican War, in favor of abolishing slavery in the District of Columbia, and to provide federal money for national infrastructure.

Though they had never been in each other's presence before, Lincoln had had a long relationship with Adams and knew a great deal about him. Lincoln was fifteen when Adams became president in 1825, twenty-three when he became the most famous member of the House of Representatives, and in his late twenties when Adams became a nationally prominent opponent of slavery. In 1828, Lincoln would not have been old enough to vote for Adams' re-election—living with his parents in Indiana, he had turned nineteen that February, when the voting age was still twenty-one—but he was already a political partisan. "We had political discussions from 1825 to 1830," a friend recollected, "the year Lincoln left for Ills. We attended them—heard questions discussed—talked Evry thing over and over." In 1828 they would have talked about Andrew Jackson against Adams. In his early years, another of Lincoln's friends recalled, "say from 1820 to 1825," Lincoln "was tending towards" Jackson's party, the Democrats. "He afterwards Changed—Parties at this time ran Jackson—Adams and others." The young Lincoln, who loved humorous and satirical political songs, may not yet have renounced Jackson when he sang, probably in 1824, "let ould acquaintance be forgot / and never brout to mind / and Jackson be our president / and adams left behind." But in the election of 1828, had he been of age, he would have voted for Adams.

In 1832, when ex-president Adams was elected to serve in Congress, twenty-three-year-old Lincoln had recently moved to New Salem, Illinois, in Sangamo County (later Sangamon). He worked against Jackson, who was running for a second term, and voted for Henry Clay, the candidate of the newborn Whig Party, the leader to whom and the party to which the young Lincoln now committed himself. In the year that Lincoln moved to New Salem, Jackson had stared down South Carolina, which had proclaimed that states had the right to nullify laws passed by Congress. On this issue, Lincoln agreed with Jackson, Adams, and Clay. Nullification was an abomination. The Constitution was a permanent pact. Yet he disagreed with Jackson on every other major issue. As a young Whig, he was already committed to Clay's and Adams' vision of America's future: the Bank of the United States should be rechartered; there should be a national monetary policy and a tariff to protect American industry; federal funding should help build roads and canals, and dredge rivers and harbors; the federal government should support education, technology, and science; the Constitution should be broadly interpreted as a living document; slavery should be eliminated from the District of Columbia; and all the states should someday be free of human bondage.

Lincoln had ample opportunity to follow state and national politics. An avid newspaper reader, he also served as the New Salem postmaster from 1833 to 1836. The postmaster could read what he pleased and then pass along the item to its intended recipient. Lincoln read the classical canon, Shakespeare, Byron, and Burns. They taught him about life, character, human nature, and poetic language. But he also read the *Louisville Journal*, the *St. Louis Republican*, the *New York Telescope*, and the Washington *National Intelligencer*. These provided an education in topical politics, political issues, and political rhetoric. Louisville had a presence in New Salem and a stronger presence in Springfield. So, too, did St. Louis. Later, Lincoln subscribed to the *National Intelligencer*, the premier Whig newspaper, of which "he was a warm admirer," and which published long extracts from congressional debates and speeches. He had ample opportunity to read Adams' words. And articles from the *National Intelligencer* were frequently reprinted in other newspapers he read.

There were some local New Salem and Springfield subscribers to the *Congressional Globe*, the official record of congressional activities. In late 1835 the obscure postmaster wrote to its publisher, "Your subscriber at this place . . . is dead; and no person takes the paper from the office, Respectfully, A. Lincoln P.M." In Springfield, to which he soon moved, the *Globe* provided the text of reference for discussions of congressional activities. A controversial presence in House debates, Adams often hand-delivered the texts of his speeches to the *Globe* offices. It published many in full, sometimes in special editions that went to its subscribers. Lincoln read, in full or in excerpts, in the *Globe*, the *National Intelligencer*, and other newspapers, what Adams had to say about the political issues of the day.

Lincoln's most regular source of news was the weekly *Sangamo Journal*. For over thirty years, he was a loyal reader. Distributed in every town in Sangamo County, the paper began publishing almost at the time Lincoln came of age, four months after he settled in New Salem. He and the *Journal* matured together, a sympathetic fit. In 1834 he acted as its business agent in New Salem, its masthead briefly listing his name. He frequently published in its columns under his own name and anonymously, in addition to reading it every week. It was the news source that he went to first throughout his Illinois life. And for all his Springfield life, its office, not far from his own home, was another home to him. Its editors were his friends and supporters. It was at the *Journal* office that he nervously waited for the results of the election that made him president.

Like all newspapers of that era, it was unabashedly partisan. So, too, were its readers, and it would be hard to find a political view published in the *Sangamo Journal* with which Lincoln would not have agreed. Its news columns, especially its frequent accounts of congressional debates on the issues of the day, were deeply infiltrated by its Whig editorial positions: it opposed slavery, rejected abolition, supported colonization, advocated federal support for infrastructure, endorsed Whig candidates, and looked to Congressman John Quincy Adams as a uniquely moral voice in national politics and a living link to the Founding Fathers. Stories about and references to Adams appeared regularly. The newspaper felt "a conscious pride" in his words and achievements.

IN EARLY 1832, Lincoln published his first article in the *Journal*. For bread, he worked as a clerk at Denton Offutt's general store in New Salem. There was no New Salem newspaper, and Offutt advertised his wares in the *Journal*, which carried advertisements, local and foreign news, agricultural instruction, state and local political news and announcements, and long excepts from and sometimes entire speeches by the political luminaries of the day. Lincoln had an announcement to make: he was a candidate for the Illinois House of Representatives. His well-written and humorously humble announcement took its conventional place in the *Journal*, which published many similar announcements. Probably Lincoln hand-delivered it to the newspaper's office in Springfield on the day on which he wrote it. The editor, Simeon Francis, was soon to became a friend, a supporter, and a publisher of Lincoln's editorials, letters, and occasional pieces, some of them anonymous. Lincoln soon had authorial stars in his eyes, a possible career or at least avocation as a writer. His announcement of candidacy was unusually good copy for this pedestrian genre. It had a distinctive stylistic touch.

When, on April 22, 1832, Lincoln left New Salem, to try his hand at soldiering in the Black Hawk War, he may have just read or even had with him the April 19 issue of the *Journal*. If so, he would have read a laudatory article about one of the newspaper's two great heroes, John Quincy Adams. The other was Henry Clay. Having just taken up his seat in a Congress controlled by his political enemies, Adams had been, to his dismay, appointed to the Committee on Commerce. He had expected to be appointed to the Committee on Foreign Relations. The pro-Jackson majority and its Speaker took some satisfaction in putting down Adams, whom they had never expected to see in the halls of power again. The *Journal* understood this to be the petty insult it was. It took the opportunity to refer "readers to the discussion" of "Mr. Adams' motion in the House of Representatives," praising Adams' "talents, patriotism, and moral purity." He "possesses a greater moral power than any other man in the nation." Adams was to turn insult into advantage. Over the next few years, he used the committee as a platform to launch his minority report on commerce and manufacturing, a widely read, praised, and influential anti-Jackson essay that became the touchstone for Whig views on the economy. The *Journal* was delighted and paid close attention.

If Lincoln missed this issue of the *Journal*, it seems likely that he caught up on back issues when, in mid-July 1832, he returned to New Salem. The May 3 issue had left Lincoln's name out of the list of eight candidates for the state legislature "who were on the frontier periling their lives in the service of their country." Someone had noticed the omission, perhaps Lincoln, or at least someone attentive to his interests. The *Journal* happily published a correction. It had omitted, the editor wrote, "by accident the name of Captain Lincoln, of New Salem." There's little reason to believe that Lincoln, except when away from Springfield, ever missed any issues of the *Journal*. Like most authors, he particularly savored every issue in which his own prose appeared. As visitors often noticed and his wife deplored, he would often, at home or in his office, stretch his long legs out from a chair or stretch himself out on the floor with a newspaper in his hands, riveted to what he was reading. Like most newspapers of the day, the *Journal* published weekly letters from its Washington correspondent and long extracts from congressional debates and speeches. Lincoln had many opportunities to read Adams' own words.

Years later, when Lincoln had his first actual sight of Adams, he already would have had a visual image in mind. In March 1833 the *Sangamo Journal* contained a vivid, worshipful pen portrait of Adams from an anonymous letter writer. It extended physical description into moral and historical touchstones. "To avoid the crowded scene of the senate I repaired to the House of Representatives," the narrator wrote, "and there found John Q. Adams on the floor, speaking against the reduction of the Tariff on imported goods." There were, the writer noticed, a few members gathered around Adams and listening intently.

> *To the left and behind him sat a knot of Nullifiers, lounging carelessly on the seats and conversing loudly, to the great annoyance of the House. Mr. Adams is a stout, well-set man, about 60 or 62 years of age, with a pale complexion and bright dark eyes, from one of which frequently drops water. His head is bald—his voice is tremulous and broken, but clear—he stands erect, and has a manly appearance, by his gestures, he suited the action to the word; and he raised his hands (which shake a little with age) in the most impressive manner. He quoted the opinions of Washington, Marshall, Hamilton, Henry, and a host of other patriots—showing that the great object in forming the Constitution—its whole spirit and language, proved that it was formed for the whole people of the United States—to bind the states together as one nation. . . . I have never seen, and never again expect to see, anything so touching and impressive as the eloquence of Mr. A. on this occasion; his appearance was more than human, and his eloquence more than reason. On returning from the House through the Rotundo, I cast my eye on Trumbull's painting of the declaration of independence; I there marked his father, standing with a bold and graceful mien, defending human rights—much like his son on this trying day.*

The *Journal*'s readers had in hand Adams' warning the previous week to the nullifiers and the nation: "Should a conflict ensue," he told Congress, "and South Carolina be unaided by any other State, which I can hardly believe, it will require an immense expenditure of blood and treasure to enable [South Carolina and its friends] to succeed against us. We may be exterminated, but subdued—never!" Lincoln was not in Congress when Adams spoke these prophetic words, but it seems likely that, as a devoted *Journal* reader, he read them. And if he missed this issue or this column, he would have had many other opportunities to read similar warnings and predictions. To what extent did they stay in his strongly retentive memory? Impossible to say. He was, though, over time, to develop a train of similar evidence, logic, and conclusions, with the same touchstones—the Founding Fathers, the Declaration of Independence, the Constitution, and the Northwest Ordinance—and also to argue that the United States was an undissolvable Union: nullification and arbitrary secession were illegal. Unlike Adams, Lincoln was to maintain until the last possible moment that "we are not enemies, but friends." By birth and affiliation, and especially in personality, his approach differed; and his timing, position, and context, despite similarities, were significantly different from those of 1833. His challenge was very different from Adams'. As a congressman, Adams could only speak and vote. Lincoln was forced to act, and inaction would be action of its own kind. But the principles were the same.

While the *Journal* proclaimed the achievements and distinction of "the most remarkable man of his age," as it described Adams in October 1835, the hyperpartisan newspaper had two reservations. The great man was not entirely trustworthy when it came to political allegiances. He was "possessed of a mind stored with learning—vigorous, active and energetic,—he has acquired undisputed laurels in the walks of literature . . . he has searched into the hidden recesses' of science—weighed the problems of the mathematician—communed with the poets and philosophers of former days . . . an advocate at the bar—a debater in the Senate Chamber—a foreign ambassador—at the head of the Department of State—and raised to the highest station in the world. In each of these spheres of action, the powers of his great mind were brought to sustain him." He never deviated from what he believed to be right. "Confiding in the strength of his own powers, he has invariably sustained his opinions and actions, with arguments at once logical and apparently irresistible." But he was neither always friendly nor always loyal to those who had supported him. He was not a party man. He was too independent. He had turned on former friends, his voice and tone acerbic, denunciatory. He could not be trusted to function effectively in a national party effort such as was demanded of all Whig loyalists as the election of 1836 approached.

Quoting at length the words of the *Missouri Republican*, the *Journal* feared that Adams actually would support Martin Van Buren rather than Henry Clay. "We shall not be surprised if, at the next session of Congress, Mr. Adams brings his talents and influence to bear in favor of Mr. Van Buren, as a northern man,—one who would foster the interest of the North, and one who would check the influence of southern 'machinery.'" In fact, Adams did nothing of the sort, and Van Buren was as much a Southern as a Northern man. Adams quietly supported Clay, partly because, as a former president, he hesitated to be overtly partisan in a presidential election, and mostly because he did not wish to be associated fully with Clay's conservative views on slavery and colonization. In a fervently partisan political culture, the *Sangamo Journal* and Lincoln demanded absolute loyalty to the Whig cause.

Neither Lincoln nor the *Journal* shared Adams' detestation of partisan politics. It was not part of their DNA. For Whig interests to ascend, elections on every level had to be won, power attained, particularly in Congress and the presidency. Adams had to face only his Massachusetts constituency. And he was not someone who could help Whig candidates win elections in most parts of the country, including Illinois. As much as the *Journal* lauded what Adams had been to the nation throughout his career and continued to be on many issues of importance to the Whigs, particularly the tariff, the national bank, infrastructure, education, the annexation of Texas, the right of petition and debate, and slavery as an immoral institution, there was a divide between the *Journal* and Adams that could not be crossed. It was an unbridgeable divide for Lincoln also. That was abolition.

With few exceptions, almost entirely in the Northeast, no Whig candidate for high elective office could hope to be elected if he supported abolitionism. It was acceptable to oppose slavery on moral grounds, to be an antislavery moralist. It would be politically fatal to advocate immediate or even imminent emancipation. That was a semi-fantasy to be fulfilled sometime in the far distant future. On this topic, Lincoln and the *Journal* could have no use for Adams. On every other issue of importance to Whigs, Adams was a presence. On the immorality of slavery, the *Journal* quoted Adams; on abolition, hardly at all. By the late 1830s and early 1840s, Adams semi-disappears from the *Journal*. And despite all the public policy positions they have in common, Adams makes only a few appearances in Lincoln's letters, speeches, and essays—so few that the absence is striking.

Like most of his contemporaries in the country as a whole and especially in Illinois, whose southern and central sections were most like Kentucky, Lincoln believed that America was for white people; that abolition would greatly increase the free black population; that black labor would drive down white wages; that the white and the black races were not compatible; and that the best hope for an all-white America was encouraging, through assistance and exhortation, as many blacks as possible to return to Africa. Lincoln sincerely believed this. As is often the case, sincerely held beliefs and political expediency merged. Abolitionism as a national doctrine was widely unpopular, sometimes violently opposed. But it had made enough inroads in Massachusetts so that it was not an automatic kiss of death, especially for a politician of Adams' stature. Free blacks in Massachusetts, though often discriminated against, had most of the same legal rights as white citizens. Adams believed that blacks in America, slave and free, were here to stay. Lincoln, at that time in his life, did not.

When, in March 1837, Lincoln co-introduced in the Illinois legislature a resolution condemning slavery as immoral, he knew where both he and the *Sangamo Journal* stood on slavery and abolition. They deplored and opposed *both*: they believed that the Constitution allowed the national government to control slavery, preferably with the consent of its residents, *only* in the District of Columbia. Otherwise, wherever slavery already existed, it was legally untouchable. It could be deplored but not altered. The Constitution prevented that. And, as Lincoln well knew, abolitionism was, for any Whig, the third rail of politics. To touch it meant death. He was interested in higher office, not political suicide. And most of the citizens of the Midwestern states strongly opposed any civil rights for free blacks, a state matter. As a candidate for office, Lincoln, as did the *Journal*, opposed Illinois free blacks having the right to vote or to sit on juries or to testify against white citizens, and he opposed marriage between mixed-race couples. He fully embraced Illinois' discriminatory black code. On January 6, 1836, he voted, the *Journal* reported, with the 35–16 majority in the Illinois legislature: "Resolved, That the Elective Franchise SHOULD BE KEPT PURE FROM CONTAMINATION BY THE ADMISSION OF COLORED VOTERS."

TWO

The First American Martyr

On the night of November 7, 1837, in the Mississippi river town of Alton, a Christian minister of the Presbyterian faith, a thirty-five-year-old man of medium height, muscular and broadly built, with a dark complexion and blacks eyes, found himself with a rifle in hand in a stone warehouse. He was a proponent of nonviolence. But an armed mob, fueled by alcohol and anti-abolitionist bravado, was attempting to set the warehouse on fire. They wanted to destroy a printing press placed there for safekeeping. It had arrived the night before by riverboat from Cincinnati. The Reverend Elijah Parish Lovejoy, editor of the *Alton Observer,* had already had three presses destroyed, one in St. Louis, where he had edited the *St. Louis Observer,* and two in Alton. In each case, a mob had broken the press into pieces. In Alton, the pieces had been tossed into the river.

The minister with the gun was not alone. About nineteen armed men had rallied to his mission: to prevent the replacement press from being wrecked. In the darkness, voices rose from about two hundred men: Give us the press! Then: Burn them out! Shots were fired toward the warehouse, quick small flashes of red-and-yellow light. Shots from inside retaliated, apparently not aimed at anyone in particular. The message: the press would not be given up without a fight. There was a cry in the darkness. A man in the surging crowd had been killed. A ladder topped by a flaming torch began to rise toward the warehouse roof.

ELIJAH PARISH Lovejoy's roots were in New England. Born in 1802, in the part of Massachusetts called Maine, he was the son of a pious mother and a Congregationalist minister. In 1827 the well-educated young man left to pursue a mission. He had been offered a teaching position in the nearby Baptist academy, Waterville College, where he had been a star student. An excellent Latinist, he was put in charge of his mentors' Latin school. He did not feel, though, spiritually prepared. His training had provided him with Christian beliefs, but he felt an absence in his heart. When his college mentor advised him to go west, he packed his bag and went in search of a promised land where he might find himself and fulfill his mission to make his fellow citizens better Christians through education. The best way to do that, he believed, would be to found a school to teach Christian ethics.

In the spring of 1827 the young man sailed to Boston. He then walked to New York, where he sold newspapers door-to-door, earning enough to keep himself alive. He then walked to Illinois. Soon he headed for St. Louis, a raucous, slave-based frontier city of about six thousand people. The premier river city north of New Orleans, it was a chaotic, semi-anarchic avenue to the South. It was also the gateway to the West. Commerce was king. Its fountain of life, the Mississippi, flowed by with steady determination. Its junction with the Missouri welcomed flatboats journeying toward the Rockies. Its waterfront was the most energetic west of the Atlantic, except for the Crescent City, seven hundred miles south. It was also a tense, rough town with a volatile mixture of businessmen, brokers, traders, gamblers, prostitutes, riverfront toughs, slaves, slave owners, free blacks, immigrants from the East Coast, Catholics from European countries, and a Protestant middle class of various denominations attempting to create traditional institutions and civic respectability. Two sets of groups competed for power: the Irish- and German-Catholic majority and the minority Protestant establishment; and the few antislavery advocates against the slave-favoring and slave-holding majority. To the Methodists, Baptists, and Presbyterians, Catholics were un-American heathens; Protestantism was inseparable from patriotism. To the proslavery majority, abolitionism was a deadly disease, spread by infected Easterners.

When he arrived in St. Louis, Lovejoy was not an abolitionist. In principle, he was opposed to slavery. He hoped that one day it would come to an end through Christian persuasion. He assumed that, in the meantime, most masters would treat their slaves kindly. He did, though, have strong political views. A Whig in the making, he supported the presidency of John Quincy Adams and Henry Clay's "American System." When Andrew Jackson became president in 1829, Lovejoy opposed his anti-Indian and anti-bank policies. Washington, D.C., seemed to Lovejoy a cesspool of unchristian behavior, a government run by exponents of the spoils system, who made party loyalty the ultimate standard. Lovejoy joined the cohort of those who demanded reform of individual and communal vices. Reform societies were sweeping from east to west: against intemperance, swearing, Sabbath breaking. He joined the Missouri and Illinois Tract Society, distributing hortatory pamphlets and preaching biblical fidelity. Committed to personal and public reform, he attended lectures by visiting preachers, and supported the formation of a Lyceum Society.

When, in August 1830, the publisher of the *St. Louis Times*, an anti-Jackson newspaper, offered Lovejoy its co-editorship and half ownership, he accepted. He wanted a public voice and a larger audience. But no matter how strongly he editorialized that Jackson and the Democrats were defiling the civic temple and advancing policies that undermined the prosperity of the nation, his instincts and training told him that individual souls had to be saved before the soul of the nation could be redeemed.

Yet textbook salvation and redemption seemed irrelevant, overly abstract theological concepts. His editorials seemed stale Christian pieties. Spiritually restless, he searched for something more. He found it in January 1832. A charismatic visiting preacher at St. Louis' First Presbyterian Church moved him deeply. Like many others, Lovejoy responded to the power of the new approach to religious experience preached by the most famous revivalist of the day, Charles Finney, and his cohort of itinerant preachers. It was time to illuminate the ancient Puritan darkness with new light. America was not a place for theological gloom, for the doctrine of election, which claimed that only the chosen could enter heaven. Everyone could be saved, Finny preached. Good works were essential, and Christian duty required a commitment to reform. First came conversion, the lighting of the inner light: Jesus was your personal savior. Then came the obligation to encourage individual conversion and national reform. Lovejoy began to see himself as a saver of souls, with a message.

But what would that message be? And how could he best prepare himself to communicate it? Conversion was far from enough. His Christian duty was to make the world a better place. He would, like Finney, use his voice and pen to illuminate souls and teach public piety. He felt, though, insufficiently prepared. In early spring 1832, he enrolled in the Princeton Theological Seminary in New Jersey, the nation's premier orthodox Presbyterian school. He stayed for a year and a half, concealing that he had hardly any interest in theology and that he had already rejected Calvinism. He was tacitly taking sides in the first stage of a divisive battle in the Presbyterian world. It would be won in the next few decades by the anti-Calvinists and their vision of an America in which Christians pursued moral justice and social reform. Ordained as a minister in 1833, he tried his hand as a guest preacher in Newport, Rhode Island, and then in New York City. When he got a letter from a group of St. Louis Presbyterians urging him to edit their reform newspaper, he felt called. The paper would promote "religion, morality and education." It would "exert an influence in favor of the benevolent institutions of the age." It would speak his language. "They are impatiently calling me to the West," he wrote to his brother Owen, "and to the West I must go."

When Lovejoy arrived in St. Louis in September 1833, the newly founded *St. Louis Observer* and its editor had at best a minor presence. The paper, founded to advance "Christian politics, the diffusion of religious intelligence, and the salvation of souls," proclaimed in its masthead "Jesus Christ and Him Crucified." A wealthy Presbyterian banker and a small number of paid subscriptions financed its existence. Lovejoy supplemented his income by itinerant preaching for the American Home Missionary Society. At best, each job was exhausting, a nonstop schedule that had him editing, writing, and responding to angry readers splitting theological hairs, orthodox Presbyterians versus new-light Presbyterians. For half the week, he traveled alone on primitive roads to preach in rural towns. His preaching converted no one. The newspaper had little influence. Its weekly formulaic Presbyterian pieties were irrelevant, as Lovejoy realized, to moral reform and to the larger life of St. Louis.

When, on a Sunday in October 1834, Catholic St. Louis celebrated, drums beating, cannons blasting, the consecration of its first cathedral, Lovejoy objected. It was a profanation of the Sabbath, an insult to God and true Christianity, the building itself a visual representation of the threat to American values posed by this foreign religion. Filled with righteous energy, he elevated what had been his mild anti-Catholicism into an all-out attack on the Catholic faith. To his supporters who advised a more temperate tone, he editorialized that "we believe the cause of Truth" demands attacks on this alien ideology, "the Mother of Abominations." The Catholic community responded furiously. Threats came orally and in writing. Lovejoy was "a slanderer, a calumniator, a libeller." Warned that he had gone a step too far even for his supporters, that he might be attacked physically, he embraced the danger. Though essentially a pacifist, he was happiest when engaged in warfare in the service of God. Like most religious newspapers of the time, the *Observer* mixed religion with politics. Sectarianism required political action, and St. Louis elections pitted Catholic Democrats against Protestant Whigs. Lovejoy insisted at the start of his editorship that he would "studiously avoid giving occasion of offence to any. Peace will be" the aim of the *Observer* "as far as that is consistent with the defence of the Truth." Local and national laws, he believed, gave his newspaper the right to be as anti-Catholic as it liked. So did Jesus' statement that "I did not come to bring peace, but a sword." For Lovejoy, the ultimate sword was the Word.

In 1834–1835, the *Observer* published one editorial after another mincing no words about the evil of slavery. Like many Whigs, Lovejoy strongly opposed it as an evil to be condemned by all Christians. But he also opposed immediate emancipation. He had antislavery beliefs but not an antislavery agenda. Still, his vehement opposition to slavery began to seem to many of his St. Louis neighbors indistinguishable from abolition. For many pro-slavery Southerners, it was a distinction without a difference. For Lovejoy, there was a difference. The Negro, he argued, was a human being who, under God's dispensation, deserved freedom and self-determination. But eventually, not now. And gradual colonization, under the leadership of the American Colonization Society, branches of which were springing up throughout Missouri and Illinois, was desirable. It would liberate free blacks from their widespread mistreatment, preventing a likely civil war triggered by a slave insurrection. Emancipation should be gradual, with compensation to slave owners. In the meantime, it was not only necessary but desirable that slaves be treated humanely; they should be educated into literacy, especially for religious purposes; and free blacks should be treated fairly. Immediate abolition would be counterproductive, he feared. Abolitionists were intemperate radicals who might, at least in the short run, make conditions worse for the slave population.

Slowly, though, he began to see things differently. He had at first believed that slaves were treated decently. Mostly, he was not looking closely. A few incidents that became public in talk and print distressed him. When the *St. Louis Times* argued that it would be acceptable for a Sunday school that admitted Negro children to be closed by mob violence, Lovejoy objected: that would be not only lawless but unchristian. Mobs throughout the country were creating law by public opinion and force, with the tacit approval of the Jackson administration and the Supreme Court. And, Lovejoy observed, those who opposed Bible literacy for slaves were winning that argument, as Southern states, including Missouri, began instituting harsher control over all aspects of slave life. He began to read abolitionist literature and listen to abolitionist arguments. He was, by mid-1835, with hesitation, inconsistency, and qualification, becoming an abolitionist. When he editorialized that "something must be done speedily on this all-important subject," pro-slavery St. Louis concluded that it had an abolitionist in its midst. Lovejoy's nuanced qualifications seemed to his pro-slavery neighbors either purposeful evasions or outright lies. Moderates who were cool to or against slavery, including many Presbyterian supporters of the *Observer,* began to worry that Lovejoy was becoming an uncontrollable verbal incendiary. His flaming sword might result in their house being burned down. Supporters cautioned him; opponents threatened.

His lengthy columns became even more forceful. Slavery was a moral and religious evil. It would have dire consequences for the nation. He urged "gradual emancipation" on the model of the British West Indies. But what did "gradual emancipation" mean? Lovejoy meant immediate legal emancipation but with practical limitations: the master-slave relationship would be continued until the slave population was adequately prepared for freedom. Since that seemed to the pro-slavery mentality to be almost the same as immediate abolition, pro-slavery Missourians concluded that Lovejoy was an abolitionist. When copies of the *Emancipator*, America's first abolitionist newspaper, turned up in nearby Jefferson City, he was blamed, though he protested that he had had nothing to do with it. "I have never, knowingly, to the best of my recollection, sent a single copy of the *Emancipator* or any other Abolition publication to a single individual in Missouri, or elsewhere," he wrote. Few believed him. "Yet I claim the right to send ten thousand of them if I choose, to as many of my fellow-citizens. Whether I will exercise that right or not, is for me, and not for the mob, to decide. . . . I do but exercise a right secured by the solemn sanction of the Constitution." For many, this was tantamount to an admission: if he had not himself distributed the *Emancipator*, he had conspired with those who had done so. And if he hadn't done so already, he was likely to do so in the future. Obviously, he was an abolitionist. When he said that a slave insurrection was likely, his warning was widely taken as encouragement for an insurrection. Public opinion, he in turn was warned, would take the law into its own hands. Best to let the subject alone.

He would not. After delivering a fiery antislavery sermon, Lovejoy barely escaped being tarred and feathered. When he proposed a convocation of Missouri's antislavery Presbyterian ministers to support a series of antislavery resolutions, they declined. Attending commencement exercises at Illinois College in Jacksonville, invited by its president, Edward Beecher, the son of Lyman Beecher, New England's famed preacher, and the brother of Harriet Beecher Stowe, he and his views were warmly welcomed. But Beecher urged caution. He, his faculty, and their students were antislavery. But how far to go in regard to abolition? How much should public opinion and the possibility of violence be taken into account? Lovejoy was clear about where he stood on this. He desired to offend no one. He abjured violence. But the constitutional protection of free speech was the ultimate and universal shield. On this there could be no evasion, no trimming, whatever the consequences to him personally.

"I can make no compromise between truth and error, even though my life be the alternative." Religion and moral absolutism were inseparable.

THE SAME Protestant absolutism that had made him fiercely anti-Catholic had, by late 1835, made him equally absolute about freedom of the press and abolition. Though he was willing, if necessary, to be a martyr for these causes, he assumed that truth and the Constitution would prevail. But when the antislavery Missouri Presbyterian Synod rejected his pro-abolition resolutions and condemned abolitionism as an "unjustifiable course," St. Louis Presbyterians took this as justification for looking for a way to shut down the *Observer*. The *Missouri Republican* warned that "the long nights are again approaching," the rapes, murders, thefts, and fires that almost everyone, whether slave owner or not, whether pro-slavery or indifferent about slavery, believed would be inevitable if the slave population was stirred up by agitators. In October 1835, a large meeting of St. Louis' respectable citizens passed resolutions opposing civil rights for free Negroes and condemning abolitionism. Their target was the *Observer*. If Lovejoy did not silence himself on the subject or take the newspaper to a state where slavery was illegal, there would be consequences. To his critics, constitutional principle was an unsatisfactory response to threats to public safety. His claim that free speech had no legal limits, that it was a sacred right protected by the Constitution, had no currency among pro-slavery forces. He was a danger to public safety. And they had a counterargument: the Constitution protected slavery as a lawful institution.

During the last two months of 1835, Lovejoy responded eloquently. Evidence, reason, and Christian good, he hoped, would change people's minds. It was his right as an American, he insisted, to speak his mind. Free speech was sacred. The *Observer* published numerous articles on the slavery issue, including antislavery editorials in which Lovejoy continued to oppose "*immediate and unconditional emancipation*. . . . We are entirely convinced that such a course would be cruel to the slave himself, and injurious to the community at large." In the antislavery world, this was not an extreme position. In St. Louis, it was abolitionist talk. A meeting of prominent citizens told him that "the public mind is greatly excited." Would he please shut up! No, he responded: "I have sworn eternal opposition to slavery, and by the blessing of God, I will never go back. . . . We must stand by the constitution and laws, or ALL is GONE." But the free press argument had little power against pro-slavery feeling and concern about public safety. Even the *Missouri Republican*, a Whig antislavery newspaper, was critical: Lovejoy had made the *Observer* a focus of controversy that damaged the reputation of St. Louis.

The newspaper's financial backers requested Lovejoy's resignation. When they declined to make payments on a promissory note, ownership reverted to the sponsoring banker. To Lovejoy's surprise, the new owner declared that the *Observer* should continue publication with Lovejoy as editor. "Nothing could have been more unexpected to me. It was as life from the dead, as light out of thickest darkness." The new year suddenly glowed with promise. But not in St. Louis. Would he move the paper across the river to the free state of Illinois, where there existed a sizable antislavery Presbyterian clergy, and to a comparatively liberal city, Alton, dominated by Whig Protestants who would welcome his press? He hesitated. But his benefactor's question was a demand. If he refused, that would be the end of the *Observer*. The next day, he was in Alton, preparing to publish there. Then a letter arrived from St. Louis, urging him to return. His benefactor had had a change of mind. Lovejoy would have another chance in St. Louis.

Missouri, though, had little tolerance for more of Lovejoy. The previous November, he had observed that "we are getting quiet again. The Lynchites are getting ashamed of their doings. The Papists, the Irish, and the proslavery Christians finding that I am not to be driven nor frightened away, are beginning to feel and act a little more reasonably. A large majority of the Protestants in the city are decidedly with me." Eager to impose hope on recalcitrant reality, he assumed that, when he returned to St. Louis in February 1836, he could safely resume his antislavery editorials. "Our creed is that slavery is a *sin*—now, heretofore, hereafter, and forever, a sin . . . whoever has participated, or does now participate, in that sin, ought to repent without a moment's delay." He made no new converts in St. Louis.

IN LATE April 1836, Francis McIntosh, a free mulatto from Pittsburg employed as a cook in the Mississippi River steamboat commerce, objected to the attempt of two policemen to arrest two unruly sailors and helped them run off. With a legal warrant, the policemen arrested McIntosh. He would be lashed at least twenty-five times at the whipping post. Drawing a knife, he stabbed both policemen. One died immediately; the other pursued McIntosh, shouting for help, and then collapsed. A crowd of about fifty took up the chase. Caught, McIntosh was taken to jail. A large crowd then attacked the jailhouse, removed McIntosh, and carried him to a vacant lot. Tying him to a tree, they killed him. Accounts of how they killed him differ. Lovejoy's detailed report in the *Observer* describes the one feature of McIntosh's death widely agreed on: chained to the tree, while still alive and able to speak, he was set on fire. Then "a rabble of boys, who had attended to witness the horrid rites, commenced amusing themselves by throwing stones at the black and disfigured corpse. . . . The object was to see who should first succeed in breaking the skull!" It was widely agreed that the act of the mob was reprehensible, but was it excusable—and how soon could the episode be made to disappear so that St. Louis' civic reputation and commerce would not be damaged?

In mid-May, a well-connected and inventive St. Louis judge, an Irish-Catholic with the appropriately Dickensian name of Luke E. Lawless, assembled a grand jury. Who was responsible, and should indictments be brought against anyone? After a dramatic lecture-tirade about the evils of abolition and the culpability of the *Observer,* Lawless instructed the grand jury to keep in mind three things: McIntosh was a white-hating murderer who'd deserved to die, though the way he had been executed was "cruel and unusual punishment"; the good citizens of St. Louis "must already regret what they have done"; and McIntosh's "execution" differed distinctly from most other instances of mob action. It had been provoked by criminal acts. In fact, Lawless proclaimed, pro-abolitionist editorials published in the *Observer,* a copy of which he held up in court, had encouraged Negro insurrection. Thus, the *Observer* was to blame even more than the direct perpetrators. No individual had personal culpability. The grand jury would best fulfill its duty by encouraging the state legislature to pass anti-abolitionist legislation. There were no indictments.

MOST OF St. Louis breathed a sigh of relief. Lovejoy responded in late June with a blistering editorial, granting that McIntosh had deserved to die, "but not this way"; that the Court had supported lawlessness; that its pro-slavery decision was evil; that Catholicism condoned slavery; that, though he did not seek martyrdom, he would rather be "chained to the same tree as McIntosh and share his fate, than that the doctrines promulgated by Judge Lawless from the bench should become prevalent in this community." It was Lovejoy's swan song in St. Louis. He now realized he could no longer work or live there in safety. In the same issue, he announced his decision to move his printing press to Alton, though he insisted it was strictly on pecuniary grounds. That night, the *Observer* office was broken into. Files were ripped, printing materials and furniture destroyed. Oddly, the printing press itself was not damaged. Lovejoy shipped it to Alton by steamboat in late July 1836. Arriving on the Sabbath, it was held over on the wharf. Early in the dawn of the next day, a group of unidentified men seized the press, broke it apart, and shoved the pieces into the dark river.

Alton civic pride was outraged. This could be tolerated in Missouri but not in the free state of Illinois. That night, a meeting of leading citizens, gathered at the Presbyterian church, assured Lovejoy that this was not the Alton way. He was promised that a replacement press would be protected if he assured them that he was not an abolitionist. As strongly opposed as he was to slavery, he could guarantee, he told them, that he never had been and was not now an abolitionist. In fact, he felt much less inclined than ever before to discuss slavery at all. Though he reserved his right to speak freely on any topic, the *Observer* would be, he promised, primarily a religious journal. The meeting resolved that the *Observer* would receive the full protection of the law if it sustained its character as a religious journal. Lovejoy, though, had made his views crystal clear in St. Louis. The *Observer* "has kindled up a fire in Missouri that will never go out, until Popery and Slavery are extinct," he had written. "And, moreover, I hope [slavery's] very death will tell with effect upon the cause of human rights and religious liberty." The citizens of Alton would have had reason to think, whatever its editor now said, that in its second incarnation the *Observer* might also "kindle up" a fire in Illinois.

Elijah Lovejoy expected to find a home for himself and his views in Alton. He was unappreciative, perhaps unaware, of the strong pockets of pro-slavery feeling in Illinois, especially in its southern and central parts and bordering the Mississippi. Some Presbyterian ministers tacitly accepted abolitionist doctrine. Others, such as Edward Beecher, were vocal advocates, though cautious. But they were a minority in Central and Southern Illinois, where many favored leaving slavery alone. Dominated by moderate Whigs, antislavery forces worried that an abolitionist paper would incite damaging controversy. Alton had prospered in the first three decades of the nineteenth century. Its river location had attracted shipping, boatyards, warehouses, produce from the interior, and a slaughterhouse for hogs. Serviced by a mix of skilled and unskilled workers; financed and administered by investors and entrepreneurs; guided by a professional class of lawyers and doctors, a clerical establishment, and two newspapers, its businesses flourished. New England values dominated the town's leadership, though far from entirely and not on the subject of slavery. The working class feared black competition for jobs. Few residents favored civil rights for free blacks. The few black faces in Alton maintained the darkness of subservient bodies. Southern influence was strong, racism widespread. And by the late spring of 1837, the city was feeling the shock waves of the depression sweeping from the East Coast to the Midwest. The last thing Alton's governing elite wanted was an exacerbation of community tension. They had no doubt that an abolitionist newspaper would do that.

In September 1836, the *Observer*, its replacement press purchased in Cincinnati and paid for by Northern Illinois supporters, began to publish again. By the end of the year, Lovejoy, in his best high tone of rationality, moral rigor, and Christian piety, renewed his attacks on slavery: "The duty of Christians is clear: Restore the slave to HIMSELF; give him back those rights which belong to him, as he is MAN, and which cannot be taken away, without robbing both him and his GOD." At the same time, the entire nation's newspapers were focusing on a sensational variation, being enacted in Washington, of the national antislavery drama. Responding to Congressman John Quincy Adams' submission of thousands of antislavery petitions, many calling for ending slavery in the District of Columbia, the House of Representatives voted on a resolution to censure the former president. Almost every newspaper in the country ran accounts of the drama.

The *Observer* was no exception: "Let every freeman in this republic remember," Lovejoy wrote, "that so long as Slavery exists in the District of Columbia, he is himself a slaveholder, and a licenser of the horrid traffic in slaves, carried on under the very shadow of the Capitol's walls. We have a right to interfere there, and that right brings with it a solemn duty, which we may not innocently neglect. John Quincy Adams presented the petitions of more than one hundred thousand freemen last year. . . . With proper effort we can furnish thirty thousand from this state." In fact, if it had been relevant to his mission, Lovejoy also could have collected in Illinois many more than thirty thousand *pro-slavery* signatures. Many would have come from Alton and Upper Alton. Filled with reforming fervor, Lovejoy organized a Lyceum that hosted a series of debates on slavery. And he worked tirelessly through the spring to convince clergymen from around the state to meet in Alton to vote for antislavery resolutions.

By summer 1837, no one in Alton could believe that the *Observer* was exclusively a religious journal or that its editor was not an abolitionist. When, in July, the paper called for a statewide antislavery convention and the formation of an "Illinois State Antislavery Society," a firestorm erupted. Influential citizens called for an "ANTI-ABOLITION MEETING for the purpose of suppressing Abolitionism in our town." That meant Lovejoy and the *Observer*. Two evenings later a large group assembled at the Market House. They were, they proclaimed, friends of the *Observer* and of free speech. But they opposed "the arid dissemination of the highly odious doctrines of modern Abolitionism . . . which has stolen on this community in direct violation of a sacred pledge." They called on the citizens of Alton "to express their disapprobation of the course pursued by the Rev. E. P. Lovejoy . . . in publishing and promulgating the doctrines of Abolitionism, and that, too, in violation of a solemn pledge . . . when an exile he sought their protection, that he would not interfere with the question of Abolitionism, in any way whatever, and that his intention alone was to publish a religious journal." Lovejoy had lied to them.

A committee was formed to draw up resolutions: "That we, as citizens of Alton, are aware that the Rev. E. P. Lovejoy still persists to publish an Abolition paper, to the injury of the community at large, and as we deprecate all violence of mobs, we . . . politely request a discontinuance of the publication of his incendiary doctrines, which alone have a tendency to disturb the quiet of our citizens and neighbors." That its attendees abhorred mob violence did not prevent the Alton meeting from creating a statement that implicitly warned that if the *Observer* continued to advocate abolition, mob violence would result. It was a warning and a threat, similar to the resolution that had been directed against Lovejoy in St. Louis. Public opinion hardened. The *Observer* had to fulfill the purpose the town approved of, or it had to go. The message, spread in casual talk by nervous and angry people, was sometimes fueled by alcohol, bravado, and racism. In late August, three attempts were made by unidentified men to destroy the *Observer* press. The first two fell short. A mob made a third attempt. Lovejoy told them, "I am in your hands, and you must do with me whatever God permits you to do." When he solicited subscriptions for a replacement press, money came from around the country. Alton and Lovejoy were now on the national antislavery map. Six hours later, the replacement was in ruins. At least it had been a "quiet and gentlemanly mob," the disheartened mayor later said. Elijah's two younger brothers, Joseph and Owen, took to guarding him with pistols and muskets.

Edward Beecher came from Jacksonville to help Lovejoy organize a statewide antislavery society, as if this were the right time and place. At Beecher's urging, they issued an open invitation: all who supported free speech were welcome to come to Upper Alton in late October to participate in organizing the Illinois Antislavery Society. At the same time, in Springfield, twenty residents signed an open petition in support of the formation of an antislavery society. Twelve members of Springfield's Second Presbyterian Church attended the Alton meeting. When the seventy-five or so distinguished participants from Alton, Springfield, and other cities, who were attending the meeting, saw a large group of proslavery anti-abolitionists file into Alton's Presbyterian church on October 28, they were shocked. The group was led by a well-known politician from Coles County, the newly elected attorney general of Illinois.

Thirty years old, Kentucky born, articulate, ambitious, and vociferously racist, Usher F. Linder knew Illinois politics and its players, including his former legislative colleague from Sangamo county, twenty-eight-year-old Abraham Lincoln. On opposite sides of the political divide, they were to be cordial professional colleagues over the next decades: Lincoln handled Linder's cases in Sangamo County; Linder, Lincoln's in Coles. A pro-Jackson Democrat, Linder had an explosive temper and a taste for alcohol. His intelligence, political savvy, and fiery rhetoric made him, in the 1850s, Stephen Douglas' valued operative in Illinois. Linder now dominated the Alton meeting. Outmaneuvering the hapless Beecher, he wrote the convention's concluding resolutions, which sidestepped the initial purpose for the meeting. The next day, the antislavery core met in a private home. A mob, organized by Linder, attacked the house, pounding on its doors. While Alton's mayor called out forty constables to clear the street, Lovejoy and Beecher created the Illinois Antislavery Society.

Beecher stayed on briefly in Alton. He hoped that there would be a new birth of Christian tolerance and commitment to free speech. But when he spoke about slavery at another meeting, he met strong resistance. A rock came hurtling through the window. Guards with weapons escorted the congregation out. The mob withdrew. A small group of Lovejoy's supporters faced off with a crowd of anti-abolitionists at the wharf as each steamer docked. When would the new printing press arrive? What boat would it be on? Another public meeting pitted Beecher against Linder, with both sides heavily represented by large numbers of uncompromising opponents. A committee of so-called neutrals, formed by common agreement, refused to take a stand for legal protection of the *Observer*. A new committee, representing both factions, was led by the anti-abolitionist and pro-colonization Cyrus Edwards, Madison county's state senator. Related by marriage to Springfield's Mary Todd, Edwards was the brother of the ex-governor and now senator Ninian Edwards. Cyrus Edwards' committee failed to reconcile the Linder and Lovejoy factions. Lovejoy refused to terminate the *Observer* or leave the city. Supported by public opinion, his opponents made clear that they would not let the *Observer* be published. If it attempted to publish again, the replacement press would be destroyed.

FRIENDLY AND watchful eyes, peering through the moonlit darkness at three o'clock in the morning on November 7, 1837, saw the *Missouri Fulton* come into sight, steaming up to Alton. One of Lovejoy's supporters, Winthrop Gilman, who owned the stone warehouse at the wharf and had made it available to safely store the press, had provided an advance lookout. Lovejoy had been alerted to the *Fulton*'s departure from St. Louis two days before. About thirty armed friends of free speech, having organized into an unofficial militia, awaited its delivery. Mayor John Krum, who had been told the likely date of delivery, had met with the city council. It declined to authorize the appointment of special constables to keep the peace. As the *Fulton* approached Alton, the mayor was awakened. He refused a request to authorize the Lovejoy militia to police the wharf. When Lovejoy and Beecher were notified, they anxiously made their way through dark, silent streets. To their great relief, there was no crowd outside the warehouse. They helped carry the press up to the top floor, the third. At daylight, they felt triumphant—and relieved. The militia dispersed. Beecher left for Jacksonville.

By late afternoon, rumors of an impending attempt to destroy the press reached Lovejoy and his associates. They gathered at the warehouse, the press safe upstairs. As night fell, it became increasingly likely that at some time that night or the next day, a group of men, no one knew how many, would attempt an attack. Heavy drinking and loud talk in the town's taverns made that clear. Some who had determined to protect the press were abolitionists; others, defenders only of free speech. The three Lovejoy brothers were both. One of the leaders called for volunteers to stay the night. Fourteen men stepped forward. Winthrop Gilman went to the mayor to ask his opinion as to whether those who called themselves a militia and were there to defend his and Lovejoy's property were acting legally. The mayor said that they were.

On the street, crowds of volatile men, about two hundred strong, were inciting themselves to action: they would teach the abolitionists a lesson. Their city was being stained by a newspaper that encouraged a Negro insurrection; that advocated that the daughters of white men be raped by or married to niggers; that would force them to compete for jobs with niggers; and that advocated civil rights and equality for a despised and inferior race. They would destroy the press. Hearing the street voices, Gilman hurried back to the warehouse. The hapless mayor, hoping for the best, followed the mob to the warehouse. The nervous defenders heard the thud of stones bouncing on the ground or hitting the building. Glass shattered. Muskets flamed. A man in the crowd fell, bleeding from a gunshot wound. As he was carried away, he died. The mayor, trying to stop a barefoot man from joining the mob, was asked, "How would you like a damned nigger going home with your daughter?"

The mob shouted: Burn down the building! Destroy the press! The ringing of the bells of the Presbyterian church attracted more angry men. From inside the warehouse, a man could be seen climbing a ladder against the windowless side of the building. With a flaming torch in his hand, he reached the roof. The wood shingles took the flame and nourished it. A number of Lovejoy's supporters ran out, fired at the incendiary on the roof, and ran back in. Lovejoy and four others hurried out to make one last effort to stop the arsonist and put out the fire. "As they emerged . . . into the brilliant calm moonlight, shots were fired from behind a shelter, and five balls were lodged in the body of Mr. Lovejoy." He "had strength enough to run back and up the stairs, crying out, as he went, 'I am shot! I am shot! I am dead!' When he reached the counting-room, he fell back into the arms of a bystander and was laid upon the floor, where he instantly passed away without a struggle and without speaking again."

THREE

A Difficult Year

On an ordinary Saturday in late January 1838, twenty-nine-year-old Abraham Lincoln stepped up to the platform of the Springfield, Illinois, Baptist church to deliver a lecture. His audience was the Young Men's Lyceum. Always a nervous speaker, he preferred to have a well-revised, polished text, and he had one now. He had friends in the audience, some of them founding members of the speaking association: his law partner, pro-slavery John T. Stuart, who had just taken the novice lawyer into his firm; Dan Stone, a businessman and legislator with whom Lincoln had, ten months before, coauthored a resolution in the Illinois State legislature stating that slavery was an evil but that abolition was equally bad; and his friend Simeon Francis, the editor of the *Sangamo Journal*, all middle-of-the-road Whigs.

The young lawyer had never before delivered a lecture. Despite the church setting, this was an occasion for Lincoln, who had no religious affiliation, to speak on a secular topic that many newspapers, including Springfield's *Sangamo Journal*, had been full of for much of the previous year. His subject, the complete text to be published in the next issue of the *Journal*: "The perpetuation of our political institutions." It was a stock political topic of the day: let me tell you how and why our political institutions are under attack and how we can save them. Many Americans believed there was good reason to worry that some of the written and unwritten covenants created by the Founders of the republic were no longer fully enough determining the tenor of American public life. There seemed to be a caustic, cold anxiety in the national air.

The year that had just ended had been especially difficult for Illinois and for Lincoln. It had been a "winter of starving time," so cold that "a man riding a horse from Chatham to Springfield to procure a marriage license . . . was so firmly frozen to the saddle, that he and the saddle were carried into the house and thawed next to the fire." As the year ended, Lincoln was unhappily in love. His standing as a state legislator, traveling the unpaved frozen roads between the state capital in Vandalia and his new home in Springfield, had not impressed the woman he courted, Mary Owen. He mostly kept his depression at bay while he slogged out his low-earning contributions to Stuart's law firm. And he found his most secure anchor in his legislative tasks.

Through most of 1837 he led the effort to move the state capital to Springfield; he strongly supported the Illinois State Bank; and he involved himself in a prolonged controversy about the legitimacy of a deed in an inheritance case, publishing satirical letters in the *Sangamo Journal*. As a Whig newspaper, the *Journal*, like Lincoln, had no doubt that the Van Buren administration, doubling-down on the anti-bank, anti–paper money, and anti-business policies of the Andrew Jackson administration, was responsible for the start of the worst economic depression in early American history. Illinois seemed likely to default on its infrastructure projects; the existence of the state bank was under threat; the state and national economies were starved for capital; businesses and farms were closing, tax receipts plunging, the federal government unable to pay its bills. Congress seemed paralyzed. The economic ideology of the Democrats required that government not interfere with the business cycle: austerity, patience, and a return to hard currency would make the economy healthy again. The *Journal* carried lengthy reports of Washington speeches and debates, often quoting John Quincy Adams on banking, financial regulation, and monetary issues. Anti-administration and pro-Whig views dominated its pages.

For the *Journal* and other Whig partisans, it was also a political opportunity. They hoped that placing the blame where they believed it lay would increase Whig representation nationwide and elect a Whig president in 1840. On the same Saturday that Lincoln rose to address the Springfield Lyceum, the *Journal* reprinted an editorial from the *New York Express*. Headed "THE CLOSING YEAR," it summarized the anger, disappointment, and sense of national crisis about the economy felt by most Whigs and many Americans. And it made clear its view about who was responsible. The year 1837 was remarkable, the editorial began,

> *as beginning the Administration of an Executive educated in a new school of politicians,—among wily and designing demagogues—who have lost all good impressions of their ancestors and all care for the paternity of their government. The merchants will remember it as the Iron Age of our history; the mechanic will remember it as the year which threatened him with beggary and want, and the poor man will think of it as the year of despondency. It has been a season for making and unmaking of Executives,—of unparalleled distress among the entire business community, the year of SUSPENSION,—not merely of the payments promised by nearly a thousand Banking Institutions, but a suspension of nearly all the avenues of prosperity, which promised us national and individual wealth [a year in which the national government has become almost bankrupt]. . . . He who has survived it, and escaped unscathed from its evils, may survive almost anything, in the history of human events, and to such a survivor, it is as I have said, the year of jubilee, while to others it has been the beginning of the seven years' bondage.*

It was far from a year of jubilee for Lincoln. Still, he had survived it satisfactorily; the year was highlighted by his recent admission to the bar.

When he stepped to the Lyceum platform, he believed that he had a relevant message, and that he had a local role, minor as it was, in delivering the news. His message had nothing to do with the economy. Instead, it focused on a series of events, which had begun a few years before and had reached, in November 1837, a notorious apogee with the murder of Elijah Lovejoy. They were events that, in the view of Lincoln and many Americans, represented a change in the values of the nation that would have long-lasting consequences. Bad as it was, the current economic depression was temporary. But "the increasing disregard for law which pervades the country," he told his audience, "the growing disposition to substitute the wild and furious passions, in lieu of the sober judgment of Courts," the murderous acts of "savage mobs" that, in New England, in the South, and in Missouri and Illinois, had taken the law into their own hands, threatened the rule of law and the constitutional basis of public safety. These mobs "spring up among the pleasure hunting masters of Southern slaves, and the order loving citizens of the land of steady habits." In Mississippi, an extrajudicial mob had hanged gamblers legally at work and lynched Negroes suspected of favoring insurrection. In St. Louis, Francis McIntosh had been burned to death by a mob instead of turned over to the authorities for lawful prosecution.

Even if he had limited himself to the years 1835 to 1837, there were at least a half dozen examples that Lincoln could have cited. They included Southern mobs burning abolitionist pamphlets, a race riot in Washington, D.C., and the burning of a Catholic convent in Boston. "Whatever, then, their cause may be, it is common to the whole country," Lincoln remarked. And "it would be tedious, as well as useless, to recount the horrors of all of them." Mob law was no law at all, he emphasized. And though he did not hesitate to state that agitation about slavery and racial hatred was one of the incitements to mob violence, it was the extrajudicial violence he condemned, not slavery. "Mobism," he lamented, "in Charlestown [Massachusetts] . . . burns a Convent over the head of defenceless women; in Baltimore it desecrates the Sabbath, and works all that day in demolishing a private citizen's house; in Vicksburg it hangs up gamblers, three or four in a row; and in St. Louis it forces a man—a hardened wretch certainly, and one that deserved to die, but not thus to die—it forces him from beneath the aegis of our constitution and laws, hurries him to the stake and burns him alive."

Had Lincoln read Lovejoy's editorial about the McIntosh incident, "Awful Murder and Savage Barbarity," or anything written or published by Lovejoy? The editorial about McIntosh was not reprinted in the *Sangamo Journal*, and it's unlikely that Lincoln had access to a religious weekly as obscure as the *Observer*. But the major St. Louis newspapers were available in New Salem and Springfield, and one of the most trenchant sentences of Lovejoy's May 1836 editorial is close to Lincoln's language in his address to the Springfield Lyceum: "We must stand by the constitution and laws," Lovejoy wrote, "or ALL is GONE." The week after Lovejoy's murder, the *Sangamo Journal* reprinted from the *Alton Spectator* Mayor John Krum's accurate account of the mob violence that had killed Lovejoy and destroyed his press. The November 18 issue contained a Stuart and Lincoln advertisement for their legal services. It's likely that Lincoln read Krum's narrative. When, in December 1837, an Alton grand jury, impaneled to consider indicting the defenders of Lovejoy's press, had heard a racist harangue by the lead prosecutor, Attorney General Usher F. Linder, it was also impaneled to consider charging members of the mob. It was a spectacle in judicial absurdity. In the end, the grand jury declined to indict either faction. Though the *Journal* did not reprint an account of the hearings, other regional newspapers did, and it may not have been possible for Lincoln to avoid knowing about what was a topic of print in St. Louis and of conversation in Springfield.

The subject of Lincoln's speech was the threat to the perpetuation of U.S. institutions, particularly the law and the courts, and the right to have the laws protect one's person and property. By itself, it was a fairly safe topic. Lincoln's approach was safe and conservative. It was also intellectually and rhetorically impressive for a twenty-nine-year-old self-educated lawyer on the provincial frontier. "By such examples, by instances of the perpetrators of such acts going unpunished, the lawless in spirit, are encouraged," he summarized, "to become lawless in practice; and having been used to no restraint, but dread of punishment, they thus become, absolutely unrestrained. Having ever regarded Government as their deadliest bane, they make a jubilee of the suspension of its operations; and pray for nothing so much, as its total annihilation."

Americans were given to "wild and furious passions," Lincoln observed, and counterproductive hatreds, especially for those with whom they disagreed, the worst of our politics virtually a blood sport for self-serving and unhinged people. Disrespect for the law, for the collective democratic will as embodied in legitimate, time-honored institutions, and antigovernment hostility that preferred no national government rather than even the small government of the 1830s threatened American prosperity. Eventually, he warned, political polarization would lead to autocratic government, even to tyranny, probably of a military sort, a Caesar or a Napoléon to bring order out of chaos. He and his fellow Whigs had in mind the example of Andrew Jackson, the anti–George Washington of Whig history. We need, Lincoln concluded, to replace the Founding Fathers with a new generation that will also use "reason, cold, calculating, unimpassioned reason" for "our future support and defence. Let those [materials] be molded into *general intelligence,* [*sound*] *morality* and, in particular, *a reverence for the constitution and laws*. . . . Let every American, every lover of liberty, every well-wisher to his posterity, swear by the blood of the Revolution, never to violate in the least particular, the laws of the country; and never to tolerate their violation by others."

The latter expostulation, though rhetorically effective, was in fact overly prescriptive and undiscriminating. There could be little to no disagreement about the pernicious corrosiveness of mob violence. But "never to violate in the least particular, the laws of the country" and apparently "never," at any level, even of sympathy, "tolerate their violation by others"? Lincoln noticeably steered away from what an outspoken minority, and he himself to a limited extent, believed: there were bad laws and bad lawful institutions. The primary example was the Constitution's legalization of slavery. That previous March, Lincoln had put on record in the state legislature his belief that slavery was immoral. But what to do about slavery, how to eliminate it, was another matter. For Lincoln, until late 1862, voluntary manumission, persuasion, colonization, and the ballot box were the only legal instruments for correcting or eliminating slavery—calmly, carefully, rationally, and over the very long haul. Abolitionists, Lincoln believed, had the potential to make all voices shrill, passions rise, the particulars of the law irrelevant, and blood flow.

Not surprisingly, in his Lyceum address Lincoln only glancingly referred to Lovejoy's murder. Alton was less than seventy miles from Springfield. Across the Mississippi, St. Louis was twenty-four miles from Alton. A triangle can be drawn with Springfield as its northeastern point; its northwestern point, Mark Twain's Hannibal, Missouri. At the triangle's apex, descending southeast, is Alton. Lincoln lived the geography and culture of the Illinois portion of the triangle. Activities in St. Louis were well known in Springfield. Still, all Lincoln had to say in his Lyceum address about Lovejoy's murder and the destruction of his printing press he relegated to an indirect mention, a phrase hanging onto his larger theme: "Whenever this effect shall be produced among us; whenever the vicious portion of population shall be permitted to gather in bands of hundreds and thousands, and burn churches, ravage and rob provision stores, throw *printing presses into rivers, shoot editors* [my italics], and hang and burn obnoxious persons at pleasure, and with impunity; depend on it, this Government cannot last." Though registering the oddity of this, Lincoln's modern editor rejects the possibility that Lincoln was "being politic," surmising that "it seems possible that he chose a subtler way of pricking the conscience of his audience than by direct denunciation." Not likely. Lovejoy and Lovejoy's murder were not comfortable topics for Lincoln to partner with. His views about abolition and his politics made that impolitic.

In this, Lincoln had considerable support among his Springfield contemporaries. When twelve members of the Second Presbyterian Church set out for Alton in October 1837 to participate in Beecher's and Lovejoy's antislavery convention, they did not represent many of Springfield's citizens. This was a newly formed breakaway church; its small congregation probably contained most of the overt abolitionists in Springfield. There had been anti-abolitionist demonstrations when the Illinois Presbyterian Synod met there earlier in the year. Afraid that abolitionism was about to have a riotous presence, numbers of residents threatened violence and repression. Five days before the Alton convention met, Illinois Supreme Court judge Thomas C. Browne, a prominent Springfield citizen, chaired a meeting to put on record how strongly Springfield's elite deplored abolitionism. Browne already had become a mentor to Lincoln; the senior judge was a welcome friend to the young lawyer. Lincoln's leadership in moving the state capital to Springfield had brought him to the attention of the local elite. And he was soon to sign, along with a long list of Springfield notables, a promissory note to guarantee payment for the land to be used for the site of the new statehouse. Judge Browne was, in 1842, to be one of the few guests at Lincoln's wedding. Standing behind the groom as he took the marriage oath with the words "With this ring I thee endow with all my goods, chattels, lands, and tenements," Browne, known for his bluntness, blurted out, "God Almighty, Lincoln, the statute fixes all that."

The Springfield anti-abolition meeting on October 23 resolved "that as citizens of a free State and a peaceable community, we deprecate any attempt to sow discord among us, or to create an excitement as to abolition which can be productive of no good result. Resolved, That in the opinion of this meeting the doctrine of immediate emancipation of slaves in this country (although promulgated by those who profess to be Christians) is at variance with Christianity, and its tendency is to breed contention, broils and mobs, and the leaders of those calling themselves abolitionists, are designing, ambitious men, and dangerous members of the society, and should be shunned by all good citizens." No doubt at least one of the Christians referred to was Lovejoy. "Resolved, That the proceedings of this meeting be published in the Sangamo Journal and Illinois Republican." They were published on Saturday, October 28, two days after the Alton convention met.

On the day that Judge Browne called the anti-abolition meeting to order, Lincoln was in Springfield. No list of the attendees exists. Possibly he did not attend. The resolutions the meeting drafted appeared in the *Sangamo Journal*, directly beneath one of Lincoln's long letters about a controversial local matter. It's hard to imagine he could keep his eyes off either column, and Lincoln had said much the same about abolitionists to the Illinois state legislature the previous March. Reporting the resolutions of the Springfield meeting, the *Sangamo Journal* made clear its detestation of abolition and abolitionists. Public opinion, it editorialized, "is likely to check at once the perfidy of these fanatical men." Emancipation would be a disaster for the South and for the nation. That Lincoln considered Lovejoy one of these "fanatical men" seems an inevitable conclusion.

Much as he had to say about lawlessness in his Lyceum address, Lincoln made no allusion to the congressional debates in progress during the first half of 1837 that focused dramatically on his topic. John Quincy Adams had narrowly escaped a vote of censure that winter. His theme was congressional lawlessness, the insistence by a Southern-led majority that, despite the Constitution, the House of Representatives not accept any petitions about slavery. On the same day that Lincoln delivered his Lyceum address, Adams' mind was on the furor that he anticipated would erupt when he introduced another batch. An additional thirty-one antislavery petitions had arrived in his mail the previous day. He spent the evening "assorting, filing, endorsing, and entering them on my list, without completing the work. With these petitions I receive many letters, which I have not time to answer. Most of them are so flattering, and expressed in terms of such deep sensibility, that I am in imminent danger of being led by them into presumption and puffed up with vanity. The abolition newspapers the *Liberator, Emancipator, Philanthropist, National Enquirer,* and *New York Evangelist,* all of which are regularly sent to me contribute to generate and nourish this delusion, which the treacherous, furious, filthy, and threatening letters from the South on the same subject cannot sufficiently counteract. My duty to defend the free principles and institutions is clear; but the measures by which they are to be defended are involved in thick darkness. The path of right is narrow, and I have need of a perpetual control over passion." By late the next day, he had 120 petitions in hand.

The *Sangamo Journal* reported in detail on Adams' trial by pro-slavery fire during 1837–1838. To Adams, it was Congress that was being lawless. Under Southern leadership and with Northern Democratic collaboration, it was acting as an organized mob. And it was encouraging if not condoning the violent acts of anti-abolitionist mobs. Lincoln shared Adams' belief that slavery was against nature and nature's God. Lincoln would not go the next step, though, from antislavery moralism to antislavery activism. In fact, he did not believe that there was a desirable next step other than the eventual voluntary removal of all free blacks and all emancipated slaves to some actual or invented ancestral home. Unlike Adams, Lincoln would not touch the third rail of American politics. He easily brushed off the charge, which he continued to reject until the last years of his life, that because he thought slavery immoral he was necessarily an abolitionist. From the start of his public life, he helped keep this distinction clear by saying, in his address to the Lyceum, little to nothing about Elijah Lovejoy or about the many other incidents in which mob violence had arisen almost exclusively as racist hostility to pro-abolition ideas and acts.

A TENSE crowd of partisans on both sides of the abolition issue pushed into Boston's Faneuil Hall on the first day of the second week of December 1837, exactly one month and a day after Lovejoy's assassination. Much of the nation, especially the business-intense New England and Middle Atlantic states, was licking the wounds of a difficult year. The entire country felt the economic pain. Businesses were failing, banks closing. Large numbers of unemployed workers loitered on urban streets. Farmers were desperate. There was reason to be angry at those who advocated that the two or more million black slaves, mostly in the South, become free agents seeking employment and a place of equality in the American sun.

Though abolitionists were a minuscule minority in Boston, they had a more concentrated presence there than anywhere else in the country, with the exception of Quaker Philadelphia. To most people, "abolition" meant "immediate abolition." By "emancipation," most meant freedom in the distant future, compensating slaveholders and filtering manumitted slaves through a slow process of acculturation that would civilize them. Gradual emancipation would equip them eventually to go to a country of their own. The idea had its adherents even in the South, where the American Colonization Society gave cover to slaveholders who wanted the satisfaction of being morally antislavery but to keep their slaves indefinitely. Abolition, almost always accompanied by the word *radical*, was not popular even in Boston; emancipation more so, though many were indifferent and even more were hostile to proposals favoring freedom for an inferior race that they believed hardly qualified to be called human.

The crowd that entered Faneuil Hall on December 8, 1837, split itself into a small number who favored abolition and a large number who did not. The majority divided into those who accepted slavery as it was, called Cotton Whigs, mostly well-to-do businesspeople benefiting economically from the slave-based cotton industry; and those who, on moral grounds, wanted slavery ended gradually. Each group had people who favored long-term colonization. But the ostensible occasion for this mass meeting was not the topic of slavery: it was freedom of the press. And the meeting had been called, against considerable opposition, because of Elijah Lovejoy's murder.

There was little sympathy or even connection between Springfield and Boston, though both were Whig cities. The city on the Atlantic was the center of elite American culture, history, and wealth; Springfield, a mud-and-wooden-plank provincial backwater. Newly designated the state capital, with a small-city Midwestern future, it would never be Boston, New York, or Chicago. Its future prosperity would be the offspring of the growth of state government and the afterlife of its most famous citizen. When Daniel Webster visited in June 1837, it was a grand civic occasion Such visitors were rare. Lincoln probably came to the grove where Webster spoke. Ralph Waldo Emerson lectured in Springfield in January 1853, a celebrity occasion that Lincoln attended. Like Lincoln, Webster and Emerson opposed slavery. Neither was an abolitionist, though Emerson's vague rhetoric might have allowed him to be thought one. Even in Boston, moderates such as Emerson preferred to claim Lovejoy as a martyr for freedom of speech. The minister's abolitionist views could be disregarded. "I sternly rejoice," Emerson wrote in his journal in late 1837, "that one was found to die for humanity and her rights of free speech and opinion."

The voices of the small cadre of abolitionists in Boston were rarely heard in Springfield. Such names hardly appeared in the *Sangamo Journal* in the 1830s and '40s. Even Lovejoy was, on the whole, too hot to handle. No meeting occurred in Springfield to defend freedom of the press, let alone to protest Lovejoy's assassination. Other than reprinting the account by the mayor of Alton, the *Journal* had nothing to say about Lovejoy's death. Springfield's leaders wanted nothing to do with pro-abolition and anti-abolition tension. In Boston, Lovejoy and abolitionism had a public voice, though there were loud counter-voices. Still, in Massachusetts the law itself did not make blacks second-class citizens. Equally important, public opinion defended free speech and personal security. In 1831, abolitionists had initiated their own newspaper, the *Liberator.* Its outspoken editor, William Lloyd Garrison, a working-class young man with a thin, meek appearance, his fingers stained with printer's ink, combined Christian values with personal courage. A radical by temperament, he denounced Whigs and Democrats equally on the two issues that mattered most to him: abolition and women's rights.

Lincoln's Springfield world, in contrast, directed considerable venom at abolitionism. Its cohort of middle-of-the-road anti-abolitionist Whigs, led by the *Sangamo Journal,* had no alternative but to give Boston's John Quincy Adams prominent billing and high praise. The former president's congressional pronouncements on the tariff, the national bank, and infrastructure were music to their ears. So, too, was his opposition to the expansion of slavery, especially the potential annexation of Texas, constantly advocated by Southern leaders during the 1830s and '40s. But the *Journal* had little to say about Adams' abolitionist sympathies. And despite every other public policy affinity, the laudatory pen portraits, and the positive accounts in the *Journal* of Adams' congressional battles, Lincoln made so few references to Adams in what survives of his letters and lectures that it is hard not to conclude that the exclusion was purposeful. Abolitionists such as Garrison have almost no presence at all. In these years, Illinois, a border state like Kentucky, had many formidable anti-abolitionists on every level of society, including some among Lincoln's friends, extended family, political allies, and political opponents. Even those who, like Lincoln, were morally opposed to slavery believed, unhesitatingly, that the United States should be a white man's country exclusively.

Those who took their seats in Faneuil Hall in early December 1837 knew that there would be at least verbal fireworks. All would have felt, with some degree of emotional intensity, the mythic presence of Boston's orators of Revolutionary days. Fiery James Otis and volatile John Adams had, in that same place, advocated bold action for American independence. Portraits of Otis, John Hancock, and the most defiant Son of Liberty, Samuel Adams, blessed Boston's civic futurity. What is now a food-and-trinket emporium was still a hallowed hall dedicated to public meetings, an eighteenth-century gift to the city from its wealthiest merchant, Peter Faneuil. William Ellery Channing, Boston's senior Unitarian minister, had issued the call for the meeting. A leader of Calvinism's transformation into a Unitarianism emphasizing God's love, he confidently expected public approval for a resolution affirming free speech.

When the Boston Town Council refused a permit for the meeting, Channing was shocked. Others were not. The council and the newly elected Massachusetts attorney general, James T. Austin, feared, even expected, that the meeting would advance abolitionist propaganda, a verbal assault on Boston's peace, an affront to many citizens who feared the South would retaliate against their business interests. "The rich and fashionable belong to the same caste with the slaveholder," Channing had written, "and men are apt to sympathize with their own caste more readily than with those beneath them." A prudent moralist, Channing abhorred slavery. It caused him moral pain. He also anticipated how much pain immediate abolition, which he opposed, would cause to "the rich and fashionable," including many of New England's most successful merchants and financiers. When he appealed the council's decision, under pressure to appear nonpartisan, the council granted the permit.

In his best clerical and ameliorative manner, the bald, bespectacled Channing, who had preached hundreds of sermons and chaired many meetings, called to order what the *New York Evening Post* called one of the largest crowds ever to assemble in Faneuil Hall. A number of resolutions were proposed: "Freedom of speech and the press [require] that the citizen shall be protected from violence in uttering opinions opposed to those which prevail around him," and legal enactments that guaranteed freedom of speech were "the only forms though which the sovereignty of the people is exercised." No one objected to the resolutions. They condemned "lawless force" on all sides. On the face of it, the resolutions were innocuous enough, obvious statements of basic first principles. For many, the resolutions were acceptable pro forma givens. For others, they were either too weak or too strong. If the former, why did they not specifically mention Lovejoy and slavery? If the latter, were they an implied approval of Lovejoy and condemnation of the pro-slavery mob?

Led by Channing, the moderates in the hall would have been happy to leave the subtext submerged. The previous August, Channing had written a public letter to Senator Henry Clay, the Whig champion of moderation. "A spirit of lawlessness pervades the community," Channing wrote, "which, if not repressed, threatens the dissolution of our present forms of society. Even in the old states, mobs are taking the government into their hands, and a profligate newspaper finds little difficulty in stirring up multitudes to violence." The issue was the possible annexation of Texas, which, Channing feared, would create violent conflict between pro-slavery partisans and those who opposed slavery's extension. That was not, though, the subject of the Faneuil Hall meeting. It was Channing's hope that the issue of free speech and lawful assemblage, to which everyone paid at least lip service, could be separated from the issue of slavery. Could an uncomplicated pro–free speech resolution be passed?

Prepared for this moment and primed for rhetorical warfare, James T. Austin, rising from his seat in the balcony, demanded that he be recognized. No one could deny this, certainly not the pacific Channing. An energetic speaker, with a touch of the demagogue, Austin had recently published a pro-slavery pamphlet. "Suppose," Austin had written, that blacks "emerge from Slavery, intelligent, moral and industrious, with all the capacity and inclinations of the white man. They would be negroes still. Two distinct classes of men could not live upon terms of equality in the same country and under the same government. The more their intelligence, the greater would be the mutual hostility of the two races; and the final possession of power would be the result of a war of extermination, in which one or the other race would perish. Is it supposed they could amalgamate? God forbid!" Our pure white daughters would give birth to "thick-lipped, woollyheaded children of African fathers." Rather than that "the negro should be seated in the halls of Congress and his sooty complexion glare upon us from the bench of justice, rather than he should mingle with us in the familiar intercourse of domestic life and taint the atmosphere of our homes and firesides . . . debased and degraded by such indiscriminate and beastly connexion . . . —I will BRAVE MY SHARE OF ALL THE RESPONSIBILITY OF KEEPING HIM IN SLAVERY." Elijah Lovejoy, Austin told his Faneuil Hall audience, "was like a man who insisted on breaking open cages containing wild beasts and setting them free to prey on the populace. . . . The people of Missouri had as much reason to be afraid of their slaves," Austin insisted, "as we should have of the wild beasts of the menagerie." Much as mobs are to be deplored, Lovejoy had been to blame for his own death.

This was, essentially, the view of most of those assembled in Faneuil Hall and most white Americans, North and South, whether in Boston, Springfield, or Charleston, whether because of self-interest or racism or the belief that slavery was ineradicable—or some combination of any or all of these. Austin expressed what most Americans believed: abolition would result either in a race war in which one race would exterminate the other or in a mixed-race society, destructive to both races. The underside of the argument—widely expressed in working-class bars and in the streets; in jokes, racial taunts, anti-black laws, and mob attacks on "nigger lovers"; in serious pamphlets, books, and speeches by the literate elite; and in political campaigns throughout the country, especially in Congress—

was: if there is a Negro insurrection, your daughters and wives will be raped by black men; if there is "amalgamation," your daughters will give birth to "woolly-headed children." From the most virulent pro-slavery racist to moderate antislavery Democrats and Whigs, this threat, no matter the degree of moral condemnation of slavery itself and no matter the political calculation, was deeply felt in the gut, beyond anything to do with rationality or religion. To anti-abolitionists there were only two alternatives: the perpetuation of slavery forever or gradual colonization.

How to end slavery, if one favored ending it at all, seemed a question without a satisfactory solution. Christian antislavery moderates, like Channing, felt its moral repugnance. How to solve a seemingly unsolvable problem, a stain on Christian values and the Christian conscience? Others who disapproved of slavery took refuge in less intellectual balancing acts: frustration, postponement, acceptance, evasion, resignation, and the American Colonization Society. Even for those who advocated immediate abolition, its aftermath was difficult to envision. What could be done to make two million ex-slaves productive citizens of American society? How much money would it take? Who would pay? How long would it take? Where would they live? And if they lived in integrated communities, how would it be possible for the two races to live peacefully together? No one had convincing answers. For abolitionists, the moral imperative dominated. But what would come next, if there was to be a next, was less concrete. James Austin could speak to his Faneuil Hall audience with self-assured specificity. His bigotry and belligerence created clarity: the real issue, he emphasized, was not free speech but slavery. The next day, the *Boston Daily Evening Transcript* had it right: "The speech of Attorney General Austin reflected the true spirit of the meeting and the citizens of Boston."

As soon as Austin took his seat, a slim, dark-haired, thin-faced man stood up. Twenty-seven-year-old Wendell Phillips, who had not intended to say anything at this meeting, surprised himself and everyone else. The son of a distinguished Boston lawyer, civic leader, and philanthropist, Wendell, like his widely respected father, was a Harvard graduate and a lawyer. John Quincy Adams had heard "the youngest son of my old friend and associate, John Phillips, perform admirably" at the Harvard graduation ceremony in August 1831. The descendent of a pious Congregationalist family—the Phillips clan arrived with the first settlement of Massachusetts—the young man had won plaudits at college. With a cultured voice, self-possession, and high-caste idealism, he seemed to some too much the Brahmin snob, to others a gifted young man in search of a mission. Six years before, William Lloyd Garrison had begun publishing the *Liberator* a stone's throw from the Phillipses' Beacon Street mansion. Wendell Phillips had been interested but far from fully convinced. His conservative Whig family disapproved. His long-widowed mother, the respected matriarch of the family, thought the *Liberator* abominable and abolitionists seditious troublemakers. When Garrison was attacked by a pro-slavery mob as he was about to speak to the Boston Female Antislavery Society, Wendell would have been almost in sight of the uproar. The wealthy abolitionist bluestocking whom he married in 1836 and of whom his family disapproved may have been at the meeting. Phillips soon became active in Boston's small abolitionist circle.

When he stood up to answer Austin at Faneuil Hall, Phillips was in the process of beginning a lifelong commitment to the abolitionist cause. He had become convinced that racial injustice was at the heart of everything wrong with America. His speech that day, though, was not about slavery. It did not mention the word or allude to the institution. From the moment he rose, he could see and hear that most of his audience was hostile. Voices from the crowded hall urged him to sit down and shut up: an abolitionist was not welcome to speak! Equally loud but more dignified voices demanded respect for free speech. "No gag!" they called out, using ex-president Adams' widely publicized exhortation, his refrain in Congress all through 1837.

At his moment of oratorical inauguration, Phillips took the high road of discretion. He stuck to the topic of free speech. "As much as thought is better than money, so much is the cause in which Lovejoy died nobler than a mere question of taxes." The issue now, Phillips proclaimed, is even more central to our secular and religious values than

> *taxation without representation. James Otis thundered in this Hall when the King did but touch his pocket. Imagine, if you can, his indignant eloquence, had England offered to put a gag upon his lips. [Great applause.] The question that stirred the Revolution touched our civil interests. This concerns us not only as citizens, but as immortal beings. Wrapped up in its fate, saved or lost with it, are not only the voice of the statesman, but the instructions of the pulpit, and the progress of our faith. . . . It is good for us to be here. When Liberty is in danger, Faneuil Hall has the right, it is her duty, to strike the key-note for these United States. I am glad, for one reason, that remarks such as those to which I have alluded have been uttered here. The passage of these resolutions, in spite of this opposition . . . will show more clearly, more decisively, the deep indignation with which Boston regards this outrage.*

The indignation was real, though thinner on the ground than Channing had expected, and mostly among the elite. Probably Garrison, who pulled no punches on free speech, slavery, immediate abolition, or women's rights, was not at the Faneuil Hall meeting. On that day, Phillips, who would have many occasions in the next decades to speak his mind about abolition and slavery, had gone as far as he judged it safe to go. Lovejoy was indeed a martyr to free speech, but the real text would be eloquently delivered on other occasions at other times.

The national Whig establishment also had gone as far as it could safely go when it deplored Lovejoy's assassination and affirmed the right of free speech. In the press and the pulpit, Whig spokesmen accompanied the affirmation with the warning that those who used the right of free speech to discuss slavery and advocate abolition were dangerously reckless. Free speech best fulfilled the country's values and contributed to its prosperity when under the control of voluntary restraint. Abolitionists were sowing the wind. They would reap the *whirlwind*. Lovejoy's death should be deplored, mob violence condemned. But those who advocated abolition, though exercising a constitutional right, were troublemakers, the creators of a symbiotic dynamic with those who felt threatened by insurrectionary language and resorted to violence in self-defense. Newspapers from St. Louis to Boston to Charleston and in any other loop around the country, with some exceptions in New England and the Middle Atlantic states, concluded that abolitionism was a threat to civic order and the perpetuation of the Union. This was Lincoln's position in 1837. Antislavery moralists and champions of free speech warned that the extremes threatened the existence of the center.

IF SLAVERY were to continue in place, John Quincy Adams believed, eventually the center would not hold. In early spring 1838, he had the courage to do what no other moderate Whig, from Channing in Boston to the unknown Lincoln in Illinois, would consider safe. In response to a request from Elijah Lovejoy's brothers, he wrote a learned and brilliant introduction to their edition of their murdered brother's memoir/biography, which had been synthesized from his letters, editorials, and poetry, and from newspaper articles and commentary. It was, Adams argued, slavery that had made Elijah Lovejoy the "first American martyr." Unlike either Channing or Lincoln, Adams had become a convert to abolitionism, though he also had no clear idea of how the practical transition from slavery to citizenry could be effected. His conviction that, sooner or later, slavery would produce a slave insurrection or the breakup of the Union, or both, dominated his mind and feelings. He also had the political independence to speak his mind, his congressional district the only electorate he would ever need to face again. Though divided over abolition, the district was overwhelmingly antislavery. It opposed the suppression of free speech on any subject. It also respected the Adams family tradition of service and appreciated the advantage of having an ex-president represent it in Congress. In 1838, at the age of seventy-one, with no higher office possible and no need to solicit support from a national coalition or constituency, Adams was freer than most of his political contemporaries to be himself on the subject of slavery, to be what his family values, his conscience, his learning, and his personality required.

In mid-January 1837, Adams, in Washington, had received a letter from an unknown young man named Joseph Lovejoy. Adams had never heard the name Lovejoy before. Joseph's older brother had, the previous year, moved his pro-abolition newspaper from St. Louis to Alton. With his brother Owen, Joseph had trekked across the country from the Lovejoy family home in Albion, Maine, to join Elijah. Joseph's letter focused not on slavery but on the widespread corruption of government officials. It emphasized one of Adams' lifelong themes: the corruption that political parties imposed on American political life. "Could the *People* be shown," Joseph Lovejoy wrote, "the moral corruption and depravity of these men by whom they have in a measure been led they would at once put a stop to all the political juggling, and the country would once more be found in a happy and prosperous condition."

It was also a fan letter. Adams, Lovejoy believed, was one of the few honest politicians in Washington. That the day "is dawning when this will take place I am happy to perceive, by the triumph with which you have attained over your enemies." Lovejoy was alluding to the congressman's opposition to the gag rule. "In the last session when we were in danger of being carried away captive, you interposed your arm and saved us." The latter phrase arose from the depths of Lovejoy's immersion in the Old Testament. Like many of his abolitionist contemporaries, he had a biblical and apocalyptic imagination. Abolitionists were, he believed, like the ancient Hebrew prophets: modern-day embodiments of God's word and God's gift of freedom to every human being. They were all in danger, as was the country itself, of being carried off, like the ancient Hebrews, into captivity, to be enslaved in Babylon or kept in bondage in Egypt, slaves to the dominance of the slave power. Their commitment was existential, one of life or death.

As always, his desk piled high with letters, Adams answered every one. In April 1837 he responded to Joseph Lovejoy. The young man's words had touched a chord. After all, Adams had for decades been urging young Americans to become morally engaged with the life of the republic, its history, its government, and the threats to its well-being. An unreconstructed New Englander but also a fervent nationalist, Adams looked to the West as the proving ground of America's character. Its future was there. He may never have heard of Alton, Illinois, but he undoubtedly knew that there was an Adams County, Illinois, created in 1825 and named after him. In it was a city on the Mississippi called Quincy. And though he was never to travel any farther west than Ohio, he had a great interest in Western expansion (to be accomplished, he hoped, without war or slavery), and the expectation that promising young men would come out of the West to lead the nation to a better way and a better time.

The Washington leadership was not as pervasively corrupt, Adams assured Joseph Lovejoy, as widely believed. "I hope and believe that your impressions of deep and general corruption among the leaders of the great parties of this country are the result of your anxiety and exaggerated fears for the virtues of the people." Striking a long-standing theme of his father's generation that he felt universally valid, he preached a post-Calvinistic sermon about American materialism. "Corruption is too often the consequence of great prosperity and for the last twenty-two years we have been visited with the temptation of that state, as no people ever were before." An all too prosperous America had become an embodiment of material self-indulgence. Through the agency of parties, politics had become a vehicle of corrupt self-interest. "That some relaxation from the virtues of our earlier age has followed cannot be denied, and party spirit the most infectious of all corruptions of a free people has undoubtedly tainted the political morality of almost all the public men now the leaders of the Union." There is "little to choose between them. To purify and refine their characters, the trial of *adversity* must come, as I have no doubt it will, and *that* will sift the wheat from the chaff and restore many of the principles of Republican virtue, proclaimed in the Declaration of Independence."

When, in November 1837, Adams read the horrendous news of the anti-abolitionist Alton mob's murder of Elijah Lovejoy, he assumed that "this Lovejoy" was the man who had written him the letter "which I answered in April." The name had stayed in the back of his retentive memory. He was unaware that there were three brothers. "One of the leading abolitionists of the time . . . he was a man of strong religious, conscientious feeling," Adams wrote in his diary, "deeply indignant at what he deemed the vices and crimes of the age. Such men are often fated to be martyrs." Adams of course would have understood that, in the larger context, it made no difference which of the Lovejoy brothers had been murdered. The event spoke to larger issues. It was "the most atrocious case of rioting which ever disgraced this country." And the incident epitomized the extent to which the proponents of the gag rule and their allies were willing to go, including the almost daily death threats that Adams received in the mail. On the subject of slavery, he had reason to conclude, there was no personal security or security for free speech and the perpetuation of the Union. He assumed that there would be more martyrs to come. Those who loved him worried that he would be one, that there was an assassin's bullet ready to fly at him, whether in the streets he walked or the theaters he attended so regularly (especially when any Shakespeare play was being performed), or even in the corridors of Congress.

Late in December, the Washington reporter for the *Sangamo Journal* told its Springfield readers that the apoplectic turmoil in Congress about the gag rule and slavery now reflected the national discourse. In the Senate, "I never saw Mr. Calhoun so much agitated." In both houses, Southern voices threatened disunion. As usual, Henry Clay attempted to calm the waters, to protect both slavery and the Union, to find some middle ground. "Clay repudiates the idea that the Union can be dissolved either by abolition or anti-abolition, by any faction or excitement." For the moment, the dramatic action was in the Senate. "In the House of Representatives, Mr. Adams has commenced his presentation of abolition and anti-Texian memorials, and they were all of them after a hard struggle laid on the table. The question of reception was raised in regard to the abolition petitions. . . . Much is to be feared from a continuation of discussion about slavery even among the people," the *Journal* correspondent continued, "and for some weeks past, there has been so much agitation on the subject in Boston, and in other places that another Alton tragedy has been looked for. The consequences of the introduction of the topic into Congress would be fatal to the harmony of that body."

Yet there had been no harmony in Congress for years on anything to do with slavery, and the only way to maintain even a semblance of harmony was to exclude the subject altogether. Indirectly, the *Journal* was supporting the gag rule and a gradual suppression of the significance of Lovejoy's assassination. It was the overwhelmingly popular view everywhere except in the Northeast, where there was public opinion on both sides and where a small number of abolitionists, white and black, were, short of physical suppression, not to be silenced. A resolution passed at a public meeting of the "COLOURED CITIZENS OF NEW YORK" in late November 1837, at Reverend Theodore S. Wright's First Colored Presbyterian Church in Harlem, unflinchingly stated the position of the American Abolition Society and of a substantial number of black Americans: Lovejoy had been assassinated "in sustaining the liberty of the press and the holy principles of Abolition, to which he was honored of God to become the first Martyr in this nation." Heartened by the widespread attention paid to the Alton events, Joseph and Owen Lovejoy were not supporting silence about their brother's death and the cause for which he had died. In the South, moderate elites balanced the view that Elijah had been responsible for his own death with condemnation of mob violence. Free speech, except on the subject of slavery, readily lent itself to support everywhere. That mob violence was pernicious seemed self-evident. But slavery itself was kept offstage as much as possible, even in the North.

Within a month of Elijah's death his brothers began to collect materials for a memoir, a privately published book of vindication to be distributed as widely as possible in as large a print run as funds would allow. They had much of the manuscript in hand by late February 1838, hoping to publish in March. In late February, Owen visited Washington. Adams, who "was very glad to see me and treated me very kindly," Owen wrote, learned that there had been three Lovejoy brothers. Joseph also made his first trip to Washington. He was "introduced to J. Q. Adams, had him alone an hour or two—was charmed with his immense resources. He was very social and kind and feels deeply interested in the Alton matter." Adams agreed to write an introduction. In New York, Owen anxiously waited for Adams' manuscript. If it didn't come soon, they would try someone else. Then, late in March, Adams' introduction was in Owen's hands. "It is done at last," Owen wrote to his mother. He had six thousand copies printed, then headed west to Illinois. Starting in the 1850s, he became an active facilitator of the Underground Railroad and then a fervent Lincoln Republican. Serving in Congress in the years leading up to and during the Civil War, he would become a living memorial to his brother's martyrdom.

The six thousand copies of *Memoir of the Rev. Elijah P. Lovejoy; Who Was Murdered in Defence of the Liberty of the Press. At Alton, Illinois, Nov. 7, 1837* prominently displayed on its title page "Introduction by John Quincy

Adams." It was a coup for the brothers. After all, the congressman was a busy man besieged by moral and political obligations. No doubt, though, he felt compelled to speak out once again, the Lovejoy example and his own mission dovetailing beyond any pressure of time and energy that the elderly Adams might have felt. The Lovejoy brothers had come to the right man. Joseph's letter of the previous year had turned out to be an unintended introduction to the task, and in visiting Washington the brothers had benefited from Adams' open door. Anyone had access to him, either by mail or in person. This had been Adams' commitment since his induction into government service. And Elijah Lovejoy had been a martyr to two things Adams cared deeply about: freedom of the press and antislavery. They were subjects about which Adams already had said much and now had more to say.

The subject was human freedom, the form a vigorously written and readable essay of about 2,500 words. The argument was simple, the exposition compelling: "The absolute despotisms of antiquity," Adams wrote, "under which the lives, persons, and property of the subject were utterly unprotected from the will of the despot, vanished very early by the adoption of the Christian faith as the religion of the Roman empire. But that life, liberty, and pursuit of happiness were inextinguishable rights of all mankind, had never been proclaimed as the only rightful foundation of human association and government, until the Declaration of Independence, laid it down, as the corner stone of the North American Union. It was a discovery in the combined science of morals and politics."

The two originators of the rights and principles of freedom that the modern world proclaims as its highest obligation to every individual are the Christianity of its inspired founder and the principles of the Declaration of Independence. Christianity "commands obedience to the laws. It enjoins reverence to the powers that be—but it lays down first principles, before which, carried to their unavoidable conclusions, all oppression, tyranny and wrong must vanish from the face of the earth. That all mankind are of one blood, and that the relation between them is that of brothers. That the rule of social intercourse between them is that each should do to all, as he would that all should do to him. This is Christianity—and this is the whole duty of man to man." It forbids war, and it forbids slavery. "The second great victory of the Christian system of morals was over oppressive governments—and that victory has not yet been consummated." It was a work in progress even in the United States. But "it is the pride and glory of the confederated North American Republic, that in the instrument of their first association they solemnly declared and proclaimed these truths, derived by clear unequivocal deduction, from the first principles of the Christian faith, to be self-evident—and announced them as the first principles both of their Union and of their Independence."

Still, first principles need effective implementation. As he had been articulating for decades, the flaw was in the implementation. The Constitution had perpetuated slavery in a series of compromises between the North and the South. The task of creating a nation in which powerful constituencies demanded accommodation as the price of assent had resulted in a contradiction so morally corrosive and materially divisive that the existence of the Union could not indefinitely continue without correction. Matters would only get worse. Ultimately, the power of first principles would implode the structures that defied them. Governments over historical time, "whether civil, ecclesiastical, or military," have been agents "of tyranny and oppression," Adams argued, but not "the most pernicious. . . . The laws of war, and the institutions OF DOMESTIC SLAVERY, have been far more effective instruments for converting the bounties of the Creator to the race of man into a curse, than all the tyrannies of emperors and kings that ever existed upon earth. War is a perpetual violation of the right of human beings to life, liberty, and the pursuit of happiness." Slavery is "the base-born progeny of war."

For decades, Adams had helped lead the United States through the complicated international and political minefields of the African slave trade. Slavery itself was the crime, the original sin. It was "politically incompatible with a free Constitution, and religiously incompatible with the laws of God. . . . That an American citizen, in a state whose Constitution repudiates all Slavery, should die a martyr in defence of the freedom of the press, is a phenomenon in the history of this Union. It forms an era, in the progress of mankind towards universal emancipation." It marks an "epoch in the annals of human liberty." Lovejoy's assassination was like the "shock as of an earthquake throughout this continent, which will be felt in the most distant regions of the earth." He is the "first American Martyr to *THE FREEDOM OF THE PRESS, AND THE FREEDOM OF THE SLAVE.*"

THE MAN who was to become the second American martyr to the freedom of the slave probably never read Adams' introduction to Elijah Lovejoy's memoir. Adams and others anticipated that there would be more martyrs to come. Adams worried that he himself might be one. Lincoln's path to martyrdom was, of course, totally different from Lovejoy's, and the story of how an anti-abolition moderate Whig, by conviction and personality embracing compromise and conciliation, and America as a white man's country, was elevated to the highest level of presidential immortality by an assassin's bullet and a war he did everything he could to avoid has its twists, turns, and ironies. Lincoln of course knew about Lovejoy's death, which he deplored in his brief allusion to the martyr in his Springfield Lyceum address. Whatever he thought beyond that, he kept his public and rhetorical distance.

In 1908 a letter from Lincoln came to light that revealed that he had had much more to say about Lovejoy than the meager allusion in his 1838 address. The letter's discovery was a wish come true for those eager to emphasize Lincoln's commitment to emancipation and black citizenship, and to create a mythical Lincoln who throughout his life dedicated himself to the high ideal of the Declaration of Independence and applied it to all races without qualification. That he had never believed that the principle applied to American blacks had the potential to create an undesirable counternarrative. Popular history and national mythmaking prefer simple stories. The Lincoln letter that the *Belleville* (Illinois) *Weekly Advocate* published in April 1908 filled in and completed a heretofore puzzlingly incomplete Lincoln/Lovejoy story. It came from a collection of notes and letters originating with James Lemen, a Revolutionary War veteran who settled in Illinois early in the nineteenth century, the founder of the first Baptist church in the state and a prominent opponent of slavery. His notes and letters, republished in 1915 with a scholarly introduction as *The Relations of Thomas Jefferson and James Lemen in the Exclusion of Slavery from Illinois and the Northwest Territory with Related Documents 1781–1818*, provides an account of Leman's secret Jefferson-sponsored mission to do everything in his power to keep slavery out of Illinois. Among the letters in the collection attesting to Lemen's antislavery credentials were two written in 1857, one by Stephen Douglas, the other by Abraham Lincoln.

"Friend Lemen," Lincoln wrote from Springfield on March 2, 1857, to the son of James Lemen, thanks "for your warm appreciation of my views in a former letter as to the importance in many features of your collection of old family notes and papers." He would

> *add a few words more as to Elijah P. Lovejoy's case. His letters among your old family notes were of more interest to me than even those of Thomas Jefferson, written to your father. . . . Both your father and Lovejoy were pioneer leaders in the cause of freedom, and it has always been difficult for me to see why your father, who was a resolute, uncompromising, and aggressive leader, who boldly proclaimed his purpose to make both the territory and the state free, never aroused nor encountered any of that mob violence which both in St. Louis and Alton confronted or pursued Lovejoy, and which finally doomed him to a felon's death and a martyr's crown. . . .*

> *Lovejoy, one of the most inoffensive of men, for merely printing a small paper, devoted to the freedom of the body and mind of man, was pursued to his death; while his older comrade in the cause of freedom, Rev. James Lemen, Sr., who boldly and aggressively proclaimed his purpose to make both the territory and the state free, was never molested a moment by the minions of violence. The madness and pitiless determination with which the mob steadily pursued Lovejoy to his doom, marks it as one of the most unreasoning and unreasonable in all time, except that which doomed the Savior to the cross. If ever you should come to Springfield again, do not fail to call. The memory of our many "evening sittings" here and elsewhere, as we called them, suggests many a pleasant hour, both pleasant and helpful. Truly yours, A. Lincoln.*

The letter is a forgery. Lincoln was in Chicago, not Springfield, at the beginning of March 1857. The vocabulary, the syntax, the sentence rhythms, and the lengthy (here omitted) comparison drawing on the New Testament, comparing James Lemen to the apostle John and Lovejoy to Peter, has no parallel in anything Lincoln ever wrote. He knew his Bible better than that. A master of American colloquial prose, Lincoln could no more write like this than a donkey can sing on key. His genius with language never allowed him to write in this flat, fawning, conventional style and tone. The forgery highlights the assumption that Lincoln and Lovejoy had so much in common that surely Lincoln had more to say about him (and favorably) than his brief allusion in the 1838 Springfield address. It assumed that Lovejoy's assassination must have had a great impact on young Lincoln's views about slavery. In fact, Lovejoy and Lincoln were worlds apart on how to deal with slavery. Most post–Civil War recollections of Lincoln are voluntary or requested responses to the question "Ah, did you once see Lincoln plain?" The self-serving optics were, for many, irresistible. Reflected glory and modified history create a powerfully satisfying delusion.

FOUR

A Field of Blood

In the early 1780s the almost seventy-year-old Congregational minister of Byfield, a small town in Essex County, Massachusetts, was accused by one of his deacons of being a "man stealer." Moses Parsons owned one slave. The deacon's accusation stunned him. His crime, the town was told, "ranked with the most enormous crimes that Scripture gives us any account of." The minister, who had moved to Byfield in 1774, was to die there in 1783, at the age of seventy. Thirty miles northeast of Boston, the quiet village had an abolitionist deacon in its midst: the deacon did not hesitate, despite the disapproval of most of his neighbors, to condemn to hell the Harvard-educated, highly respected minister for what he believed was a crime against God.

In 1780, Massachusetts had adopted a constitution, written by John Adams, assisted by a committee that included Moses Parsons' son Theophilus, later to be the chief justice of the Massachusetts Supreme Court. It declared "all men are born free and equal." They "have certain natural, essential, and unalienable rights." In 1783 the state Supreme Court declared slavery illegal. Moses Parsons, his grandson wrote in 1859, summoned his three "slaves into his sitting-room, and there, in the presence of his children, declared to them that they were free." The two who worked alongside the minister on his farm immediately decamped. His house slave, Violet, a dark-skinned black "of pure African descent," who had come into his possession as a very young girl, declined. "'No, no, master,' said she, 'if you please, this must not be. You have had the best of me, and you and yours must have the worst. Where am I to go in sickness or old age? No, master; your slave I am, and always will be, and I will belong to your children, when you are gone; and by you and them I mean to be cared for.' She lived in the family until she was nearly ninety," a part of its daily life, warmly remembered by Parsons' descendants as a family member.

A law-regarding churchman, the minister was deeply offended by the deacon's accusation. After all, Parsons had offered Violet her freedom. Since she had chosen to stay, the absence of a legal document testifying to her status did not justify denouncing him as a sinful slave owner. The minister "invited" the deacon "to ascertain [Violet's] wishes." She emphatically rebuked the antislavery deacon in language unfit to print, apparently having adopted the flinty New England view that neighbors should mind their own business unless called on for help. The parish sided with Parsons. It temporarily suspended the deacon's fellowship in the church, a severe criticism of his tone rather than his substance.

Violet was an independent spirit, and practical. She embraced the only family she had. Over her lifetime, with their assent, she assimilated into the family ethos. Its spirit and reputation became inseparable from her own. "It was not merely that she identified her interests with those of the family," Moses' grandson wrote, "but she believed that she was one of us. She remembered nothing of parents or relations of her own blood; she grew up with my grandfather's children, a child with them." She fell "into an indefinite sort of notion that she was of our kith and kin. . . . And so Violet, the slave, the servant, the friend, lived among us and died." The president of Harvard officiated at her funeral, "and she was buried with every circumstance of expense or ceremony which could have taken place had she been a daughter of the house; and her remains now rest in the family tomb."

Violet's narrative and her decision to remain in the Parsons family were put into words by others. The words, though, have the ring of truth. After all, what did her legal status matter if she continued to be treated with respect and be well taken care of? On her own, she would be relatively helpless. And no one in Byfield or in Massachusetts was, by the late eighteenth century, defending slavery, though many felt its existence elsewhere was not their concern. Emancipation created a financial problem for slave owners and former slaves: state law required that a slave seeking legal freedom bring suit, automatically to be decided in the plaintiff's favor. But the process would have bureaucratic costs; they would have to be paid by someone. Violet was unlikely to be able to pay. Parsons was suffering the loss of the market value of his slave property. Local and personal considerations dominated such individual manumissions. Statewide, the larger concern was that emancipation would attract impoverished blacks from other states to be supported at the taxpayers' expense, that abolitionist activity would disrupt national unity, and that investments in businesses connected to the slave economy would be at risk. There were unlikely, though, to be slave entrepreneurs in Byfield.

In 1785, when the ill will the deacon caused had died down, "the ex-deacon, who was, I believe, a very good man," Parsons' grandson wrote, "but probably not quite so much better than his neighbors as he thought himself, made full and formal acknowledgment that, in his treatment of the Reverend Moses Parsons . . . he had urged his arguments against the slavery of the Africans with excessive vehemence and asperity, without showing a due concern for his character and usefulness as an elder, or for the peace and edification of the church." He was then "restored to full fellowship." His neighbors had not been keen on having stones thrown at them, and post-Revolution Massachusetts was in the process of eliminating the problem. Many of Byfield's residents apparently felt that this time of transition called for moderation and respect, especially for those, like Parsons, who had had to implement the change.

In most other states, change came more slowly, mostly at a glacial pace. To men like Byfield's deacon, for whom the imperative was apocalyptically insistent, it moved excruciatingly slowly. New Jersey and New York, for example, would take decades from the end of the Revolutionary War to become entirely slave free. Much of the rest of the country took even longer. In the late 1850s, the ameliorative candidate of the newly formed modern Republican Party was to say that it did no good to throw stones at slave owners. Respectful persuasion was best. Only time, education, and a change of heart would end slavery in the South. The larger problem seemed insoluble.

A MARRIAGE between a black man and a black woman took place in January 1784 in the home of the most distinguished resident of Braintree, Massachusetts. It was not a sight that anyone there would have witnessed before: a free black woman and a free black man married by a Congregationalist clergyman in the home of a well-known white family. The family patriarch was John Adams, the U.S. minister to the Netherlands, now in Paris and Amsterdam on matters of peace, trade, and finance, and soon to be appointed minister to the Court of St. James's. Sixteen-year-old John Quincy, his eldest son, was with him. Three other children remained at home. His wife, Abigail, had arranged that the marriage take place in her own front parlor. The officiating clergyman was Anthony Wibird, the seventh minister of the First Congregational Church of Braintree. Through his sermons and rituals he had ministered to the Adams family for almost thirty years.

The previous September, the Reverend William Smith, Abigail's father, had died. His will, dated the last day of September 1783, revealed the awkwardness of the transition into legal emancipation in Massachusetts. With her two sisters, Abigail had grown up in a household in which there were at different times three or four slaves, the men doing the vegetable gardening and other heavy chores, and a female, named Phoebe, working in the house. One of the male slaves, between 1764 and 1766, had carried private courtship letters between Abigail Smith and John Adams. What Reverend William Smith thought of slavery nobody now knows. Like many New England clergymen of the period, he was comfortable enough with the institution to own slaves. The Puritan God had not commanded abolition. It was, until the ruling of the Massachusetts Supreme Court, a local and individual matter. As in the Parsons household, some slaves, particularly female servants, were familiar, valued, everyday presences. Some considered themselves and were considered family members. Like Parsons' Violet, Phoebe had been William Smith's slave since childhood. She had been in the family at least since Abigail was a little girl, and Smith had officiated at her first wedding, her marriage to a free black resident of Boston.

The minister now, in his will, disposed of Phoebe. "I give unto my Negro Woman Phoebe her freedom," he wrote, "in case she should chuse it; but if she should not Chuse it I do then give the said Phoebe unto either of my Daughters. And it is my will that one hundred pounds be retained out of my estate, and that to such my daughter with whom the said Phoebe shall live, the annual interest thereof shall be paid so long as she shall live with her if by sickness, or age the said Phoebe shall become a charge to her; or otherwise my Executors shall have full liberty to apply the said one hundred pounds or any part thereof for [her] comfortable maintenance and support." But it was not possible in Massachusetts legally to remain a slave after 1783. Still, no one other than a fanatical deacon would have maintained that a former slave could not decline to do the legal paperwork and remain with the person who had previously owned her. Smith could have avoided the issue by selling her out of state at any time up to 1783, using a middleman to take her to where she could be sold and deliver to Smith what was due him. He chose otherwise, accepting his responsibility for the post-slavery maintenance of Phoebe.

Still, Smith apparently believed it was his right to give her the choice. If she did not choose freedom, he assumed he could dispose of her as if she were still a slave, as a gift or bequest. In either case, she might benefit from the handsome sum of £100. His choice of language speaks to the world he had lived in all his life. Whatever her decision, Phoebe would be either a pensioned-off retainer or a sponsored dependent, with or without a legal document stating that she was free. Unlike Parsons' Violet, Phoebe chose to activate her freedom. Continuing to live in Weymouth, having been set up in her own housekeeping by Abigail and her sisters, supported by the interest on Smith's bequest, in early 1784 she decided to marry again. Since there was at the time no minister in Weymouth, Abigail said to her longtime slave—servant? family member? obligation?—why not take your vows in my front parlor? "I gave them the liberty," she wrote to her husband, "of celebrating their nuptials here, which they did much to their satisfaction."

Abigail had another helpful scheme in mind. After years of separation, it had been decided that she and her daughter Nabby would join John Adams in Europe. The two younger sons would stay behind, under the care of Abigail's sisters. Whether to undertake a dangerous winter crossing or wait till spring created a season of anxious deliberation. Abigail, though, had a solution to one issue: what to do with the family's Braintree house, one of two adjacent buildings on the Plymouth Road, in the other of which Abigail's sister Mary lived. "I have determined to put into this House [my] Pheby," she wrote to her husband in February 1784, "to whom my father gave freedom, by his will, and the income of a hundred a year during her Life. . . . I proposed to her taking care of this House and furniture in my absence." Phoebe accepted. "The trust is very flattering to her, and both her Husband and She Seemed pleased with it. I have no doubt of their care and faithfullness, and prefer them to any other family."

Abigail knew Phoebe well, her character and trustworthiness. As house-sitters, the newly married couple were to have all the rights that went with the house, including the garden vegetables for home consumption, sale, or barter. No limitations were imposed. Phoebe and her husband were free to continue their lives in their usual ways, including having a black couple live with them between working assignments. When, in June, Abigail and Nabby sailed for Europe, Phoebe and her husband had to have been delighted to be the occupants, rent free, of a handsome, well-furnished house. Apparently, some neighbors were displeased that a black couple not only occupied the Adams house but conveyed the impression that they were there as independent providers of a mutual service. Abigail's sister praised Phoebe's competence. She "keeps [your house] in nice order. . . . She looks happy." And she would in fact have been happy, Mary continued, "if some of the Neighbours did not trouble her. She says She Believes they think that you left her your Almoner, for she cannot think that they can Suppose her able to supply all their wants. They impose upon her sadly." Though slavery had ended in Massachusetts, long-standing attitudes had not.

Mary had otherwise only good things to report. The next summer she wrote that "your sable Tenants almost maintain themselves by selling" a fine crop of grain and corn. From London, Abigail regularly expressed tender concern. "How does Pheby. Does her income make her comfortable. If it does not, I would willingly contribute towards her support." Mary reassured her: "Abdy and Phebe do very well and live very comfortably. She has her health better than She used to do. She washes for some of the Neighbours. She does So for me." But "she complains that she cannot get work enough to do." Her husband is "always Puddering about but does not bring much to pass." Phoebe continued to work at her usual menial jobs, her husband to putter, as the tenants of the Adams ancestral home for much of the next decade.

Ten years later, Abigail, now the wife of the first vice president, had had enough of Philadelphia, America's temporary capital. She preferred to spend the winter of 1797 in Quincy. Phoebe may or may not have been still living there. As with most of her black contemporaries, history remembers her only through her interaction with the literate white world. There's not another word about her in the available record. From her temporary residences in New York and then Philadelphia, Abigail, though, had much to say on the subject of black character: the superiority of black servants to white, the inferiority of the white working-class work ethic south of New England, and the different gradations of blackness she encountered. "I had rather," she told Mary, "have black than white help, as they will be more like to agree with those" black servants she had brought from Massachusetts who had absorbed the New England work ethic. "I have a very clever black Boy of 15," named Prince, "who has lived with me a year and is bound to me till he is 21, my [white] coachman will not allow that he is a negro, but he will pass for one with us." Mary scouted black servants and farmhands from the Boston area to work for the Adamses. Emancipation, Abigail observed, bred self-sufficiency and responsibility, a commitment to productive work. Slavery bred slackness, and the closer one came to the South, the less productive black labor became.

In Quincy in February 1797, before leaving for the newly established permanent capital, Abigail had a direct confrontation with prejudiced neighbors. "I have been much diverted with a little occurence which took place a few days since," she wrote to her husband, "and which serve to shew how little founded in nature the so much boasted principle of Liberty and equality is." One of the Adamses' black farmhands wanted his son to attend a newly opened evening school that was teaching arithmetic to boys apprenticed to local employers. It would cost a shilling a week. The pupils would bring their own firewood and candles. One of Abigail's young black apprentices had for some time been attending the Quincy town school about which she had "heard no objection. . . . 'Go with my compliments to Master Heath,'" Abigail told Prince, "'and ask him if he would take'" the young boy. "He did and Master Heath returnd for answer that he would." The boy began attending the school. The next week, Abigail's neighbor James Faxon, whose sons attended the same school, "came in one Evening and requested to speak to me . . . to inform me" that if the Negro boy continued to attend the school "it would break up the School for the other Lads refused to go." What? Abigail responded: "'Has the Boy misbehaved? If he has let the Master turn him out of school.' 'O no, there was no complaint of that kind, but they did not chuse to go to School with a Black Boy.' 'Do they object to going to church with him?'" Abigail asked. Since they sit separately in church, why not in school? And "'did these Lads ever object to James playing for them when at a dance? How can they bear to have a Black in the Room with them there?'"

"'O it is not I that object,'" Faxon responded, "'or my Boys. It is some others.' 'Pray who are they? Why did not they come themselves?'" Whereas segregated seating in school, as in church, was acceptable to Abigail, exclusion from opportunity was not. "'The Boy is a Freeman as much as any of the young Men, and merely because his Face is Black, is he to be denied instruction? How is he to be qualified to procure a livelihood? Is this the Christian principle of doing to others, as we would have others do to us?'" Faxon was quick to be officious. "'O Mam, you are quite right. I hope you wont take any offence.' 'None at all Mr. Faxon, only be so good as to send the young men to me. I think I can convince them that they are wrong. I have not thought it any disgrace to my self to take him into my parlour and teach him both to read and write. Tell them Mr. Faxon that I hope we shall all go to Heaven together.' Upon which Faxon laugh'd, and thus ended the conversation. I have not heard any more upon the subject."

The subject, though, could not be repressed, then or in the future. The contradiction between "all men are created equal," to which the Revolutionary War had been dedicated, "the so much boasted principle of Liberty and equality" that Abigail threw back in the face of the national hypocrisy, and the reality of slavery and racism would always be an embarrassment, a moral conundrum, and a complication for the Adamses. They had no doubt that it was incompatible with the principles on which the Revolution had been based.

WHEN IN 1766 the Stamp Act, a London-mandated tax on printed materials, intensified the feeling of many American colonists that they were being treated by the British government as second-class citizens, some resorted to slave/master language to express their anger. Parliament, they protested, was treating them as if they were slaves, not freeborn Englishmen. The spineless West Indian colonists, John Adams wrote in his diary, had surrendered "the Rights of Britons" and deserted "the Cause of Liberty." Americans would not do that. The West Indians were "Meeching, sordid, stupid Creatures, below Contempt, below Pity. So craven were they, they deserved to be made Slaves to their own Negroes," who seemed "to have more of the Spirit of Liberty than they." They deserved a black insurrection, Adams fulminated, so little did they value their own liberty. Those Americans who accepted London's new rules deserved to be slaves.

Such rhetoric hardly distinguished between slavery as metaphor and slavery as reality. Outrage at what seemed an infringement of natural and legal rights could exploit language that in any rational consideration had no right to be used. The use of the word *slave* to express the feelings of many colonists in the revolutionary struggle inevitably contributed, after independence had been won, to the moral discomfort felt by some citizens of the new nation when, during the Articles of Confederation and Constitutional conventions, the intractability of the slavery problem became apparent. Slavery as reality, not as metaphor, had always been condemned by the Adamses. "I wish most sincerely there was not a Slave in the province," Abigail wrote to her husband in 1774. "It allways appeard a most iniquitious Scheme to me—fight ourselfs for what we are daily robbing and plundering from those who have as good a right to freedom as we have. You know my mind upon this Subject." Those who owned slaves, she speculated, could not cherish freedom as much as those who did not. "I have sometimes been ready to think that the passion for Liberty cannot be Eaquelly Strong in the Breasts of those who have been accustomed to deprive their fellow Creatures of theirs. Of this I am certain that it is not founded upon that generous and christian principal of doing to others as we would that others should do unto us."

Worst of all, for those Northerners involved in nation thinking and nation making at the highest level, their Southern counterparts, with whom on other grounds they were collegial, were all slave owners. The South was indeed a foreign country. And the mentality of many slave owners appeared to some Northerners, even in the cooperative revolutionary period, that of masters of the universe looking down on inferior creatures. Virginia and South Carolina oligarchs radiated an aura of superiority, the slave-owning elite's belief that its privilege was deserved, its culture superior. Many of the Northern elite felt, as John Quincy Adams later complained, that the Southern elite in Congress spoke and acted as if the South were to the North as slave owners to their slaves. If the Adamses had been asked to use one word to describe the Southerners they knew, it would have been *arrogant*. To Northerners, sensitive to the virtues of their own culture and to the master/slave terminology they had exploited in rebelling against British tyranny, Southern condescension felt like personal insult. It implied tyranny and enslavement, metaphors rather than realities, but metaphors with an emotional sting. At the same time, Adams and his Northern colleagues knew that the creation and the continuance of the United States depended on compromising with Southern interests, including the perpetuation of slavery in the states that chose to keep it.

Also, they early on discovered that slavery was a subject open for discussion in national forums only at great risk. Every Southern state would sustain its allegiance to the Union only if its primary economic and social institution remained inviolate. That was clear to most Northern delegates during the Articles of Confederation debates in the summer of 1776. For John Adams, the Confederation Congress, at which he took detailed notes, especially about whether slaves would be taxed as property and which states would pay more or less of the nation's bills, was an eye-opener. For the first time, he observed firsthand Southern values and views about slavery. No negotiation was possible. South Carolina's Thomas Lynch made the Southern position clear, as Adams recorded: "If it is debated, whether their Slaves are their Property, there is an End of the Confederation. Our Slaves being our Property, why should they be taxed more than the Land, Sheep, Cattle, Horses, and Freemen cannot be got, to work in our Colonies." Benjamin Franklin answered Lynch: "Slaves rather weaken than strengthen the [?] there is therefore some difference between them and Sheep. Sheep will never make any Insurrections."

The next year, in Baltimore for the Articles of Confederation debates, Adams recorded a striking difference between "the Manners of Maryland" and the culture of New England. Maryland's agrarian society has "but few Merchants. They are chiefly Planters and Farmers." Most important, "the Lands are cultivated, and all Sorts of Trades are exercised by Negroes . . . which has occasioned the Planters and Farmers to assume the Title of Gentlemen, and they hold their Negroes and . . . all labouring People and Tradesmen, in such Contempt, that they think themselves a distinct order of Beings. Hence they never will suffer their Sons to labour or learn any Trade, but they bring them up in Idleness or what is worse in Horse Racing, Cock fighting, and Card Playing." The South's slave owners, he concluded, consider themselves "a distinct order of Beings," superior to those who value the Puritan work ethic and labor as farmers, farmhands, traders, shopkeepers, craftsmen, clerks, teachers, journalists, shipbuilders, clergymen, bankers, businessmen, investors, brokers, and lawyers in an economic structure in which worth is defined by labor, whether of the body or the mind. Northerners were not and could never be, in Southern eyes, "gentlemen." A gentleman did not work for a living.

Abigail could be equally expressive. "Having had a full view of Southern politicks and Southern Elections," she wrote from Quincy to her husband in May 1794, "I begin to *think* we are much the greatest part of the union. much as [they] hold Britain in disdain and abuse her constitution, they have adopted the most pernicious part in the most corrupted Stage [Congress]—a packe of Negro drivers, they deserve chains themselves."

In 1801, preparing to leave Washington after a narrowly lost election, the result of the South's slave-generated electoral votes, John Adams had a dark but accurate overview of the state of the nation, with one exception. Like many others, even some Southerners, he believed that "the practice of slavery is fast diminishing," that the age of reason and humanism, despite the compromises of the Constitution, was in the process of eliminating it. Slavery also seemed an unviable economic institution. He was not, though, in favor of immediate emancipation. "The Abolition of Slavery must be gradual and accomplished with much caution and Circumspection. Violent means and measures would produce greater violations of Justice and Humanity, than the continuance of the practice." He could not, of course, know that the recent invention of the cotton gin would transform the slavery-cotton nexus into the major asset of the South, productivity migrating from the farmed-out tobacco soil of Virginia to the rich cotton-producing earth of the Deep South. Cotton wealth was soon to increase the already substantial Southern clout in Washington. Cotton would make secession seem economically viable, and Adams could not anticipate that in the next fifty years the slave population would grow to four million.

As to many of his contemporaries, it seemed to John Adams that slavery was so obvious a moral injustice and economic stupidity that it would die a natural death. Better to let it die on its own than to make changes that might alienate enough Southerners to threaten the existence of the Union, already threatened by various evils that "are growing, (whereas the practice of slavery is fast diminishing,) and threaten to bring Punishment on our Land, more immediately than the oppression of the blacks." Like many Northerners raised in the Protestant dissenting tradition, Adams had his list of national flaws, some of which have resonance for modern-day Americans. As great an evil as slavery was, it was not, he believed, the only, let alone the most imminent, threat to the Union. "That Sacred regard to Truth in which you and I were educated, and which is certainly taught and enjoined from on high, Seems to be vanishing from among Us. A general Relaxation of Education and Government. A general Debauchery as well as dissipation, produced by pestilential philosophical Principles of Epicurus." In Virginia and other Southern states, the condition of "the common Sort of White People," the working and the nonworking poor in states with extreme income inequality, seems "more serious and threatening Evils, than even the slavery of the Blacks, hateful as that is." At the end of the eighteenth and into the nineteenth century, this seemed a plausible emphasis.

SLEEPING IN his family home in Scarborough, Maine, an eleven-year-old boy was awakened late in the night on March 19, 1766, by his pregnant mother's screams, his sibling's cries, and his father's loud resistance to thirty drunken men, disguised as Indians, breaking into the house. Hatchets were thrown through windows, papers burned, furniture destroyed. The perpetrators, later called "a Mob" by one of Massachusetts' most promising young lawyers, rifled the homeowner's papers, "and terrifyed him, his Wife, Children and Servants in the Night. It is enough to move a Statue, to melt an Heart of Stone, to read the Story." Though John Adams was arguing for his client in a suit for financial restitution, he was not exaggerating. The invading vandals belonged to the Sons of

Liberty, a secretive loose confederation of anti-British colonists, some of whom desired both liberty and loot. And they were especially intent on showing who was boss, to force the well-educated and wealthy to know that they would not allow themselves to be condescended to and exploited anymore. The object of the attack was John King. His eleven-year-old son, Rufus, was to become a U.S. senator from Massachusetts and New York, twice the American ambassador to the Court of St. James's, twice the Federal Party's candidate for president, and, in 1820, to deliver a powerful antislavery speech to the U.S. Senate.

John King probably would not have approved of his son's 1820 antislavery speech. Actually, nothing is known about his views on the subject. He did, though, own numbers of slaves. Like Moses Parsons' and William Smith's slaves, they were treated as servants and almost family members. A second-generation Bostonian of English background, King had moved in the 1740s to Scarborough, a prospering town just south of Falmouth (later renamed Portland). A businessman, he had interests in ships, shipbuilding, lumber, lumberyards, and farmland. Many townspeople thought well of him. A civic leader and a pious Congregationalist, he was a wealthy, committed, and unrepentant Tory Loyalist. His politics and prosperity, which included profitable moneylending, motivated the attack on his home. He had made enemies, one of whom claimed that King had gotten "his Estate by wronging the Poor, and now we found you out, and your reign is but short."

Self-styled Liberty men, harboring economic and class grievances, often stretched law and order to make prerevolutionary statements and used anti-British sentiment as the cover for terroristic acts, settling personal scores and expropriating property. The protests against the Stamp Act provided convenient cover. To the Sons of Liberty, those who cooperated with the act were traitors, slaves to George III and enemies of the people. With a conservative's passion, John King believed that the law was sacred: every citizen was obliged to render to Caesar what was lawfully due. He detested the disguised and masked men who walked or rode in the night, who taught the lessons of destruction and fire, of shattered glass and violated homes.

When he tried to have the perpetrators brought to justice, King was rebuffed and threatened. Anonymous voices in Scarborough warned that he would have his ears cut off if he did not desist. Local authorities refused to cooperate. At his own cost, he gathered witnesses, pushing the recalcitrant legal process to grind its wheels less slowly; and a grand jury in Falmouth eventually indicted fourteen of the alleged criminals. Try as he might, though, he could get little redress. His property was attacked again, his barn set on fire, the vandals hiding in the nearby bushes, mocking his wife's cries of distress. Self-styled Liberty Men continued to harass the Kings. Life in Scarborough, where everyone knew the perpetrators, was tense. They attended the same church, went to the same town meetings. "Mrs. King," noted for her piety, "refused to take Communion as long as the rioters were permitted to do so." The court case, directed at one of the most openly hostile Liberty Men, dragged.

In 1774, King, who had been trying for vindication for seven years, found the young John Adams to represent him before the Falmouth Superior Court. A well-known advocate for independence, Adams could not be accused of harboring Tory sympathies. At the same time, no one could doubt his commitment to the absolute right to a fair trial regardless of political views. After all, he had defended the five British soldiers accused of murdering Boston citizens in 1770 in what became known as the Boston Massacre. That John King was a Tory sympathizer was irrelevant. He and his family had been victims of criminal acts.

For the jury, Adams painted in lurid language what the King family had experienced that night. Some of the horror story that he delivered to the court he included in a private letter to his wife. It also contained a larger statement about principle. "I am engaged in a famous Cause, the Cause of King, of Scarborough vs. a Mob." It was also a "Cause" on a higher level. In a revolutionary period, with a sizable minority favoring loyalty to Great Britain, there would be complicated challenges to law and order. Revolutions were often, Adams well knew, unjust to those who did not agree or who simply got in the way. But justice to the individual was still paramount. The law was not to be taken into private hands. "These private Mobs, I do and will detest." This applied also to affairs of governance and state. There had to be just cause. And the bar should be high. "If Popular Commotions can be justifyed, in Opposition to Attacks upon the [British] Constitution, it can be only when Fundamentals are invaded, nor then unless for absolute Necessity and with great Caution. But these Tarrings and Featherings, these breaking open Houses by rude and insolent Rabbles, in Resentment for private Wrongs or in pursuance of private Prejudices and Passions, must be discountenanced, cannot be even excused upon any Principle which can be entertained by a good Citizen—a worthy Member of Society." John King, Adams argued, deserved the protection of the law and restitution.

The times, though, were against what King had assumed would be the lawful protection of property and legal justice. He got neither. As the colonies moved toward rebellion, tolerance for dissent decreased. What side one took in the political schism began to determine the degree to which one had access to the rule of law. From King's point of view, this legitimized lawlessness. To submit to the Stamp Act was to be a law-abiding citizen. Civilization required that one affirm the obligation of every citizen to obey lawfully constituted authority. King had much to lose from anarchy, let alone revolution. He had dedicated his life to playing by the rules. Unlawful violence was anathema to him. Government existed to protect property and civil rights. And there were proper places to contest what seemed unjust laws: the colonial courts and the executive; in London, the Parliament and the court, where colonial representatives could attempt to influence imperial decisions. King belonged to that cohort of colonists who, also preferring minimal taxation and colonial self-governance, believed that the colonies got their money's worth from the British imperium in external protection. He gave highest priority to two values: the protective umbrella of British power and the supremacy of the law.

Matters got worse for John King in the last two years of his life. He never voluntarily recanted his loyalty to British rule. For him, it was a practical and a character-defining commitment, a test of loyalty to the extended family. He could not understand why anyone would forgo the advantage of being the subject of a beneficent imperium, especially since the cost of rebellion would be bloodshed, destruction, and anarchy. An eighteenth-century man, he considered it imprudent. In the increasingly volatile atmosphere of Massachusetts in the mid-1770s, he paid a heavy price for his views. Liberty Men in Scarborough assumed that he would collaborate with the enemy. When lumber on a ship he owned sailed into British-occupied Boston Harbor, it was sold to build barracks for the British troops. A drunken crowd of anti-British Scarborough patriots, assuming that King had sold the lumber by prearrangement, broke into his house, demanding that he renounce his Tory views. Refusing, he was forced by a form of torture to recant. It was less than waterboarding but sufficient to break him. At the age of fifty-seven, a month before Concord and Lexington, he died. His equally conservative son would have entirely different political views and a happier life.

A DISASTER struck the Adams family in April 1803. It was about money, a resource that no generation of the family had much of. Most of it was invested in local property. When the London bank, Bird, Savage and Bird, in which Abigail and John Adams' cash savings had been placed, failed, John Quincy brought the painful news to his parents. He had been entrusted with the handling of the account. "I feel myself in a great degree answerable for this calamity.... The error of judgment was mine" in not long ago having moved the funds to another bank, though there had been no reason to suspect that the bank might default. "Therefore I shall not refuse to share in the suffering."

They had counted on the principal and interest from the $14,000 as their retirement fund, their only significant source of cash income after March 1801, when John Adams relinquished the presidency's $25,000 annual salary. He could not know that his successor, Thomas Jefferson, needed the money even more than he did. But he did know that the Constitution and his opponents' Southern strategy had made Jefferson's election possible by counting slaves as people when it suited them and as property when it did not. By virtue of the compromise that had resulted in the Constitution's three-fifths stipulation, the South had extra votes in the Electoral College. To add insult to injury, the former friends were not on speaking terms, especially because Jefferson and his supporters, the "real and haughty Aristocrats," in Abigail's phrase, had managed to make stick the charge that Adams was a monarchist, an all-purpose term of insult made against Federalist leaders.

John Adams' savings were now lost. Once they left office, presidents were entirely on their own, as Jefferson and Monroe were to experience unhappily as bankrupts. In order to pay checks outstanding against his London account, Adams had to consider doing what he hated: selling some of his residential, farm, and business property. Rents and profits from these properties were modest; the remedial American banking system did not make personal loans; most mortgages were privately held, the lending done by individuals. Most wealth came from inheritance, marrying up, speculation in Western lands, and commerce: trade, shipping, banking, and insurance. The Adamses were people of the small farm, not the plantation; of the law office, not the countinghouse. How could they sustain their retirement years without selling land that represented the family's rootedness in local soil?

Rufus King, John King's son, came to the rescue. The eleven-year-old boy who in 1766 had feared for his and his family's lives had never forgotten John Adams' legal representation of his father in 1774. A friend of the Adams family, he was in a position to help. At his father's death, he had not inherited much. From early on, though, he had a knack for making money as a lawyer and an investor, a talent hyper-accelerated by his marriage to the daughter of a rich New York merchant, a member of the wealthy Alsop family of New York and Connecticut. The marriage was a success in every way, including the Alsop family's preference that King move from Massachusetts to New York City, where his connections, his wealth, and his achievements as a Federalist politician-lawyer soon made him one of New York State's first two U.S. senators and then President Washington's minister to Great Britain. He had remained in London from 1796 to 1803, one of the few Federalists whom Jefferson kept on after the election of 1800.

Like the Adamses, King had had no reason to believe that Bird, Savage and Bird would close its doors. For more than a decade, the bank had handled European financial transactions for the U.S. Treasury. Whether King had any reason except loyalty to help is unknown, but as an intimate friend and political soul mate of the family, he assured the Adamses, before departing from London in May 1803, that he would provide a bridge loan to help make good the outstanding checks. In the meantime, John Adams began to sell some of his small parcels of Boston and Quincy property to repay King. But "whether it will ever be in my power to repay . . . your act of friendship, in taking the heavy charge of the bills, and saving me from the additional burthen of protest damages I know not," John Quincy wrote to King. "That I shall ever retain a grateful sense of your kindness I do know."

Twenty-one years old in 1776, King had not hesitated to align himself with the patriot cause. A student at Harvard from 1774 to 1777, with disruptions because of wartime turmoil and time in Scarborough when his father died, he had been infuriated by the British occupation of Boston.

Personal attacks by those who assumed that he was a Tory sympathizer incensed him. Grievances against his father were imposed on the son. Over time, he successfully defended himself, but it was a nasty experience. Long before he graduated, he was a determined supporter of the Revolution. Graduating at the head of his class, he moved to Newburyport, a prosperous coastal port town northeast of Boston, to study law in the office of thirty-seven-year-old Theophilus Parsons, whose nearby father, Moses, was, in a few years, to ask his slave Violet if she desired her freedom. An engaging, clever, and dynamic lawyer, Parsons had already risen high in his profession. Almost twenty years later, he was to become John Quincy's legal mentor.

This was a small world. Those at this level of education and professional life all knew one another. Mostly all Federalists, they had as their highest priority the rule of law. They were to align themselves with the various factions in what became, in essence, the party of George Washington, Alexander Hamilton, and John Adams. Conservative by training and instinct, most Federalists required recalibration to get from devotion to the law to open rebellion. The solution was to view the Revolution as political, not social. The previous regime's time-honored values—common law, statute law, the protection of private property, respect for the individual, British standards of justice and culture, rule by the best and the brightest—would continue, they assumed, to be the values of the new country.

Rufus King, Theophilus Parsons, and John Quincy Adams never had any doubt about where they stood on the issue of slavery. But its elimination was not their highest priority. That was the perpetuation of the Union, whose very creation had been divisively debated in 1787–1788 and approved by a slim majority. Adams, King, and Parsons strongly supported it. Newly returned from Europe and a Harvard student, John Quincy at first had his doubts, mostly because he thought the proposed Constitution did not provide for a strong enough executive. He soon convinced himself into approval, mainly through discussions with his cousin William Cranch, later the chief justice of the U.S. District Court in Washington, with whom, in 1837, he was to consult on the Dorcas Allen situation. It seemed to John Quincy the best that could be agreed to at the time. Of these partisans, only Rufus King was a delegate to either assembly, in his case the Confederation Congress *and* the Constitutional Convention. An active player at both, he supported the creation of a permanent Union with a central government that would provide economic, social, political, and military security for the new country. From the start, those who favored a strong central government opposed those who did not; those favoring centralized power tended, on the whole, at least in principle, to be against slavery; and the anti-Federalists would participate in a Union only if the Constitution made slavery exclusively the business of the states. Rufus King shared the Adamses' view that the protection of slavery was the price of having the Constitution at all. At almost all costs, they wanted a central government that could raise revenues, facilitate commerce, and provide for national security.

When, in March 1789, the newly created Congress met in Philadelphia for its first session, Rufus King of New York took his Senate seat. The country's first vice president, John Adams, presided. It was a time of firsts, but the issues that dominated were mostly those that had already been the subject of hard bargaining and volatile debate. It was now necessary to implement the Constitution's guidelines for governance. Words on a page had to be translated into institutions, policies, and laws. Almost everyone recognized that, in places, the compromise text crafted in 1787 was so general and evasive that interpretation, presupposition, and what the document omitted made differences about implementation inevitable. King and other Federalists fulfilled the bargain they had agreed to in order to get the votes necessary for ratification: they voted for amendments guaranteeing the individual rights and government limits they had agreed to support as reassurance to those who feared an all-powerful federal government. The issue now, in 1790 and 1791, was how to implement the Constitution's stipulations about voting, taxes, and the court system. There was a lot of tweaking to be done. Money and power were at stake.

Writing in December 1791 from Philadelphia to her cousin Cotton Tufts, Abigail Adams observed that the most determining issue, especially from the New England point of view, was and continued to be representation. And that was inseparable from the South versus the North, especially about slavery as an economic and political asset. After all, Northerners had argued, if slaves were property, why should they be counted for congressional and Electoral College representation? Yet that arrangement was enshrined in the Constitution, and that reality, it was clear, was not to be changed under existing circumstances.

Whether slavery would be forbidden in the territories that various states had ceded to the federal government had been settled by the Confederation Congress in 1787, when it passed the Northwest Ordinance, prohibiting slavery north of the Ohio River. Fortunately, the new Congress did not have to deal with that, though much of the South soon felt buyer's remorse, which would, over time, become outright opposition and denial. The Southern elite regretted it had not been paying close enough attention in 1787: many had assumed that the relatively powerless Confederation government could do little to enforce the Northwest Ordinance. Others, like Jefferson, thought it a good humanitarian idea, though they were later to change their minds. But what was clear to King and the Adamses as the First U.S. Congress came to a close was, as Abigail noted, "the great fish have a wonderfull appetite for the small fish, and the old dominion [Virginia] Strugles hard for an over balance in the scale. what is surprizing, is to see Some persons helping them, who mean well, but do not seem to apprehend the weight of the Negro Representitives as mr King calls them. the black cattle in the Northern states might as well claim to be represented."

Still, anxiety about the continued existence of the Union, not slavery, dominated the Federalist frame of mind, and Southerners' assumptions of superiority could be tolerated, though resented. The crucial question for King, the Adamses, and their cohort was how much Southern dominance they would have to put up with to keep the Union intact. Slave representation always stuck in the craw, especially when the additional votes made a crucial difference, as they were to do in the election of 1800. But it was a done deal, almost impossible, under foreseeable circumstances, to reverse. And when Southerners, already overrepresented in the new government, threatened that if they did not get their way in additional matters (such as their preference that the federal government have a weak judiciary or almost none at all), they would leave the Union, it felt to many Northerners like blackmail. And it left those opposed to slavery in moral discomfort as well as at a political disadvantage. The indefinite protection of slavery had been the price of creating the Union and now seemed to be the price of perpetuating it. All the leverage of overrepresentation was with the South, and there were no solutions on the horizon except the increasingly unrealistic expectation that in this Enlightenment world even slave owners would come to see that slavery was incompatible with a modern society.

NO MATTER how far away he was from the domestic scene, whether in The Hague or Berlin, John Quincy Adams throughout the 1790s worried most about whether the United States would continue to exist. Would it last into the new century? He observed strong countervailing forces, misguided and self-serving. Secretary of State Thomas Jefferson and his friends were the vortex of the danger, though the Adamses partly exempted Jefferson's most brilliant friend, James Madison, who seemed to have enough common sense about government not to be entirely pulled into the Jefferson orbit. And the Jefferson faction seemed to be growing stronger, so much so that in 1796 John Adams, Washington's heir apparent, only barely defeated Jefferson for the presidency. Moreover, because the creators of the Constitution had not anticipated the birth of a party system, he found himself with Jefferson as his vice president, a semi-enemy within the camp. Adams and Jefferson's friendship from their shared European years was soon over.

There were now two flash points: the Francophile and Anglophobic views of the anti-Federalists, beginning to call themselves Republicans, and their strong belief that the federal government should keep its hands off everything except the powers explicitly granted by the Constitution, interpreted in the narrowest way. There were anti-Federalists all over the country, stressing one or both of these flash points. They were growing in number, partly because of their populist appeal to democracy, while also maintaining an elite leadership and a commitment to slavery. Their strength came from Virginia, the wealthiest Southern state. Always, whether explicitly or not, Virginia and its allies emphasized that those states that had slaves had the right to continue to have them and that any new state, the Northwest Ordinance aside, should have the right, if it wanted, to become a slave state. There were many twists and turns, many complications, as John Quincy Adams recognized, in this ideological scenario. The twists and turns were to continue for another sixty years. But the essential point was clear: if the North wanted the Union to continue to exist, it needed to toe the Southern line, especially about states' rights and slavery.

Still, much of the threat to the perpetuation of the Union, in the view of most Federalists, came from the intensity with which Jefferson and his followers loved the revolutionary government in France, not from anything to do with slavery. The new French regime was heir to the monarchy that had helped the United States gain its independence. France and the United States had been allies against Great Britain. Many Americans acknowledged that a debt was owed. As the election of 1796 came to a head, the dominant question was: to what extent was the United States obligated to support France in its war against Great Britain? Also, ideological preferences aside, how much sympathy did one feel for French direct democracy and how much for balanced British constitutionalism, and what policy toward these warring giants was in America's best interest? The Jefferson cohort explicitly preferred France. It identified with the ideology of the French Revolution. It stressed that the United States had a moral and a treaty obligation. Federalists responded that no country had the obligation to go against its vital interests; neutrality was the best policy. To support France against Great Britain would almost certainly mean war with Great Britain, and "that a dissolution of the union would be the consequence . . . I think is very probable," John Quincy wrote in June 1796, "but the dissolution of the union is perhaps rather a subject of hope than of fear to those who are hurrying the Nation to its disgrace and calamity."

It seemed to the Adamses that the anti-Federalists loved France more than the Union. For most Federalists, the only revolution they approved of was the American. That the Jeffersonians were transforming it into a social revolution, with democracy as an excuse for class warfare, seemed to carry across the Atlantic a whiff of the guillotine. Jefferson's leadership could result, the Federalists feared, in mob rule, governance by the least educated, and a direct democracy that would, as in France, have a weak executive and judiciary. And behind it all, the New England Federalists observed, was the hypocrisy of the slave master who espoused democracy. Worst of all, the Jeffersonians seemed willing to leave the Union if they did not get their way. But "all my hopes of national felicity and glory," John Quincy affirmed, "have invariably been founded upon the continuance of the Union. I have cherished these hopes with so much fondness, they have so long been incorporated into my ideas of public concern, that I cannot abandon them without a pang, as keen as that of a dissolving soul and body. . . . We shall proceed with gigantic strides to honour and consideration and National greatness, if the union is preserved, but that if it is once broken, we shall soon divide into a parcel of petty tribes at perpetual war with one another." The stinging irony was that the most vocal advocates of French-style democracy were Southern slave owners. Their commitment to slavery was as strongly felt in 1796 as it was to be sustained in 1861. In the meantime, it seemed best, "much as I must disapprove of the general tenor of Southern politics," to "yield to their unreasonable pretensions, and suffer much for their wrongs, than break the chain that binds us altogether."

From abroad, John Quincy watched, with a time delay of about two months, his father's presidency buffeted and bruised in the battle between those favoring neutrality and those advocating an active alliance with France. And as was always hereafter to be the case, all eyes were on the next election. Jefferson wanted to be president: that, he hoped, would enable his vision to become the American reality. When, in 1798, the Adams administration and a Federalist Congress, attempting to prevent sabotage of its neutrality policy, instituted the Alien and Sedition Acts, these acts seemed more aggressive than the Constitution would normally have allowed. They made citizenship more difficult to attain, facilitated deporting noncitizens, and forbade writing or printing "any false, scandalous and malicious writing" against the government. The anti-Federalists of course rebelled, a partisan response to partisan repressive laws. Virginia and Kentucky passed resolutions of defiance, covertly written by Jefferson and Madison. The legislatures of ten of sixteen states disapproved of the Alien and Sedition Acts. In defiance, Southern Republican leaders claimed that they had the right to leave the Union; they would do so if these laws were not repealed. Each state, they declared, since the constitutional bargain was between the states, had the right to nullify any federal law it decreed unconstitutional.

To the Federalists, nullification seemed the road to chaos: any part could overrule the whole. It was democracy as dysfunction, an instrument of passion rather than reason. Disguised as the voice of the people, it rejected compromise and the rule of law, the principles that kept government and its constituencies in orderly harmony. And those who espoused nullification and this form of democracy were themselves fatally flawed. "If the negro keepers will have French democracy," John Quincy Adams wrote, "I say let them have it." The contradiction between owning slaves and espousing democracy seemed palpably obvious, "the inconsistency of holding in one hand the rights of man, and in the other a scourge for the back of slaves." Yet, even to moderate Southerners, who in principle disapproved of slavery, the compatibility of freedom and slavery seemed an obvious given. Freedom was the birthright of the superior race. God and nature's God had made the white race supreme, the black inferior, suited in mind and body for enslavement.

To the Adamses, the Virginia and Kentucky resolutions seemed a prelude to possible Southern secession. In mid-1799, the Virginia legislature went the next step. The Virginians passed motions, Rufus King reported to John Quincy, implying that they would "attempt to arm their militia against the general government." How much of this was saber rattling rather than actual desire to fight was difficult to determine. But it was serious enough to remind some New Englanders that, ten years before, they had feared they were making a pact with the devil: they had agreed to the slavery elements in the Constitution as a necessary evil in the service of a higher good. But many were also aware that slavery would, if not corrected, play the devil with the country's future. It seemed possible, in 1798–1799, that that future had come.

Rufus King believed that "an appeal to arms will before long be made." John Quincy agreed. An armed conflict "between the Ancient Dominion and the Union" was certain someday to happen. And Virginia's constant threats were like fire to kindling. Eventually there would be a conflagration. And "a separation is the greatest calamity that can befall us. . . . Nothing could make it excusable, and we can never be safe so long as any attempt for it shall not be considered as treason." By December 1800,

John Quincy, frightened by extreme Republican and Federalist partisanship, found it impossible "to avoid the supposition that the ultimate necessary consequence, if not the ultimate object of both the extreme parties which divide us, will be the dissolution of the Union and a civil war."

A small but elite group of ultraconservative New England Federalists, led by their hero, Alexander Hamilton, conspiring against the more moderate John Adams, seriously considered a movement to take New England out of the Union. In the spring of 1801, as the House of Representatives struggled to break the Electoral College tie between Jefferson and Aaron Burr, John Quincy worried that they both might want "to dissolve the Union." If so, "in God's name, let the Union go. I love the Union as I love my wife. But if my wife would ask and insist upon a separation, she should have it, though it broke my heart." In 1803–1804, when the purchase of a vast new territory seemed likely to diminish New England's influence in the Union, Josiah Quincy, an influential Bostonian, warned the House of Representatives that "if this bill passes, the bonds of this Union are virtually dissolved; that the States which compose it are free from their moral obligations, and that, as it will be the right of all, so it will be the duty of some, to prepare definitely for a separation—amicably if they can, violently if they must." Both extremes were looking into the abyss.

Everything John Quincy thought and felt compelled him to discourage disunion, though it seemed to him that there would be at some future time a heavy price to pay for territorial integrity; and his perceptive mother, in February 1802, tautly expressed, with a phrase from Milton's *Paradise Lost*, the heavy melancholy of her grim prediction, which her husband and eldest son shared: "There is a darkness visible upon all our national prospects," she wrote, "which cast a Gloom upon my declining days. What of Life remains to me, I should rejoice to pass in tranquility; but danger takes rapid strides, and faction and party Rage will soon involve us in a civil war: or a Lethargy and Stupor render us fit subjects for Southern despotism; the rising Generation will have more dangers to encounter than their Fathers have surmounted; such are your prospects my Son." As long as an uncompromising South insisted on having its way in sustaining its extreme version of states' rights and perpetuating slavery, the Union would be in perpetual danger. And as long as the compromising North permitted Southern dominance, its own best virtues would be vitiated. It would see its own freedom shrink, its energy diminish, its spirit decline.

At the end of that year, John Quincy's rising political star brought him to Plymouth, Massachusetts to deliver an oration memorializing the anniversary of the first landing of the Pilgrims. He had much to say, mostly a message of urgency and hope. "Two centuries have not yet elapsed since the first European foot touched the soil which now constitutes the American union—Two centuries more and our numbers must exceed those of Europe herself. . . . Perceive in all their purity, refine if possible from all their alloy, those virtues which we this day commemorate as the ornament of our forefathers." He and his audience assumed that these virtues were most gathered and sustained in the Northeastern part of the country. "Bind your souls and theirs to the national union as the chords of life are centered in the heart, and you shall soar with rapid and steady wing to the summit of human glory. . . . Let us all unite in ardent supplications to the founder of nations and the builder of worlds, that what then was prophecy may continue unfolding into history—that the dearest hopes of the human race may not be extinguished in disappointment, and that the last may prove the noblest empire of time." Early the next year, when the Massachusetts legislature elected him a U.S. senator, no one could have anticipated that the United States was soon going to purchase a vast Western and Southern territory that would exacerbate deeply troubling questions about the future of what John Quincy hoped would be "the noblest empire of time."

A DEFINING moment in the life of all Americans occurred in Paris on April 11, 1803. The "noblest empire of time" was about to undergo what the Founding Fathers had not anticipated: immense expansion. Robert Livingston, Jefferson's minister to France, walked into a meeting with Napoléon's treasury minister, hoping that the great man, the wizard behind the curtain, had instructed François de Barbé-Marbois to accept the American offer of $10 million for the city of New Orleans. Though a small tract of land for the money, from the American point of view it would be worth every penny. In French hands, New Orleans was a threat to American prosperity and security. Without it, there would be no egress into the Gulf of Mexico for American ships except by French permission. To have an imperial European power hemming in the United States on its southern and western borders seemed a nightmare in the making. It would curtail westward expansion. Even worse, it threatened territorial shrinkage. Napoléon, his armies pressing on America's boundaries, might think it a happy addition to the glory of France to conquer the United States.

All Jefferson had in mind was New Orleans itself. To think beyond that would be unrealistic. Why would Napoléon want to divest himself of a huge source of potential wealth and power? Livingston had been instructed to try for just New Orleans, a slim possibility but worth pursuing. To Livingston's shock, François de Barbé-Marbois announced that the United States could have the entire Louisiana Territory, a vast, mostly unmapped landmass extending far to the west and north on the west side of the Mississippi River, for $15 million, only $5 million more than just the city. The wizard behind the curtain had impetuously but definitely decided that he would withdraw all his forces and resources from the Atlantic world to concentrate his war machine on the European theater. He had good, though not perfect, reason.

During the 1790s, led by its majority slave population, a bloody revolution in Haiti, then known as St. Domingue, had transformed that fertile sugar-rich country, France's most profitable New World colony, into a bloodstained hell. Napoleon tried to reassert French control in 1802. Not even his heavy commitment of French troops could reestablish white dominance. Disease and black nationalism destroyed Napoléon's invading army. Making matters more difficult for the emperor, President Jefferson, fearing that Haiti's example might lead to a slave revolt in the American South, declared American neutrality. The United States would not help France in any way. Napoléon had wanted to restore slavery and French rule in Haiti. Jefferson had wanted to protect and retain slavery in the United States. Napoléon failed, Jefferson succeeded. Napoléon then said, Take the whole damn thing! I'll use the money to fight the British. Jefferson said, We'll buy it. The difficulties the purchase might give rise to were not relevant. It was enough to seize the moment and possess what the mercurial Napoléon had so unexpectedly offered.

When John Quincy Adams' stagecoach brought him, on the early evening of October 20, 1803, onto the dusty streets of the nation's village-like capital, the newly elected senator was one day too late to cast his vote for or against the Louisiana Territory purchase. He would have voted, he soon made clear, for the purchase, despite the opposition of every other New England Federalist senator and the Massachusetts legislature. It seemed to him a national security necessity. It was also compatible with his vision of a union eventually extending from the Atlantic to the Pacific, of a prosperous and mighty transcontinental nation. He agreed with his fellow Federalists that New England's power in the national decision-making processes would be diminished by the inevitable creation of new states. But that was the cost to be paid for the greater good.

There was another obstacle, though: the purchase (legally known as a cession, a government's attainment of territory by purchase or gift, to be distinguished from possession by conquest) had no sanction in the Constitution. Was not an amendment required that would give legal sanction to all such cessions? Equally important, what was the totality, Adams asked, of what the United States had purchased? It had purchased land, but the land was already occupied, so it had also purchased people: tens of thousands of French- and Spanish-speaking white Catholic residents; a recent influx of white French-speaking refugees from Haiti; and a large number of people of color, a multiracial population of every conceivable variation of degree between dark-skinned and white, including a small community of free blacks and a huge slave population, about half the size of the total, most living on the sugar plantations dominating the economy of the countryside and the Mississippi River Valley. Beyond New Orleans, to the west and north, were an undetermined number of people of European extraction, mainly trappers and hunters, at work in a territory so immense that no one knew how far it extended. And in that vast interior lived an unknown number of red-skinned people.

Where in the Constitution, whether one favored narrow or expansive interpretation, Adams asked, was there a provision for purchasing territory? And since the United States was also purchasing the people who lived there, was that not trafficking in human beings without their consent? And since it was assumed that many new states would be created from the Louisiana Territory, would they be free or slave states? On the answer to that question depended the balance of power between North and South. Adams went to see the secretary of state. James Madison dismissed Adams' scruples, though acknowledging that he had a point. The Constitution did not allow for this situation, the secretary agreed: the legality of the purchase would best be affirmed by a constitutional amendment. Had the administration, Adams asked, arranged to have a member of the Senate propose an amendment? If not, he would feel it his duty to do so. Under these unusual circumstances, Madison responded, it would best be addressed by consulting with the sentiment of the country. To wait might jeopardize the purchase. In effect, Jefferson and Madison, otherwise in favor of strict construction, had decided that it was in the country's interest to make this a political rather than a constitutional process. The sentiment of the country was in favor of the purchase itself. So was the majority of the Senate. And, in fact, so was Adams.

But Madison's answer appalled Adams. It was as if the secretary of state shared the view of one of the signers of the Constitution, who, when asked, as the Louisiana Purchase became a national controversy, whether its authors in 1787 had considered including a provision about the cession and purchase of new territory, responded, "I knew as well then as I do now, that all North America must at length be annexed to us. Happy, indeed, if the lust for dominion stops there. It would, therefore, have been perfectly Utopian to oppose a paper restriction to the violence of popular sentiment in a popular government." Still, it seemed to Adams and most Federalists rank hypocrisy by an administration elected on the platform of strict construction to have the executive and legislative branches of the federal government enact, because it was the expedient thing to do, what the Constitution did not allow. Where, Adams wanted to know, were Jefferson's principles now? And why didn't the secretary of state cite the 1795 cession by Spain to the United States of the Mississippi Territory as a possible precedent? Was it because that had been a boundary adjustment about territory the United States believed it already rightfully owned? Consequently, it hadn't needed a constitutional amendment? That example would highlight why an amendment was necessary now. How could the principles of the Founding Fathers permit the people of Louisiana to be conscripted into the Union without their consent? How could the president and Congress, in a country founded on opposing taxation without representation, require by fiat that the people of the new territory, mostly non-English-speaking, become U.S. citizens required to pay taxes to a government that they had not elected and to which they had not given their consent? Wasn't a vote or plebiscite called for as well as a constitutional amendment that would set out the guidelines for Congress? To decline to seek an amendment seemed an act of hypocrisy by those who otherwise had prided themselves on constitutional scrupulosity.

Adams, as he pondered what to do, had more than his usual number of restless nights in October and November 1803. In late October, the Senate authorized the president to appoint all executive and judicial officers for Louisiana until Congress could pass permanent enabling legislation for governance. Having determined that his conscience on the matter could not be satisfied otherwise, Adams proposed adding to the bill the phrase "consistently with the Constitution of the United States." It was immediately rejected by Jefferson's large majority. The president had decided that he would not risk losing Louisiana by putting the purchase through the time-consuming amendment process. Napoléon might as quickly change his mind and decide *not to* sell as he had made up his mind *to* sell. That the chief executive would be empowered to make all appointments and laws for the territory, without congressional oversight or consent, as if the Constitution were irrelevant, seemed acceptable to Jefferson and Madison. To Adams, who believed the amendment would have been quickly enough approved by a country strongly in favor of the purchase, Jefferson's course was an ultimate hypocrisy. In the end, it appeared to him another testimony to the slave-owning mentality: we strongly favor strict construction and states' rights when these profit us, but not otherwise. And would the members added to Congress from the new states formed from Louisiana be more likely to vote with or against New England priorities and values? The answer was obvious, especially on the key issue of slavery and representation. Through the early winter of 1804, as the Senate debated an enabling act, Adams' scruples were voted down time after time.

Over the next three months Jefferson's majority accomplished for Louisiana what its predecessors in 1787 had enshrined in the Constitution. It was never in doubt. The Louisiana Territory, after some twists, turns, and minor limitations, would be given the same constitutional status as the Northwest Territory, with one important difference: slavery would be permitted throughout. Through January and February 1804, the Senate engaged in sharp debate about how much slavery should be permitted and where these slaves should come from—exclusively from other states or also from the international slave trade—and with what limitations, if any. The Northwest Ordinance had seemed to antislavery Federalists a reasonable compromise. It required that the Northwest be reserved for free labor. The reservation, as much as it had to do with slavery, also entailed a host of associated issues: commerce, banking, manufacturing, tariffs, the distribution of power between the states and federal government, and the host of lifestyle and public policy issues on which the North and South differed.

Louisiana was different, though. Slavery flourished there, especially in the area dominated by New Orleans and in the Lower Mississippi Valley. It was a long-standing part of French and Spanish New World culture. Its leadership had been augmented by the influx of slave owners fleeing from Haiti. And sugarcane, its major crop, depended on slave labor, a necessity, so slave owners proclaimed, since only Negroes, they believed, were capable of laboring in that hot, humid climate. To the north and west were the likely new states that the South expected would become, mostly, slave states. These would be a profitable destination for excess slaves from Virginia and Maryland. "The real reason," John Quincy remarked in his diary, "why the senators from the Southern States" at first "desired the prohibition of the foreign importation of slaves into Louisiana, was that such action would raise the price of their own slaves in the market, and give them a chance to get rid of dangerous slaves." Diffusion would also make insurrections less likely. This was Jefferson's hope. The doctrine of diffusion made sense to him. This was to be, as he looked westward, his "Empire of Liberty."

Others had a different view. Louisiana "is to be," the Boston *Columbian Centinel* asserted on July 2, 1803, "a field of blood before it is a cultured field; and indeed a field of blood while it is cultivated." Is it "for such an extension of human liberty and of human happiness that we are called upon for such sacrifice?" From the New England point of view, it would be New England tax dollars that would pay most of the $15 million purchase price. The South, by always opposing attempts in Congress to impose direct federal taxes, had cheated on the constitutional bargain by which the North had agreed that slaves would become part of the electoral base of the South, adding to its representation in Congress and the Electoral College, in return for which the federal government could raise direct taxes on property of various kinds, including slaves. Otherwise, all federal revenue would have to come from a tariff or import tax on foreign goods, which in practice would be paid mostly by the Northern commercial states.

In the fall of 1804, John Quincy cogently emphasized the point in a series of articles in the Boston *Repertory*: the three-fifths compromise had turned out to be no compromise at all. It was a bad deal for the North. "Every planter south of the Potomac has one vote for himself, and three votes in effect for every five slaves he keeps in bondage; while a New England farmer, who contributes tenfold as much to the support of the government, has only a single vote. . . . At the time the Constitution was formed, this provision was submitted to on the ground that the burden of taxation should be apportioned to the benefit of representation. The experience of fifteen years, however, has proved the error of these calculations." In effect, "four-fifths of the burdens of this government must be supported by the States which have no representation for slaves. . . . We are doubly taxed, and they are doubly represented. . . . The ten states which have no representation for slaves in . . . 1802 . . . contributed three-fourths of the net revenue collected by impost, tonnage and navigation. . . . And the seven states, whose slaves count to make members of Congress, contributed only one-fourth. Or to be more perfectly accurate, the whole amount of net revenue collected from that source throughout the United States was $8,359,227.96 of which sum $6,103,898.69 was collected in the ten slaveless states. This is the proportion of taxation and contribution to the public burdens." Yet the free states, with much the larger white population, "have only seventy-eight members in the House of Representatives, where the others have sixty-four, fifteen of whom are added in consequence of the black population." In 1798, in the one instance in which Congress had legislated a direct tax on property, the South had declined to allow it to be collected. The North felt betrayed.

There was an additional sacrifice. Those who opposed slavery and the slave trade would pay most of the moral cost of bringing more slaves and new slave states into the Union. As a currency, the moral cost was difficult to quantify, but it was real. In Congress, Southerners opposed attempts by antislavery senators such as Adams to limit the sale of slaves into Louisiana: new residents could bring their slaves, but slaves from outside could not be sold into Louisiana. Opposed by all the Southern senators, the limitation was ultimately rejected. Louisiana became a participant in the national slave market. But what about slaves from abroad? Even South Carolina had at first opposed the importation of slaves purchased on the international market, concerned that more slaves from Africa would increase the chance of slave insurrections. It soon changed its mind, rushing to cash in on the increased demand for slaves, whether home bred or imported, in the new territory. The more slaves and the fewer Native Americans, the better, more land and more slaves the South's economic nirvana. "The natives of the soil," the *Columbia Centinel* lamented, "a numerous race. who have never injured us, and never will until encroached upon, must be driven out. . . . And still a more numerous race from Africa must be violently brought to toil and bleed under the lash."

The lash had begun to bite more sharply than ever before against the moral skin of antislavery New Englanders and Pennsylvania Quakers, among others. Such sufferers lived in a body of the imagination, an alternative body that itself became corporeal in its identification with the bodies of actual slaves. It was, though, a body they could sometimes escape. But in 1803–1804, with Louisiana its focus, the body became unitary and inescapable, not only for immediate practical reasons but also because many were keenly aware that the empire of slavery, the "field of blood," was expanding, and that the blood of the lash and the blood of the Union would, eventually and inevitably, someday be mingled. Adams did his best to stop the bleeding. A few others also did, but the numbers in Congress were heavily against them. So, too, were the administration and the sentiment of the country. And their own motives were not entirely unmixed. They felt New England's power draining away.

The rejection of John Quincy's constitutional scruples left him so disgusted with Jefferson's hypocrisy that he was one of five senators out of twenty who, on February 18, 1804, voted against the entire bill to put a governing structure in place. "It is forming a government for that people without their consent and against their will." This seemed the first step for the United States in becoming a colonial power, like the European countries it reviled. And that disregard of the "consent of the people" so revolted Adams that he voted against all the individual provisions as they came before the Senate, including one that would have partially curtailed slavery, which he was quite right to suspect would soon be gutted anyway. He thought it too weak, but he also believed that Congress had no right to pass any provisions at all without the consent of the people of Louisiana and without a constitutional amendment that would provide a template for the future acquisition of territory. At some level, it could be argued that the United States was treating all the people of Louisiana like slaves.

If he had had his way, there would have been no actual slaves brought or sold into Louisiana, and the slaves already there would, over time, have been emancipated, though he recognized that the centrality of slavery to the Southern economy made his preferences impossible. But it was possible to take a stand on principle, even though his vote, viewed out of context, might create the impression that he approved of slavery in the Louisiana Territory. Nothing was further from the truth, and few of his contemporaries misunderstood his position. He saw nothing but future trouble, especially in regard to other likely acquisitions arising from the way Louisiana had been made part of the United States, and that the spread of slavery would constantly threaten the balance of power between the North and South. He could already see, and in the next three decades with ever-greater clarity, as far as Missouri, Texas, Mexico, California, and Oregon. And the process of acquisition was already inseparable from its moral and economic substance, which was slavery. That substance contained the greatest threat to national unity. There was indeed, distinctly visible, blood on the horizon.

FIVE

The Distant Goal

A few months before Rufus King made the speech of his life to his fellow senators in February 1820, eleven-year-old Abraham Lincoln, in Spencer County, Indiana, gained a beneficent stepmother. In late 1819, Sarah Bush Johnston had married Thomas Lincoln in Elizabethtown, Kentucky. Both had been longtime residents of that border state. Thomas Lincoln had returned to ask for Sarah's hand in marriage, a second wedding for both of them. By 1820, Kentucky had been a member of the Union for twenty-eight years. The place of Abraham Lincoln's birth, it was always to have special significance for him. The woman he was to marry was also born there, the year before his father remarried; Henry Clay, his ideal political leader, was Kentucky writ large; and it was the only slave territory he had ever visited as an adult, once in 1841 and then again in 1847, when he came as a congressman to the nation's capital. In his presidency, he was to be preoccupied with Kentucky's shaky allegiance to the Union.

Like the nation as a whole, in 1820 Rufus King was preoccupied not with Kentucky but with the huge spaces of the Louisiana Purchase north and west of the state of Louisiana, especially the territory called Missouri. It had petitioned to become the second state to be formed from what Napoléon had so unexpectedly sold to the United States in 1803: the future states of Missouri, Arkansas, Iowa, Kansas, Nebraska, and

Oklahoma; parts of North Dakota, South Dakota, and New Mexico; and all of Montana and Wyoming. In 1820, Eastern eyes could hardly glimpse the most distant of those places. They would come vividly into focus, especially Kansas and Nebraska, when Lincoln, more than thirty years later, was to confront the subject of Rufus King's speech. In 1820 all eyes were on Missouri, and everyone knew that much more than Missouri was at stake. Whether it was to be admitted to the Union as a slave state or a free state might determine how far the "field of blood" was to be extended.

Sixty-five years old, in rich black set off by white in a portrait by Gilbert Stuart, a wreath of brown curls defining his baldness, Rufus King, with a friendly but sharp gaze, was not to live long enough to see that his antislavery speech would be to no avail. None of the politicians listening would have doubted that the venerable New Yorker, still essentially a Federalist, adhering to a party that now hardly existed, fantasized that the Federalism that had created the Confederation Congress and the Constitutional Convention might be resurrected, its former presidential and vice presidential nominee finally taking his place as the successor to Washington and Adams. It was Rufus King who in 1795 had provided the language of the Northwest Ordinance, mandating that the states formed from the Northwest Territory eventually be slave free. No one misunderstood his position on the slavery issue: he was against its extension. He was, though, far from a radical.

A wealthy New Yorker, with roots in Federalist civil society and humanism, and with a deep respect for church, God, and country, he was committed to the national balance that would keep the Union harmoniously intact. King hoped for slavery's eventual extinction, but he believed that immediate abolition was impractical, divisive, and dangerous: the end of slavery would evolve from individual manumissions. In the meantime, since a large part of the country accepted that the Constitution gave the original slave states the legal right to maintain slaves as property, he advocated only that slavery not be allowed in any states to be added to the

Union. Congress, he believed, had the right, by constitutional provision and precedent, to make all rules and regulations necessary to govern the territories. "Slavery, unhappily, exists within the United States," he told his fellow senators in 1820. "Enlightened men, in the States where it is permitted, and everywhere out of them, regret its existence among us, and seek for the means of limiting and of mitigating it." That was not the dominant view in the South.

In early 1818 the single delegate from the Missouri Territory had petitioned Congress to admit it as a state. A preliminary enabling bill had been enacted. Everyone granted its admission likely. Discussion, though, soon became heated. Slavery was well entrenched in parts of Missouri. Its admission as a slave state might give additional advantage in Congress to Southern views and values. The Louisiana Purchase, from King's perspective, had given slavery the opportunity to grow from a geographically limited evil to a nationally dominant monster. What would happen, he and others had been asking since 1803, to the Northeast's moderate, pro-business, antislavery voice in Congress when the inevitable admission of new Southern and Western states added more voices and votes to the imbalance already existing because of the three-fifths clause in the Constitution? King's signature was on the Constitution. Unhappy at its concessions, he had accepted its compromises. It was that or no union at all. And in 1804, he had agreed with John Quincy Adams that the Louisiana Purchase required a constitutional amendment, that slavery ought to be limited in the new territory, and that the three-fifths rule made a mockery of equal representation, an otherwise fundamental principle of the American republic. All that had been to no avail.

Neither he nor most others had foreseen in 1787 the radical recasting of the union that would result from the purchase of new territories. No one had the possibility of new territories in mind. The Louisiana Purchase changed everything, and in 1818 buyer's remorse, dating as far back as the Constitutional Convention, and Northern anxiety about slavery and Southern power began to find their voice. In mid-February 1819, an antislavery congressman from New York, James Tallmadge, shocked his colleagues when he introduced a bill in the House to amend the Missouri Enabling Act: no new slaves would from the moment of its final passage be allowed into Missouri, and all children born to slaves after Missouri's admission would become free at the age of twenty-five. Since there had been no head counts and little awareness among the leadership about extension anxiety, the unprepared Southern power base was caught off guard. Tallmadge's amendment narrowly passed. Shock waves radiated through the South.

Henry Clay, now the powerful Speaker of the House, was stunned. So were all the Southern members of Congress. The conflict over Missouri had been under way in heated debates for almost a year, some of it centered on the admission of Alabama to the Union in December 1819. That had reestablished parity between slave and free states: eleven each. The antislavery and pro-slavery rhetoric was increasingly hot and heavy, and the Tallmadge amendment made it explosive, with the usual threats from both sides to pack up their bags, if they did not get their way, and go home. Most but not all of the exodus-mongering came from the South. It fully expected Missouri to become the twelfth slave state. Clay now had to deal with the unexpected, his inventive political mind already at work on what would become the contours of the Missouri Compromise. The House but not the Senate admitted the slave-free state of Maine to the Union at the beginning of January 1820. If the Senate agreed to admit Maine without also admitting Missouri as a slave state, the balance would be in favor of the North. The national balance could be sustained only by pairing Maine and Missouri. By itself, though, this would not meet the challenge of the Tallmadge amendment. Since the majority of the Senate had no intention of prohibiting slavery in Missouri, it forced a pause by refusing to concur with the House vote. That left statehood for Maine and Missouri unresolved.

When Rufus King stepped to the podium of the Senate on February 11, 1820, he expected to be a voice of sensible persuasion, a precise, enlightened, and sound exponent of Northern Federalism and antislavery conviction. Why should there be slavery in Missouri at all? he asked. Neither history nor the Constitution required it. "Freedom and slavery are the parties which stand this day before the Senate; and upon its decision the empire of the one or the other will be established in the new State which we are about to admit into the Union." It would also be established beyond Missouri. Much of the West, he feared, would become an "empire" of slavery. Expansion should be stopped: liberty was the founding principle of the country. His argument and tone were to have their fullest expression in Lincoln's speech at the Cooper Union forty years later: for Missouri, substitute Kansas-Nebraska. Lincoln was to cover the same ground, though in even greater historical detail. Although there is no proof that he read King's 1820 speech, he expressly approved of its being cited, with a substantial quotation, in notes that he found "exceedingly valuable," published with the official text of his speech. Charles King, the president of New York's Columbia College, the "son of *the* Rufus King of revolutionary memory," as Lincoln was to describe him to Edwin Stanton, may have been in the audience.

STATE BUSINESS was much on Secretary of State Adams' mind in early 1820. Still, he went to the Capitol in the early afternoon of February 11 to hear Rufus King's speech. "His manner is dignified, grave, earnest, but not rapid or vehement, though there was nothing new in his argument." Everything that could be said by way of argument about slavery had already been said, and during the next forty years nothing new in substance or reasoning was to be added. Rufus King, Adams noted in his diary, "unravelled with ingenious and subtle analysis many of the sophistical tissues of the slave-holders. He laid down the position of the natural liberty of man, and its incompatibility with slavery in any shape. He also questioned the Constitutional right of the President and Senate to make the Louisiana Treaty; but he did not dwell upon those points, nor draw the consequences from them which I should think important in speaking to that subject. He spoke, however, with great power, and the great slave-holders in the House gnawed their lips and clenched their fists as they heard him."

They also responded, to Adams' ongoing chagrin, with great rhetorical force, avatars of the irony that, in Adams' view, those with the worst arguments and the weakest evidence had the greatest oratorical talent, exemplified by Virginia's mad but brilliant John Randolph. "I heard him between three and four hours. His speech, as usual, had neither beginning, middle, nor end. Egotism, Virginian aristocracy, slave scourging liberty, religion, literature, science, wit, fancy, generous feelings, and malignant passions constitute a chaos in his mind, from which nothing orderly can ever flow." Yet other Southerners were gifted orators. "With the exception of Rufus King, there is no senator . . . from the free States able to cope in powers of the mind with William Pinkney or James Barbour. In the House . . . the freemen have none to contend on equal terms either with John Randolph or Clay."

And King, Adams observed, made the mistake of reckoning "more upon the apparent ardor of the popular sentiment against slavery in the North than it is worth. The question to the North and in the free States is merely speculative. The people do not feel it in their persons or their purses." They would not risk either money or security for a moral position. "On the slave side it comes home to the feelings and interests of every man in the community. Hence, if this question is ultimately decided, as it will be in favor of slavery in Missouri, the people in the free States will immediately acquiesce in the decision, and it will be impossible to keep the controversy alive." He had no doubt, though, that eventually there would be even more bitterly divisive opportunities for conflict about which compromise would prove impossible. "A dissolution, at least temporary, of the Union, as now constituted, would be certainly necessary, and the dissolution must be upon a point involving the question of slavery, and no other. The Union might then be reorganized on the fundamental principle of emancipation."

The secretary of state had been listening to the Missouri debates from the sidelines. For the previous two years, he had been negotiating with Spain to purchase Florida and the Spanish possessions west of the Louisiana Purchase. The Adams–Onís Treaty, which ceded Florida to the United States and decided Spain's territorial boundaries in Spanish Texas, had seemed firmly in place in 1819. Then it ran into trouble over false Spanish representations about Florida land titles. By early 1820, it seemed to Adams unlikely that the treaty would be approved, partly because "the North and East . . . do not wish ever to have Florida as another slave State and the South and West . . . wish to have all the territory to the Rio del Norte for more slave States."

Still, President Monroe and Secretary of War John Calhoun, slave-owning Southerners, strongly supported the treaty. "I believed it now, as when it was signed, an acceptable bargain," Adams told Ninian Edwards, the slave-owning senior senator from Illinois. Politicians ambitious for higher office, such as Clay, were making disapproving noises. So, too, were those who had hoped the treaty boundary would include Texas. The treaty, it seemed to Adams, had become a hostage to the Missouri debate, a domestic topic inappropriate for the secretary of state to make public comments about. Congressmen, dropping by the State Department library to consult historical and legal records, solicited Adams' views. And since the secretary of state was inevitably thought of as a possible future president, what more natural than to engage him in private discussions on the hottest political topic of the day?

Missouri was, in Adams' mind and heart, an increasing preoccupation. It touched on two aspects of slavery that had been part of his official responsibilities since 1814. In Ghent, negotiating to end the War of 1812, he had been instructed to demand that the British pay compensation for slaves taken out of the United States during the Revolutionary War. That unresolved issue had been a long-standing irritant in British-American relations. Slaveholders believed themselves entitled to reparations. Whether the slaves had been conscripted, persuaded, or self-liberated was at issue. Adams had been required to argue views incompatible with his own views on slavery. The documents and testimony that the British demanded were not easy to come by. And there was insurmountable British reluctance to return former slaves to slavery, an impractical alternative anyway, twenty-five years after the exodus. The issue was not to be settled until 1826, when the John Quincy Adams administration, negotiating with a British government eager to partner with the United States against the international slave trade, agreed to pay reparations of over a million dollars. National pride and the Southern pocketbook were satisfied; a pesky issue for Adams was finally put to rest. No former slave was to be repatriated into misery.

The international slave trade also had been a subject of hot discussion at Ghent. In general terms, the two countries had agreed to cooperate to end it. Both considered it a form of piracy. In 1808 the United States had made American participation illegal. Americans, though, continued to ply the profitable trade: financing it, outfitting ships, sailing those ships, and selling slaves in Cuba and parts of the American South, claiming that the slaves were native born. Rogue slave ships fraudulently flew the American flag, preventing searches by British warships. When, in 1818, Britain began to pressure the United States to partner directly with it to stop the slave trade, many Americans, including Adams, had an irresolvable conflict: how could the United States allow British ships to search American vessels even if they were transporting slaves illegally when the United States had declared war with Great Britain in 1812 because it had been arbitrarily searching American ships for British naval deserters? It was a painful complication for Adams. Doubtful about the soundness of any arrangement that might be seen as an infringement on American sovereignty, Monroe and Adams were not ready to allow the British to search ships flying the American flag, even in exchange for allowing Americans to search British ships. Neither was the American public.

Adams' portfolio restricted his public statements to foreign affairs. But Missouri was an issue about which everyone had something to say, even if only privately. Ex-president Madison agreed with Monroe "that a coupling of Missouri with Maine, in order to force the entrance of the former thro' the door voluntarily opened to the latter is, to say the least, a very doubtful policy." But practicality was more determinative than doubt. "It would be better," Monroe wrote in the two days between the start and the end of Rufus King's speech, to adopt the compromise "than break the union." The Southern phalanx, including ex-president Jefferson, was in place on the issue. Many Northerners believed slavery a small price to pay for the union's perpetuation. And when the junior senator from Illinois, Jesse B. Thomas, Kentucky born but antislavery, introduced an amendment that could attract majority support, a compromise seemed certain. It was a structurally elegant resolution of the issue: Maine would be immediately admitted as a state; Missouri would be allowed to create a state constitution, whose approval would trigger Missouri's admission; and slavery would be excluded north of the 36th parallel, except for Missouri. The result would divide the country between slave and free states on an east-west line at the 36th parallel. Numerical parity would be maintained. It was, Adams granted, impractical "to proscribe slavery . . . in Missouri." But the provision "excluding the introduction of slaves into future Territories . . . will be a great and important point secured." This last compromise was carried, Adams wrote in his diary, "by a vote of ninety to eighty-seven in the House . . . after successive days and almost nights of stormy debate." Then the House passed the bill as a whole, but stripped of any vestige of the Tallmadge amendment: 37 of the 42 votes against it came from Southerners who would never agree to any territorial restriction on slavery.

A fearful Jefferson wrote to Monroe that "this Missouri question by a geographical line of division is the most portentous one I have ever contemplated." What he objected to and most worried about was the east-west line preventing slavery north of the 36th parallel. It would cause future trouble. Southerners were likely to feel that their rights as property-owning citizens had been abridged. It was, Jefferson wrote, "the knell of the Union. It is hushed indeed for the moment. But this is a reprieve only, not a final sentence." Jefferson had no reservation about most if not all of the Louisiana Purchase states becoming slave states. And King's speech infuriated Southerners who were eager for more slave states, hoping these would give them the numerical advantage in Congress. Jefferson responded to Monroe with his lifelong semi-paranoid political partisanship: "King is ready to risk the union for any chance of restoring his party to power and wriggling himself to the head of it." Adams had a calmer, more balanced assessment of King's ambition and the politician's life. He "is one of the men who have been held up as candidates for the Presidency, and certainly one of the men the most qualified for it. . . . He has had many vicissitudes of political fortune, ebbs and floods of the tide of popularity. He has been more than thirty years in the first line of American statesmen, and lives in continual expectation of a chance which may raise him to the summit of our public edifice."

Speaking a few days before the Senate was to vote on a newly amended version of the Missouri bill, King hoped that slavery would be excluded from the new state. For if slavery "be permitted in Missouri with the climate, and soil, and in the circumstances of this territory, what hope can be entertained that it will ever be prohibited in any of the new States that will be formed in the immense region west of the Mississippi?" King made his case: the slave states already had more than their fair share of representation; the South had broken the constitutional agreement by making internal taxes impossible; more slave states would endanger the Union because slaves were more of a drain than a benefit to prosperity and security; and the United States would be even more in hypocritical betrayal of its underlying foundational values if it allowed slavery to spread. Adams agreed in full. King, though, gave no weight to Southerners' threats to leave the Union. Adams did. Unchangeable aspects of Southern life, even more fundamental than money and power, made a future rift inevitable. It was embedded in the character of the Southern elite. They could never accept territorial limitations on slavery. "The discussion of this Missouri question has betrayed the secret of their souls . . . their souls pride and vainglory in their condition of masterdom . . . they look down upon the simplicity of a Yankee's manners, because he has no habits of overbearing like theirs and cannot treat negroes like dogs. It is among the evils of slavery that it taints the very sources of moral principle. It establishes false estimates of virtue and vice; for what can be more false and heartless than this doctrine which makes the first and holiest rights of humanity to depend upon the color of the skin?"

Northern antislavery representatives hated the compromise, and it seemed particularly galling that the votes of cooperative Northern congressmen had made this possible. "And so it is that a law for perpetuating slavery in Missouri, and perhaps in North America," Adams privately commented, "has been smuggled through both Houses of Congress. . . . I have been convinced from the first starting of this question that it could not end otherwise. The fault is in the Constitution . . . which has sanctioned a dishonorable compromise with slavery. There is henceforth no remedy for it but a new organization of the Union, to effect which a concert of all the white States is indispensable. Whether that can ever be accomplished is doubtful." Other Northerners rejoiced that the bullet had been dodged. Some Southerners saw it as a victory for slavery, though many abhorred the 36th parallel restriction. At the beginning of March 1820, the Senate concurred with the House. "I consider myself and associates as conquered," Rufus King wrote to his son. "The slave States," assisted by Northern collaborators, "have subdued us." But both Adams and King believed there would be other shoes to fall. Ultimately, they were certain, the compromise would not stand, though when and how it would fall, they could not know. With slavery cut off from northern expansion, it seemed inevitable to Adams that the South would place even more emphasis on Texas and the Southwest—and on Cuba, Mexico, and Central America. There would be future union-threatening conflicts.

Almost immediately, the pro-slavery Missourians began fulfilling Adams' prediction. In St. Louis, in mid-July 1820, the state convention charged with creating a constitution based on republican principles added a provision that no one had anticipated. It rubbed into the sensitive eyes of antislavery Northerners a compound of salt, bitterness, and foreboding: "It shall be . . . the duty" of the Missouri state legislature, the constitution stipulated, "as soon as may be, to pass such laws as may be necessary . . . to prevent free negroes and mulattoes from coming to, and settling in this state, under any pretext whatsoever."

To Northerners, this seemed astoundingly offensive and patently illegal. It was the opposite of "republican," inconsistent with the U.S. Constitution, which specifies: "The Citizens of each State shall be entitled to all Privileges and Immunities of Citizens in the several States" and "Full Faith and Credit shall be given in each State to the public Acts, Records, and judicial Proceedings of every other State." In St. Louis, this was not seen as a problem. After all, Negroes were not citizens. But in Massachusetts, New York, and Pennsylvania, they were, even if with limited civil rights and oppressed by local prejudices. That the proposed Missouri constitution also forbade any future legislature from emancipating slaves was bad enough. It was not, though, illegal by anyone's reading of the Constitution. But forbidding Negro or mulatto citizens of another state to move into Missouri was, by every Northerner's understanding, constitutionally illegal. Everyone granted, Adams and King acknowledged, that the new "Missouri question of the present session," when Congress assembled in the fall of 1820, "was a totally different question from that of the last."

Somehow this affront to the Constitution and the free states had to go away. It rubbed salt in the wounds of those who had hoped that Missouri would be admitted as a free state. And it was a problem to those Northern congressmen who had reluctantly, against the wishes of their constituents, agreed to its slave status in the interest of national harmony. The exclusionary provision made it difficult for them to approve the Missouri constitution. For two years, there had been angry editorials, bitter speeches, and popular discontent on both sides of the issue. Then the matter had seemed, at long last, to be settled. Unexpectedly, it had again become volatile.

Adams poured his angry heart out privately. "The article in the Missouri constitution," he told Pennsylvania congressman Henry Baldwin, who was to be in 1841 the only Supreme Court justice to favor returning the *Amistad* prisoners to slavery, "was directly repugnant to the rights reserved to every citizen of the union in the constitution of the United States. Its purport went to disfranchise all the people of color who were citizens of the free states . . . and if I were a member of the legislature of one of those states, I would move for a declaratory act, that so long as the article in the constitution of Missouri depriving the colored citizens of . . . Massachusetts, of their rights as citizens of the United States within the state of Missouri, should subsist," so, too, would "the white citizens of the state of Missouri . . . be held as aliens within the commonwealth of Massachusetts, not entitled to claim or enjoy within the same any right or privilege of a citizen of the United States." If Congress allowed the Missouri provision to stand, he would, in Massachusetts, forbid "any person whomsoever to claim the property or possession of a human being as a slave, and I would prohibit by law the delivery of any fugitive slave upon the claim of his master. All which I would do, not to violate, but to redeem from violation, the constitution of the United States."

Southerners were quick to assert that this was buyer's remorse, the heartburn of those rendered powerless by the coalition between the South and West and its Northern facilitators. Still, it was necessary to find some practical legislative mechanism to put Missouri in the slave state column. By a typically clever maneuver, Henry Clay solved the problem. For the House Speaker and the soon to be born Whig Party, it was politically necessary to condemn slavery as immoral and also to accept its ongoing legal existence. Without that, there could be no Clay presidency, just as forty years later there could be, absent that paradoxical accommodation, no Republican Party and no Lincoln presidency. With his usual tactical cleverness, Clay maneuvered into existence a joint House and Senate committee stacked with members who wanted to settle the issue expeditiously. The committee reported a resolution in favor of admission, provided that Missouri's constitution "never be construed to authorize the passage of any act by which any citizen of either of the States of the Union should be excluded from the enjoyment of any privilege to which he may be entitled under the constitution of the United States."

An act of legislative hypocrisy, it was a protective screen allowing Missouri to do as it pleased. As everyone recognized, it was totally unenforceable. The House narrowly approved the resolution, 86 to 82; the more pro-slavery Senate, 28 to 14. After the vote, Rufus King sat in the office of his friend, the secretary of state, adjusting to the new reality. "Upon the Missouri question," Adams wrote, "he has much cooled down since last winter. The question is now not the same as it was then, and is much more clear against Missouri. But he has discovered that the people of the North, like many of their Representatives in Congress, flinch from the consequences of this question, and will not bear their leaders out."

It had been a personal and politically losing battle for King, and he would have nothing more to say about it in the seven remaining years of his life. Adams was to have much to say. He had worked with Clay at the Ghent treaty negotiations. He shared Clay's vision of a strong national union. They were to work closely together again. But he disapproved of Clay's legislative ruthlessness, and he was furious at the disrespect shown to the constitutional guarantee of free transit of every citizen from one state to another. It was clearly Missouri's intent to do as it pleased, and he predicted that other states would do the same. Much as he accepted the necessity of the Missouri Compromise, he detested its necessity and the means that had brought about its passage. "So polluted are all the streams of legislation in regions of slavery, that this bill has been obtained only by two as unprincipled artifices as dishonesty ever devised: one, by coupling it as an appendage to the bill for admitting Maine; and the other, by this outrage perpetrated by the Speaker upon the rules of the House." The compromise had been "smuggled through Congress." It bought time probably not worth buying.

Slavery "perverts human reason, and reduces man endowed with logical powers to maintain that slavery is sanctioned by the Christian religion, that slaves are happy and contented in their condition, that between master and slave there are ties of mutual attachment and affection, that the virtues of the master are refined and exalted by the degradation of the slave; while at the same time they . . . burn at the stake negroes convicted of crimes for the terror of the example, and writhe in agonies of fear at the very mention of human rights as applicable to men of color." He had "since the Missouri debate . . . considered the continuance of the Union for any length of time as very precarious."

Would it not be better to bite the separatist bullet now? Perhaps, then, no actual bullet need be fired. Why not bring together a convention of the people, just as had been done in 1787, and rewrite the Constitution? Or, if that proved not doable, would it not be better for the fourteen free states, by consent of all parties, to go their own way, to form a slave-free republic? But, he mused, it was already too late for that. The moment had passed, and he could not avoid recognizing, in the depths of his nationalistic soul, that there were important interests, many of which he shared, that could best be advanced by the perpetuation of the national union. Still, in the late fall of 1820, the possibility of peaceful corrections could be seen only in the union's rearview mirror. The Louisiana Purchase and the Missouri Compromise were irrevocable deals. Slavery had triumphed. But, Adams speculated, "perhaps it would have been a wiser as well as a bolder course to have persisted in the restriction upon Missouri, till it should have terminated in a convention of the States to revise and amend the Constitution." This new country "of thirteen or fourteen States unpolluted with slavery" would have "a great and glorious object . . . rallying to their standard the other States by the universal emancipation of their slaves. If the Union must be dissolved, slavery is precisely the question upon which it ought to break. For the present, however, this contest is laid asleep." It would, he knew, awaken.

IT AWAKENED on a small scale four years later, soon after John Quincy Adams was elected the sixth president. With trepidation, he placed his hand on the Bible and swore his presidential oath, but he had no desire to touch the third rail of American politics: slavery and emancipation. His views were well enough known anyway. As secretary of state, he had had nothing to say in public about the subject, but he had privately expressed himself in conversation frequently enough for the Washington world to have no doubt that he opposed slavery on moral grounds and wished to see it eliminated as soon as possible. Anyway, he had nothing constructive to offer on the topic. His hope that he would be Monroe's successor had required that he not further alienate Southern moderates, of whom there were fewer and fewer. At best, a Southern moderate was someone who opposed slavery in principle but happily profited from it. Missouri was now a slave state. Representation in the Senate was in equal balance. The House tipped toward the North. In both chambers, though, there were enough Northerners who, in deference to self-interest, political advantage, or racism, kept any discussion of slavery for most of the 1820s to a low murmur.

In the Northeast, the late-eighteenth-century emancipation momentum gathered legislative focus. In 1821, the year after the admission of Missouri, New York gave free blacks the right to vote. In 1827 it ended slavery, over forty years after Massachusetts. Public opinion and the legislative wheels in the North had been grinding slowly, but they had been turning. The South mostly ground its slavery wheels in the opposite direction. In 1822, Denmark Vesey, a free black carpenter, the founder of the first African Methodist Episcopalian church in Charleston, South Carolina, alarmed the South into anxious alert and increased repression. It was discovered that he was organizing a large cohort of black slaves to rebel. Vesey and five others were hanged. Southern representatives in Congress and the press denounced, with evocations of mayhem and rape, all antislavery advocacy.

In the election of 1824, with Missouri in place and the country mostly quiet on the subject, Adams had no reason to say anything about slavery. His three major opponents were wealthy slaveholders, William Crawford of Georgia, Andrew Jackson of Tennessee, and Henry Clay. It was not held against them. A founder, in 1816, of the American Colonization Society, Clay kept his slaves hard at work on his Lexington, Kentucky, plantation. The main mission of the society was, over time, to persuade as many free blacks as possible to resettle in a distant country. For some, though, the society had a distinct whiff of compensated emancipation, the start of a solution to the slavery problem; for others, in the North especially, it had the potential to keep communities as white as possible; for many Southern supporters, it would help relieve the South of its troublesome free black population. Among its founding bedfellows were John Randolph, John Marshall, Francis Scott Key, and Daniel Webster, united by their conviction that blacks had no future in America.

President Monroe and his secretary of the treasury, William Crawford, strongly supported the society. Lincoln became a committed member in the 1840s. Adams thought it a cruel joke, an absurd impossibility.

Acting in accordance with the Constitution, in February 1825 the House of Representatives elected Adams president. With the assist of the three-fifths provision, Andrew Jackson had gotten a plurality of the Electoral College votes. Indirectly, his own slaves had voted for him. No candidate, though, had received the necessary majority. The state of Indiana, where the Lincoln family lived, gave its popular and electoral votes to Jackson. What young Lincoln, three days later to celebrate his sixteenth birthday, thought of that, no one knows. To say the least, he was not uninterested in politics and oratory. He had already memorized some of Clay's speeches. "Often for amusement for his play fellows—neighbors and friends made quite good stump speeches . . . between the ages of 15 and 20." That Jackson owned slaves provided no obstacle to his election. Every presidential candidate Lincoln was to vote for until 1860, other than John Fremont, the Republican candidate in 1856, owned slaves. And though there was antislavery sentiment in Illinois, pro-slavery feelings or indifference dominated. Actually, antislavery forces had had to work hard to prevent Illinois from passing a pro-slavery constitution in 1818. But it also made no difference to Jackson's electoral chances in Illinois and Indiana that he believed slavery to be God's and nature's directive. The issue, so to speak, was not on the ballot. Even in the Northern states, only an insignificant number of votes were determined by the candidates' views on slavery.

In the House election, each state having a single vote, Illinois, Ohio, Kentucky, and Missouri, under Clay's charismatic influence, gave their votes to Adams. With thirteen votes, a majority of the states, Adams was elected. William Crawford's supporters, hating Jackson even more than Adams, refused to switch to Jackson. Clay, hostile to Jackson, whom he thought reckless, ignorant, and a potential rival for Southern and Western votes, preferred Adams, whose political views he mostly shared. And when Adams selected Clay to be his secretary of state, the Jackson coalition was outraged. In the House, Adams' supporters had a tiny majority. In the Senate, Jackson's coalition had a tiny majority. Its mission was to make life miserable for Adams. They would do everything in their power to make him a one-term president.

Searching for an issue around which to rally popular support, they found two. One was a gift of the Constitution. Why not proclaim repeatedly that a corrupt bargain between Adams and Clay had stolen the election from the American people? After all, though the Constitution required that the House resolve an election left unresolved by the Electoral College, was it not undemocratic *not* to elect the candidate who had gotten the most popular votes? The relentlessly repeated canard that Clay had betrayed democracy for a handful of silver and that Adams was an illegitimate president became, starting in late 1826, a powerful populist sound bite. In fact, Clay supported Adams because he believed him best qualified to be president and because they agreed on most public policy issues. Clay despised Jackson. As these things often go, Clay's hope for the presidency in the future was best served by his collaborating with Adams rather than assisting Jackson to attain an office from which he would do everything in his power to harm Clay.

The other issue Adams gave them: in late 1825 he accepted an invitation to send delegates to a conference of the recently independent South and Central American republics to be held in Panama in 1826. Spain, it was feared, might try to repossess what it had lost. France and Spain still had imperial ambitions in the southern hemisphere. Great Britain continued its efforts to dominate trade with South America. In 1823, Monroe and his secretary of state had collaborated on a statement demanding that the Old World keep its hands off the New. The Panama Conference was designed to advance the principles of the Monroe Doctrine, with an emphasis on hemispheric cooperation and solidarity. It was hoped that it would, in a modest way and as a first step, represent a united front against the threat of renewed European colonialism. Adams' secretary of state, an early, consistent advocate for American recognition of the new South American nations, strongly approved. So did Adams. Clay expected easy Senate confirmation of the president's two nonpartisan nominees. Adams was wary.

When the upper house, its slim anti-Adams majority intent on mischief making, requested that the president send it the documents exchanged between the administration and the conference organizers, the president saw trouble coming. The Senate, he acknowledged, had the right to see the documents in closed session. When, at the instigation of the pro-slavery Jackson and Crawford coalition, the Senate voted to require that the president make the documents public, he refused. The "Rules of the Senate," he pointed out, were clear on the matter. Documents that were part of an ongoing diplomatic discussion were required to be held in confidence. In retaliation, the Senate narrowly voted to require the president to stipulate in writing which documents required confidentiality and which did not. Angry, Adams refused. It seemed an insult to the prerogatives of the presidency, and would, he told the Senate, set a precedent damaging to the conduct of foreign affairs. Frustrated, the anti-Adams senators denounced what they claimed was an affront to the Senate.

Yet there was a deeper, more explosively emotional subject instigating the Senate majority. More than a conflict between two branches of government was at issue. It was the subject of slavery, at first somewhat disguised and distanced. It soon became the fire pit of every incendiary statement invoking hell and brimstone in the Senate chamber. And it centered on American policy toward the government of the western portion of the island of Hispaniola, soon to be called Haiti. The issue had clutching, painful roots in American history, its tentacles reaching back to the Washington administration, the election of 1800, the Louisiana

Purchase, and the Missouri Compromise. And it was traumatic for many Southerners. The black republic of Haiti had accepted an invitation to send delegates to the Panama Conference, the conference organizers thinking it appropriate and reasonable to invite their sister republic. Yet, if the United States also accepted the invitation, would it not be the case, Southern members of Congress asked, that the American delegates would have to sit in the same room with the black Haitians? And would that not be a de facto recognition of the black republic, a recognition that the United States had refused since Haiti became independent in 1804? And would it not follow that Haiti would appoint diplomats to the United States? And would it not, then, be the case that those diplomats would think it their right, and would not diplomatic protocol affirm they had the right, to walk *as equals* the same Washington streets as every white American who lived in or resided temporarily in the nation's capital? Their presence, their touch, would pollute white purity. It was not a matter of politics or diplomacy or international law. It was a matter of visceral disgust.

There was a relevant, well-known backstory. The Adams family had played an important role in American-Haitian relations from the start. So, too, had Thomas Jefferson. Did Southerners in Congress in 1825–1827 remember, or had they been reminded by their elders, that the sixth president's father had, twenty-five years before, supported the Haitian Revolution and might have, if he had been re-elected, recommended recognition? And would not the slave-holding elite remember John Adams' antislavery views and have reason to believe that his son shared them? The suspicion that, in accepting the Panama invitation, John Quincy favored closer relations with Haiti, even recognition, was not a paranoid fantasy.

For almost two hundred years, Haiti, originally called St. Domingue, France's most wealth-producing colony in the West Indies, had supplied the majority of the world's sugar. French, Spanish, and British interests had competed for territory and markets. The American colonies, and then the United States, with the advantage of proximity, managed for most of the eighteenth century to navigate between and around the mercantile restrictions of the European powers. Trading food, timber, and other commodities for sugar and molasses was immensely profitable. The most capable smugglers on the planet, Americans dominated trade in the Caribbean. In the early to mid-1790s, the slave population of St. Domingue, led by competing black warlords, seized its freedom. Over the next ten years, with different races and factions alternating dominance, St. Domingue, amid fire and carnage, slowly moved toward independence. By the late 1790s, revolutionary France, its policies as shifting as Haitian realities, approved of black rule in Haiti, but it also had reason to worry that the regime would eventually declare total independence. The Washington and Adams administrations also had choices to make. The United States wanted to protect its lucrative trade as France's colony moved toward independence. The new government in St. Domingue, as the United States demonstrated good faith, gave American trade special privileges. There were, though, two tense issues. First, how could the United States and St. Domingue become closer trading partners and not provoke British and French hostility? Both Britain and France, with powerful navies, thought nothing of seizing American merchant ships. Second, how to minimize Americans' fears, mainly Southern but to a lesser extent Northern also, that support for François-Dominique Toussaint Louverture's black government would compromise the ideology and security of American slave owners?

John Adams had never made his detestation of slavery a secret. "I have," he wrote, "through my whole life, held the practice of slavery in such abhorrence that I have never owned a Negro or any other slave, though I have lived for many years in times when the practice was not disgraceful, when the best men in my vicinity thought it not inconsistent with their character." He had, though, accepted the fait accompli of the Constitution and the difficulty of eliminating an institution deeply embedded in Southern life and an essential part of the national economy. As president, he hoped to sustain American trade with St. Domingue and also enhance American security with a stronger presence in the Caribbean. But would not a special relationship with Toussaint's St. Domingue require that America, with its strong pro-slavery constituency and racist ideology, shake hands with, if not embrace, a black republic and black leaders? And would not a war with Great Britain or France be a disaster? The United States claimed the right to trade freely with both countries and their colonies. But the British and French each thought they had a right to America's exclusive cooperation. France believed the United States owed it a moral debt and had a treaty obligation. Great Britain took the view that cultural consanguinity and common safety ought to produce Anglo-American cooperation. The opposing views were mirrored in American domestic politics. Jefferson and much of the South, with some allies in the North, favored a tilt toward France; the Federalists favored Great Britain. When the United States declined to assist France, French warships began seizing American ships, especially in the Caribbean.

In the mid-1790s, President Washington had dipped his diplomatic toe in Haitian waters. He had wanted to facilitate trade. But even Caribbean waters were too cold, despite the zealous efforts of his secretary of state, Massachusetts antislavery ultra-Federalist Timothy Pickering. The cautious president feared having diplomatic relations with former slaves. When newly elected president Adams, in March 1797, kept Washington's Cabinet in place, Pickering now had a president who agreed with him about slavery: an evil to be eradicated, if only the means could be found. With Adams' consent, as France ratcheted up pressure, confiscating more ships and cargo, Pickering became the facilitator of a semi-secret pro-Haitian policy. With a quasi-war in progress between France and the United States, Adams struggled to negotiate a resolution: to get reparations for confiscated ships; to keep the British from seizing American ships; to assert neutrality; to keep flowing into the government coffers revenue that came from international trade, which paid most of the nation's bills; and also not to alienate the Southern, pro-French political elite and his own anti-French Federalist colleagues. It was a difficult balancing act.

In late December 1798, a back-channel negotiator from St. Domingue, representing Toussaint, quietly entered Philadelphia. At an out-of-the way dinner, negotiations began. It was the initiation of a remarkable dialogue between a country whose constitution privileged slavery and the black leaders of a country that had recently abolished it. Soon a talented consul, Edward Stevens, given tacit ministerial powers and dispatched to St. Domingue, brilliantly kept American interests in active and constructive balance with the competing factions in Haitian society. At the same time, the most powerful warship in America's small navy, the U.S.S. *Constitution*, patrolling Haitian waters, did battle with an aggressive French warship. The result was a decisive American victory. The *Constitution*'s commodore, Silas Talbot, on Adams' instruction, protected St. Domingue from French and British recolonizing efforts. Edward Stevens kept Adams well informed and committed.

So, too, did American sea captains, many from New England. Between 1779 and early 1801, the harbors of Cap-Français and Port-au-Prince flaunted, from the masts of merchant ships, American flags by the hundreds. Though New England traders dominated, the mid-Atlantic states also benefited. So, too, to a lesser extent, did the Southern states and seaports. With the spotlight on the domestic conflict between pro-French and pro-British enthusiasts, and with everyone profiting from trade with the French colony, the complications were mostly overlooked, though not entirely. Some Southerners feared their slaves would be misled into rebellion by black troublemakers or antislavery Northerners inspired by the example of emancipated blacks in St. Domingue. And would not antislavery Americans want to extend diplomatic recognition to St. Domingue when it threw off its colonial yoke and declared itself an independent nation?

In London, Adams' minister to the Court of St. James's, the estimable Rufus King, energetic and immensely competent, sought to create an expanded opportunity for the United States to play what he believed its rightful role in the Caribbean and South America. Appointed in the last summer of Washington's administration, the Anglophile, cultured King had happily resigned his Senate seat, moving himself and his family to London for a seven-year engagement. His mission was to demonstrate to the British elite that an American envoy deserved its attention and respect. He had been trying, with little success, to get the British to implement all the provisions of the 1795 Jay Treaty, a controversial attempt by the Washington administration to avoid a new war with Great Britain. The Jefferson faction hated the treaty, believing it a betrayal of France. Most Federalists supported it, including twenty-eight-year-old John Quincy Adams, called to London from his ministerial post in Holland to be helpful to the American negotiators in whatever ways he could. Though the Jay Treaty had made no substantive breakthroughs, it had nudged Great Britain to move a little less slowly toward fulfilling the terms of the 1783 Treaty of Paris, which had ended the Revolutionary War. Most important, the Jay Treaty had decreased the possibility, for the time being, of the United States' having to fight both European imperial powers.

It also cleared the way for King, in 1798 and 1799, to find common ground with Great Britain over St. Domingue. In effect, London would do nothing to impede American trade. More openly than the John Adams administration, it would support the Haitian independence movement, to be realized, it was assumed, when Toussaint felt strong enough to come fully out of the French closet. King in London and Adams at The Hague thought alike: independence for the French colony would benefit both countries, though President Adams prudently resisted inflaming any further the nascent but strong opposition of Southern proslavery and pro-French factions. Haitian independence would be a blow to France, a victory for Federalist and British interests. Soon, on his own initiative, but then with the president's approval, King went the next step, starting discussions with London about the desirability of Spain's South American colonies' becoming independent. Full eviction of Spain and France from the Americas was a consummation devoutly desired by Great Britain and the United States. It would leave both hemispheres, King and his British counterparts agreed, secure monopoly markets for British and American trade. And it would, from the point of view of the Federalists and the British, advance their antislavery values, a marriage of American Federalism and British constitutional monarchy in serving both Mammon and God simultaneously. On this, Adams, King, Pickering, Hamilton, and most Federalists would have shaken hands in brotherly harmony

In May 1800, Adams, fed up with Pickering's covert alliance with those in Adams' own party opposing his attempt to keep the peace with France, discharged him. The ex-secretary of state and Alexander Hamilton, Washington's ex-secretary of the treasury, then began to campaign vigorously, though partly behind the scenes, against Adams' re-election. Their political maneuvers, the long delay that trans-Atlantic travel imposed on news of the administration's diplomatic success in Paris, and the three-fifths rule cost John Adams the election. It also damaged the Federalist Party beyond repair. Predictably, Jefferson and the new administration, though favorable to South American independence as an interest rather than a priority, opposed Haitian independence. The notion was to them an abomination. Though Jefferson, for convenience, kept King on in London, Anglo-American discussions about South America ceased. They were to be revived twenty years later by President James Monroe and his secretary of state.

By March 1801 the world had changed for the Adams family, for

Toussaint, for Rufus King, for Jefferson, and for St. Domingue. In January, the House of Representatives had narrowly elected Jefferson in a twice-contested election. John Quincy Adams returned from Holland, discharged by the Jefferson administration, which had no more use for the services of the person Washington had said would one day be found "at the head of the Diplomatique Corps." Jefferson had little use for almost all other aspects of the Washington legacy. When, in 1802, malaria, yellow fever, and a black army destroyed an army that Napoléon, having decided to re-impose slavery, had sent to reconquer Haiti, the emperor threw up his hands. On January 1, 1803, the island republic declared its independence. On April 7, 1803, a few days before the French foreign minister shocked Robert Livingston with Napoléon's offer to sell the Louisiana Territory to the United States, Toussaint Louverture, having been betrayed under a flag of protection, died in a French prison. Napoléon had washed his hands of Haiti and Louisiana, and for the next sixty years American presidents, except for John Quincy Adams, wanted to have nothing to do with a free black republic. Anyway, Haiti, its economy destroyed, was no longer an important trading partner. Most American entrepreneurial eyes turned to the near Southwest and to the extended Mississippi River Valley. Their rich bottomlands were in the process of creating a cotton boom that made slavery a seemingly irreplaceable pillar of American prosperity.

Markers, paving stones, and gravestones were being laid firmly in place on the path that led through Haiti to the Louisiana Purchase, the Missouri Compromise, Kansas-Nebraska, and the Civil War. In July 1802, Jefferson let his Federalist minister in London know that the United States abhorred the example of a slave republic. His vision for America's future required that, eventually, every Negro in America be colonized to some distant place, perhaps a territory in the far western wilderness or in Africa. As starters, he proposed that "slaves guilty of insurgency might be transported" to one of those distant places—and then free blacks. The

This 1856 wood engraving in *Harper's Weekly* of a slave who has murdered two of her four children to release them from slavery provides a representation of Dorcas Allen's similar crime in 1837. [*Library of Congress*]

Solomon Northup (from his *Twelve Years a Slave*) being beaten by "a man whose whole appearance was sinister and repugnant. His name was James H. Birch, as I learned afterwards—a well-known slave-dealer." It is the same James Birch who, four years earlier, had purchased Dorcas Allen and her children. [*Library of Congress*]

Probably the same Washington, D.C., slave pen in which Dorcas Allen and her children were imprisoned in 1837. [*Library of Congress*]

John Quincy Adams, depicted by Edward Dalton Marchant in 1843, six years after the Dorcas Allen episode and two years after Lincoln visited the Speed plantation in Louisville, Kentucky. [*National Portrait Gallery*]

The first known image of Lincoln, made in 1846/1847, five years after his encounter with a slave coffle on the Ohio River and shortly before his election to Congress. [*Library of Congress*]

This 1848 watercolor by Henry Lewis shows an almost pastoral Alton, Illinois, an image-making attempt to help the city put behind it the murder of Elijah Lovejoy. [*Missouri Historical Society*]

"The Pro-Slavery Riot of November 7, 1837. Death of Rev. E. P. Lovejoy."
[*Missouri Historical Society*]

The only extant image of Elijah Lovejoy, in silhouette, an immortal ghostly shadow of "the first American martyr." [*Missouri Historical Society*]

Wendell Phillips in the 1850s, at the height of his oratorical powers. The photograph by Matthew Brady highlights his self-assured idealism. [*Library of Congress*]

John Adams, in 1784, after a portrait by John Singleton Copley. "I have through my whole life, held the practice of slavery in such abhorrence that I have never owned a Negro or any other slave, though I have lived for many years in times when the practice was not disgraceful, when the best men in my vicinity thought it not inconsistent with their character." [*National Park Service, Adams National Historical Park*]

Abigail Adams, painted by Gilbert Stuart between 1800 and 1815. How is it, she asked, that the white school boys in Quincy never objected to her black servant "James playing for them when at a dance"? How can they object to his attending school with them? [*National Park Service, Adams National Historical Park*]

Rufus King's father and his family were subject to a similar attack in Falmouth [Portland] by Liberty Men enforcers and vandals. "These private Mobs, I do and will detest," John Adams wrote. [*Granger Collection*]

From New England to Virginia, Loyalist sympathizers like John King suffered, between 1765 and 1783, humiliation, intimidation, and torture by pro-independence patriots. [*Library of Congress*]

John Quincy Adams as secretary of state, painted by Charles Robert Leslie in 1816, the year of the founding of the Colonization Society. [*Granger Collection*]

Sixty-five-year-old Senator Rufus King in a portrait by Gilbert Stuart at the time of the Missouri Compromise debates in 1820. [*National Portrait Gallery*]

The only extant image of Charles Fenton Mercer, a principal leader of the American Colonization Society. This 1841 portrait by James Reid Lambdin is of Mercer in his early sixties. Born during the Revolution, Mercer lived until three years before the Civil War. [*Philadelphia History Museum*]

[From the Rail Road Journal.]

LIBERIA.—The last number of the African Repository and Colonial Journal, contains with other interesting intelligence relating to Liberia, a well written diary, kept by Mr. J. Mechlin, upon a recent expedition to explore the country adjacent to Mesurado, and learn its adaptation to agricultural purposes. After ascending the river Mesurado for some distance, the exploring party crossed the country to the sources of the Junk river, which is described as being not more than three yards wide and two feet deep at the deep at the point of embarkation, in a canoe, but gradually expanding, until, at ten miles from its source, the stream is 150 yards wide, and deep enough to float a vessel of a hundred tons. At this point, the party embarked in a barge, and the scenery is thus describ-

"As we descended the river, it grad
ually expanded, and at the distance
25 miles from its source, we found
fully a mile wide; it is very windin
in its course, in some places describ
ing three-fourths of a circle, and
others, the shores, swelling out on on
side, and receding on the other, form
ed a series of graceful curves, which
at every turn, offered to our view
continued succession of objects, eac
presenting new beauties to admire. W
passed several villages, delightfully si
uated on the banks, and embosomed i
groves of plaintain, banana, and palı
trees. The shores were covered wit
vegetation, splendid beyond descrip
tion. Trees of singular form and fol
iage, springing from a deep, rich soi
reared their heads to an amazin

the soil gave a depth and vividness to the green, which was finely relieved by the varied hues of the flowers that decked the forest, and the surface of the stream, as smooth as a polished mirror, reflected with the utmost minuteness the variegated beauties of the vegetation that clothed its banks. As we approached a native village, groups of inhabitants would assemble on the shore, inviting us by their gestures to land; occasionally, a light canoe might be seen shooting across the stream, while overhead, troops of monkeys pursued their pretty gambols among the trees: in short, every thing combined to give animation to a landscape, the beauties of which, description can never equal."

A land so beautiful, and soil so luxuriant, is almost sufficient to tempt a white emigrant to leave our colder skies and less kindly vegetation for its sun-

"The houses are placed without any attention to order or regularity, and are generally of a circular form, with high conical roofs, thatched with leaves, and are very dry and comfortable: the eaves project a considerable distance beyond the walls, and form a shade in which the natives, during the heat of the day, recline on rude couches formed of banks of clay, hardened in the sun, and covered with matts; the spaces in front of the houses are swept twice a day; and no offals of any kind or dirt is suffered to be deposited within the limits of the town; in fact, no place presents an air of greater neatness than a well ordered African village."

The nations of this region are now anxious than otherwise, that the colo-

and, as the Monrovians see
with them a share of the e
the country whence they em
settlements will doubtless
tended into the interior, t
luxuriant region here descr
Mecklin mentions elsewh
Journal that several of the
the country, who formerly
gainst the emigrants, are n
to place themselves under
tion of the colony; a fact e
itable to the energy and mo
the latter in its collisions
tives, and chastisement of
lence.

Beautiful Liberia, a paradise even for white men. The *Sangamo Journal* reprinted this article from the *Rail Road Journal* on March 15, 1832. It was one of many touting the magnificent attractions of the colonization destination that Lincoln is likely to have read. [Sangamo Journal *article, March 15, 1832.*]

A "Life Membership Certificate" for the American Colonization Society, circa 1840, signed by its president, Henry Clay. [*Library of Congress*]

governor of Virginia, James Monroe, urged this solution, Jefferson told King, and requested that the president look into it. "The course of things in the neighboring islands of the West Indies" appears "to have given a considerable impulse to the minds of the slaves in different parts of the US," and "a great disposition to insurgency has manifested itself among them." American slaves are vulnerable to contamination by the Haitian example. They need to be suppressed and dispersed, and white dominance should be reestablished in Haiti. In the United States, emancipation, Jefferson counseled, if it is ever to occur, must go hand in hand with colonization.

Almost within rock-throwing distance, Haiti was dangerously close. Twenty-five years later, Secretary of State Henry Clay, attempting to take advantage of proximity, proposed that white America might best be served by encouraging free blacks to emigrate there as an alternative to an African destination. Troublemaking slaves might be chained to the decks of the same ships that brought free blacks to Port-au-Prince. Let black troublemakers join their soul mates in Haiti. His presidency already burned by the Panama Conference imbroglio, John Quincy Adams raised no objections. Dismissive of the American Colonization Society, he thought colonization impractical and morally repugnant. But when Clay raised the possibility of the United States recognizing Haiti, Adams demurred on political grounds. It was untimely and certain to be counterproductive. "Can the people of the South," asked Georgia senator John M. Berrien, "permit the intercourse which would result from establishing relations of any sort with Haiti? Is this emancipated slave, his hands yet reeking in the blood of his murdered master, to be admitted into their ports, to spread the doctrine of insurrection, and to strengthen and invigorate them, by exhibiting in his own person an example of successful revolt?" The fear and anger Berrien's words expressed had to be taken, Adams knew, with deadly seriousness.

WHEN THIRTY-YEAR-OLD Abraham Lincoln opened his copy of the *Sangamo Journal* on March 2, 1839, he would not have been surprised to see two of its five pages devoted to the full text of a speech by Henry Clay. Delivered to the U.S. Senate in early February, it was "On the Subject of Abolition Petitions." John Quincy Adams had been presenting petitions to the House of Representatives by the hundreds. Surprised or not, Lincoln would have been pleased. The *Journal*'s publication of the full text signaled that it was an important expression of a view that its editor and many of its Springfield readers shared. Full publication was also a political statement: if Americans wanted a constructive, experienced, and moderate Whig president, Henry Clay was the paragon of that mold. The speech would have lifted the spirits and confirmed the correctness of moderate anti-abolition Whigs such as Lincoln. But it would not have altered Lincoln's and the *Journal*'s decision not to support Clay for the 1840 nomination.

A little over a year before, Lincoln had given the first major speech of his life to the Springfield Young Men's Lyceum. Its only publication was in the *Journal*. Clay's Senate speech dominated the national press. Lincoln's obscure address had a different emphasis. Though it had nothing overt to say about abolition, abolitionists, or abolitionist petitions, it implied that they had contributed to the interactive dynamic of lawlessness that he believed threatened the nation's unity and peace. Like most Americans, he wanted the abolitionists to shut up and go away. Embedded in the congressional maelstrom, Clay, unlike Lincoln, was responding directly to the pro-slavery–antislavery drama triggered by petitions and agitation from Alton, Illinois, to Charleston, South Carolina, to Washington, D.C. The very existence of the union is threatened, Clay claimed, by abolitionism; abolitionists should "pause in their mad and fatal course," their "wild and ruinous schemes," which "threaten to deluge our country in blood"; and the abolition petitions constantly submitted to Congress, most notoriously by Adams, "may prove but prelude to the shedding of the blood of their brethren."

Neither the *Sangamo Journal* nor Whigs such as Henry Clay approved of antislavery petitions. On this issue, the otherwise highly regarded ex-president turned congressman needed to be muffled. Adams was a danger to national Whig ambitions. A few days before Lincoln read Clay's speech, he had advised a meeting of Springfield Whigs, preparing for the 1840 presidential campaign, to draft an address calling for "all the opponents" of the Van Buren administration "to unite upon the common platform of Union and Compromise." Lincoln, Clay, and most Whigs defined compromise in the same way: North and South should respect the constitutionality of their respective institutions. As little political fuss as possible should be made about slavery. Cotton was increasingly king. And Northern insurers, brokers, bankers, factors, merchants, machinists, manufacturers, traders, shipbuilders, politicians (many of them Whigs), and huge numbers of workers were deeply vested in the dominant source of national wealth: slavery and cotton. Slavery put money into innumerable pockets. And the urgency of emancipation, even for those such as Clay, who hoped it would happen eventually, had its sharp edge blunted by the widespread conviction that Negroes were an inferior race and the practical problems almost insuperable.

There were other issues: the tariff, the national bank, and federal funds for infrastructure. But on these issues, contentious as differences between Whigs and Democrats occasionally became, there were paths to compromise. Both sides had enough overlapping interests to ensure that controversial legislation did not produce absolute alienation. South Carolina had seriously threatened to leave the Union in the early 1830s. Ostensibly, the issue was the tariff. It soon became clear that what drove South Carolina's antiunion extremism was its commitment to protect slavery. The vehicle to do that was the doctrine of nullification: each state, South Carolina claimed, had the right to nullify congressional legislation. It had in mind the tariff, Native American lands, and antislavery legislation. Nationalists, whether slave owners or not, united against that. It was a step too far. How could there be a meaningful Union if nullification were allowed? Other ways existed to accomplish the same aims, and Federalism lived on in the Whig and moderate Republican commitment to oppose the nullification doctrine. National unity and economic well-being required it. Clay, Adams, Jackson, and the young Lincoln could shake hands on that.

Henry Clay often seemed to be the man of the hour, the exemplary crafter of the fine compromise. And once again, in 1839, compromise was needed. Though there was no crisis at hand requiring legislative legerdemain, he had no doubt that his talents as a man of reason, prudence, and amiability, powered by his golden voice and lifelong good luck, made him the right leader for the times, the pacifier and persuader, the protector of the Union. If his party were to be united behind him, he would find ways, he believed, to keep the country together, to prevent it being sacrificed to the violence of slavery or antislavery extremism. After all, having established a national reputation as a leading legislator and the primary facilitator of the Missouri Compromise, he had become the shining star in the Whig firmament. His supporters ranged from the border states to the agricultural fields of the West. He had deep pockets of strength in the Upper South. He had the allegiance of many businessmen and bankers in the North. And if Clay had had any awareness of Lincoln's existence, he would have assumed that the young Illinois politician, like all progressive Whigs, was a fervent supporter. They agreed about public policy on every major issue. Lincoln had been, from the start of his career, a strong advocate of Clay's "American Plan": federal money for infrastructure, a national bank and banking system, and a tariff to protect and encourage domestic industry.

Yet had Clay been slightly less self-confident by nature, he would not have been as surprised as he became when most Whigs in 1839 agreed to support ex-general William Henry Harrison for the presidency. As a Whig elector, Lincoln enthusiastically committed himself to Harrison. A *Sangamo Journal* editorial, perhaps written by Lincoln, boasted that choosing Harrison would "proclaim to the world, that poverty shall never arrest virtue and intelligence on their march to distinction." Both claims were nonsense. Harrison was a sixty-seven-year-old upper-class ex-Virginian, the owner of a huge Ohio property, whose military exploits in the War of 1812 were minimal and whose intelligence no one but a fellow politician, creating a sound bite, would ever have emphasized. His record as an Indian fighter had been exaggerated into falsehood; his military record was mediocre to bad. Desperation, though, drove the Whigs to a down-market consensus: the choice of a man with neither the personality nor the intellect to be an outstanding president. It was an attempt to out-Jackson the Jackson example against a vulnerable Martin Van Buren, widely blamed for the recent depression. Even worse, the ticket had in second place a slave-owning former Democrat from Virginia, John Tyler. Apparently, no one thought to ask whether Tyler agreed with any of the basic Whig public policies. An ultraconservative states' rights advocate, he did not. None of this, apparently, made a difference to Lincoln's commitment to Harrison.

And, unlike Clay, Harrison was indifferent to slavery's immorality. It was, he believed, rightfully to be a permanent feature of American life. When governor of the Indiana Territory, he had lobbied for repeal of Article 6 of the Northwest Ordinance, prohibiting slavery. He had favored legalizing slavery in all the Western states, on economic grounds. Lincoln did not allow his disagreement with Harrison over the morality of slavery to influence his decision to support Harrison's candidacy, and the differences existed mainly in principle. When, early in the year, Lincoln had the opportunity to move from principle to practice, he found it expedient to stand on the politically comfortable middle ground. He voted in the

Illinois General Assembly for a resolution condemning the governor of Maine for not adhering strictly to the pro-slavery provisions of the Constitution. Then he changed his mind, concluding that it was "better to postpone the subject indefinitely." But when, the week before Clay's anti-abolition speech to the Senate, the Illinois legislature considered an anti-abolitionist resolution, Lincoln voted with the majority against it. This was not the same, of course, as voting in favor of abolitionism. In the best of all possible Whig worlds, the less involvement with the issue the better.

When Clay addressed the Senate on February 7, 1839, every senator in his seat, the galleries packed to hear the master orator, he still expected, as many Americans hoped, that he would be the Whig nominee and the next president. An objective observer would have had reason to doubt this. Still, what he had to say counted. His importance could not be underestimated. Without party unity, which required a cooperative Henry Clay, Whig prospects would be less than sanguine. As the paragon of senior Whig leadership, the embodiment of the middle way, sectional harmony, and economic progressivism, Clay was the Whig ideal and idea man. He embodied the sparkle of Whig personality and policy, the avatar of constitutional fidelity and progressive policies: the supremacy of the legislature, economic nationalism, and a united country—and the Whig middle way on slavery. This meant maintaining slavery's place as an economic and constitutional reality while at the same time condemning it on moral grounds.

Moral rectitude, though, was not the prelude to action or even to verbal activism. "Slavery is undoubtedly a manifest violation of the rights of man," Clay had written previously. "It can only be justified in America, if at all, by necessity." But necessity, he emphasized in February 1839, had already made its decision. The facts were the facts. "Congress has no power, as I think, to establish any system of emancipation, gradual or immediate, in behalf of the present or any future generation." It was not possible to undo history, to change the law, to defy economics. "That it entails innumerable mischiefs upon our Country I think is quite clear," even entails dangers to the peace "in particular parts of the Union." But not, Clay believed, if his advice were to be followed: the Southern states were taking, and should take, more effective steps to protect against the possibility of slave insurrection. The danger came now not from homegrown Southern insurrectionists or from ameliorants, like most Whigs, who favored colonization. It came mostly from Northern agitators, "the inconsiderate and misguided individuals" such as those, like Adams, who were petitioning Congress to abolish slavery in the District of Columbia.

Adams often walked from the House to the Senate to hear speeches of interest. Apparently, he did not on this Thursday in February. Preoccupied with a meeting on the James Smithson bequest, he submitted five resolutions urging that the money be used to create the museum Smithson had intended. Adams had almost every day for the first months of the year devoted himself to House business: tariffs, budgets, the Treasury, banks, and infrastructure. And his chairmanship of the Committee on Manufactures occupied much of his time. Though his heart was in some of this, it was, in fact, given mostly to the drama of Congress' reaction to the antislavery petitions he submitted on the first Monday of each month. In January, he had submitted one hundred; ninety-five on the subject of slavery. One, likely to be particularly dear to his heart, called for the "recognition of the republic of Hayti." He would have remembered his father's antislavery views, his support of the Haitian Revolution, and the hostile response to his own acceptance of the Panama Conference invitation.

"There was, on January 7," Adams had written in his diary, "a petition from the State of Maine, with seven distinct prayers, five of which were the slavery interdicts, then for the recognition of Hayti, and then to rescind the gag." When he had begun to read them, he was interrupted by the Speaker, James K. Polk, who ruled him out of order. He then began to read a petition "from William Lloyd Garrison and sundry inhabitants of Boston, praying for the removal of the seat of government to some place north of the Potomac, where the Declaration of Independence is not considered as a mere rhetorical flourish . . . and moved that Garrison's petition should be referred to a select committee with instructions to enquire and report to the House their opinion of the constitutional power of Congress to remove the seat of government. . . . I said it was a grave and serious question, and, if Congress had the power, this petition was an offer of compromise as a substitute for the abolition of slavery in the District, which deserved to be considered. The petition was laid on the table."

It was a grave and serious question, Henry Clay agreed as he began his speech to the Senate. His golden baritone filled the hall, the gliding tones expressing his persuasive powers, his sweet reasoning, his graceful language, the accomplished orator's confidence that he could make the galleries weep, his fellow senators see the light, and voters crown him with electoral approval. Talking, as he usually did, from bullet points on slips of paper, he ornamented his argument with anecdote, metaphor, and personal experience, including enough fact and data to support his broad claims. His rhetoric flowed along channels of attractive sound. Finding the point at which rhetoric and exhaustion created a peroration, he felt none of his powers fail him. It was Henry Clay at his best. All eyes were on, all ears attentive to, the famous speaker. His subject was the history of slavery, its moral repugnance, its economic necessity, its long existence in the United States, the constitutional compromise, the hope for the distant day when colonization would free America from this incubus, and, most important, the danger of antislavery agitation. "Anxious as I always am," he concluded, hitting the politician's high note of humble self-sacrifice, "to contribute whatever is in my power to the harmony, concord, and happiness of this great people, I feel myself irresistibly impelled to do whatever is in my power, incompetent as I feel myself to be, to dissuade the public from continuing to agitate a subject fraught with the most direful consequences."

The agitators could be reduced to bullet points, categories from the benign to the mistaken to the dangerous. "The first are those who, from sentiments of philanthropy and humanity, are conscientiously opposed to the existence of slavery, but who are no less opposed, at the same time, to any disturbance of the peace and tranquillity of the Union, or the infringement of the powers of the States composing the Confederacy." In the second class are those who defend the right of petition, who may or may not favor abolition. The third is the most dangerous, a class that most Southerners would have assumed included Adams. They are the

> *ultra abolitionists, who are resolved to persevere in the pursuit of their object at all hazards, and without regard to any consequences, however calamitous they may be. With them the rights of property are nothing . . . the acknowledged and incontestable powers of the States are nothing; civil war, a dissolution of the Union, and the overthrow of a government in which are concentrated the fondest hopes of the civilized world, are nothing. A single idea has taken possession of their minds, and onward they pursue it, overlooking all barriers, reckless and regardless of all consequences. With this class, the immediate abolition of slavery in the District of Columbia, and in the Territory of Florida, the prohibition of the removal of slaves from State to State, and the refusal to admit any new State, comprising within its limits the institution of domestic slavery, are but so many means conducing to the accomplishment of the ultimate but perilous end at which they avowedly and boldly aim,—are but so many short stages in the long and bloody road to the distant goal at which they would finally arrive. Their purpose is abolition, universal abolition, peaceably if it can be, forcibly if it must.*

And, he continued, they dangerously appeal to the ballot box rather than to the Constitution, to the manipulation of public opinion that makes the popular will more determinative than the law, threatening to break the sacred agreements embedded in the nation's founding document. And to raise the likelihood of bloodshed and destruction. "I am, Mr. President," Clay boasted, "no friend of slavery. The Searcher of all hearts knows that every pulsation of mine beats high and strong in the cause of civil liberty. Wherever it is safe and practicable, I desire to see every portion of the human family in the enjoyment of it. But I prefer the liberty of my own country to that of any other people; and the liberty of my own race to that of any other race." If we are to have immediate emancipation, which the abolitionists advocate, either the black race or the white race will rule. For "the liberty of the descendants of Africa in the United States is incompatible with the safety and liberty of the European descendants. Their slavery forms an exception—an exception resulting from a stern and inexorable necessity—to the general liberty in the United States." And slavery now was an economic necessity, the aggregate value of all slaves the single largest repository of wealth in the country. "We did not originate, nor are we responsible for, this necessity. Their liberty, if it were possible, could only be established by violating the incontestable powers of the States, and subverting the Union. And beneath the ruins of the Union would be buried, sooner or later, the liberty of both races. . . . I beseech the abolitionists themselves solemnly to pause in their mad and fatal course; and to reflect that the ink which they shed in subscribing with their fair hands abolition petitions may prove but the prelude to the shedding of the blood of their brethren." Two weeks later, in late February 1839, Adams proposed to the House of Representatives a constitutional amendment to abolish slavery.

SIX

The African Mirage

Late on a February night in 1816, three drunk Virginians had an intemperate political argument. One of them, Philip Doddridge, blurted out fighting words: Thomas Jefferson was "a consummate hypocrite!" Delegates to the Virginia House of Delegates, the three men were roommates, sharing an apartment in Richmond while the legislature was in session. A wealthy lawyer and planter from Albemarle County, the owner of fifty slaves, Dabney Minor was Jefferson's neighbor and close friend. A member of the Virginia elite and an ardent Republican, Minor thought Jefferson could do no wrong. Philip Doddridge, from across the mountains in what is now West Virginia, and Charles Fenton Mercer, from Loudon County in Northern Virginia, belonged to the small remnant of Virginia Federalists. Mercer owned a few slaves by inheritance. Doddridge, a self-made man, probably owned none. Neither admired the former president.

Thirty-eight-year-old Mercer, short and still slim, with light hair, a friendly smile, and a gloomy view of life, was a lawyer and subsistence planter who had been struggling for years to settle his improvident ancestors' and relatives' debts. And he was, unlike his equally drunk friends, an intellectual with formal credentials, a graduate of the College of New Jersey, later renamed Princeton, with a graduate degree in law. Impressed by what he had seen in the North, he advocated that Virginia create a system of free public schools and encourage economic diversification, especially industry. Like most Virginia Republicans, especially its governing elite, ex-president Jefferson rejected appeals to economic diversification. Industry and manufacturing were undesirable. The planter class wanted Virginia to remain agricultural forever. That meant plantations worked by slaves.

Mercer's attempts to get the Virginia legislature to support free public education, encourage industry, and fund infrastructure projects all decisively failed. The Jeffersonians were having none of it. As far as they were concerned, the Loudon County Federalist deserved denunciation: anyone who disagreed with Jefferson's vision for America's future was, by that alone, an enemy of democracy, probably a secret Tory and an aristocrat. Just as much an elitist as Jefferson, though of a different kind, Mercer himself did not believe the ballot box sacred or that the uneducated should be permitted to vote. Jefferson leaned slightly more toward a broader franchise on the assumption that voters, North and South, would follow his lead: it was his job to make policy; the voters', to agree to it. And as much as he disapproved of slavery in principle, if Virginia were to remain a pastoral paradise uncontaminated by smokestacks and money-grubbing commerce, it required slaves to work the land. He had over his lifetime about four hundred of them. Having retired from the presidency in March 1809, he watched broodingly and protectively over his legacy.

The next morning, a sober Charles Fenton Mercer asked Philip Doddridge, a short, broadly built, outspoken lawyer, what he had meant by accusing the ex-president of being "a consummate hypocrite." He did not assume that the charge had anything to do with slavery. That Jefferson had a slave mistress would not particularly have bothered Mercer or Doddridge, though neither would have approved. Newspaper rumors about Sally Hemings during the 1800 election campaign did Jefferson no damage among his supporters. His admirers, like Dabney Minor and their Albermarle County circle, knew of Sally Hemings, though probably not the intimate details. Jefferson's Hemings family connections would have been noticed by people visiting Monticello regularly. But Mercer, a closeted gay man, would never have criticized Jefferson simply because he owned slaves and had a slave mistress. And Virginians who professed lives of Christian piety would have had nothing to say, publicly at least, about that, given its prevalence. As Federalists, Mercer and Doddridge had voted in 1800 for John Adams, not Jefferson—but that had had nothing to do with slavery. Like Jefferson, they were against slavery in principle. They wished it could somehow be made to go away. Like Jefferson, they saw it as a problem without a practical remedy, though Doddridge had had what seemed to him a glimpse of one. Mercer wanted details. Why was Jefferson a "consummate hypocrite"?

Because, Doddridge responded, when the Virginia legislature in late 1800 had in secret session revived the idea of colonization for all blacks, and Virginia's governor, James Monroe, requested that the newly elected president look into it, Jefferson had done nothing practical to push the possibility forward. As a member of that legislature, Doddridge hoped that colonization might be coupled with gradual emancipation. Twenty-five years earlier, in 1776–1777, the rulers of Virginia, gathered in a special convention in which Jefferson played a leading role, had included in their revision of Virginia's legal code a proposal to expatriate all blacks at the conclusion of a process of gradual emancipation. One of many proposals, it was not approved. By the time Jefferson, in 1785, made his ideas on emancipation with colonization public in his *Notes on the State of Virginia,* he no longer thought it as good an idea as he had ten years before. Most of his fellow slave owners never had liked it. The emancipation part had been an idealistic pipe dream, and emancipation without colonization was inconceivable. But selective colonization without emancipation was not.

Suddenly, in 1800, the idea of selective colonization became alive again. In August, Richmond had almost been put to the torch by rebellious slaves. Virginia's white masters fantasized that, had the rebellion succeeded, they might have been made, if their lives had been spared, the slaves of slaves. Terrified by Gabriel's Conspiracy, as the slave insurrection was called, the legislature looked for remedies. Why not colonization? But for whom? Non-slave-owning Federalists such as Doddridge hoped colonization might include the eventual expatriation of all Negroes. If not, as the slave population increased, sheer numbers would make colonization impractical. Few Virginians, though, agreed with him. Jefferson no longer did, or he did so as an ideal that he had no practical way to implement. And he needed to be careful, whatever scheme he pursued, not to alienate his constituency, the planter class to which he belonged.

It was comparatively easy for Doddridge, from west of the mountains where slavery was minimal, to advocate a slavery-free America. But that even he was short on specifics did not make his views less objectionable. Most elite Virginians wanted to keep their slaves. Their way of life required that. How could the proprietor of Monticello, the advocate of an agrarian ideal that required black field laborers, envision an existence without slaves? And, as a parallel consideration, was it not evident that the money required to compensate owners and pay for removal was far beyond the capability of the federal treasury, even if all other conditions could be met? In any case, how would that work? Would American blacks of every description be forced into colonization? And what if they chose not to go? About to ascend to the presidency, resigned to the gap between the ideal and the practical, Jefferson narrowed the focus of colonization. It needed to be decoupled from general emancipation. Responding to Monroe and those traumatized by Gabriel's Conspiracy, he agreed with the majority of the legislature: find a place to which to transport slaves guilty of, or even only suspected of, insubordination. Such Negroes, from troublemakers to revolutionaries, should be eliminated, through either execution or removal. That should be the immediate aim of colonization.

It should have nothing to do with emancipation. That was for a different era, a future generation.

But to where to export them? Haiti was a possibility, or Sierra Leone, on the west coast of Africa, where the British had established a colony for free blacks. In London, Rufus King, ordered by Jefferson to look into this, reported back that the British had said, "No, thank you." They were having enough trouble financing and securing Sierra Leone. They did not want it to become a dumping ground for Negro troublemakers and criminals from America. Where else, then? The unexplored vastness of the American West seemed to Jefferson a possibility, both before and especially after the Louisiana Purchase. But wasn't that reserved for white Americans? And how could there be an "Empire of Liberty" if it contained independent Negro enclaves? That would limit white expansion and provide an example that might undermine slavery in the South. Detesting what he considered Jefferson's hypocrisy in general, Doddridge felt self-righteously comfortable denouncing him as "a consummate hypocrite" on slavery. The Virginia legislature had in 1800 pointed the way when it revived the idea of colonization for all slaves. But Jefferson had not, Doddridge explained to Mercer, gone down that road in any practical sense. Always ready to deplore slavery on moral grounds, the president was never prepared to do anything about it.

When the incredulous Charles Fenton Mercer, never having heard of this secret session of the Virginia legislature, gained access to its records, they confirmed what Doddridge had told him. He became preoccupied with colonization. A narrowly focused version seemed to him a grand idea. Unlike Jefferson, he had little in the way of governing responsibilities. With his own small estate managed by a few slaves, and without a wife or children, he had ample time for political interests and public policy passions. He was to follow his service in the state legislature with thirty years representing his Northern Virginia district in the House of Representatives, a congressman given to outbursts of energy and implosions of depression. His district valued his education, upper-class status, and commitment to capitalism, colonization, and funding for infrastructure. Like other former Federalists, he eventually became a Whig, and Lincoln occasionally read his name in the *Sangamo Journal* in the 1830s. Though he made enemies among his fellow Southerners who thought him too Northern, he remained on good terms with many post-Jefferson Republicans, particularly Madison and Monroe, both of whom gradually embraced some policies for which they had previously condemned the Federalists. Mercer, though, wanted more. He wanted for the South what most of the South did not want: literacy, capitalism, and a diversified economy. To Jefferson, he seemed an enemy of the good life, of ennobling agriculture and pastoral bliss.

LIKE MOST Federalists and then Whigs, Mercer had no particular plan for eliminating slavery, though by the beginning of the nineteenth century it had less and less economic importance in Northern Virginia. Much of the soil had been depleted by two hundred years of mineral-leaching tobacco crops. Now the rich soil of Georgia, Alabama, and Mississippi, cultivated by thousands of former border state slaves sold southward, had begun to provide most of the raw cotton that European looms transformed into cloth for the world marketplace. Still, the decreasing number of slaves in Virginia did not make slavery less central to the well-being of the planter elite, and no public antislavery activity could be conducted safely anywhere in the South. Mercer's antislavery views did not alienate his constituency, partly because he rarely expressed them. And he was on safe ground giving indirect support to those who hoped, even expected, that colonization would someday result in the United States being a Negro-free country, that the entire black population would someday be thousands of miles away in a land of its own.

Mercer made sure, taking up the colonization cudgel in 1816, that everyone knew that the society he was organizing rejected abolition. Called the American Colonization Society, it would, he assured prospective members in Washington, Baltimore, Philadelphia, and New York, be dedicated exclusively to solving the most pressing problem of the day: how to rid the South and North of free blacks. They were, he proclaimed, a dirty, dissolute, impoverished population (of about 250,000), a burden to taxpayers, and a source of crime and disease. Their existence undermined the livelihood and dignity of Northern workingmen. Easily radicalized, they were a threat to the security of Southern communities. Free blacks inspired black slaves to think that they, too, could become free. Inferior racial aliens, they could never be assimilated. On this, Jefferson, Mercer, and most white Americans agreed. In December 1816, the Virginia Assembly, persuaded by Mercer, found it sensible to resolve that the federal government should find land in the American West or in Africa to which to deport this alien population. If Virginia was in favor, Mercer argued, why should the federal government hold back?

Filled with missionary zeal, Mercer became a salesman for an idea easy to sell in the border states, in the nation's capital, and in Northern cities. In Virginia, the idea, familiar already, seemed likely to be helpful: it would get rid of troublemakers. Maybe even, down the line, it would help rid the state of excess slaves, with adequate compensation for slave owners. In the Deep South, it had only minor attraction; it was worth considering if limited to deporting troublemaking slaves and free blacks as long as it was not expected to be the prelude to emancipation. In Northern cities, it appealed to the white working class eager to eliminate black competition, to taxpayers afraid of black poverty and crime, to various casual racists of all sorts, and to evangelical Christians eager to Christianize Africa. It also appealed to antislavery moralists, some of whom thought it would be a good thing even as a limited palliative, and those who hoped that it would culminate in the expatriation of all black Americans. In Washington, Mercer found converts among the governing class, North and South, mostly antislavery moralists who shared his view that, while slavery was a sin, it was a sin more readily to be lived with if American life were liberated from the presence of all free blacks, unwelcome aliens infesting Northern and Southern cities.

Enterprising and persuasive, Mercer soon had a national organization under way, with a roster of distinguished supporters. Supreme Court justice Bushrod Washington, the great man's nephew, agreed to become the society's first president. A small cadre, led by Mercer and Robert Finley of New Jersey, did the initial organizing. James Madison, Henry Clay, John Marshall, John Randolph, John Taylor, William Crawford, Daniel Webster, Francis Scott Key, James Monroe, and John Tyler, among other public luminaries, became founding or early members. Its Washington headquarters buzzed with optimistic activity; annual national meetings were held in the hall of the House of Representatives. Chapters were initiated in hundreds of cities and towns, including Springfield, Illinois. To its converts, the American Colonization Society was both a noble cause and an affirmation of racial purity. A benevolent society in an age that increasingly loved societies, it addressed potential members with bombastic self-congratulations. At last something practical could be done about ridding America of pernicious racial aliens, at the same time helping them to a better life. And it was even construed by some antislavery moralists as a first step toward eventual emancipation.

Membership in the society didn't alone reveal whether someone was pro- or antislavery. The glue that bound members together was their commitment to white supremacy and a black-free America. Ex-president Jefferson's unofficial approval hovered in the background, expressed in private letters circulated widely enough to help validate the society. Antislavery Republicans and Federalists, slave owners and non–slave owners, found common ground in a project that could easily mean different things to different people. To Jefferson, writing in 1817, a new country "on the coast of Africa" was an essential early step in the "gradual emancipation" that he had always hoped would solve the slave problem. But who would pay for the purchase of the land? Impossible, he knew, to get agreement among the states to share the cost. Indeed, Virginia and South Carolina had different priorities. And if the federal government were to pay the costs, wouldn't that provide the basis for a huge expansion of the central government at the expense of states' rights? "Personally," Jefferson concluded, "I am ready and desirous to make any sacrifice" to rid Virginia of free blacks by establishing them "elsewhere in freedom and safety." Slave emancipation might slowly follow. But "I have not perceived the growth of this disposition in the rising generation, of which I once had sanguine hopes." Was he himself willing to sacrifice Monticello and his slave-supported way of life? It was airy talk rather than political initiative. Emancipation was a long-term nonstarter. "No symptoms inform me that it will take place in my day. I leave it, therefore, to time, and not at all without hope that the day will come, equally desirable and welcome to us as to them." Still, "perhaps the proposition now on the carpet at Washington to provide an establishment on the coast of Africa for voluntary emigrations of people of color, may be the corner stone of this future edifice." That future was, conveniently, very far off.

By 1817 the American Colonization Society had a national presence. There were, though, two troublesome questions: how many free blacks would voluntarily agree to be deported, and who would pay for it? And since none of the society's leaders had the stomach for involuntary expulsion, the free black population needed to be shown that expatriation was in its self-interest. Mercer was disappointed to discover that the vast majority of free blacks believed that they were not Africans but Americans, some with lineages predating those of most white Americans. Why, skeptics asked, would they want to go to an undeveloped foreign land, which would have less to offer and more dangers for them to confront than where they already were? Besides, transporting and resettling large numbers to Sierra Leone or even Haiti would, so the money multipliers calculated, cost huge sums in a tax-averse, cash-poor country with a sizable national debt. Donations and subscriptions could never pay that bill.

Mercer believed he had an answer. The national government should help pay some of the cost. His colleague, Virginia congressman John Randolph, wasted no time before formally requesting federal funding, and in 1817 the American Colonization Society asked Congress for money to purchase land in Africa. Strongly supporting the request, Henry Clay assured the South that this was not a wedge to pry open the slavery can of worms. Still, even a hint of a connection between colonization and emancipation created a shadowy fear in many Southerners' minds. No money was authorized.

When, in 1819, the Missouri crisis struck fear into the heart of the national Republican establishment, Mercer saw another opportunity. The nation was dividing along sectional lines, slavery and plantation agrarianism versus antislavery free soil and capitalism. It began to seem that the Union could not long accommodate such incompatible economic systems. Why not, then, put off the long-term problem by simultaneously admitting Missouri as a slave and Maine as a free state? Clay's compromise legislation did that. But soon another dagger threatened to kill accommodation. The proposed Missouri constitution contained a provision forbidding free blacks to immigrate into the state, but how could the North possibly tolerate a ban on its blacks moving into Missouri? North and South were, in 1820, at each other's throat. Again, Clay's legislative maneuvers helped pull back the dagger. But, Mercer again asked Congress, would it not be sensible, since it would alleviate the free black problem everywhere, to fund colonization with federal money, even if it was not strictly consistent with limited government and states' rights?

THROUGH CALM seas or choppy waters, whether the rain beat down or the sun blasted steamy wooden decks, the slave ships kept coming.

There was money to be made. Profiteers, with ships built in East Coast ports from Baltimore to Savannah, slipping out under false pretenses, brought enslaved Africans across the Atlantic to the southern coast of the United States, defying the 1808 law prohibiting the importation of slaves from abroad, bringing this illegal cargo ashore in out-of-the-way places, mostly unseen by the monitoring authorities. Even many Southerners did not approve. It was one thing to deplore federal intrusion on local institutions. It was another to make matters worse by circumventing the prohibition on importing slaves. To most border state slave owners, such smuggling diminished the market value of the slaves they already owned. And to antislavery moralists, whether slave owners or not, the larger the slave population, the farther off the already distant day of emancipation. But to slave profiteers, with a market in the Deep South, it was exclusively about money. And their challenge was to get non-English-speaking black Africans through the coastal sieve, past federal authorities, to local markets, where legal restrictions and moral scruples could be evaded. But the federal authorities also had a problem. What to do with the cargoes they captured?

Mercer saw an opening. His attempts to get Congress to provide funds for the society to purchase land in Africa had failed. In general, Congress had little to no will to appropriate money for anything other than basic necessities. And the use of federal money to transport free blacks to Africa, undesirable as that population was, did seem to many Southerners an opening wedge. Initiatives against slavery itself might be next. Still, the problem needed to be solved. What to do with the African blacks captured off the southern coast? Bring them to the nearest port, of course. But what then? Washington had no mechanism in place to determine whom they belonged to or even if they were slaves at all. How, then, to classify them? And Congress had neither money nor mechanism to return them to the place from which they had come. So what to do other than turn them over to the local authorities nearest the capture?

But, as Mercer pointed out, each state had its own laws regarding such black aliens. South Carolina, Georgia, and Louisiana handled the problem each in its own way. The result was legal chaos, an affront to rational administration and American justice.

In fact, Southern attitudes and legal edicts from Charleston to New Orleans were clear and consistent: regardless of where they had come from and why they were here, these captured blacks were assumed to be slaves. They should be treated as property. After some form of due process, limited to the interests of slave masters, they should be disposed of, with the least possible cost to taxpayers, by sale or expulsion. Sale was preferable. In the end, the unintended consequence of the enforcement of federal law was that most became slaves in America. A typical notice of "Sale of African Slaves" appeared in 1819 in a prominent Southern newspaper: "On Tuesday, the 4th of May next, in the town of Milledgeville, will be exposed to public sale, to the highest bidder, between thirty to forty prime African slaves, which have been taken possession of by the state of Georgia in consequence of their having been introduced contrary to the law of the State, and of the United States. Indisputable titles will be made, and prompt payment required. By order of the Governor."

Why not, Mercer proposed, authorize funds for the president to "make such regulations and arrangements, as he may deem expedient," to return to Africa on U.S. warships those Negroes who had been brought onto American soil from a captured slave ship and establish "a government agency on the African coast for resettling victims of the slave trade?" Colonization, which required land purchase, was never mentioned. On the face of it, the Slave Trade Act, passed by Congress in early March 1819, applied only to African Negroes captured at sea. It authorized $100,000 to cover expenses. A triumphant Mercer knew that he had the possibility of more than the bill literally provided. It seemed a small step from resettling illegally imported Africans to offering free blacks the opportunity to immigrate to the same place. Could the language of the bill be interpreted to allow the money to be used for both purposes, including the purchase of land? Could he persuade strict constructionists, some of whom, such as President Monroe, belonged to the American Colonization Society, to see it his way? A committee of the society's prestigious Washington chapter went to see the president. Yes, he agreed. This was an opportunity to rid the country of the free black population. He would take it up with his Cabinet.

WITH HIS mind on other things, including negotiations with Spain about Florida, Secretary of State John Quincy Adams had had no occasion or reason to make public his thoughts on the Colonization Society until mid-March 1819. At the White House for a brief meeting with the president, he was not surprised to hear that a committee had urged Monroe to approve the purchase of "a territory on the coast of Africa to which the slaves who may be taken under the late Act may be sent." Twelve months before, the secretary of state had taken part in a discussion with William Crawford, the secretary of the treasury, and George Hay, President Monroe's live-in son-in-law, in which the society had been mentioned. Colonization seemed to Adams, as he made clear on later occasions, morally repulsive and practically untenable.

The president had a question for him: did the legislation allow the $100,000 to be used to purchase land? Absolutely not, Adams replied. "I thought it impossible that Congress should have had any purchase of territory in contemplation of that Act." And the colonization project itself was in his view an intellectual, moral, and political muddle. "This project is professed to be formed," depending on whom you listened to, "1, without intending to use any compulsion upon the free people of color to make them go; 2, to encourage the emancipation of slaves by their masters; 3, to promote the entire abolition of slavery; and yet, 4, without in the slightest degree affecting what they call a certain species of property that is, the property of slaves." How absurd! And who are these diverse colonizationists? They

> *are men of all sorts and descriptions . . . some exceedingly humane, weak-minded men, who have really no other than the professed objects in view, and who honestly believe them both useful and attainable; some, speculators in official profits and honors, which a colonial establishment would of course produce; some, speculators in political popularity, who think to please the abolitionists by their zeal for emancipation, and the slaveholders by the flattering hope of ridding them of the free colored people at the public expense; lastly, some cunning slave-holders, who see that the plan may be carried far enough to produce the effect of raising the market price of their slaves.*

Equally offensive, would not the result of the government's creating an African country be an American colony, dependent on American funds and protection? The name "Colonization Society" implied that. The United States would become a colonial power, no different from Spain, France, and Great Britain. And though Adams believed that none of the society's members had this in mind, would that not, he asked the president, make the United States no better than the country it had gained its independence from? The president had his counterargument ducks in a row. Colonization had, he responded in his soft Southern voice, "been recommended by a resolution of the Virginia Legislature." Many in Virginia sincerely desired "the gradual abolition of slavery." That was testimony to "the excellent and happy condition of the slaves in that State . . . the kindness with which they were treated, and the mutual attachment subsisting between them and their masters." In fact, Monroe continued,

> *after the close of our Revolution many persons had voluntarily emancipated their slaves, but this had introduced a class of very dangerous people, the free*

> *blacks, who lived by pilfering, and corrupted the slaves, and produced such pernicious consequences that the Legislature were obliged to prohibit further emancipation by law. The important object now was to remove these free blacks, and provide a place to which the emancipated slaves might go: the legal obstacles to emancipation might then be withdrawn, and the black population in time be drawn off entirely from Virginia.*

When the Cabinet met, "it was soon settled," to Adams' satisfaction, "that the Slave-Trade Act gave no authority to the President to purchase a territory or establish a colony in Africa." It authorized him only "to take measures for removing beyond the limits of the United States the negroes who may be taken, as imported contrary to the law, and to appoint an agent to receive them in Africa." It seemed as if Adams' position would hold. And opposition to colonization made strange bedfellows. The influential George Hay, a pro-slavery Virginian and former member of the state legislature, who often carried the day with his father-in-law, was waiting in the secretary of state's office in late April 1819, furious at the president's continued advocacy for colonization. It would, Hay believed, lead to emancipation. That, ultimately, was, he believed, what colonization was about, and if the Virginia legislature, tricked by Mercer, had the opportunity to vote again, it would now oppose colonization. Hay "bitterly repented his vote."

Shocked by the vehemence of Hay's view, Adams took a deep breath. What disturbed him most was that apparently sincere people could not see that "their project of expurgating the United States from the free people of color at the public expense, by colonizing them in Africa, is . . . upon a par" with the proposal by a well-known explorer "of going to the North Pole and travelling within the nutshell of the earth." It was both stupid and cruel. "I believed," he told two pro-colonization clergymen who came to solicit a contribution from him, "that the mass of colored people who may be removed to Africa by the Colonization Society will suffer more and enjoy less than they would if they should remain in their actual condition in the United States . . . [that] their removal will do more harm than good to this country, by depriving it of the mass of their industry, and thus that the result of the whole, to both parties, will be evil and not good." Usually charitable, Adams refused to give the clergymen anything but his opinion and the promise that he would not speak publicly against them.

In mid-December 1819, the Cabinet, to Adams' distress, reversed itself. Crawford, "ready to make a Colony out of the law of the last session," now sided with Monroe. Attorney General William Wirt, persuaded by Crawford, reversed his position. The society members had been "indefatigable in their efforts to get hold of the funds appropriated by that Act," Adams noted in his diary. They had early on gotten the ear of the president, now of Crawford. And William Wirt, the attorney general, had now decided that it would be lawful to use some of the money to finance moving free blacks to an African homeland. Adams again "objected that there was no authority given by the law to spend money to maintain the blacks in Africa at all." But the society's proponents, as "ravenous as panthers," in Adams' phrase, for the $100,000, prevailed. Strict constructionists, Adams knew from his Louisiana Purchase experience, were able to be less strict when loose construction served their interests.

The initial money, everyone understood, would be far from enough. With sour vindication, Adams was to observe in the next thirty years frequent attempts to tap the public treasury for the society's activities. They all failed. Some newspapers touted African settlement as an earthly paradise. Its proponents advertised the prospective experience as blissful for free blacks. Liberia was "a land so beautiful and soil so luxurious," Lincoln's newspaper, the *Sangamo Journal*, glowed. It was "almost sufficient to tempt a white emigrant to leave our colder skies and less kindly vegetation, for its sunny clime and gorgeous forestry." It was "a landscape the beauties of which description can never equal." Many Americans, like Lincoln in the 1830s, found the society's platform credible. Others did not. "Colonize the blacks! A man might as well colonize his hands," Wendell Phillips was to write, though in a different context. But in the furtherance of an all-white America, colonization had enough plausibility to attract a wide swath of people in the North, including some abolitionists, such as Elijah Lovejoy and Gerrit Smith. Many antislavery Whigs became enthusiasts. Still, even for moderate antislavery racists—North and South; Whig, Democrat, or Republican—it was at best a hope, not a practical opportunity. If it were to be voluntary, it would never work. Forced expulsion was out of the question, and no one wanted to pay for it. Private contributions were meager, more tax dollars unforthcoming. "Tax us today for the transportation of our free negroes to Africa," one South Carolina congressman warned, "and tomorrow we will have to pay for the emancipation of our own slaves." In the border states, enthusiasm rapidly diminished. It disappeared in the Deep South. The free black community, with a few exceptions, emphatically rejected colonization.

Solicited over and over again to put his name and money behind the society's efforts, Adams did not change his view over the years. In fact, it hardened. "I freely gave my opinion," he wrote a few weeks after Lovejoy's assassination in 1837, "that the whole colonization project was an abortion; that as a system of eventual emancipation of the slaves of this country it was not only impracticable, but demonstrated to be so; that as a scheme for relieving the slave States of free negroes its moral aspect was not comely, and it was equally impracticable. I held this opinion when the existence of the Colonization Society was first made known to me. . . . Every day's experience had confirmed me in it from that time to this." No one could convince him otherwise. The Negro was here to stay, he had no doubt, even if simply as a practical matter, and why any free black would voluntarily export himself to a primitive African environment seemed beyond common sense and experience. So why the willingness among otherwise smart, experienced, humane, and even learned people to indulge in the colonization fantasy? Behind it all, Adams believed, was the widespread inability to accept that America already was and would always be a multiracial country.

HENRY CLAY never gave up hope that colonization would solve America's black problem. Free blacks would go first; then, eventually, some slaves, through voluntary manumissions by antislavery owners, and, as a distant though unemphasized possibility, government-sponsored emancipation with total compensation. Gradually, over a hundred years or more, three to four million slaves would emigrate to a black homeland in Africa, the Caribbean, or South America.

In 1827, at the eleventh anniversary of the society's founding, Clay gave his most impassioned, frequently quoted speech exhorting the country to get behind the colonization effort. No one need fear, he assured the South, that the society actually favored abolition. The general view, that "the purpose of the Society is to export the whole African population of the United States, bond and free," is wrong. "That is not what the Society contemplates." There was only one question: "Is it practical . . . to colonize annually six thousand persons [a year] . . . without materially impairing or affecting any of the great interests of the United States? This is the question presented to the judgments of the Legislative authorities of our country. This is the whole scheme of the Society." It could all be reduced to arithmetic: the exportation of six thousand free blacks a year, the exponential growth of the white population, an increase in slave manumissions, and the slower growth of the slave population would result, in a century or so, in the elimination of the free black population and a reduction in the slave population to make it minuscule in relation to the population as a whole. Dying a natural death, slavery would be less and less an issue. All it would take would be a government subsidy of $100,000 a year. To many, this seemed magical arithmetic.

Still, Clay insisted, "the Society's plan is not visionary, but rational and practicable."

Clay was better at rhetoric than arithmetic. "There is a moral fitness," he proclaimed, "in the idea of returning to Africa her children, whose ancestors have been torn from her by the ruthless hand of fraud and violence. Transplanted in a foreign land, they will carry back to their native soil the rich fruits of religion, civilization, law, liberty." The skeptics "must do more than put down the benevolent efforts of this Society. They must go back to the era of our Liberty and independence, and muzzle the cannon which thunders its annual joyous return. They must revive the slave trade, with all its train of atrocities. . . . They must blow out the moral lights around us, and extinguish that greatest torch of all which America presents to a benighted world, pointing the way to their rights, their liberties, and their happiness." Furthermore, "they must penetrate the human soul, and eradicate the light of reason and the love of liberty." They must "repress all sympathies, and all humane and benevolent efforts . . . in behalf of the unhappy portion of our race who are doomed to bondage." Slave owners were not to blame; they are we and our friends. "Cursed with this greatest of human evils," they deserve "the kindest attention and consideration. Their property and their safety are both involved. . . . Let us continue to appeal to the pious, the liberal and the wise. Let us bear in mind the condition of our forefathers, when, collected on the beach of England, they embarked, amidst the scoffings and the false predictions of the assembled multitude, for this distant land; and here, in spite of all the perils of forest and ocean, which they encountered, successfully laid the foundations of this glorious Republic. . . . [L]et us [redouble] our labours, and invoking the blessings of an all-wise Providence, I boldly and confidently anticipate success."

It was a speech that Lincoln was unlikely to have read in Indiana at the age of eighteen. But he knew it well enough in 1852 to quote it at length. Widely published, it was an address that he had in hand when writing a eulogy for his recently deceased mentor. Whether he read Clay's next speech to the Colonization Society, marking the occasion in 1837 of the society's twenty-first annual meeting and Clay's elevation to its presidency, would have made no difference. Clay had nothing to add to his 1827 message: slaveholders had no reason to fear the society; it had nothing to do with emancipation; and abolitionists were as evil as slavery itself. If the society should provide a model that future generations might make use of, and if voluntary emancipation should ever take place, fine and good. But the society addressed itself only to the situation of free blacks. It coerced no one. Yes, very little immigration to Liberia had occurred. But a good start had been made in a multigenerational enterprise. Most important, the great project would be accelerated if only state legislatures and the national government saw the wisdom of allocating funds for it.

If Clay had not become so closely associated with colonization, he might have been elected president in 1844. He lost, a bitter disappointment to every Whig, by the smallest of margins, to James Polk. Ohio stuck with him, though not one other Western state did. And his advocacy of colonization ensured that he would not carry a single Deep South state. Only three border states gave him their electoral votes, and his proposal that the proceeds from the sale of public lands be used to support colonization lost him many votes in the West.

A member of Springfield's Clay Club, Lincoln campaigned vigorously for his leader. Campaigning also on behalf of his own political future, he accurately blamed Clay's electoral defeat on the irony that antislavery Whigs in New York did not vote for him because, as a colonizationist, he wasn't antislavery enough. With not even 40,000 more popular votes than Clay, Polk was president. The slavery issue, even in the tepid form of colonization, had proved to be a political trap and a moral conundrum. Best, Lincoln wrote in October 1845, for "us in the free states," in deference "to the Union of the states, and perhaps to liberty itself (paradox though it may seem) to let the slavery of the other states alone; while on the other hand, I hold it to be equally clear, that we should never knowingly lend ourselves directly or indirectly, to prevent that slavery from dying a natural death—to find new places for it to live in, when it can no longer exist in the old." This included Texas. Clay shared this view, but it was a losing position during the 1840s, and Clay's defeat eliminated any possibility of obtaining federal funds for the Colonization Society.

On what basis did Clay and Lincoln think that slavery would ever die "a natural death"? There was reason to believe that the opposite was the case. States rich in cotton, sugar, and slaves were growing richer. The claim by pro-slavery Southerners that slavery was competitive with, even superior to, free labor, despite constant counterclaims by Northern Whigs and free soil advocates, was proving to have some merit. And the claim that it would eventually die a natural death provided, at best, moral cover for those who decided not to oppose it actively. The claim had little evidentiary credibility. Lincoln agreed fully with Clay's denunciation of abolitionists in his February 1837 speech, which the *Sangamo Journal* reprinted in full, but he could also readily deduce from the results of the 1844 election that Clay had gotten the worst of both worlds: too moderate to be favored by pro-slavery Southerners and so hostile to abolitionists that he lost votes in the North. At the same time, he alienated the constituency in both parties that craved westward expansion, regardless of slavery. It created a dilemma for antislavery Whigs. Could one be antislavery and still win a national election?

In Quincy, Massachusetts, on November 11, 1844, John Quincy Adams, though not especially enthusiastic about Clay, voted the straight Whig ticket. He was already aware that Polk had carried New York and the election by a tiny margin. It was, Adams understood, a momentous and determinative election, one that soon precipitated a war with Mexico and which would make a civil war about slavery, which he had long anticipated, even more likely. Having a true Southerner to vote for, an unqualified supporter of slavery and slavery expansion, the South emphatically rejected Clay, moderation, and compromise. "It is the victory of the slave element in the constitution of the United States," Adams wrote in his diary. "Providence, I trust intends it for wise purposes, and will direct it to good ends." It was the same sentiment that Lincoln was to express in his Second Inaugural Address twenty-one years later. It was a "Providence" that Adams had more consistent trust in than Lincoln, but one they both struggled to understand.

NEWLY ELECTED congressman Abraham Lincoln, soon to leave for the nation's capital, walked into a Coles County, Illinois, courtroom in October 1847 arm in arm, though perhaps not literally, with his colleague and friend Usher F. Linder of Elijah Lovejoy notoriety. They were about to be co-counsel in defense of a slave owner named Robert Matson, who spent half the year in Illinois and half in Kentucky. Five of Matson's slaves, whom he had brought from Kentucky to work on his farm in Coles County, claimed, with the help of local antislavery activists, that under Illinois law they were free. Exactly what Illinois law was, under the circumstances, was in dispute. Were they free because Matson had domiciled them in Illinois for almost two consecutive years? Were they free because they had been brought from slave to free soil for whatever length of time, no matter how short? Did Matson's claim that he had brought them to Illinois as temporary workers have any relevance? And did federal law and precedent have any jurisdiction, or was this entirely an Illinois matter? Lincoln had agreed to team up with Linder in defense of Matson's claim that his slaves were still slaves.

When Linder had left Alton almost ten years before, he had been puffed up with pride and extravagant in his racial nastiness. He had helped hammer nails into Lovejoy's coffin, both on the streets and in the courtroom. With energetic hostility, inspired by his hatred of abolitionists and abolitionism, he had led the attempt to prosecute the men who had armed themselves to defend Lovejoy's press. A petition from sixty pro-slavery residents had urged his participation. An Alton grand jury brought an indictment under an Illinois statute that seemingly made it a crime for an organized group to resist a mob: the crime of "violent riot" apparently could apply to victims as well as perpetrators. Lovejoy's associates had "unlawfully, riotously . . . and in a violent and tumultuous manner" defended their property. By implication, it was they who were responsible for Lovejoy's death, all damages, and the loss of life on both sides.

Seriatim, another Alton grand jury indicted a list of people purported to have attacked the warehouse. Linder now acted as their defense lawyer. Both trials were great performance opportunities. The attorney general treated both juries to impassioned pro-slavery rants. The argument was simple: all blacks were primitive inferiors whom God and nature had made for the purpose of serving their white masters; the Constitution sanctioned slavery; antislavery speech and actions endangered public peace, sectional harmony, and national security; consequently, the Lovejoy faction was responsible for all the violence that had occurred. Lovejoy had gotten what he deserved. He had come to Alton "to teach rebellion and insurrection to the slave," Linder told the jury, "to excite servile war; to preach murder in the name of religion . . . and to spread desolation over the face of this land."

Most of Alton's citizens wished the whole mess would go away. The national publicity was devastating. Both juries, in sequence, declined to convict either Lovejoy's colleagues or his killers Why damage their city even more? To have brought in a conviction against either side would have generated additional adverse attention and, in the inflammatory atmosphere of 1837–1838, might have attracted more advocates of confrontation to Alton's streets. A verdict against either, the juries decided, was not in the city's interest. Linder himself probably cared less about the outcome than about publicity and self-promotion. And by late February

1838, when Lincoln stepped to the podium to deliver his address to the Springfield Young Men's Lyceum, he would have known the results of the Alton trials. Linder himself was in Springfield.

Those on either side who had hoped for vindication were disappointed. Certainly Joseph and Owen Lovejoy were. Since the pro-slavery faction believed Lovejoy had gotten what he deserved, it could put the incident to bed with a sense of satisfaction. The hated abolitionist was dead, and the trials had been an excellent showcase for pro-slavery propaganda. That was clearly Linder's view. Though national attention would soon move to other scenes of conflict about slavery, the image for many Northerners of Lovejoy as a martyr became a permanent trope, especially for abolitionists and even for some antislavery moderates. Whig ideology and political opportunism, though, found it convenient to stress that Lovejoy had died a martyr not to antislavery but to freedom of the press. That was Lincoln's entire emphasis in February 1838.

Racism aside, Linder had injected himself into the Alton turmoil out of ego and for political advantage. When, in early 1837, his Democratic colleagues in the Illinois legislature elected him attorney general, he had happily taken up his more prestigious, better-paying duties. In his mind, his office entitled him, at the request of Alton's pro-slavery citizens, to become the prosecuting attorney of the surviving Lovejoy group. The spotlight would shine on him. High elective office would be next. In the state legislature, he had met, the year before, another young politician with whom he exchanged banter and debate. Though they were on opposite sides of the aisle, there was a mutual attraction between Linder and Lincoln. They were exact contemporaries, born in 1809 in Harden County, Kentucky, a short distance from each other. Border state Southerners, they both migrated to Illinois via a residence in Indiana. As young men without money, status, or formal education, each had embraced the law, Lincoln in Sangamo County, Linder in nearby Coles. Lincoln was prudent, deliberate, even plodding; Linder, boisterous, spontaneous, and transparently ambitious. Different as they were, they seemed to get along well. Lincoln was equally ambitious, and he and Linder were soon on the same political page when, in late 1838, Linder switched to the Whig Party.

Mercurial and impulsive, Linder lacked "plain, common horse sense." Otherwise, a contemporary claimed, he had "all the qualities of a great man and a great lawyer," without, paradoxically, being one. He was "vain, but just enough to spur him on to action," a late-nineteenth-century legal historian remarked in a brief biography. Proud, boastful, and self-destructive, he was, on the Central Illinois judicial circuits, a companionable associate, amusing and unpredictable, sometimes a colleague, sometimes an adversary. He and his fellow lawyers and the judges traveled together, often sharing bed and board, the rough conditions of frontier accommodations. During prosperous days, he dressed in high fashion, and he was flamboyantly imprudent. He earned handsomely and spent profligately, and he drank a great deal. Often drunk, he had an explosive temper, especially when he felt his honor impugned, his self-importance denied. At his best, he was social, amiable, and amusing. At his worst, he was reckless and violent. With gun in hand, once in Alton and numbers of times thereafter, he was barely prevented from killing men who had insulted him. Deserving of reproach, he found reproach unbearable. Everyone granted that he had talent. Before a jury, in the legislature, and on the political trail, he was dazzling. He never needed a text. With a gift for courtroom tricks and maneuvers, an impassioned and sincere orator, he was convincing enough always to convince himself, though he may not always have believed everything he said—except on one subject: slavery and race. On that he was deeply sincere.

Between 1838 and October 1847, Linder and Lincoln were often enough in each other's company. Having resigned as attorney general in the summer of 1838, Linder had returned to private practice. He had left Alton for Springfield early in the month Lincoln made his debut before the Young Men's Lyceum. Returning to Coles County, which now had a

Whig majority, he settled in Charleston, the county seat, which Lincoln visited regularly. Flexible in almost everything except his expectation of success, Linder announced that he was available for elective office. Hoping it would increase his chances of being elected to something, he had joined the Whigs. He made fiery anti-Democratic speeches. Every public policy he had argued against as a Democrat he now argued for, transforming himself from a Democratic demagogue to a Whig rabble-rouser. Lincoln approved. When it seemed that Linder might be physically attacked in Springfield by incensed Democrats, Lincoln helped escort him to safety. In 1846, after numbers of failed attempts at elective office, Linder was at last returned to the state legislature. In Springfield, he once again became as well known for heavy drinking as for fiery rhetoric. On the wagon and off, pro-temperance and then a flaming drunk, an avid Democrat, now a fiery Whig, Linder had only one immovable bottom line: his belief in slavery and his detestation of free blacks. In Coles County, he had become Lincoln's go-to person. Lincoln handled some of Linder's business in Springfield.

In mid-October 1847, Lincoln walked into the Coles County Courthouse to argue that the five black people claiming they no longer belonged to Robert Matson were still indeed his slaves. What was on his mind? And why had he agreed to act as Linder's co-counsel? He knew the facts: the five blacks were Jane Bryant, married to a free Negro who worked for Matson, and her four children. Matson may have had sex with Jane. One or more of the children may have been his. Mary Corbin, Matson's housekeeper and common-law wife, had strongly urged that Jane Bryant and her children be sold into Deep South slavery. Jane claimed that under Illinois law she was a free person. She had been there for almost two years. With the help of two antislavery Coles County men, probably abolitionists and conductors in the Underground Railroad, she fled. By hiding Jane and her children, her supporters, if Jane was indeed a slave, had broken Illinois law. Matson pursued her to her hideout. When everything short of force failed, he asked the court to intervene. He wanted his property back.

But what if it could be proved that Jane was already a free person, no longer Matson's property by virtue of her residence in Illinois? Matson then would have no claim on her. Instead of being both property and a person, she would be a person only. Or could Matson's attorneys prove that she was still a slave, in the permanent situation of all slaves, property when it suited the owner, persons when it did not?

Morally opposed to slavery itself, Lincoln apparently had no hesitation representing a client who owned slaves. Characteristically closed-mouthed, he kept his counsel and conscience about what he was doing. And there were complications. He had first become aware of the Bryant case when Linder asked him to serve as co-counsel. He accepted. After all, that is what lawyers do: they earn fees by defending clients, and he had been used to cooperating with Linder on all kinds of cases. They, in fact, had also been opposing attorneys, including on a case that had been tried the day before the Matson trial began. Acting for the defendant, Lincoln had lost. The next day, they were co-counsel. Lincoln had already acted "in four cases involving slavery." In three, his role is obscure. In the fourth, the Illinois Supreme Court agreed with him that there was no evidence that the black woman at issue was a slave. Consequently, she could not be sold, and the monetary claim at issue was denied. The case, though, revealed nothing about Lincoln's views.

To his surprise, soon after accepting Linder's request, Lincoln was asked to join Jane Bryant's defense. He could not, he told Bryant's supporters. He had already agreed to act on Matson's behalf. Apparently conflicted, he then tried, unsuccessfully, to back out of his commitment to Matson. No one knows the reasons for these contortions. Did he feel uncomfortable acting for Matson? Is that why, given the opportunity, he tried to change sides? Was he aware from the start that Matson's case against Bryant was weak and likely to be rejected by the court? Did remuneration play any role? Or had friends or supporters on both sides of the case, who included Linder, appealed to him on personal grounds, creating divided loyalties and interests? What is clear is that when he had the chance to change sides, he did not. He also did not withdraw, which he had every right to do. After all, the only loss would have been a modest fee. Withdrawal, though, might have been viewed as an antislavery statement, perhaps too bold for Lincoln's Whig ambitions. He also might have felt it would be a betrayal of his legal ethic: even a pro-slavery client deserved the benefit of the law. And when the law and its procedures conflicted with moral values, the law had priority. That was the implication of Lincoln's Lyceum address. The proper protest against a bad law was to work, peacefully, to change it.

The Matson trial attracted attention, but not nearly as much as a special convention to create a new state constitution that had been held in Springfield during the summer months of 1847. Not a delegate himself, Lincoln was as observantly aware of the convention as he was, in October, actively engaged in the Matson trial. By the mid-1840s, Democrats and Whigs were of the same mind: the 1818 constitution, Illinois' first, badly needed revision. As its 162 delegates toiled from early June through late August, the convention did not have high on its agenda the issue of slavery or the condition of free blacks in Illinois. The issue was thought to be not the status of black residents but how many black people were in Illinois' future. Over two-thirds of the delegates had been born in states in which slavery was legal. A small minority favored making slavery legal in Illinois. No one, though, thought this likely to happen: Illinois had been and would continue to be, in theory, a free state. Anyway, other issues preoccupied the delegates. Since the depression of 1837, the state had been in a severe fiscal crisis, its debts far greater than its revenue. How to fix that? And how to prevent it happening again? Also, the state's government and banks needed to be modernized.

At home in Springfield during the convention, Lincoln had his particularly lawyerly concerns. "It is considered as almost settled," he wrote in late June 1847, "that they will *not* prohibit Banks; that they *will* establish a poll tax; *will* restrict the number of members of both Houses of the Legislature to 100; *will* limit their *per diem* to $2 or 2.50—and make it still less after the first forty days of the session. So far as I have mentioned, I am pleased. Some other things I have fears for. I am not easy about the *Courts*. I am satisfied with them as they are; but shall not care *much* if the judges are made elective by the People, and their terms of office limited. I fear, however, something more," which would be "much worse": the creation of a large number of "puppy courts" to handle small civil claims and criminal trials "in all cases not capital." Even worse, "a Migratory Supreme Court and *Salaries* so low as to exclude all respectable talent. From these, may God preserve us." A member of the legal establishment, he had a vested interest in keeping its power and organization much as they were. Though not a delegate, he was a presence in the background, and the convention met within a stone's throw of where he lived and worked. He knew and talked to many of the delegates. In early August, he hosted about twenty of them at his home.

Sangamo County had been allowed four delegates. They were all politically active Whigs, three of them close friends of Lincoln's: his brother-in-law Ninian W. Edwards, at whose home he had been married; James Matheny, an intimate friend for twenty years and a witness at his wedding; John Dawson, his legislative associate in the effort to move the state capital to Springfield; and Stephen T. Logan, his senior law partner for three years. Like his father, the former governor and senator, Ninian Edwards had no serious argument with slavery. He had slaves disguised as servants at his home. Neither did Ninian's brother Cyrus Edwards, a delegate from Madison County, the father of a young woman with whom, years before, Lincoln had been infatuated. Cyrus, who had owned slaves, reportedly still had indentured Negro servants. The four were probably among the twenty guests at the Lincoln home in early August, when they could hardly have avoided discussing the work of the convention. So, too, was Judge David Davis, a delegate to the convention from McLean County, originally from a slave-owning Maryland family, whom Lincoln later rewarded with a seat on the U.S. Supreme Court. All were politically sensitive Whigs. All were colonizationists. Like Lincoln, they rejected slavery in principle but deplored abolitionism. They favored the black codes and the exclusionary law that the convention soon recommended to voters. The one abolitionist delegate, Daniel Whitney, from Northern Illinois, probably had not been invited to the Lincoln home.

Having delayed as long as it could, when the convention finally took up the free Negro issue, it disposed of it expeditiously. The black codes would remain in place. All Democrats and most Whigs favored racial exclusiveness, Illinois as a white man's state with a minimal Negro population, tightly controlled by a black code. The delegates were united on the slavery issue: it should be prohibited. And there was general agreement on denying civil rights to free black residents.

But what to do about allowing or forbidding free blacks from other states to move into Illinois? A heated five-day discussion of what provisions the new state constitution should have about new black residents ensued. The majority had not the slightest doubt: out-of-state blacks should be excluded. Otherwise the state would become a magnet for fugitives and a dumping ground for elderly former slaves who would become a charge to the taxpayer. Illinois would become a haven for a growing population of free blacks, widely believed to be a shiftless, lazy, immoral, and often criminal population. Counterarguments invoked the "full faith and credit" clause of the U.S. Constitution requiring each state to respect "the public acts, records, and judicial proceedings of every other state." How, then, it was argued, could Illinois deny entry of free blacks from other states? Some delegates appealed to the Declaration of Independence, to national integrity and honor, to justice and humanity. Black codes, yes. Exclusion, no. Daniel Whitney made an impassioned antislavery speech. It was a federal matter. The U.S. Constitution forbade exclusion.

The convention, restating the 1818 free state provision based on the Northwest Territory prohibition, overwhelmingly agreed to prohibit slavery in Illinois. There was, equally, no disagreement, except from Whitney, about depriving free blacks of civil liberties. In the end, only the exclusionary clause met serious opposition, though far from majority disapproval. In late August, the convention voted 90 to 53 to put before the state in a separate vote its recommendation that additional black settlement in Illinois be prohibited by statute, to be passed by the legislature rather than embedded in the new constitution. It was a strategy to give the voters the chance to approve the new constitution without an exclusionary provision, while at the same time instructing the legislature to pass an exclusionary law. It also encouraged an end-run around the likelihood that Congress would object to a state constitution in conflict with the federal Constitution. The 53 nays included many who preferred having the exclusionary law embedded in the state constitution. For never-to-be reconstructed racists, that would be a guarantee of its permanence.

The next year, in March 1848, 80 percent of the state's voters approved the new constitution. And almost 70 percent voted in favor of instructing the legislature to pass an exclusionary law. It made "Illinois the only Free State forbidding blacks to settle within its borders." Sangamo County outperformed the state as a whole. It's likely that the 80 percent in favor of the new constitution included the county's four Whig delegates. It would have been, essentially, a no-brainer. It suited them ideologically, politically, and morally. It was another attempt to keep Illinois and America as white as possible. If Lincoln had been in Illinois rather than in Washington in early March 1848, he almost certainly would have voted with his Sangamo colleagues for the new state constitution. Pro-slavery and antislavery moralists were united on this. Would Lincoln have been among the 70 percent who voted for the exclusionary referendum?

WHEN THE Matson trial began in October 1847 most of the convention delegates had been gone from Springfield for six weeks. Lincoln himself had, so to speak and then literally, his bags packed. He and Mary were soon to leave for Kentucky, then Washington. His early October court travels brought him in mid-October to the two-story brick courthouse on Charleston's village square a few days before the trial began. No transcript was kept. No record survives. The only extant comment on the trial from a participant was made by one of the opposing lawyers, Orlando B. Ficklin. A longtime friend of Lincoln's, now a Democratic congressman who had recently defeated Usher Linder, Ficklin was a capable lawyer. He had served with Lincoln in the Black Hawk War and the Illinois state legislature.

The two-day trial had extralegal complications on the courthouse steps and nearby streets. Tension between pro-slavery and pro-abolition opponents threatened to become violent. Guns were visible. Would this be another Alton? The presence of two estimable Illinois Supreme Court justices, Chief Justice William Wilson and Associate Justice Samuel Hubbell Treat, one a Whig, the other a Democrat, helped keep the conflict confined to the courthouse and the law.

Every seat in the first-floor courtroom was filled when Lincoln and Linder made their way in. Matson simply wanted his property back, Linder argued: The U.S. Constitution required that his client be made whole. It sanctioned slavery. It made property sacrosanct. It provided for the return of runaways. Jane Bryant and her children were fugitive slaves. Not to require that they be returned defied the national compact; it would be another intensification of the national disharmony bred by abolitionists. Brushing aside Linder's argument, Ficklin cited the Northwest Ordinance, the Illinois Constitution, and Anglo-American precedents. Challenged to deal with the facts of this particular case, Lincoln stressed Matson's claim that he had frequently stated publicly that Bryant was in Illinois temporarily. There were witnesses. But was that claim relevant? Lincoln labored to convince the court that Matson's statements were sufficient grounds on which to determine that Jane Bryant remain a slave. To Ficklin, Lincoln appeared ill at ease, spiritless, unenergetic. Years later, Stephen Logan remarked that if Lincoln "believed his client was right, especially in difficult and complicated cases . . . he was the strongest . . . lawyer he had ever met—or if the case was somewhat doubtful but could be decided either way without violating any just, equitable or moral principle, he was very strong—but if he thought his client was wrong he would make very little effort." Lincoln never afterward said or wrote, as far as we know, a word about the Matson trial.

The judges had much to say: they were concise and unequivocal. Illinois law, its 1818 constitution, and legal precedent were clear on the distinction between a slave briefly in Illinois and a slave kept in residence. If "briefly" could be or should be defined by an exact time, by no stretch of its meaning could almost two years come within the definition. Matson's claim, no matter when and or how frequently made, that he intended to keep Jane in Illinois only briefly, that she was a seasonal worker or a slave in transit, was irrelevant. The fact, the judges declared, was that she had been kept in Illinois long enough for her to be liberated from the statutory limitation. Consequently, she was not a slave. And those who had helped her in her flight from Matson had not committed a criminal act. Whatever Matson claimed, Bryant was no longer a slave and had not been a slave for quite some time, and Matson was responsible for the court costs of all the parties.

Probably it had been an agonizing two days for Lincoln. The facts denied him a credible argument. What did he feel about the verdict? Impossible to know. He must, though, have known almost from the start that he couldn't win. He had to know Illinois precedents and that "intent" could not be a winning argument. An astute, logically obsessive lawyer, he had to have known that Matson had kept the Bryants in Illinois long enough to make it a fact that they were not in transit or temporary. Why hadn't he, from the start, advised Matson to accept the reality and cut his losses? And why submit himself to the humiliating experience of arguing a case he would have to lose? The answer, if there is one, resides in the complicated recesses of Lincoln's relationship with Linder, his sense of himself as a lawyer, his attempt to balance his moral antislavery position with his anti-abolitionism, and his conviction that America was and always should be a white man's country. Slavery was morally wrong. Free blacks, though, needed to go someplace else, preferably to Africa.

IN THE early evening of January 18, 1848, a huge crowd took possession of the House of Representatives, the largest venue in the nation's capital. By 7:00 P.M., neither seating nor standing room was available. "The hall and every avenue leading to it was filled to suffocation by an eager crowd of both sexes," *Niles' Register* reported. "Several females fainted in consequence of the pressure, and had to be carried from the hall," a gender-inflected trope that mid-nineteenth-century American journalists found irresistible whenever evoking the spectacle of any large space fully occupied by both sexes. John Quincy Adams declined to attend. Ill much of the day, he would not have attended even if he had been well. These annual gatherings of the Colonization Society seemed an exemplification of a delusion, a waste of time and money. And this was a triumphal meeting, a celebration of the society's thirtieth anniversary. An overflow crowd of Washington celebrities, politicians, and delegates from various states bustled into the hall, eager to affirm the society's importance, which was indicated by the presence of its most distinguished member, its newly elected president.

"Calls were . . . made from all parts of the hall, for Henry Clay, who rose and addressed the meeting." He had done this, memorably, twice before, in 1827 and 1837, when he still had reason to hope that he might be president of much more than just the Colonization Society. Even in 1848 he hoped, unrealistically, for one more chance. Time had stoked much of his incandescent energy. At the age of seventy-one, with little flesh on his tall frame, his lungs infected by slowly progressing tuberculosis, and depressed by the death of his son and namesake in the Mexican War, he still radiated optimism about colonization. So did his audience, which probably included thirty-nine-year-old Abraham Lincoln, who had arrived in Washington the previous month. Though still sustaining his lifelong reverence for the Whig luminary from his wife's hometown, he had already decided not to support Clay for the 1848 Whig presidential nomination.

Two months before, after a lifetime of worshipping Clay, Lincoln had been for the first time in the great man's presence. On their way to Washington, the Lincolns had taken a circuitous route, via Lexington, Kentucky. On a cold, dark day in mid-November 1847, a large number of Clay enthusiasts, having for decades been hoping that their neighbor would be president, had gathered for an oratorical feast in support of their native son. Standing in a large crowd under the portico facade of the Market House in downtown Lexington, Lincoln could see his hero clearly. Having had a lifelong infatuation with Clay's prominence, Mary Lincoln was also in the audience. Perhaps Joshua and James Speed were there. And probably Lincoln's father-in-law, with whom the Lincolns were staying, attended to by slaves and warmly welcomed by a family of Clay partisans who, like their leader, were antislavery in principle but not in practice.

The Mexican War and the upcoming presidential election were in the anxious air. Attentive to the words of his political mentor, Lincoln heard in Clay's almost three-hour speech a political and moral message with which he agreed: condemnation of the illegality and immorality of the

Mexican War and a scathing denunciation of the Polk administration. These were Lincoln's views also; his own anti–Mexican War speech in Congress two months later would be hardly different in substance from Clay's speech in Lexington. There was, though, an important difference: Lincoln was not running for the presidency. Just another congressman, pledged not to run for re-election, he could speak his mind. At most, he might alienate some pro-war Whigs in Illinois. Clay's outspoken opposition to the war, embodied for the first time in his heartfelt Lexington speech, added to his enemies those from both parties who had supported the war; it seemed hypocritical to others; and it further encouraged the Whig political machine to turn to General Zachary Taylor, a Mexican War hero who seemed likely to defang criticism of Whig opposition to the war and take attention away from divisive internal issues such as slavery. Toward the end of November 1847, the *Sangamo Journal* (now the *Illinois Journal*) reported on Clay's speech. On the same page, in a banner box, it announced, "For President—Zachary Taylor."

Lincoln was also on board. But he was still and always on board with Henry Clay about slavery and colonization. If Clay's rhetoric was too high flown and formal for Lincoln's colloquial idiom, it was occasionally barely so. For the first time, he now saw and heard Clay speak. His living presence must have had for Lincoln its distinctive power: Clay's tired, elderly face, his rich baritone, an embodiment of ambition and mortality, an object lesson for a man inwardly attuned to the poetry of transience, to the balance between thwarted ambition and pride, achievement and death. Before, Clay had been, for Lincoln, exclusively words on a page. "I have brought with me no rhetorical bouquets to throw into this assemblage," Clay told his neighbors and friends that November. "In the circle of the year, autumn has come, and the season of flowers has passed away. In the progress of years, my spring time has gone by, and I too am in the autumn of life, and feel the frost of age." In those commonplaces, Lincoln would have recognized sincere emotion, the great orator's ability to give life to ordinary language, to appeal to and engage his audience's feelings with biographical touchstones. Lincoln was learning. Listening to Clay in mid-November 1847, he had a foretaste if not a preview of the speeches he was to develop, starting in the mid-1850s, which reached their apogee in his presidential years, on the two great themes of Clay's speech: war and slavery.

It was a brilliant antiwar speech, a prelude to the creation, less than ten years later, of the Republican Party and the Lincoln presidency. It was also an antislavery speech. Though the specific instance was the Mexican War, its concept and arc were antiwar in the universal sense. The Mexican War, Clay argued, was an aggressive war, initiated for territorial gain, an example, among others he cited, of the most deplorable of human activities, even more reprehensible in this case, as the United States had already been blessed with vast lands. A Whig Party, divided on the war, now bore almost as much blame, Clay had the temerity to tell his colleagues, as the Democrats. How could the country extricate itself honorably from a war it had initiated at great loss of life and treasure on both sides? Who would compensate whom? And would not there be a desire to make Mexico pay for a war it had not started? That impoverished nation would be forced to pay in the only currency it had: territory. And that would exacerbate an existing American problem: slavery. It would become even more divisively damaging than it had been. "Among the resolutions, which it is my intention to present for your consideration, at the conclusion of this address, one proposes," he announced, "to disavow . . . any desire, on our part, to acquire any foreign territory whatever, for the purpose of introducing slavery into it."

Clay was articulating, in 1847, a morally sound and politically unpalatable twofer: a condemnation of the Mexican War and of slavery expansion. "My opinions on the subject of slavery are well known," Clay continued. "They have the merit, if it be one, of consistency, uniformity, and long duration. I have ever regarded slavery as a great evil, a wrong, for the present, I fear, an irremediable wrong to its unfortunate victims. I should rejoice if not a single slave breathed the air or was within the limits of our country." It was not, though, a pro-emancipation speech. "Here they are, to be dealt with as well as we can, with a due consideration of all circumstances affecting the security, safety and happiness of both races." In brief, there seemed no way short of turmoil, misery, insurrection, and death for the moral imperative to overcome the demographic, social, and economic reality.

As Lincoln listened, he stood, as he well knew, in sight of and a stone's throw from the Lexington slave market, with its holding pens and transfer stations. He stood not far from dozens of plantations worked by slaves on whose labor the prosperity of Central Kentucky, portions of the other border states, and all of the Deep South depended. He had been a monthlong guest at one of them in 1841. Like Clay, he accepted that slavery was exclusively a state matter. And there were only two ways forward. The first was to accept the status quo and keep it in place for as long as necessary—slavery where it was and not beyond, with gradual, voluntary, and compensated emancipation and colonization the ultimate goals. "*Resolved,*" Clay advised, "That we do, positively and emphatically, disclaim and disavow any wish or desire, on our part, to acquire any foreign territory whatever, for the purpose of propagating slavery, or of introducing slaves from the United States, into such foreign territory." The second was the American Colonization Society. "A scheme of unmixed benevolence has sprung up," Clay told his Lexington audience. "About twenty-eight years ago, a few individuals, myself among them, met together in the city of Washington, and laid the foundations of that society. . . . The Colonies, planted under its auspices, are now well established communities, with churches, schools and other institutions appertaining to the civilized state." This was mostly a colonizationist fantasy. But falsification sustained the hope and the mission. It also sustained Clay.

Still, it repelled at least one reader of his widely published speech. He had never been and would never be in Clay's presence, though he would be in Lincoln's. It's unlikely that Frederick Douglass and Lincoln ever spoke about Clay. And Lincoln never read the open letter to Clay that Douglass published in early December 1847 in the inaugural issue of his abolitionist weekly, the *North Star*. For Douglass, with little confidence in Clay's soundness on any issue with moral content, Clay had a consistent record of compromising away any alleviation, let alone curtailment, of slavery. He was, in effect, a great evildoer. And what was colonization? A self-indulgent attempt by racists to maintain America as a white man's country while also protecting slavery, an anodyne of self-congratulation for those who denied that Negroes are worthy of basic human entitlements. The colonization cure would be worse than the disease of slavery. America was a multiracial country already, Douglass insisted. Colonization was nonsense. "We live here—have lived here—have a right to live here, and mean to live here," he was to later write.

In December 1847, sentence by sentence, he eviscerated Clay's argument. "I wish to remind you that you are not only in the '*autumn*' but in the winter of your life. . . . For fifty years . . . you have been a slaveholder. . . . Emancipate your own slaves. Leave them not to be held or sold by others. Leave them as free as the father of his country left his. . . . Make the noble resolve, that so far as you are personally concerned, 'AMERICA SHALL BE FREE.'" Douglass would have been pleased to learn that Clay did free some of his fifty slaves. But since he mandated their colonization, requiring that they themselves earn the money for their passage to Africa, Douglass would have thought it the same old game.

Lincoln was in the process of embracing the mission that Clay espoused and Douglass abhorred. Not that slavery's expansion or the colonization project dominated his consciousness. He showed up in the House of Representatives on its opening day, December 6. He voted against tabling petitions to abolish slavery in the District of Columbia, which he soon spoke out in favor of. But most Whig votes about slavery were perfunctory attempts to prevent the party's divided views from undercutting its larger political goal: the election in 1848 of a Whig to the presidency. The Mexican War was one of the linchpins, and Lincoln followed the dominant Whig strategy of denouncing Polk's war and supporting Zachary Taylor. In late December, he made his move, introducing resolutions to require that Polk inform the House whether the exact "spot" on which American blood had first been shed was or was not on territory claimed by Mexico. Though Congressman John Quincy Adams made no explicit reference to Lincoln's resolutions, he also denounced Polk for withholding information that Congress had a right to have. On January 12, 1848, Lincoln addressed the House at length. Adams and the other antislavery and anti–Mexican War Whigs were in full agreement and probably approved of his tone, humor, and passion. Henry Clay had also come up to Washington. "There is too much fog here for me to see anything clearly and distinctly," he wrote to a friend. "The Whig Party has not settled definitely on any course in regard to the Mexican War." It actually had, threading the needle of condemnation of Polk's war and support for the troops. Slavery was on the legislative and policy table only in regard to how to deal with the territory to be extracted from Mexico.

And what Lincoln would have heard, if he had been in the audience for Clay's anniversary speech to the American Colonization Society in mid-January 1848, would not have been news to him. He had heard a version of it in Lexington, and the main thrust of Clay's position on slavery, abolitionism, free blacks, race relations, and colonization was part of the ideological and political air he had been breathing for years in Illinois, part of his consciousness and his belief system. He believed Clay right on all the basic points, probably even independent of Clay's influence. But Clay's influence is inextricably embedded in the Lincoln saga. He truly believed in Clay's message and in the man, his rhetoric, his evocation of transience and departure, his synthesis of the universal and the personal, and his charismatic presence. Lincoln could not, of course, in 1848, have anticipated that, in 1850, Clay would be a major player for one last time.

"Go on, then, gentlemen," Clay concluded in January 1848. "Go on in your noble cause. For myself, I shall soon leave you and this stage of human action forever. I may never occupy this chair again; but I trust that the spirit which originated and which has sustained this Society will long survive me, and that you may long continue, now that our African republic is at length born, to discharge the office of guardianship, and aid and co-operation, and ever lend to the interests of African freedom, civilization, and social happiness your best energies and most fervent prayers. From this auspicious hour, even to the end of time, or until the great object of the amicable separation of the two races shall have been fully effected, may others spring up to take your places, and to tread in your steps." In tone, Clay's farewell resonated with self-eulogy. In substance, it was the familiar story.

LINCOLN WAS soon to take up both the elegiac tone and the colonization project. In the 1850s and thereafter, he was to identify himself explicitly with the colonization effort, though he did not officially become a member of the society until 1856. The eulogy came first. In July 1852, bells tolled throughout the nation and dark cloth draped its body. Its most consequential National Republican and then Whig leader, the man who would be president but never was, who was more than a president for millions of Whigs, died at the age of seventy-five. He had dragged his tubercular body up to Washington to die in place, so to speak.

Lincoln was in Springfield. A public meeting, mainly of Whigs, chose him to deliver a eulogy memorializing their fallen leader. Naturally, he accepted. Valued as a Whig stump speaker and behind-the-scenes operative, the ex-congressman had no clear path to political office, though his well-recognized oratorical skills kept him in demand. And he had no explicit issue to attach to his political persona. One was, nevertheless, beginning to appear, though it was not fully visible until 1854. Like the Whig Party in Illinois and nationally, Lincoln had been wandering in the political wilderness. Both he and his party seemed almost at a dead end. Clay's last political deed and his death were a help.

In 1850, a senator once more, Clay had begun the process that led to the Compromise of 1850. It contained, as was quite clear by 1852, two poison pills: the Fugitive Slave Act and the admission of California to the Union as a free state, which would lead in 1854 to the South's attempt to admit Kansas as a slave state to keep the balance between free and slave states or, even better, to create a balance favorable to slavery. The likely future attempt to repeal the Missouri Compromise of 1819 by claiming slave state status for new states north of what had been the dividing line was implicit in the Compromise of 1850, whether Clay or anyone else admitted that at the time. Between 1850 and 1854, Lincoln and many Whigs began to see that their opposition to the extension of slavery, which the Missouri Compromise had made a nonissue for thirty years, could help them rise again. It could become their defining issue. Henry Clay had been the architect of the Missouri Compromise. It had kept the peace. He had been the partial architect of the Compromise of 1850. It had bought more time, but not much. In 1854, the terms of both compromises were to be fully and explicitly exploded with the passage of the Kansas-Nebraska Act.

As he wrote his eulogy for Clay between July 1 and 6, 1852, Lincoln had his work cut out for him. A eulogy required sincere praise. His heart was in that. But how could he subtly finesse Clay's role in the 1850 compromise and also provide a path forward on the problem it had attempted but failed to solve? The answer was the Colonization Society. His audience on that warm July day, two days after the celebration of the seventy-sixth anniversary of the birth of the country a year before Clay's birth, would be sympathetic. But it was still a needle that needed threading.

At 11:00 A.M. there was a seventy-six-gun salute. "The procession, consisting of the Odd Fellows, Temple of Honor, Sons of Temperance, Cadets of Temperance, and a large number of citizens, marched to the Episcopal Church." Lincoln listened to the Reverend Charles Dresser, who had married him, perform the religious service. Everyone marched in solemn procession to the Statehouse, crowding into the main hall. Stores had closed. Business was suspended. Black drapery memorialized the great man's departure. Lincoln began reading from his text. Clearly, he had struggled with what to say, partly because of the pressure of time. But there were other obstacles, psychological and thematic, particularly the degree to which personal identification might be counterproductive. Throughout, he struggled to avoid commonplaces and to keep himself out of the narrative, though he touched a personal chord, which few of his listeners would have identified, when he remarked that Clay's rise from obscurity of birth "teaches that in this country, one can scarcely be so poor, but that, if he *will*, he *can* acquire sufficient education to get through the world respectably." And how to begin was an issue, as it always is for a eulogy. Relying on words that were not his own, he started with a long quotation from an anti-Clay newspaper, which claimed in high-blown rhetoric that Henry Clay had transcended party. It was a dubious claim in pedestrian prose, and it was a poor start. Lincoln struggled to find the right balance between praise and analysis, between partisanship and national harmony.

As he summarized Clay's life, his praise gathered strength, without full accuracy, as he reached the two achievements of most relevance in 1852, the Missouri Compromise and the Compromise of 1850. Disingenuously, though probably without full awareness, Lincoln justified the complications of Clay's role in the Missouri Compromise. "By some judicious modifications of his plan, coupled with laborious efforts with individual members, and his own over-mastering eloquence upon the floor, he finally secured the admission of the State." There was little truth in that.

Eloquence played no part. It was mostly persuasion and arm twisting. The "modifications" were linguistically clever tricks, the sleight of hand that allowed the North to capitulate to a deal that, when the tactical fog had cleared, left the North bitter, the South dissatisfied. Both soon had buyer's remorse.

And Lincoln said nothing about the second stage of the Missouri mess: the attempt in 1820 by the state's constitutional convention to prohibit free Negroes from settling in the state. Whatever the language of the state and federal constitutions, free Negroes were not and would not be, as Lincoln well knew, any more welcome in Missouri than in Illinois. Lincoln, who was selectively enthusiastic about Jefferson, then quoted the paragraph of reference on the ongoing problem, the most famous words on the subject from Jefferson's often-cited letter of April 1820. For the first time, a North–South line had been drawn: no slavery above, slavery below. It could not stand, Jefferson had predicted. "We have the wolf by the ears and we can neither hold him, nor safely let him go. Justice is in one scale, and self-preservation in the other." Clay, Lincoln declared, had perceived the danger, and "engaged his whole energies to avert it."

But what Lincoln could not bring himself to say was that Clay had failed, both in 1820 and in 1850. Lincoln could and did dress up the achievement of 1820 in laudatory language. But if it had not failed, the Compromise of 1850 would not have been necessary. And what was becoming clear to Lincoln, the Whigs, and the country was that 1850 would not hold. What could be done, what needed to be done, to prevent disaster? The exemplar was still Clay, and the answer was Clay's answer. "He ever was, on principle and in feeling, opposed to slavery," Lincoln affirmed. "He did not perceive, that on a question of human right, the negroes were to be excepted from the human race," though he himself was a slave owner. The slave owner, as a human being, Lincoln implied, needed to be understood. His was an entirely human predicament: the conflict between justice and self-preservation. If you did not see that, how could you respect and love Henry Clay? And what needed to be done was to reject, as Clay had, both extremes: the radical abolitionist and the radical slave owner. One demanded immediate turmoil and misery for the white population of the South; the other, committed to the view that Negroes were subhuman property forever to be deprived of human agency, rejected the nation's founding commitment to the belief that "all men are created equal." The moderate man in the middle was the man to be admired—and emulated. He was Lincoln's ultimate model.

And what was the solution, the way out? How could the nation find a way to let go of the tail of the wolf and still be safe? "I quote," Lincoln began the conclusion of his eulogy, "from a speech of Mr. Clay delivered before the American Colonization Society in 1827." It was a text Lincoln was to quote from again, especially in his debates with Stephen Douglas in 1858. "It sets out the main principles of the Colonization Society. Its language is the language of freedom, of liberty for everyone." And as Lincoln and Clay agreed, it affirms that slavery is an evil, a national shame inconsistent with the founding principles of the country. Eventually there must be no more slavery in America. To deny this expectation is to repudiate the events that gave birth to the country. But history, custom, and human nature will allow of only one solution: the Negro must go someplace else, to some country of his own. He should be free, but not here.

And the Colonization Society, Lincoln argued, has the preliminary answer. It is the start of the solution. It does not threaten the South. It applies no pressure. It is in business only to provide opportunity and encouragement for free blacks to live a better life in a place of their own. It says nothing officially about the emancipation of slaves. That is for a future time and a different agency. Colonization, in fact, will be a boon to many slave owners. Lincoln concluded, extending Clay's claim that there "is a moral fitness in the idea of returning to Africa her children," with his own rhetorical flourish: "This suggestion of the possible ultimate redemption of the African race and African continent, was made twenty-five years ago. Every succeeding year has added strength to the hope of its realization. May it indeed be realized! Pharaoh's country was cursed with plagues, and his hosts were drowned in the Red Sea for striving to retain a captive people who had already served them more than four hundred years. May like disasters never befall us!"

Easy to hope, but easier to worry. Lincoln's anxiety seeps through, partly diverted by ceremonial rhetoric and self-delusion. "If as the friends of colonization hope, the present and coming generations of our countrymen shall by any means, succeed in freeing our land from the dangerous presence of slavery; and, at the same time, in restoring a captive people to their long-lost father-land, with bright prospects for the future; and this too, so gradually, that neither races nor individuals shall have suffered by the change, it will indeed be a glorious consummation."

It was a consummation to be realized in a different way, as Adams had predicted. Gradualists such as Lincoln were eventually to find that gradualism had been made impossible. Probably, as Adams believed, it always was. "Let us strive," Lincoln concluded, to deserve" that "Divine Providence . . . will not fail to provide us the instruments of safety and security." Henry Clay and his Colonization Society, as one of those instruments, had not been successful. And Lincoln, in 1852, could have no idea what role he was to play, for better and worse, in obtaining the "safety and security" of his country. "Safety and security" needed to be redefined, and they were to come at a heavy cost.

SEVEN

The Constitutional Rag

At 5:00 P.M. on a cold Saturday in March 1848, the remains of John Quincy Adams were interred in a stone vault in Quincy, Massachusetts. It was in a cemetery he had wandered in many times, meditating about time and transience. Across the street, in the church whose construction the former president had funded, the Reverend W. P. Lunt had memorialized Quincy's famous son to a full house of distinguished mourners. By late afternoon, the day had been exhaustingly long for the participants. The procession to the church had been slowed down, the sun having turned frozen roads to mud. Adams' only surviving child, Charles Francis, thought the sermon "elegant and happily conceived." The text from Revelation, "Be thou faithful unto death, and I will give thee a crown of life," had to seem to the five hundred or so mourners deftly appropriate. At such a moment, everyone would have been moved by the sentiment.

The only body fully at rest had started its journey from Washington earlier in the week. For the first time in American history, a nation in mourning paid its respects to a dead ex-president traveling by shrouded train from the nation's capital to his grave site. The journey ascended entirely through a Northern landscape, as befitted the man in the coffin. In Philadelphia, the body was displayed for two days in Independence Hall. It was remarked that the presence of John Quincy Adams' spirit was palpable. Then, with mourners lining the tracks, the special train slowly moved on to Boston. The next morning, an assemblage of city and state officials, the delegation from the state legislature, and representatives of both houses of Congress, accompanied by honor guards and militiamen, marched to the railroad station. Special trains of the Old Colony Railroad took them to Quincy. Joined by members of the Adams family and townspeople, organized into a procession they marched "to the Adams mansion," Peacefield. At a quarter past two, the funeral cortege moved toward the Unitarian church. The Roxbury artillery fired minute guns. "By three o'clock all in the procession were seated in the church."

It was a nonpartisan assemblage. Not everyone shed tears. Still, it was a momentous occasion, partly local, partly national. The House of Representatives, narrowly controlled by Adams' party, had sent a delegation of thirty members, one from each state in the union, evenly split between Whigs and Democrats. The more widely publicized national funeral had occurred in Washington on February 26, three days after the eighty-one-year-old Adams died. His body had lain in state in the House Rotunda, its coffin lined with lead, his face "visible through a glass." Amid funereal pomp, after a service more impressive for its assemblage than the sermon, the corpse was taken to the congressional cemetery for temporary burial. The elite of the three branches of government, dark in Victorian mourning dress, followed the cortege. President Polk noted in his diary that it had been "a splendid pageant." Official Washington had self-consciously created a historically memorable spectacle.

Many hoped that the enactment of a more solemn ritual than had ever before memorialized an ex-president might provide a unifying occasion for a divided country. Only one previous president had died in office. Never before had an ex-president died in Washington. Adams had been, after his presidency and for eighteen years, a distinctive national presence, a singular exemplar and a living connection to the founding generation. There was magic in his name, lineage, and service. Memories of collegial years spent together on both sides of the aisle transcended ideological differences. South Carolina's John C. Calhoun, the premier pro-slavery theorist, Missouri's Thomas Benton, a vigorous proponent of Western expansion, both Democrats, and Roger Taney, Andrew Jackson's pro-slavery Chief Justice of the United States, served as pallbearers, assisted by antislavery associate Supreme Court justice John McLean and Pennsylvania's Joseph Ingersoll, Adams' fiery colleague against the gag rule and the annexation of Texas. It was a funeral of a sort that had never before occurred: the executive, the judiciary, Congress, and the general public in a performance of national unity, Americans celebrating the man and the history his life and name embodied. Whigs and Democrats, antislavery and pro-slavery, North and South—all could, for a moment, be less the partisans and more the patriots.

Walking in the funeral procession from the Capitol to the Congressional Cemetery was a man whose distinctive feature was his unusual height. He was one of about 270 congressmen in a phalanx of about 500 marchers. Was he in black mourning dress? Did he wear his characteristic black stovepipe hat? Slouching, beardless, thin, with a face almost gaunt, he may have wrapped his shoulders in a shawl to keep warm in the bright late-February weather. Thousands of citizens lined the streets. City and nation had been blessed with instant virtual attendance, from the moment Adams collapsed three days before, through the medium of the newly invented telegraph. Abraham Lincoln had gotten the news firsthand. He had been in the hall of the House when Adams fell. He would have seen the body lying in state, "the coffin . . . covered with black velvet and ornamented with silver lace." And he had been designated a member of the Arrangements Committee. As the only Whig member of the Illinois delegation, he had been added by default to a bipartisan committee of thirty. The number had been intended to apply only to the committee accompanying the remains to Quincy. "At our first meeting, the mistake was discovered," he later explained, "and . . . we delegated out authority to a sub-committee, of a smaller number of our own body, of which . . . I was *not* a member." An eyewitness to the death, Lincoln had nothing more to say about these events, and not another word thereafter about Adams.

BUT THROUGH the first three months of the winter 1847/1848 session of the Thirtieth Congress, the freshman congressman and the ex-president, sitting in the same hall in the House of Representatives, had mostly voted the same way. Assigned to two minor committees, Lincoln had only a few opportunities to make himself visible. No doubt he was noted by some, and he took the opportunity to speak his mind, always with a political inflection and with the upcoming presidential election in view. His sarcastic, piercingly logical speech on the Mexican War, defending his "spot" resolutions and excoriating Polk, attracted enough attention to make party operatives decide that he would be a useful late summer and fall stump speaker for the likely Whig presidential nominee, Zachary Taylor. Lincoln was already on record as a supporter.

Adams probably was not present when Lincoln introduced his "spot" resolutions, challenging the Polk administration to name the exact spot at which Mexican troops had infringed on American soil. He was, though, at his seat when Lincoln got the floor on January 12 and spoke at length about the war. How much Adams or anyone else in the House actually heard is open to question. The hall was a noisy echo chamber where members talked, shouted, amused themselves, wandered in and out, often absorbed in personal and constituent business at their desks, mumbling, writing and engaged in inner and outer discussions, regardless of anything else that was occurring, especially when no one of particular distinction held the floor.

The ex-president's presence was strong but not his voice or body. A series of life-threatening strokes had enfeebled him. When, in February 1847, he had returned to his seat to a round of bipartisan applause, he put his colleagues on notice: "It is with much pleasure that I again return to your midst. Had I a more powerful voice, I might respond to the congratulations of my friends and the members of this House for the honor which has been done me. But enfeebled as I am by disease, I beg that you will excuse me." He needed no other concessions, and he voted vigorously on every issue he felt passionately about: the Mexican War, funding for internal improvements, the evil of slavery. He would not have disagreed with anything Lincoln said about Polk and the war.

"Any people anywhere," Lincoln proposed to the House, "being inclined and having the power, have the *right* to rise up, and shake off the existing government, and form a new one that suits them better. This is a most valuable,—a most sacred right—a right, which we hope and believe, is to liberate the world." It justified the creation of the Republic of Texas in 1836. The only necessary condition had been the consent of the majority of those living there. That principle had justified the creation of the United States in 1776. To deny this right would be to imply that the American Revolution itself had been unlawful, that the colonists had had no "right" to rebel.

Lincoln also had in mind what Adams and many others had often proclaimed: the United States as a model for universal republicanism, for the overthrow of tyranny in an age of democratic revolutions, which had become a cliché of American self-congratulation on both sides of the aisle. "Nor is this right confined," he continued, "to cases in which the whole people of an existing government, may choose to exercise it. Any portion of such people that *can, may* revolutionize, and make their *own*, of so much of the territory as they inhabit." That of course justified the American residents of pre-annexation Texas in rebelling against Mexican sovereignty, creating a new state from what had been Mexican territory. "More than this," Lincoln continued, "a *majority* of any portion of such people may revolutionize, putting down a *minority*, intermingled with, or near about them, who may oppose their movement." Apparently, the Mexican government had been equally justified in attempting to suppress the rebellion. "Such minority," Lincoln continued, "was precisely the case, of the Tories of our own revolution." And the anti-Tory, pro-independence majority did in effect "suppress" the Tory minority. "It is a quality of revolutions," Lincoln concluded, "not to go by *old* lines, or *old* laws; but to break up both, and make new ones." Hence the United States of America.

Lincoln seems not to have been mindful of two other potential revolutions within the territory of the United States: a revolution in which millions of American slaves would do what the anti-Tories had done in 1776; and a revolution in which eight million white American Southerners would choose "not to go by *old* lines, or *old* laws; but to break up both, and make new ones." By the extension of his logic, these were also "sacred" rights. Did slaves have the *right* to do this? Did white Southerners have the *right* to do this? Lincoln's logic implied that they did. Focused on the Mexican War, he had nothing to say about the likelihood that any territory gained from the war would further exacerbate the issue of slavery extension. He was, in fact, advocating a sweeping theory of revolution. One of its manifestations was rebellion, another word for which in the South was *secession*. His argument would also justify slave insurrections. If a member of the House or reader of the speech had challenged him on this, what would Lincoln have said? Those threatening secession might have found Lincoln's words apposite and agreeable, though they were probably paying little attention: his words more than recognized revolution as a historical reality. He claimed that revolutions, including civil wars, were justified, without qualification; that a dissatisfied people have a right to assert self-governance. It is not, he proposed, a conditional right. And those who are being rebelled against, he argued, have a right to suppress rebellion.

How closely was Adams listening? He had for years anticipated either a slave rebellion or Southern secession. Would he have heard in Lincoln's words a theoretical justification for either, whatever Lincoln's intentions? From December 1847 to late February 1848, both voted the same way in every instance in which slavery was an issue but with different underlying views about how to deal with the issue as a whole and with different expectations about how slavery would come to an end. They agreed on one important localization of antislavery moralism: the Constitution gave Congress authority to legislate about slavery for the District of Columbia and the territories. Both supported petitions against slavery in the District. Lincoln, though, conditioned his support: antislavery legislation for the District needed the consent of its white residents. Adams made no conditions: the evil needed to be eradicated from the capital. Dorcas Allen had to have been in his thoughts.

Beyond that, they were in serious disagreement, the difference between an antislavery moralist and an antislavery activist. Lincoln had many times made clear that abolitionism was beyond the pale. Adams had given up denying that he was an abolitionist. He had welcomed and publicly acknowledged the help of Theodore Weld, the brilliant abolitionist author and political activist who became Adams' volunteer research assistant during the gag rule debates. Slaves and free blacks were here to stay, Adams believed. He would not support colonization. Blacks should and eventually would be citizens. Slavery, though, was the problem to be resolved—probably convulsively and violently, Adams anticipated. Peacefully, Lincoln hoped, and certainly not by a slave rebellion and not by secession. Abolitionism, which might encourage a rebellion, directly or indirectly, was to be denounced. Lincoln's strict constitutionalism and Whig moderation required that he reject abolitionism in any form. Slavery, he granted, was legal where it existed. That was that, short of developing the political muscle to change the Constitution, which neither he nor anyone else thought possible. The most that could be hoped for was containment. As long as the Senate remained evenly divided, legislation to restrict slavery was difficult; to eliminate it, impossible. There would be no internal recalibration. Everyone had the right to earn his own bread by the sweat of his brow. That was the principle. But slavery itself was not a principle; it was a fact. Only a change in public opinion, including taxpayers' willingness to compensate slave owners, might permit a recalibration. And beyond that there would be the question of where these millions of former slaves would live.

The immediate problem, though, was legal and constitutional. When the usually prudent Lincoln proclaimed, without qualification, that it was justifiable for people to rebel against the governing body to which they were subordinate, it's unlikely he had in mind slaves rebelling against masters or the Southern states seceding from the Union. Like Jefferson, when he spoke of the right to revolutionize, to assert independence and a new sovereignty, he was thinking of a right, in the American context, that *only* white people had. Anything further would not have dawned on Lincoln. And the word *only* would not have come to mind. Neither could conceive that any part of the principle or claim about the right to revolutionize could apply to Negroes in America, who both Jefferson and Lincoln hoped would eventually not be here at all. As long as they were, though, they had no place in the polity or the discourse about rights and revolution.

Adams also had nothing to say about the right of blacks to revolutionize. He simply expected it to happen, or at least to be a likely possibility. Any legitimacy to that action inhered in the right of every human being to assert control over his own mind and body, to overthrow tyranny, much as the American colonists did in 1776. Though as much a legalist as Lincoln, he identified more with black suffering, and he had enough of an apocalyptic personality to imagine that there would be some correlation between the inevitable and the desirable. His Massachusetts roots and his family history had imbued him with a visceral hatred of slavery. He was activist enough to have tried to help Dorcas Allen. Lincoln had his compassionate moments, eloquently expressed in his letter to Joshua

Speed evoking the chained slaves he had seen in 1841 (and, later, in his response to the 1850 Fugitive Slave Law). He was, though, more tied to legal literalism than Adams, and his background had not made him feel compassion for, let alone give special assistance to, an individual Negro, whether slave or free.

Both tended to treat the Constitution reverently. Both, apprehensively and critically, acknowledged its one deep flaw: its acceptance of domestic slavery. But they differed on the reason for the flaw and how to deal with it. The flaw, Lincoln argued, was mostly in the eye of the beholder who misread the history and the text. The Founders, he believed, intended slavery to be contained and then eliminated. The Constitution's tolerance for slavery was a temporary expedient. And, he argued, the founders all opposed its continued existence, let alone its spread. He was far from entirely correct. Anyway, by the late 1840s, most Southern leaders rejected that claim: to own slaves was an unalterable constitutional right granted to every state to implement or not, the bargain between the North and the South that had made the Union possible. Lincoln deemphasized the evil in the document, the compromise that had created the nation. He saw a good document that would, over time and with a change in public opinion, be purified. Adams believed the compromise to be a fatal flaw.

WHEN PRESIDENT Polk ordered troops into Mexican territory, he had, both Adams and Lincoln agreed, neither interpreted nor amended the Constitution. He had defied it. He had broken the law. The Constitution was not at fault. For Lincoln, the legal issue was less important than the political. The Constitution had not been damaged; it had been taken advantage of. The prohibition against an executive-initiated war had been unconstitutionally flouted through the agency of a lie. No national emergency required that the United States defend itself against aggression by invading Mexico. It was once again real estate, real estate, real estate. And why that particular real estate? Antislavery moralists had reason to believe that the Polk administration had as one of its motivations new territory for slavery. Territorial conquest would add new slave states to the Union. Lincoln did not make much of this. Texas as a slave state was already in the Union, and there were other free states in the anteroom to help keep the balance, especially California and Oregon. And what could be done in response to Mr. Polk's war? Politically very little, except to pass condemnatory resolutions, and it would not do to refuse to support troops in the field. Both Adams and Lincoln in 1847/1848 voted to pay for a war that was already in progress. That was a political and even moral necessity. But the war itself was a challenge to the integrity of the Constitution.

For Adams, the assault on the Constitution had been ongoing since 1803. From the start of his public life he had bewailed slavery's being embedded in the Constitution, especially the three-fifths clause. That slaves should be counted as voters had seemed a knife wound in the heart of the republic. The knife needed to be withdrawn. The constitutional evil forced on the nation as a condition of its creation needed, eventually, to be transformed into constitutional freedom. For the South, though, slavery was an absolute, an unchangeable given, as permanent as the stipulation that every state, no matter its size, have two senators. While the Constitution itself did not forbid the elimination of the three-fifths clause, its elimination had proved to be, so far, politically impossible.

The extension of slavery was another matter. On that, by any reasonable interpretation, Congress had rights. In 1803–1804, the South made clear that whatever the Constitution said on the matter, extension would depend on political power. Jefferson and the South had it. The southern part of the Louisiana Purchase would be slave territory, and as much beyond as possible, though the details were left to the future. The future came in 1819: Missouri became a slave state. Then, in 1845, came the annexation of Texas.

About Louisiana and Texas, Lincoln had little to say. He accepted the

Missouri Compromise as a necessary foundation for the perpetuation of the Union. By 1848, it was for Lincoln an incontrovertible historical fact, the foundation of Western expansion and the basis for the harmonious perpetuation of the Union—not a matter to be raked up and gone over, and not to be thought of as an offense to the Constitution. In contrast, Adams felt that the Constitution had been assaulted and abused in each of these cases. Jefferson, the so-called strict constructionist, had made an end-run, Adams believed, around the Constitution in establishing governance for and slavery in Louisiana. Admitting Missouri as a slave state had been an undesirable extension of a constitutional evil—the state constitution, forbidding free blacks to settle in Missouri, was itself unconstitutional. But the most flagrant abuse of the Constitution had been the annexation of Texas. On February 28, 1845, "the heaviest calamity that ever befell myself and my country was this day consummated," Adams wrote in his diary. By a vote of 27 to 25, the Senate adopted the House resolution to annex Texas. In Adams' view, that should have required a constitutional amendment. It was a dirty business on two counts: constitutional integrity and slavery. Led by slave owners and expansionists, the twenty-five-year effort to make Texas U.S. territory had at last succeeded.

The strong were preying on the weak, Adams lamented. The United States had cheered on the rebellion of American settlers in Mexico's Texas and the creation of the Republic of Texas. Mexico had prohibited slavery in its Texas province. An independent Texas immediately reinstituted slavery. For Adams, there was a moral component in revolutions. There had been none, it seemed to him, in the creation of the Republic of Texas, both in the state's inception and in regard to slavery. Lincoln, in 1848, had proclaimed that a minority had an unconditional right to revolutionize. Adams was much less certain. There had to be just cause and a moral standard. He believed there had been both, even if self-servingly, for the Founding Fathers. But for America to annex Texas was a double affront: a new slave state and an assault on the integrity of the Constitution. There should have been an amendment, just as there should have been for Louisiana, not legislative legerdemain.

For Adams, it was a moment of passionate despair. The annexation of Texas seemed the ultimate betrayal of the Constitution. He was not yet, or ever, on the side of those who, like Wendell Phillips and William Lloyd Garrison, considered the Constitution a pact with the devil, to be torn up and discarded so that an entirely new start could be made. But he was deeply disgusted by the triumph of willful power over constitutional principle. The end of the Union as he had known it seemed in sight. Outraged and in pain, he expressed himself privately in the puritanical language of polluted blood and biblical example: "The Constitution is a menstruous rag, and the Union is sinking into a military monarchy, to be rent asunder like the empire of Alexander or the kingdoms of Ephraim and Judah."

When, on February 21, 1848, he rose from his desk in the House and the cry went out that Mr. Adams was "sinking from his seat in what appeared to be the agonies of death," was Lincoln at his seat in the House chamber? If so, what could he have seen from so far back? Perhaps he was wandering somewhere else in the hall. Or perhaps he had left momentarily for an errand. There's no way of knowing. He had been at his desk minutes before. Like Adams, he had voted against a triumphal, chest-thumping resolution thanking military officers for "gallantry and military skill" in the victories at Vera Cruz and Cerro Gordo. The resolution ordered that eight gold medals be struck, one for each general. It passed 98 to 86.

Lincoln never, as far as we know, referred to that memorable day. If he was indeed there at the moment of Adams' fall, his silence about such an event is noteworthy. Was he uncomfortable with Adams' passion? With Adams as an abolitionist? With Adams' rejection of the American Colonization Society? With Adams' concept of constitutional evil and how to think, feel, and act about it? And did he not clearly prefer Henry Clay for his own mentor and model? Adams had for some time been thinking about and preparing himself for an American apocalypse. Given his age, he did not expect to see it with his literal eyes. But he saw it with his prophetic imagination. Lincoln, to the extent that he was thinking about it at all in the late 1840s, was thinking about how best to avoid it. This was to be his permanent frame of mind.

LINCOLN'S APOCALYPTIC imagination was limited mostly to the theater and to dreams, which, to the extent that one remembers them, are a form of theater, the inner and primal theater of anxieties, shifting scenes, illogical and irrational events. Adams recorded some of his dreams in his diary. An accomplished classical scholar, he considered Cicero his favorite author from the ancient world. In one of his most telling dreams, he envisioned Cicero forced to kill himself as the Roman Republic that he had made his lifework became an empire of tyranny. In his last years of life, as the war he presided over moved toward its conclusion, Lincoln dreamed of his own death. The war he had tried hard to avoid seemed, in his nightmares, to become the likely instrument of his own demise.

In their waking lives, Adams and Lincoln were avid theatergoers. The stage was a place where dreams and waking life coalesced. On it, they could envision their private selves and their public roles. It was a place of both immersion and escape. In their years as public figures, both went to the theater at personal risk, asserting their right to free movement. Receiving no special protection, presidents were citizens like all others, sharing, except on political or ritual occasions, public streets, public transportation, public spaces. In indoor venues, a spectator, sitting for hours, was especially vulnerable. Starting in 1834, when he became the most prominent opponent of the gag rule in the House of Representatives, Adams received letter after life-threatening letter. All came from the South. Many were obscene, slavery and racism their aggressive thrust. Lincoln received similar, even nastier threats. In race-obsessed Southerners' eyes, the Republican "baboon" was himself a "nigger."

The ultimate threat, enacted in Booth's theater, was perhaps the deadliest because it had never been inscribed in writing. No one who wrote a threatening letter to Adams or Lincoln had ever acted on it. Inveterate theatergoers such as John Quincy Adams knew they were especially vulnerable every time they went to a play. So did Lincoln, though the temper of the times—and its recourse to violence, great as it was—was less volatile in the 1830s and '40s than it became in the 1860s. An actual war made a difference. Secession could proceed by individual as well as mass violence. And what were only occasional drumbeats and half-toned bugle blasts in the 1840s became, in the 1860s, total war, to be fought by every means, including assassination. By 1865, the temper of the times was also inflected by desperation and revenge for a cause already lost.

For both Adams and Lincoln, these realities were Shakespearean. Their favorite playwright provided the template for their private and political dramas: ambition, power, conflict, and assassination. An Americanized Shakespeare appeared regularly in America's large cities, intermittently traveling to small towns throughout the country. Shakespeare also gave America, North and South, a powerful dramatization of racial anxieties. In *Othello*, a play that Adams had much to say about and Lincoln touched on indirectly, Shakespeare gave stage and dream presence to one of the most pervasive taboos of nineteenth-century American life: sexual relations between black men and white women. Adams adored Shakespeare; so did Lincoln. For Lincoln, the plays he loved were about ambition and tragedy; for Adams, about character, values, ideas, and race: Lincoln, the nineteenth-century man, born into the Romantic gestalt, though uneasy with it; Adams, the eighteenth-century man, a child of the American and European Enlightenment. Both lived Shakespeare awake and asleep, in the theater and in dreams. They vocalized the power of Shakespeare's language, reciting it to themselves or aloud to others. Lincoln, who had something of the Method actor in him, recited Shakespeare with an actor's feel for the power of the lines, with intense and personalized emotion, particularly the speeches of characters he especially identified with: Macbeth, both Richards, and Claudius. But not Othello.

Though the word *miscegenation* was not coined until 1863, white-black sexual relations had been a well-known reality of Southern life from the first importation of Africans into Virginia in the seventeenth century. Most Southern slave owners believed they could use their property in any way they pleased, including sexual relations by consent or force. Property rights were sacred, God-given, and legally ordained. How one treated one's property was mostly a personal matter. Mixed-race families and all-white families, fathered by the same person, existing side by side, were not uncommon. Thomas Jefferson married the fully white daughter of a man who had two such families. As a widower, he took as his domestic companion for thirty years the half-black daughter of his father-in-law's other family. Virginia law, for obvious reasons, never criminalized miscegenation, though, like many states, South and North, it prohibited mixed marriages until well into the twentieth century. It was legal to have sex with a slave but not to marry one. It was illegal until 1967 for a white person in Virginia to marry a free black.

Lincoln's Illinois prohibited mixed-race marriages. Repeal did not come until 1874. Well aware that there were, in fact, households in which white men and black women lived together intimately, Lincoln probably knew, as gossip had it, that it was likely that Robert Matson and Jane Bryant had had sexual relations. He was not an innocent, and he was observant. In his visit to the Speed plantation in Kentucky in 1841, he would have seen light-skinned slaves and slaves who had white skin. The mulatto world had an unmistakable presence in the South. Miscegenation was obvious—in the North also, though in smaller numbers. A supporter of his state's Black Codes, Lincoln opposed allowing a free black person to marry a white person. He had, though, little interest in and no reason to express a view about black-white sexual relations.

As a congressman in 1847/1848, Lincoln expressed no criticism of slave-owning colleagues, some of whom were fathers of mulatto children. Adams found their pro-slavery diatribes contemptible, their sexual conduct repulsive and hypocritical. When he touched on the subject, his Southern colleagues howled. Lincoln, in contrast, had no inclination to identify himself with attacks on slave owner hypocrisy. He would have much to lose politically; it would sound too much like abolitionism. Beyond that, he was, during the 1848 election, preoccupied almost entirely with the Mexican War, the administration's policies, and Whig strategies, with a glance at a moderate plan for emancipation in the District of Columbia. By background and temperament, he was able to identify with those who had inherited an economic and social world based on slavery. "I have no prejudice against the Southern people," he was to tell his audience in Peoria in October 1854. "They are just what we would be in their situation. If slavery did not now exist amongst them, they would not introduce it. If it did now exist amongst us, we should not instantly give it up. . . . When Southern people tell us they are no more responsible for the origin of slavery, than we; I acknowledge the fact." It was not a "fact" that Adams would have granted.

Was it a fact at all? By 1854, many Southerners were touting slavery as a "positive good," and there never had been any active, broadly based movement in the South to eliminate slavery at any stage in its history. It was as much a given as the soil Southerners stood on. Why would they, first-time buyers included, not happily have bought and used slaves, especially in the Deep South, which was increasing the slave population by birth and interstate purchases? And even if one could not make the unqualified claim that nineteenth-century Southerners were "responsible for the origin of slavery," an unbiased historical examination would have revealed that slavery, having been brought to the colonies by the earliest British-American settlers, was contentedly and profitably inherited by their descendants and by new colonists. In 1776 these slave owners became exclusively Americans. In 1787 they were largely responsible for the creation of a Constitution that perpetuated the legality of slavery.

For Lincoln, the question at issue was a practical one, which is also to say political: "I surely will not blame them for not doing what I should not know how to do myself. If all earthly power were given me, I should not know what to do, as to the existing institution"—except to promote colonization, whose practical limitations he recognized. To make free blacks fellow citizens was out of the question. "My own feelings will not admit of this; and if mine would, we well know that those of the great mass of white people will not. . . . Whether this feeling accords with justice and sound judgment, is not the sole question, if indeed, it is any part of it. A universal feeling, whether well or ill-founded, cannot be safely disregarded. We cannot, then, make them equals." Still, he had no hesitation in acknowledging that he *shared* this "universal feeling." It was politically desirable to do so, and he was also sincere, though he himself would never find it advantageous to initiate discussion of the topic.

It was, though, forced on him. In 1858, as a member of the new Republican Party, he attempted to unseat Stephen Douglas, Illinois' well-established U.S. senator, the embodiment of the Democratic Party's combination of pro-slavery activism and indifference to slavery. Western expansion was Douglas' highest priority, slavery a nuisance issue. Slavery should be put, he believed, very far back on the back burner. A moral issue, it actually had, he believed, no place in politics at all, though it had been forced on him as much as on Lincoln. Naturally, Douglas would not let Lincoln off the hook. The challenger's antislavery moralism could easily be portrayed as implying civil rights for free blacks, including legalizing mixed-race marriages, which Illinois' racist voters opposed. How would Lincoln defend himself against the charge? If he faltered, he would lose votes. At Charleston, Illinois, in the fourth debate with Douglas, he was ready to take the bait and turn it to his own advantage.

By tactic, personality, and conviction, he met the test. The tactic was anecdote, the tone humor. "While I was at the hotel today, an elderly gentleman called upon me to know whether I was really in favor of producing a perfect equality between the negroes and white people. [Great Laughter.]" The audience was with him, the charge preposterous. No Republican, ex-Democrat, or lingering Whig would have found it anything but ludicrous. And Lincoln would not allow the trap to close. "While I had not proposed to myself on this occasion to say much on that subject," he began, "yet as the question was asked me I thought I would occupy perhaps five minutes in saying something in regard to it. I will say then that I am not, nor ever have been, in favor of bringing about in any way the social and political equality of the white and black races, [applause]—that I am not nor ever have been in favor of making voters or jurors of negroes, nor of qualifying them to hold office, nor to intermarry with white people; and I will say in addition to this that there is a physical difference between the white and black races which I believe will forever forbid the two races living together on terms of social and political equality."

He needed to make his position even clearer. "I say upon this occasion I do not perceive that because the white man is to have the superior position the negro should be denied everything." White superiority did not reduce the Negro to a nonhuman. Race mixing, though, was another matter, and Lincoln knew how to appeal to the common ground that he and his audience, Republican and Democratic, shared, using two of his oratorical gifts: humor and the personal voice. "I do not understand that because I do not want a negro woman for a slave I must necessarily want her for a wife. [Cheers and laughter.] My understanding is that I can just let her alone. I am now in my fiftieth year, and I certainly never have had a black woman for either a slave or a wife. So it seems to me quite possible for us to get along without making either slaves or wives of negroes." He would give Senator Douglas "the most solemn pledge that I will to the very last stand by the law of this State, which forbids the marrying of white people with negroes."

Speaking in Chicago a few months before, he had said the same in a slightly different way. God and nature had some responsibility, and offered guidance: "As God made us separate, we can leave one another alone and do one another much good thereby. There are white men enough to marry all the white women, and enough black men to marry all the black women." But to state that divinity had created two different races was, in this context, to claim that divinity had also mandated they be kept separate. But what if a free white woman *wanted* to marry a free black man who desired to marry her? Or a black man a white woman? And there was mutual consent? And even if the law prevented a marriage ceremony, as it did in many states, how to prevent the practical equivalent of a common-law marriage? Lincoln certainly knew of the most common form of race mixing in the North and South, white men in intimate nonmarital relationships with mulatto women. All this he veered away from. "Why, Judge," he asserted, addressing the absent Stephen Douglas, "if we do not let them get together in the Territories[,] they won't mix there." That was the desirable focus. And he need not have said anything about miscegenation or sex between white masters and their slave property or between free blacks and whites outside marriage.

WHAT LINCOLN probably had no interest in even thinking about, Adams had been concerned about since he first read *Othello* as a young man. In 1786, while a student at Harvard, he delivered to his debating society a short essay on whether love or money "ought to be the chief inducement to marriage." His focus was *Othello*, which hardly lent itself to the subject at hand. His actual topic was interracial marriage. What to make of white Desdemona and black Othello falling in love, marrying, and sharing a marital bed? It was not a salacious preoccupation, but it was emphatically racial. As a young boy, Lincoln would have read "Othello's Apology for His Marriage" and "Othello's Address to the Venetian Senate" in *Lessons in Elocution*, a textbook his stepmother put into his hands. In February 1857, in Springfield, he probably for the first time saw *Othello* performed. The well-known actor Charles Walter Couldock put on a series of widely publicized, well-attended plays, his performance in *Othello* highly praised in Springfield's *Daily Illinois Register*. A few weeks before, Lincoln had been elected one of the eleven managers of the Illinois State Colonization Society, which had held its annual meeting in Springfield. Dedicated to facilitating the immigration of free blacks to Africa, the society's members were unlikely to have recognized the irony in the co-existence of, on the one hand, a black African general, played by a white actor whose blackface performance the audience had paid to see, speaking Shakespeare's beautiful verse, and on the other, the mostly impoverished, ill-treated free blacks on Illinois streets, let alone the enslaved former Africans in the South.

Of course, *Othello* was safer to Americans on the stage than in the street, in literature than life, though there were almost no performances of it in Southern theaters. Some Northern reviewers did express discomfort with the exhibition of a white woman and a black man in a marital relationship. Some evaded the issue with various stratagems. Others were horrified. Racism aside, if that were possible, many upper-class men, North and South, were especially revolted by the sight of a black man slapping and eventually killing a white woman, even onstage. It was the depths of dishonorable, racially transgressive conduct. No gentleman would ever do that. And the combination of dishonorable conduct and a mixed marriage threatened the bunker-like minds of slave owners, whose imaginations ran riot about both. Indeed, the play had incendiary potential for them, but it probably did not for Lincoln. There's no reason to believe that he connected the race issue in the play with slavery.

When Lincoln made a list of his favorite Shakespeare plays for James H. Hackett, the actor whose performance of Falstaff in *Henry IV, Part I* Lincoln had attended in March 1863, *Othello* was not on it. He responded to a gift of Hackett's book, *Notes, Criticisms, and Correspondence upon Shakespeare's Plays and Actors,* with appreciation and enthusiasm. When, in October, he saw E. L. Davenport play Othello at Grover's Theatre, he seems to have had nothing to say about the play. He himself was daily playing the real-life role of commander in chief of the Union army, a general of sorts. To the South, he was the "black Republican," as terrifying an example of the race threat as Othello. He had begun enlisting free black men and escaped slaves, "contraband," into the Union army. And he had recently issued an Emancipation Proclamation. The relevance of black Othello, the warrior and husband of a white wife, seems not to have registered, as far as we know, in Lincoln's consciousness. Or perhaps he was wary of being pulled any further, beyond what he had already said in 1858, into a discussion of mixed marriage or race. Behind it all, it's clear that *Othello* was not a play that had ever meant much to him, though he knew it well enough to quote lines from it occasionally.

It meant, though, a great deal to the Adams family. Hackett's book contained John Quincy's 1835 essay "The Character of Desdemona," which focuses on a subject that had distressed John Quincy's parents. Did Lincoln read it? He had it in hand. With so much pressing business to attend to, he may not have found time to read any of the Shakespeareana in Hackett's volume. Anyway, his antislavery moralism tended toward the abstract. It had a nonparticularized essence, whereas plays are concrete. Lincoln never cites specific examples of slaves who were suffering. Slaves existed, for Lincoln, as a group, a category, a collective entity, not as individuals. If he had read Adams' essay, he would have found it resonant with contemporary applications, the most specific, sophisticated, and revealing pre–Civil War expression of the interplay between antislavery moralism and racism. And all this was embodied in two dynamic, physically vital, and particularized human characters. "The play's the thing wherein to catch the conscience of the King." But not in Lincoln's case. And though *Othello* has multiple themes, it would have taken a special evasiveness or even blindness for a mid-nineteenth-century American, especially one concerned about slavery and mixed-race marriages, not to have noticed that these were central to its drama. If Lincoln noticed, he kept it to himself.

It was a theme the Adams family had grappled with for two generations. When John Quincy's parents looked to express the epitome of slaveholder immorality, they invoked what was to them the horror of racial mixing: white slave owners having sexual relations with their black slaves. Slavery was an offense against God and man. But so, too, was a mixing of the races. The Adamses condemned both. To such moralists, the deepest flaw in Southern society was its embrace of slavery. Its acceptance of miscegenation exemplified Southern hypocrisy. And Southerners, apparently, loved their slaves more than they loved the union.

To the Adamses, this was the foundational sin. Slavery, they believed, was an abomination, and they were not exclusionary racists in regard to civil rights for blacks. They supported citizenship equality, and they did not shy away from the presence of black people. Abigail's free black servant, Phoebe, had been married to the black man of her choice in the Adams' parlor, at Abigail's suggestion. But black-white sexual relations were another matter. To the Adamses, they were an abomination, an unnatural assault on the God-given distinction between the races. "It is to me, one of the most delightful Ideas that is treasured in my Mind," John Adams wrote to his wife from Philadelphia in 1796, "that my Children have no Brothers nor sisters of the half or quarter Blood. One such Consciousness would poison all the Happiness of my Life . . . and none could pierce my heart with such corrosive and deleterious Poison as this."

The remark was an indirect comment on the world of Southern slave owners and their offspring that Adams had observed in Philadelphia. Its force and emphasis, though, came not from external observation but from instinctive feeling, an imaginative projection of how he would feel if one of his children or siblings should be the parent of a mulatto child. There is no record or even suggestion of interracial sex in any generation of the Adams family. Yet John Adams' feelings are resonantly intense about the horror of it. The happiness of his life would have been destroyed. Sex between blacks and whites, let alone interracial marriage, poisoned the blood. It created mulatto children, embodiments of pollution and impurity, an existential assault on what it meant to be an Adams. And it was a horror experienced not only in the mind. The entire white body shuddered at the thought, let alone the sight.

In 1785, in London, Abigail attended for the first time a performance of *Othello*. The visual reality had an impact that the words on the page had never had. "I was last Evening . . . at Drury Lane," she wrote to her son-in-law, "and saw for the first time Mrs. Siddons," an actress of great beauty and grace. "She . . . acted the part of Desdemona. Othello was represented blacker than any African. Whether it arises from the prejudices of Education or from a real natural antipathy I cannot determine, but my whole soul shuddered whenever I saw the sooty Moor touch the fair Desdemona." Othello's "most incomparable speech ['Farewell the tranquil mind'] . . . lost half its force and Beauty, because I could not Separate the colour from the Man." Less racist than most of her contemporaries, Abigail nonetheless shuddered at the sight. Why, she asked, had she recoiled? Was it intuitive and irrational, or tribal and socially generated, or both? Othello, she observed, was generous, noble, and manly. Yet "*So powerfull was prejudice that I could not seperate the coulour from the Man.*" She would have known that the word *prejudice* had its origin in the Medieval Latin for *injustice*. She immediately struck the line through, as if to erase the evidence of what she had acknowledged: that she had been startled by, if not ashamed of, her body's involuntary response to the sight of a black man's hands on a white woman's body. She recognized that the fault might be not in her stars but in herself. Or it might be in the star under whose influence she had been born, and that she herself writ large was the society as a whole.

Fifty years after his first encounter, John Quincy returned to the same play. He could find no way to read it that allowed an escape from or an evasion of two elements that stuck in his craw: Desdemona's rejection of filial piety and the sexual relationship between Desdemona and Othello. Desdemona had succumbed, against her father's wishes, to her love for an inappropriate suitor. The sacrilege was twofold: no daughter should marry against her father's express prohibition; and no white woman should marry a black man. Like his father, John Quincy believed that nature had set up an unmistakably visual prohibition between the mingling of black and white blood, the very distinction conflating the metaphorical and the biological. For nineteenth-century Americans, "blood" was equivalent to genetic inheritance. And culture and history also prohibited race mixing. White America often placed heavy penalties on the perpetrators. But even more important, nature was opposed. And the only way Adams could keep faith with his version of Shakespeare, the wisest and greatest of poets, was to interpret the tragedy of *Othello* as an exemplification of the inevitable result of breaking nature's laws. Nature had decreed that white and black blood should not mingle. "The moral of the tragedy is that the marrying of black and white blood is a violation of the law of Nature. That is the lesson to be learned from the play."

Blacks were not, for Adams, inferior to whites. There was no superior or inferior race, though there were races, especially the white European, that had benefited from a religious, cultural, and political history that had placed them on a higher rung on the ladder of civilization. But neither John Quincy nor his parents assumed that the ladder required stationary positions. It was, to some extent, in regard to all races, potentially an escalator. American blacks, Adams knew, had given evidence that they could move up the steps, obstacles notwithstanding. But miscegenation and mixed-race marriages seemed an obstacle, not a facilitator, of cultural advancement. Racial purity and racial distinctiveness had been gifts of

God and nature. They should not be denied. And if "the color of Othello is not vital to the whole tragedy," Adams wrote, "then I have read Shakespeare in vain."

He also had no doubt that Desdemona's passion, not Othello's jealousy, was the active agent in precipitating the tragedy, a consequence of her filial impiety and sexual aggressiveness. But much as his essay gives the impression that he was preoccupied with Desdemona, it was the topic of race that most energized his concern. Race, not sexual impropriety or filial disrespect, was the issue of the day, structurally and psychologically embedded in American life. In 1832, when Adams first took up his seat in the House of Representatives, he began his attacks on the gag rule. In 1835, he published his essay on *Othello*. In 1837, Lovejoy was murdered in a race riot, the culmination of a decade of pro-slavery mob violence and volatile anti-abolitionist propaganda, part of the widespread lawlessness that Lincoln focused on in his Springfield Lyceum address. By the late 1830s, slavery and the Southern-imposed gag rule had become the obsession of Adams' public life. They were the dark poison in the white blood of his waking hours and his dreams.

He was, for himself, like most white Northerners, clear on the issue of miscegenation as a political and biological phenomenon: the high proportion of mulattoes in the South testified to the hypocrisy of the slave power—the lust, arrogance, and will to national mastery of the Southern elite. The mixing of black and white blood, whether within marriage or not, was, John Quincy believed, against God and nature. Let the races, in that regard, remain distinct. But to believe that Negroes were less than human or inferior humans was absurd: they were no different from white Americans except in the color of their skin. Since, by historical reality, free blacks were just as much Americans as any white American, they were due every consideration of human equality—civic equality as well. History, Christianity, the Declaration of Independence, and the Constitution required that. And what about the millions of enslaved blacks, property as well as people? Adams asked. The Constitution kept them in slavery. Under what circumstances could that be changed?

USHER F. Linder kept reappearing in Lincoln's rearview mirror. For the time being still a Whig, Linder found that his pro-slavery racism kept him, through the 1840s, reassessing his value to moderate antislavery Whigs and considering what advantages might accrue to him in a political world destabilized by the cross-party currents that the slavery issue had created. Deep down, he was loyal in his own way to his absolute conviction that the white race was superior to the black. Believing that slavery should exist in America indefinitely, he assumed that it would as long as radical antislavery activists were put in their place. He could abide antislavery moralists like Lincoln, wrong as they seemed to him in principle, but not antislavery activists. It was the difference between a disagreement among friends and violent conflict. In the case of Elijah Lovejoy, that meant the grave, and Linder, in Alton in 1837, had acted accordingly.

Lincoln wanted slavery to end, but the only practical and political position he and his colleagues would commit to was that it should not be extended to the territories. That was an expression of antislavery moral principle and of strategic politics. It became the Republican Party's distinctive marker, its defining and distinguishing issue. It was the electoral banner under which antislavery moralists, whether racists or not, could vote for Lincoln rather than Stephen Douglas in 1858. Except for nonextension, slavery could exist for as long as it took to work out some way of eliminating it, which seemed a long way off—to be accomplished by a change in public opinion in the South and North, and then a change in the Constitution, with the creation of some mechanism that the majority could agree on and support, including compensated emancipation. For all practical purposes, the pro-slavery racist and the antislavery moralist ended up in the same place, at least for a long time, except on the issue of extension. Lincoln, of course, could no more control Linder than he could make slavery go away. And it is difficult to discover, except in selective instances, what was really going on in Lincoln's head, about Linder or anyone else. He kept his thoughts mostly as private as his private life. When he spoke for the record or by the hot stove, he was either the advocate or the entertainer, or both. Unlike Adams, he kept no diary. He wrote few revealing letters. Those he did write and the meditative notes he composed in order to clarify his thoughts seem fragmentary embodiments of the hidden work of an active mind. Much more went on in his head and heart than we can know. So the effort to know, or guess, becomes ever the more stressful and often strained.

The area in which Lincoln reveals himself most is the political, the arena in which he most related to people, especially about the importance of winning elections. He had little to say, at least in writing, about those activities and national issues in which he did not have a direct interest. Only his Lyceum lecture in 1838, his Temperance Address in 1842, and a few speeches he gave in the 1850s have no direct connection to practical politics. Noticeably, he had nothing public to say about the widely reported *Amistad* trial. In February 1841, John Quincy Adams helped persuade the Supreme Court to conclude that fifty-three Africans aboard a ship that had drifted into American waters were free men. Abolitionists and some antislavery Whigs opposed efforts by the Van Buren administration to send the Africans back to slavery. Springfield's *Sangamo Journal*, laudatory about Adams personally but uneasy with any Whig-abolitionist alliance, downplayed the trial. Lincoln had nothing to say about it, as if it were not taking place, though he had to have been aware of it. Writing to Mary Speed in September 1841 about the slave coffle aboard his Ohio River steamship, he avoided any larger context for his description, as if the trial had not recently occurred. No doubt he detested slavery, but practical politics, especially elections, took precedence.

And he had no difficulty being friends with and collaborating in legal affairs and politics with pro-slavery racists.

When, in the presidential campaign of 1848, Linder's racist principles conflicted with the Whigs' willingness to accept abolitionist support if it was politically advantageous, Lincoln did have stringent words for his friend. Attacked by the Democrats, the Whigs felt vulnerable to the charge that they had obstructed the Mexican War effort. Attempting to straddle the fence, Linder wrote to Lincoln that he had been entirely in favor of Polk's war and also supported the anti-Polk Whig presidential candidate, Zachary Taylor. Lincoln chastised Linder: an attempt to have it both ways would damage their candidate. "You know," he assured Linder, that "I mean this in kindness, and wish it to be confidential." Linder answered with a list of heterodox views. Fearing that Linder's views might influence other influential Illinois Whigs, Lincoln responded with a long, analytical letter intended for Linder to share with others. His political energy overflowing, he attempted to stab and bleed out the heart of what, between the lines and sometimes overtly, underlay all Linder's views about the Mexican War, President Polk, and the election. Linder's extreme racism elevated ideology above practical considerations. Uninterested in racism as an ideological or a moral matter, Lincoln was not about to denounce it directly. Still, it was of paramount concern as a political consideration. The problem: Linder's views transcended party; they were beyond political modulation. He had a higher commitment to his gut belief in the rightness of slavery and the criminality of abolitionism than to party affiliation; more in common with extreme pro-slavery advocates, mostly Southern Democrats, than with moderate antislavery Whigs.

Antislavery Whigs such as Lincoln also disapproved of abolitionists, but on a different level and in a different register. Linder might oppose Polk and the Democrats for ordinary political reasons, though he sometimes had to struggle to do so. But he was, in his deepest feelings and core ideology, sympathetic to the Mexican War and the spread of slavery. And, as the election approached, he was revolted by the likelihood that the Whig presidential candidate had taken a neutral position in the hope of getting the votes of Southern and Northern antislavery moralists. The main point for Lincoln was to win the election, but Linder was aghast. Since the Democratic candidate would undoubtedly be pro-slavery, some abolitionists would vote for Zachary Taylor as the lesser of two evils. Originally from Virginia, a slave owner, and now a resident of Louisiana, Taylor was a career soldier who silently opposed almost all traditional Whig public policies but also the extension of slavery to the Western territories. A war hero without a political record, he seemed a viable candidate in the South and North. Linder expressed to Lincoln his horror at the thought that a candidate he supported would have abolitionist support.

Lincoln set him right. "Friend Linder," he responded, "your third question" is "have we as a party, ever gained anything, by falling in company with abolitionists?' Yes, we gained our only national victory by falling in company with them in the election of Genl. Harrison. Not that we fell into abolition doctrines; but that we took up a man whose position induced them to join us in his election. But this question is not so significant as a *question*, as it is as a charge of abolitionism against those who have chosen to speak their minds against the President." The opposition was tarring all who opposed the war as abolitionists. That was the danger, Lincoln warned. Linder cared less about the danger and more about even an inaccurate charge of an alliance with abolitionists. His skin crawled at the notion. To Lincoln, abolitionist votes were not a contaminant or even an itch. They were simply votes.

As the election approached, danger was arising on another front—though, like almost everything else in the 1840s and '50s, it, too, could not be separated from the slavery issue. Like all Whigs, Lincoln abhorred the entrance of a spoiler into the race, a third-party candidate. Ex-president

Martin Van Buren, whose re-election in 1840 Lincoln had campaigned against, now ran again, this time as the Free Soil Party's candidate. Van Buren had wanted his Democratic Party's 1848 nomination. After all, he had served the party well, as the main architect of Andrew Jackson's victories in 1828 and 1832 and as a loyal senator, vice president, and president. His presidency had been damaged and his re-election balked by the depression of 1837. Though he understood that economic downturns usually deprive a president of a second term, he resented what seemed to him his party's ungratefulness. In an endlessly drawn-out Machiavellian convention in 1844, the Democrats had nominated James Polk. The bitter Van Buren, who had never before opposed the Democrats' pro-slavery ideology, embraced the small Free Soil Party's opposition to the extension of slavery to the Western territories and accepted its nomination. He had almost no chance of winning, as he knew.

As the election campaign entered its final months, many Whigs feared that Van Buren might take away enough votes from Zachary Taylor to elect the pro-slavery Democratic candidate, Lewis Cass of Michigan. In October 1848, the *Sangamo Journal* detailed satirically, with biting irony, "Ten Reasons Why Antislavery Whigs Should Vote for Van Buren." If Lincoln had not been traveling from New England, where he had been campaigning for Taylor, to Chicago to attend a Whig rally, it would be only a modest stretch to think he himself had written the article. It mocked Whigs who "are so violently opposed to Slavery that they intend voting for M. Van Buren, thereby assisting in the election of Gen. Cass, who is pledged to veto any bill restricting the extension of Slavery." The *Journal* editorial did not prevent pro-slavery Cass from carrying Illinois, though he carried it by fewer than 100 votes, with the help of almost 16,000 Free Soil votes for Van Buren. Illinois' Electoral College votes went to Cass. Still, the national vote favored Taylor. With a plurality of 47 percent, he became the twelfth president of the United States. Van Buren and his running mate, Charles Francis Adams, John Quincy's youngest son, received 10 percent of the popular vote. But Van Buren had fulfilled his underlying mission: he had prevented any Democrat other than himself from being elected. And he had, unintentionally of course, helped make Lincoln a happy man. Disappointed that the Whigs had so narrowly lost Illinois, Lincoln still took great pleasure in the priority prize: his party had once again elected a president.

WAS LINDER, who never placed party first, disappointed? His immediate self-interest was with the Whigs, but his heart was extremely pro-slavery. As the calendar turned into the next decade, he switched his allegiance back to the party he had started with. Exactly when that happened is unclear, though probably it was with the passage of the Kansas-Nebraska Act in 1854. In 1853, he and Lincoln were still trading clients for mutual convenience, as they did until Lincoln's death. And there's no sign that there ever was any personal alienation. But by 1858, Linder had already returned to his first love. That was not Lincoln but Stephen Douglas. He had from their first meeting as young Illinois legislators in the mid-1830s bonded with Douglas, whose views about slavery he had more in common with than with Lincoln's, though on that subject he made even Douglas seem a moderate.

In the 1840s, Linder thought Douglas a great man and Lincoln a talented but ordinary politician. Like many, he never thought it even possible that Lincoln would one day become president. Douglas, though, especially when he began a stellar career as a U.S. senator in 1847, seemed almost a certainty. Much as Linder and Lincoln were friendly colleagues, it was to Douglas that Linder had always given his heart. "I desire," he wrote in 1874, "in these my memoirs, to lay an humble leaf of laurel on the grave of my friend. My intimacy and friendship with Douglas commenced in 1836, when I was a very young man, and he was, as it were, a mere boy. He looked like a boy . . . but when he spoke . . . he spoke like a man, and loomed up into the proportions of an intellectual giant. . . . I cannot add to his great name by anything I might say. I loved him with the love that Jonathan had for David—'A love that passeth the love of woman.' . . . My personal intercourse with him was like that of a brother, which, in one respect, I was." Not totally, though, in regard to slavery. Far to the right of Douglas' moral neutrality, Linder always thought slavery an excellent good thing. Douglas accepted it as an unalterable fact to be lived with indefinitely. There were more important issues, particularly Western expansion, with or without slavery, the position he took in the hard-fought 1858 campaign to retain his Senate seat.

Douglas had, until the summer of 1858, assumed his re-election was a certainty. He had good reason to think so: his fame and achievements as a senator seemed a solid foundation for re-election and then the presidency. Alert to the overlapping fault lines between the old Whigs, the Northern and Southern Democrats, and the fast-growing Republicans, who combined antislavery moralism and opposition to extension with the Whig Party's middle-class business-minded constituency, Douglas underestimated Lincoln. And he was only beginning to see that the divisions in his own Democratic base were irreconcilable. The Kansas-Nebraska Act of 1854, mostly Douglas' brainchild, had proved a disaster for the Democrats. The slave-owning South wanted open access to the West and Northwest. Most Northern Democrats opposed that, and of course so did antislavery Whigs and Republicans. Abolitionists were up in arms. To solve the problem, Douglas proposed a variant on an old idea, "popular sovereignty": the citizens of the place at issue would make the decision. When Southern Democrats, whose support Douglas needed, rejected "popular sovereignty," he lost a crucial part of his national base. In 1857 the Supreme Court's *Dred Scott* decision, siding entirely with the slave owners' view, made Douglas' position even more precarious: why should any Southerner accept "popular sovereignty" when the law of the land now stated that slave owners were entitled to take their property anyplace in the country they pleased?

Under pressure, Douglas agreed to debate Lincoln in order to defend his Senate seat and strengthen his presidential candidacy in 1860. The first worked out well enough for him. He narrowly squeaked by. The second was a disaster, mostly because forces greater than those of any individual had already, triggered by the passage of the Kansas-Nebraska Act, made secession and a civil war likely, as Adams had predicted. Like many others, Douglas could not see that horror as likely: people of good faith, open minds, and love for the union would work together to prevent it. And that work was essentially political, the determination to follow traditional Democratic Party principles: states' rights, local control, agrarian supremacy, Western expansion, and live-and-let-live with regard to slavery.

After all, why should anyone argue with the premise that local decisions at the ballot box should determine slavery, jurisdiction by jurisdiction? And although, as Douglas believed, disagreeing with most pro-slavery Southern Democrats, the corrupt Lecompton pro-slavery vote in Kansas deserved to be invalidated, this was no reason to conclude that popular sovereignty was invalid. Anyway, as he began to argue, no jurisdiction could support slavery unless local enforcement laws were passed, and why make a fuss about allowing the possibility of voter-sanctioned slavery in the West when climate and geography made it economically untenable? Voters would not vote against their interests, he argued. Though his Democratic base was increasingly divided, the Republican base increasingly united, Douglas expected the center to hold. It did not seem to him possible that Southern Democrats would think themselves better outside the Union than in.

Eager to make the best case for himself and his party, he agreed to participate in a series of seven debates with Lincoln, starting in Ottawa, Illinois, in late August 1858 and ending in Alton in mid-October. After all, he had good reason to expect that he could win in Illinois. From the time of its admission to the union, the state had mostly elected Democrats. Since Andrew Jackson, it had always preferred a Democratic president. And he himself had been elected senator twice before, by large margins. He also firmly believed that his approach to slavery was the most sensible, the most practical. The antislavery moralists, however moderate they tried to make themselves appear, were essentially, he implied, abolitionists who elevated personal moral conviction into Union-destroying rhetoric. The country could not keep and sustain all the good things it had and would have if it gave priority to a moral crusade in defiance of property rights and the Constitution. And if Illinois elected Lincoln, he began to argue as the debates started, they would be electing a man who would help destroy the Union. Lincoln was, in effect, a closet abolitionist.

Of course Lincoln was not that at all. But as Douglas had reason to know, he *was* a formidable debater. And he had a substantial organization of political friends to support him. Many had helped pressure Douglas into agreeing to the debates in the first place. They had cheered Lincoln and taunted Douglas in a series of speeches Lincoln gave in places in which Douglas had spoken on the same day. Was Douglas afraid to appear on the same stage as his opponent? Feeling stalked and "attacked," even when he "would be in bed asleep, worn out by the fatigues of the day," he nevertheless felt compelled to accept the challenge. Telegraphing his friend and admirer Usher Linder, who could out-harangue almost anyone, he urged Linder "to meet him at Freeport, and travel around the State with him and help to fight off the hell-hounds, as he called them, that were howling on his path, and used this expression: 'For God sake, Linder, come.'" Linder, of course, came. "Some very honest [dishonest] operator," Linder wrote in his *Reminiscences*, "stole the telegram as it was passing over the wire, and published it in the Republican papers. They dubbed me thenceforth with the sobriquet of 'For God's Sake Linder,' which I have worn with great pride and distinction ever since." Meeting in St. Louis, they traveled "down through the Southern part of Illinois, speaking together at all his meetings—as far down as Cairo and up to Jonesborough, where he and Lincoln met in joint debate."

Linder backed Douglas throughout, as his personal attendee and vocal advocate. And he probably squirmed almost as much as Douglas did when Lincoln, in late August at Freeport, forced his opponent into a defense of "popular sovereignty," revealing Douglas to be more of a moderate on the extension of slavery than Southern Democrats could tolerate. In principle, Linder sided with the extreme pro-slavery position. In practice, Douglas' popular sovereignty was the best he could get. Linder granted that the South had a constitutional right to take slaves anyplace in the United States and its territories. How could local law or the voting booth invalidate a right guaranteed by the highest law in the land, the Constitution? Seeking the conciliatory middle ground, Douglas would leave it to the voters, territory by territory, state by state. But since that would allow, if local voters assented, slavery to spread, Lincoln had the advantage, as popular sovereignty was also unacceptable to antislavery moralists, many of whom revered the example of Henry Clay, the supreme antislavery moralist, an advocate of containment and colonization.

Though Lincoln narrowly lost the 1858 election, he narrowly won the popular vote. Illinois electoral law did not honor raw numbers, just as federal election law did not. Slightly dominated by Democrats, the state legislature was the equivalent of the Electoral College. Linder was delighted. The better man and the better way forward had won. Not that he undervalued Lincoln, but he overvalued Douglas. It was also a party issue. He had returned to the party whose core values he shared, particularly on the subject of slavery. And he looked forward to what he and many others believed was certain, a united party propelling Stephen Douglas to the presidency in 1860.

Linder, though, soon began to realize, even more quickly than Douglas, that the positions the senator had staked out leading up to and in the 1858 senatorial campaign damaged his viability as a national candidate, especially if there were to be a strong Republican contender—and probably even if not. For if the Northern states all supported the opposition candidate, they could by themselves carry a majority in the Electoral College, even with only a plurality of the popular vote. An exclusively Southern candidate could not. Even more forebodingly, if the Democratic candidate could not hold the South, because the South preferred a candidate who asserted the right of slave owners to bring slaves anyplace, how could Douglas possibly win the presidency? Linder began to wonder and worry. Could the Northern and the Southern wings of the party hold together?

IN LATE April 1860, Linder, a delegate to the Democratic nominating convention, left Chicago with a group of pro-Douglas delegates traveling to Charleston, South Carolina, to help nominate the next president. They stopped over in Washington City to meet with the great man. We

> *visited our friend Douglas, at his residence, in a body, and interchanged opinions in reference to uniting the Northern and Southern Democracy. Many of us had our doubts about doing so, but Mr. Douglas, with all his great common sense, upon that subject was perfectly infatuated. We all told him that such men as Yancey and other fire-eaters who controlled public opinion in the South, were very bitter towards him in consequence of his not letting Kansas come into the Union under the Lecompton Constitution, which history has recorded as the greatest fraud ever practiced upon a free people. "Well, gentlemen," said he, "let the politicians do their worst, the Southern people will not go with them"; and went on to show us from information he had received from the South that such was the fact. And would you believe it? he convinced us all that he was right. But that was one of the saddest mistakes that Stephen A. Douglas ever made.*

It was already, in early May, hot and insect-ridden in Charleston. The huge Institute Hall felt like a literal and ideological hotbox to the Northern delegates. Linder knew from the start that pro-Douglas Democrats were in hostile territory: the site chosen for the convention indicated that the power center of the party was far below the Mason-Dixon line. Even this rabidly pro-slavery racist immediately realized that the literal heat was being stoked further by the "fire-eating" anti-Union extremists. They wanted nothing to do with Douglas and popular sovereignty; they wanted secession. No sooner had Linder and his Northern colleagues entered "the Southern States" than the ideological temperature intensified. "We began to feel that the South was lost to Douglas." In Charleston, "we found the hostile feeling towards him at fever heat. While William L. Yancey, and others of his kidney, addressed the vast crowd that gathered nightly around the Mills House to hear their inflammatory speeches, not a single friend of Mr. Douglas was permitted to speak. Several of us attempted to do so, but they drowned what we said with the beating of drums and tin pans, and the blowing of horns, and many other unearthly noises!" When they found a venue where they could be heard, "our only auditors were the NorthWestern delegation. . . . We soon learned that the Southern sympathies were not with us Northern delegates, who were friendly to Mr. Douglas. The truth is, I believe they disliked him worse than they did Lincoln."

Not that Lincoln could have gotten a single vote in South Carolina. Neither could Douglas. But whoever the Republican candidate might be did not need them. Douglas did, as Linder well knew. Douglas, though, was also committed to the territorial integrity and perpetuation of the Union. So was Linder, who was startled to learn that his Southern proslavery brethren had it in mind to be brethren no longer in the Union that the Founding Fathers had created. It was an existential shock, as it was to be for Douglas and, later, Lincoln.

With his Northern colleagues, Linder stayed in Charleston for over two difficult weeks. They were treated like pariahs, cultural and ideological strangers from an alien world. "I had not been in that convention over three days till I discovered a deep-rooted hostility and burning dislike to Northern men and statesmen." That they were pro-slavery or happy to be indifferent to slavery made no difference. It was not enough to bridge the cultural and ideological gap. They were not true enough believers. "I had no intercourse on my part with the Southern fire-eaters. I heard subdued murmurs of civil war uttered by them from various quarters. They evidently tried to frighten us, but we didn't propose to be frightened."

As partisans of Douglas, they supported popular sovereignty and believed it was counterproductive, even delusional, for Southerners to insist that slavery be allowed to go wherever any Southerner chose to bring it. Most distressingly, they saw the writing of electoral defeat on the wall if Douglas was not the candidate of a united Democratic Party.

> *We did everything in our power to compromise with them, so as to prevent the cutting up and dividing of the Democratic party. They made an offer to us that we might select the candidate for the party if we would let them make up the platform—or let them select the candidate, and we might make the platform. Inevitable defeat awaited us in the acceptance of this proposition. If they had built the platform we should have had to stand on the Dred Scott decision, the Lecompton Constitution with the right of Southern slaveholders to carry their slaves into free territory, and hold them there as such against the wishes of the people of such territories. With such a platform as this, we could not have carried a single electoral vote north of Mason and Dixon's line. Had we given them the candidate . . . the consequences would have been equally disastrous, for we would have lost the whole North and a considerable portion of the South.*

No candidate in Charleston could get the votes necessary to be nominated. "We tried every expedient to convince our Southern friends that if they did not unite with us some Northern Abolitionist would be elected President, and that no man could foresee the consequences." To the Democrats in Charleston, it seemed likely that William Seward, the antislavery ex-governor and senator from New York, would be the Republican nominee. Like his political mentor John Quincy Adams, Seward had predicted, in a widely quoted speech, an "irrepressible conflict," his way of saying that slavery and freedom could not exist together in the same country indefinitely, a variant of Lincoln's statement in 1856 that the country could not indefinitely continue half slave and half free. In Charleston, the Deep South delegates strategically collaborated on a platform that Northern Democrats could not accept: slavery legitimized in the territories, the *Dred Scott* decision affirmed. How, Linder and his Northern colleagues asked, could they win even a single Northern state? Probably the pro-secession delegates had calculated that the election of a Republican president would provoke Southern secession.

When the Northern majority, helped by border state Democrats, passed an insufficiently aggressive platform, the core delegates from the Deep South walked out. Apparently, they had planned to do so from the start. There were now two Democratic Parties. The next month, in Baltimore, the Northern wing nominated Douglas. The Southern wing went its own way, with its own candidate, John C. Breckinridge of Kentucky. As Linder feared, some "Northern Abolitionist," the phrase stressfully and misleadingly applied, would be elected president. "At that time there was not a man north or south of the Mason and Dixon's line that even dreamed of the nomination of Abraham Lincoln as the candidate of the Republican party." Linder could not have imagined that in his wildest dreams.

He could not, of course, have imagined that just three and a half years later he would be deeply grateful to President Lincoln for the freedom of his Confederate son, a Union prisoner. The president's old colleague and friend, who had himself, despite his pro-slavery beliefs, supported the Union war effort, humbly asked for his son's release. Daniel Usher had chosen the wrong uniform. His father had not, though his age made an actual uniform out of the question. And he had done the state some service, which Lincoln apparently recognized. "Your son Dan, has just left me," the president wrote to him the day after Christmas in 1863, "with my order to the Sec. of War, to administer to him the oath of allegiance, discharge him and send him to you." It was a touching gesture, an affirmation of personal loyalty and sympathy with a father's pain. Attorney General Edward Bates remarked that Lincoln released the young Confederate soldier "to gratify . . . the father, who is an old friend" and who still handled some of the legal business of Herndon and Lincoln. "A friend remembered Lincoln writing to Linder: 'I am sending your boy to you to-day as a Christmas present. Keep him at home.'"

Though he had an "utter abhorrence of Abolitionists," Linder, a nationalist in the Andrew Jackson mold, supported "a vigorous prosecution" of the war, urging in speech after speech "our young Illinois chivalry to arms." He did not buy the allegation that Lincoln was an abolitionist. He knew better. And it was "a war," Linder felt he had reason to believe, "to save the Union, and not to emancipate the negro, or to make him the equal of the white man . . . this was a white man's government, made by white men and for the benefit of the white race." He did not like the Emancipation Proclamation, which on January 1, 1863, modified the war rationale. But he begrudgingly accepted it "as a war measure, believing that it would end the war and prevent the further shedding of fraternal blood, in which belief," he later concluded, "it seems I was badly mistaken." Mistaken or not, he believed it was a step in the wrong direction. Nothing could ever make blacks equal to whites. America was and always should be a white man's country. And the proclamation had complicated America's future for the worse. How was it possible that two fundamentally antipathetic races could ever peacefully co-exist as citizens and equals? Linder thought it not only impossible but out of the question. Lincoln had his own doubts.

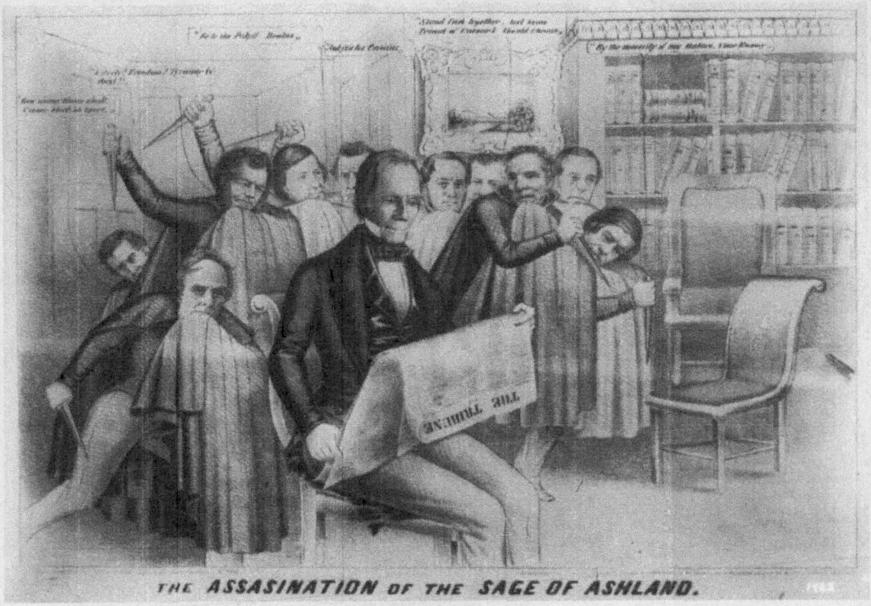

THE ASSASINATION OF THE SAGE OF ASHLAND.

An 1848 political cartoon depicting Clay, as Julius Caesar, being murdered by fellow Whigs who supported Zachary Taylor rather than Clay for the presidency. Lincoln also deserted Clay, whom he revered. [*Library of Congress*]

John Quincy Adams, in a daguerreotype by Philip Haas in 1843, much as he would have appeared to Congressman Lincoln in 1847/1848. [*Metropolitan Museum of Art*]

This nineteenth-century engraving of Shakespeare's Othello embracing Desdemona as he welcomes her to Cyprus dramatizes racial anxieties and resonates with the fact and theme of miscegenation. Even to an antislavery Northerner like Adams, mixed-race relationships were against God and nature. [*Getty Images*]

Abraham Lincoln, two weeks before the final Lincoln-Douglas debate in Lincoln's unsuccessful bid for the Senate, in a photograph taken in Pittsfield, Illinois, October 1, 1858. [*Library of Congress*]

The tired sadness of James Buchanan's face in this 1856 campaign engraving suggests the veteran pro-Southern politician's likely awareness that he would attain the presidency at a time when the problem of slavery made a stable Union untenable. [*Library of Congress*]

Andrew Johnson in 1860. The pro-Union governor of Tennessee was soon to be Lincoln's best ally in his border-state policy. An unshakable racist, he was Lincoln's choice in 1864 to become his second vice president. [*Library of Congress*]

Dominated by fire-eating secessionists, the 1860 Democratic convention in Charleston split the party into four factions and made Lincoln's election possible. [*Library of Congress*]

In this parody of the 1860 presidential candidates, they all dance to the music of the Dred Scott Supreme Court decision, which affirmed slavery's national legitimacy. The depiction of Lincoln dancing with a Negress alludes to the association of Republicans with racial mixing. [*Library of Congress*]

"Expulsion of Negroes and Abolitionists from the Tremont Temple, Boston, Massachusetts, on December 3, 1860." [*Library of Congress*]

This sharply etched photograph of Maine's Hannibal Hamlin, Lincoln's first vice president, was probably taken shortly prior to or during the war, before Lincoln replaced him in 1864 with Andrew Johnson. [*Library of Congress*]

In this heroicized 1860 depiction of Winfield Scott, the general in chief of the Union army, pro-Union propaganda assumed a quick victory over Southern treason. Its chief leaders are represented as a Civil War version of the seven deadly sins. [*Library of Congress*]

Wendell Phillips in the 1860s. [*Library of Congress*]

Lincoln, in January 1864, depicted in Matthew Brady's iconic photograph, five months before he made the consequential decision to drop Hannibal Hamlin as his running mate. [*Library of Congress*]

The cartoonist Thomas Nast depicts President Andrew Johnson as Shakespeare's Iago. He is deceiving Othello, represented as a black Union soldier being tricked into accepting policies that pardon treason and perpetuate white control in the South. [*Library of Congress*]

This cracked glass negative has scratched into the emulsion the phrase "Ex-President Andrew Johnson." The accidental crack from top left to bottom right, crossing Johnson as if to decapitate him, stands as an eerie representation of Johnson's role in the failure of Reconstruction. [*Library of Congress*]

Thomas Nast's 1865 "Emancipation" drawing, with Lincoln's face at the bottom, is a revision of his 1863 version in which Lincoln is absent. Both are otherwise identical, celebrating the blessings of emancipation in a series of happy scenes in contrast to the miseries of slavery. Nast's otherwise undated revision was probably created after the president's assassination in April. [*Library of Congress*]

Linder found an admirable example of the best sort of relationship between blacks and whites on a stopover in Atlanta in mid-May 1860, on his way home to Chicago from the convulsive Democratic convention in Charleston. "The hotel where we stopped was one of the best kept I ever saw; and an incident occurred here which I'll venture to relate, although my readers may think it of too trifling a character to find a place in these pages." Writing in 1878, Linder would have known that neither he nor his readers would think the incident trifling. It made an important point, as relevant to white America during the latter stages of the failed attempt to create a race-free South as it had been in 1860.

At dinner with his friend Thompson Campbell, Linder "noticed a very black negro man officiating as waiter, and I happened to be within hearing when the hotel-keeper, his master and owner, asked him for the loan of fifty or a hundred dollars. 'Oh! certainly, massa,' said he, and pulled it out and gave it to him." The landlord left. "I called the negro to us and asked him how it happened that he was loaning money to his master, and where he got the money, 'O, gemmen,' said he, 'I bought a ticket in the lottery and drew a prize of ten thousand dollars.' 'Well,' said one of us, 'It's a wonder he don't take it without asking it as a loan, for by the laws of Georgia both you and your money belong to him.' 'Yah! Yah! Yah!' said he; 'You don't understand my massa; he be too good a man for dat.' 'Well,' said I, 'Sambo, does he pay you back these loans?' 'Yes, sah, and offers me ten per cent interest, but I nebber takes it and nebber will.' 'Well,' said I, again, 'why don't you purchase your freedom?' After another negro laugh he replied: 'O, God bless your precious heart, how can I be any freer than I am now? I goes when I pleases and comes when I pleases, and my massa never makes any complaint; I nussed him when he was a little child and massa lubs me and I lubs him, and I will nebber leave him while I lib, so long as he is willin' to keep me.' Campbell turned to me and remarked significantly, 'I wish some of those d—d rabid Northern Abolitionists were here to hear what that nigger says.'"

EIGHT

The Ameliorative President

After two blisteringly hot days, Springfield celebrated July 4, 1860, "very quietly," the daily *Illinois State Journal*, formerly the *Sangamo Journal*, reported. "There was no general celebration by the people." With a headache and sore throat, Lincoln abstained from the politician's usual Independence Day activities. He thought he might have a low-grade version of the "hard and tedious spell of scarlet fever" that his son William had been suffering. His eldest son, Bob, was about to enter Harvard. "He promises very well, considering we never controlled him much." His longstanding intimate friend James Matheny, one of the few guests at his wedding in 1842, gave the Fourth of July oration at the fairgrounds. Lincoln stayed home. In the afternoon, the Springfield Guards paraded to the admiration of the crowd milling around on the city streets. "They then marched out to the woods, where they spent the rest of the day," probably in the shade. The "interminable popping of fire crackers during the whole day, and the shooting of rockets and other pyrotechnics at night, completed the day's performances." The editors of the *Journal* hoped that "our citizens will not permit another anniversary of our glorious Independence Day, to come and go without celebrating it in a more general and worthy manner." The concerns on the next July 4 were to be dramatically different. Union army volunteers would be marching through Springfield streets.

Sharing the widespread confidence that he would be elected president in the fall, the newly nominated Republican candidate could not have been unhappy, sitting in the shade of his porch or indoors, as he skimmed the *Journal*. It had reprinted in immediate sequence the Declaration of Independence and the Republican Party platform. The next page there was a Fourth of July editorial containing long excepts from two well-known speeches Lincoln had given in 1858. Both celebrated the Declaration as the country's founding document. Its affirmation that "all men are created equal" was the "electric cord," Lincoln proposed, that bound together all Americans, whatever their national or ethnic origin. And the argument of those who claimed otherwise was that of "the same old serpent that says you work and I eat, you toil and I will enjoy the fruits of it. Turn in whatever way you will—whether it come from the mouth of a King, an excuse for enslaving the people of his country, or from the mouth of men of one race as a reason for enslaving the men of another race, it is all the same old serpent." And the serpent must be denied, though not inconsequentially and irresponsibly crushed. The *Dred Scott* decision, Lincoln stated, was the case in point. It needed to be denied. Slavery was a form of tyranny, of denying the right of every living human being to have freedom. That was Lincoln's position. That was the position of the Republican Party and of all antislavery moralists.

But an antislavery moralist was not necessarily an antislavery activist. Most Republicans were not. All Americans, Republicans believed, should be free to make choices of employment, residence, and consumerism, free to possess the things of this world according to their means and abilities. That did not mean that free Negroes who lived in the United States should have civil and political rights. It did not mean that it was desirable for antislavery activists to agitate in destabilizing ways. And it certainly did not justify abolitionism. The Constitution's stipulation that slavery was entirely a state matter needed to be respected. Civil and political rights for free blacks were at the will of the white majority, the superior race.

The 1860 Republican platform, like Lincoln's speeches, paid homage to the Declaration of Independence. Structured as a series of seventeen declarative statements, the platform linked those statements together in an ascending series of affirmations and accusations. Its rhetorical tone and logic imitated the Declaration, suggesting that an "electric cord" connected the Declaration of 1776 and the Republican platform. The platform declared, first,

> *1. That the history of the nation during the last four years, has fully established the propriety and necessity of the organization and perpetuation of the Republican party; and that the causes which called it into existence are permanent in their nature, and now, more than ever before, demand its peaceful and constitutional triumph. 2. That the maintenance of the principles promulgated in the Declaration of Independence and embodied in the Federal Constitution, that we solemnly re-affirm the self-evident truths that all men are created free and equal . . . and that the Federal Constitution,* the Rights of the States, and the Union of the States must and shall be preserved *[my emphasis]. 3. That to the Union of the States this nation owes its unprecedented . . . [prosperity] . . . and we hold in abhorrence all schemes for disunion. . . . And . . . that no Republican member of Congress has uttered or countenanced the threats of Disunion . . . without rebuke . . . and we denounce those threats of Disunion . . . as denying the vital principles of a free government, and as an avowal of contemplated treason, which it is the imperative duty of an indignant People sternly to rebuke and forever silence. 4.* That the maintenance inviolate of the Rights of the States and especially the right of each State to order and control its own domestic institutions according to its own judgment exclusively *[my emphasis], is essential to that balance of powers on which the perfection and endurance of our political fabric depends. . . . That the new dogma that the Constitution, of its own force, carries slavery into any or all of the*

> *territories of the United States, is a dangerous political heresy, at variance with the explicit provisions of that instrument itself . . . is revolutionary in its tendency, and subversive of the peace and harmony of the country . . . That the normal condition of all the territory of the United States is that of freedom.*

No wonder most abolitionists had no trust in the Republican Party or its nominee. Though its platform affirmed in broad terms that all men are created equal, this did not include free blacks in the North or free blacks and slaves in the South. On the whole, white Americans did not believe that Negroes were equal to Caucasians. Well-known antislavery moralists such as Jefferson, Clay, and Lincoln rejected civil rights for blacks. And most Americans would not have concluded that either the Declaration or the Constitution was an umbrella under whose shelter American Negroes could find citizenship. Some Americans believed that the Declaration did not apply to slaves. Slaves were not included in "all men." Republicans, in general, took exception to this, though they accepted that the Constitution legitimized slavery at the will of the individual states. Lincoln had only a minor argument with the latter: the Constitution didn't require that it be forever and unalterable. He would leave slavery for future adjudication. And he had a minor qualification about the claim that "all men are created equal." They were created equal in their right not to be slaves but not in their right to be citizens. No civil rights for free Negroes in Illinois. There were, though, two bottom lines: no extension of slavery into the territories and no secession.

ON THAT same July 4, 1860, in a cooler climate, an extraordinary twenty-nine-year-old man delivered a brilliant address to an audience of two thousand people. The place was Framingham, Massachusetts, two of whose militia companies had fought in the Battles of Lexington and

Concord. Each year, starting in 1854, the Massachusetts Antislavery Society chose July 4 as the day to hold its annual rally in a grove called Harmony. There, in 1850, William Lloyd Garrison burned a copy of the new Fugitive Slave Law, a key component of the Compromise of 1850. All good Whigs, like Lincoln, were pledged to uphold that law. The New England states, especially Massachusetts, passed personal liberty laws and resisted.

The extraordinary man who stepped to the platform in the tree-lined amphitheater had, ironically, the same surname as two famous opponents of slavery, Stephen A. Douglas and Frederick Douglass. The mulatto son of a Virginia slave owner named William Douglas and a slave mother known as Mary, at the age of fifteen H. Ford Douglas had fled to Cleveland and freedom. He seems never to have revealed how he pulled it off. Self-taught, a habitué of the Cleveland Free Library, he discovered a gift for literacy and oratory. The Cleveland black community welcomed him. Already an outspoken abolitionist by his mid-twenties, an admirer and soon a friend of Frederick Douglass, he moved to Chicago. In late summer 1858, appalled at his adopted state's Black Code, he met briefly with the two most prominent Illinois Republicans, Senator Lyman Trumbull and senatorial aspirant Abraham Lincoln. He had a request in hand. Would they please sign his petition urging that free blacks residing in Illinois be given the right to testify before juries in cases in which they had evidence to offer regarding themselves or another person?

Trumbull and Lincoln refused. Blacks, they regularly affirmed, had the right not to be slaves, but did not have any civil rights, let alone the suffrage, in the United States. Someplace else, perhaps. H. Ford Douglas' petition went nowhere. Now an advocate of voluntary expatriation to any country treating Negroes as equal citizens, he himself went to British Canada. It seemed impossible for a literate, intelligent man like Douglas not to take at face value statements such as Trumbull's in support of his colleague as Lincoln initiated his campaign against Stephen Douglas: "We, the Republican party, are the white man's party. We are for free white men, and for making white labor honorable and respectable, which it never can be when negro slave labor is brought into competition with it. We wish to settle the Territories with free white men, and we are willing that this negro race should go anywhere that it can better its condition. . . . We believe it is better for us that they should not be among us. I believe it will be better for them to go elsewhere."

At first "elsewhere" suited H. Ford Douglas. In July 1860 he had good reason to believe that racist attitudes would always severely limit Negroes' opportunities in the United States. Colonization, perhaps to Canada or Haiti or Central America, seemed the answer. John Quincy Adams, Douglas told his audience, had said twenty years before that "'the preservation, propagation and perpetuation of slavery is the vital animating spirit of the national government,' and this truth is not less apparent today." If men like Lincoln and Trumbull preferred that as few free Negroes as possible live in Illinois, that they carry personal identity cards, and that they not be citizens in any meaningful sense, why should any black person be impressed by their minimalist position? Was their no-extension line in the sand not callously self-serving? After all, the free soil doctrine advocated free soil for white, not black, people. And blacks anyplace, including those in the territories, were to be residents without rights. "I care nothing about that antislavery which wants to make the territories free, while it is unwilling to extend to me, as a man . . . all the rights of a man. In the state of Illinois, where I live—my adopted state—I have been laboring to make it a place fit for a decent man to live in. In that state, we have a code of black laws that would disgrace any Barbary State. . . . Men of my complexion are not allowed to testify in a court of justice where a white man is a party. If a white man happens to owe me anything, unless I can prove it by the testimony of a white man, I cannot collect the debt. Now, two years ago, I went through the state of Illinois for the purpose of getting signers to a petition asking the legislature to repeal the 'Testimony Law.' . . . I went to prominent Republicans, and among others, to Abraham Lincoln and Lyman Trumbull, and neither of them dared to sign that petition, to give me the right to testify in a court of justice!"

What could one expect from Lincoln, H. Ford Douglas asked, if he became president? "I know Abraham Lincoln, and I know something about his antislavery." It is a morally self-indulgent antislavery, an egregious example of making oneself feel good without accepting the moral obligation to act. It is, partly, a politician's feel-good evasion of corrective public policy, let alone constructive action. It does nothing, Douglas argued, to make the lives of free or enslaved blacks the slightest bit better. Insofar as he deplores slavery as an evil, he will say and do nothing to prevent its indefinite perpetuation. Lincoln will risk, Douglas concluded, no political or personal capital, even to advocate that a black man as well educated as he be allowed to testify in a courtroom against a white man who has committed a civil crime or criminal act. That's the kind of antislavery person Lincoln is. And who are Lincoln's models and antecedents? Douglas asked. "I want to know," he continued, "if any man can tell me the difference between the antislavery of Abraham Lincoln and the antislavery of the old Whig party or the antislavery of Henry Clay? Why, there is no difference between them. Abraham Lincoln is simply a Henry Clay Whig, and he believes just as Henry Clay believed in regard to this question. And Henry Clay was just as odious to the antislavery cause and antislavery men as ever was John C. Calhoun. In fact, he did as much to perpetuate Negro slavery in this country as any other man who has ever lived." That was a harsh judgment on Clay. The "in fact" was a rhetorical exaggeration, but in 1860, in historical retrospect, true enough.

Six months later, anxiously awaiting his inauguration day, Lincoln gratefully accepted from an ex-Whig New York Republican the gift of a limited-edition bronze medal memorializing "the Great Compromiser." Lincoln felt "extreme gratification . . . in possessing so beautiful a me-

mento of him whom during my whole political life, I have loved and revered as a teacher and leader." H. Ford Douglas had reason to anticipate that Lincoln would now follow in his mentor's footsteps. He would find a way to compromise with the South. There would be no secession, or it would be, after a compromise, retracted. There would be no civil war. Slavery would remain. And the racism in Illinois and much of the country that deprived free Negroes of civil rights would be a permanent feature of American life. At the climax of his address, Douglas called the roll of his abolitionist heroes, asserting by association his commitment to stand with them as an heir to their leadership. And he did so with the sense that the black man in America had a special relationship with Massachusetts and New England. "What can I say, then, as a black man, other than to thank the men and the women of New England who have so nobly stood by the rights and liberties of my unfortunate race." It was an appropriate hortatory exaggeration. By 1860, slavery had been long gone from New England. The Adamses and the Parsons of Massachusetts had long ago rejected slavery. Most New England states had legislated civil rights for blacks, though local racism limited opportunities. Still, most abolitionists recognized that the New England that had given the country John Quincy Adams had far outpaced all other sections of the country in its acceptance of Negroes as equal citizens. It was in New England and its extensions that abolitionism had been allowed to breathe and then grow strong.

Invoking the names of those who had stood on the same platform where he now stood, Douglas praised his own honor roll of American heroes. "What an army of brave men the moral and political necessities of twenty-five years ago pushed upon this platform to defend . . . this last Thermopylae of the New world! Then it was that our friend Mr. Garrison could . . . brave a Boston mob, in defence of his convictions of right, in words of consuming fire. . . . Then it was that Elijah P. Lovejoy . . . gave to the cause the printed sheet and the spoken word within the very sight of the fortress of the evil doer." He now "sleeps in a martyr's grave on the banks of the father of waters. . . . These were brave men," among others. "Then, too, it was that that other good friend, Wendell Phillips, brought to the Antislavery platform the rare gifts of scholarly culture and a magnificent rhetoric. . . . Frederick Douglass, had not yet stirred the intellectual sea of two continents to the enormities of this country." And "let us not forget one other name. . . . not born to die . . . John Brown has gone to join the glorious company of 'the just made perfect' in the eternal adoration of the living God, bearing in his right hand the history of an earnest effort to break four millions of fetters, and 'proclaim liberty throughout all the land, to all the inhabitants thereof.'"

The men and women who, on July 4, 1860, gathered on the slope, overflowing the Harmony amphitheater, could not know, beyond hopes and fears, what the next years would reveal. Neither could Lincoln and Trumbull. Neither could H. Ford Douglas, who advocated that the American Negro should claim his rights as a human being and also consider geographic alternatives, either Canada or the Caribbean world, where he would have full citizenship among nonracist whites or in a black nation. The former was Douglas' preference. He was soon to find that he had another alternative. In an ironic, unintended way, it was Lincoln's election to the presidency that made this possible. The alternatives Lincoln faced and the choices he made determined H. Ford Douglas' future. Though the war that came was one that Lincoln was stuck with, it was a war that Douglas embraced. Like Wendell Phillips, he cheered secession on as the last best hope for emancipation in his lifetime. The rivers of blood that would flow seemed to him, and to most abolitionists, an acceptable and inevitable price to be paid for Negro freedom—and to repay the generations of blood that had been shed under the lash: the rapes, murders, and torture; the callous destruction of families; the transformation of human bodies into cash entities in accounting books. In 1863, H. Ford Douglas became one of the first thirty black men commissioned as officers in the Union army.

In this regard, it was to take Lincoln five years to catch up to the abolitionists, to find the compassion and the language, as he did in his Second Inaugural Address, to express what Douglas felt on July 4, 1860. And when Lincoln, in March 1865, a month before his death, looked back at why the United States had fought a bloody civil war, he was in essence in the same place Douglas was in 1860. It was indeed slavery that had made the war unavoidable, because different views about it had made disunion inevitable. But from his election to at least mid-1862, Lincoln was to hope that an end-run around slavery was possible. The South could keep slavery for some long period of time if it returned to the union. And he was to keep trying from 1862 to 1864 to bribe the South or buy out slavery and make colonization viable. Emancipation was not the goal; reunification was. Unlike H. Ford Douglas and most abolitionists, he did not think, almost to the moment of his death, that the black race had much of a future in America. Racism was too deeply embedded in the white psyche and soul.

IN THE tightly packed best acoustical auditorium in downtown Boston, a Baptist church called Tremont Temple, once a Greek Revival theater, a now rake-thin and partly grizzled Wendell Phillips, who for almost twenty-five years had been hoping for an American political and moral revolution, denounced the newly elected president. It was November 7, 1860. Abraham Lincoln, Phillips proclaimed, was "not an abolitionist, hardly an antislavery man." He was and would be "a pawn on the political chessboard." He owed his election "to no merit of his own, but to lives that have roused the nation's conscience, and deeds that have ploughed deep into its heart." It was the spirit and blood, Phillips reminded his audience, of Elijah Lovejoy, William Lloyd Garrison, and John Brown that had, indirectly, made Lincoln's election possible.

It was not an acknowledgment that Lincoln was ever to make. It was not politically apposite to do so, even if he had been capable, which he was not, of recognizing abolitionists as revolutionaries, as he readily granted the Founding Fathers had been. Why did they not also have, as he had implied in his speech to the House of Representatives in 1848, a "sacred right" to revolutionize? This was partly, it would seem, because they were abolitionists, partly because he valued stability more than anything else, his only red line a prohibition on extending slavery beyond where it already existed. His dedication was to the opportunity for white America to be its best unitary self, for the Whig values of individual initiative, economic nationalism, and rational public policy to determine America's future. His was not a revolutionizing temperament. He looked for prudent, gradual, law-affirming ways to move the nation from slavery to emancipation. For him also—as it was for the rowdy crowd that filled the streets, pushing into Tremont Temple to hear the most rousing of abolitionist orators, as it was for almost everyone—the excitement of his election was inseparable from worry about what would come next. Would there be secession? Would a compromise be hammered out at the last moment? Would markets be destabilized? Would there be a war?

Five days before Wendell Phillips' Tremont Temple speech, Lincoln had been elected chief executive with 40 percent of the popular vote, the smallest percentage ever. Though his election itself was not a surprise, there was considerable difference of opinion over what would happen next. Phillips had his preferred scenario. As an unknown young man, he had risen in Faneuil Hall, soon after Lovejoy's assassination in 1837, to defend freedom of speech, even that of abolitionists. He had then himself become an abolitionist, an electrifying orator with a radical message questioning whether a nation under a Constitution that legitimized slavery ought to endure. Wouldn't the North be better off without the South, Phillips asked. Were not moral integrity and equal rights more important than any practical consideration? And now that the secession of the Deep South states seemed likely, would not the cause of justice, human and divine, be better served by the creation of a separate Northern nation, uncontaminated by slavery? Or, alternatively and even better, would not a war in which the loyal Union states crushed the treasonous slave power be preferable to an indefinite continuation of slavery? A nationalist, Phillips preferred the perpetuation of the United States, though not under the present slave-favoring Constitution—and not under the Fugitive Slave Law that Congress had passed in 1850. The pro-slavery Constitution was now—as John Quincy Adams, whom Phillips had known and admired, put it when Texas was admitted to the Union by a legislative end-run around the Constitution—"a menstruous rag."

The question of the moment in November 1860 was: what could one expect from the new president? Phillips expected little. He had reason to believe that Lincoln would, like his predecessors, do everything he could not to challenge the existence of slavery in the South. He had, though, mustered some hope that the man he had recently referred to as "the Slave-hound of Illinois" might not be quite as retrograde as that. After all, Lincoln's party was antislavery and Lincoln himself an antislavery moralist. Still, the Republican Party movers and shakers could not be counted on for anything more than a commitment to nonextension. That was the centerpiece of their platform. They had no intention of tampering with the national status quo. Even William Seward, author of the notorious "irrepressible conflict," was now sugarcoating his abolitionism with the language of accommodation. With his party about to take power, he was toning down his rhetoric.

From Phillips' point of view, only the sword would do. And the hypocrisy of Seward's claim that the Republican Party "is a party of one idea; an idea that fills and expands all generous souls; the idea of equality,—the equality of all men before human tribunals, as they are all equal before the Divine tribunal and laws," seemed nauseatingly self-laudatory. Also, it was simply not true. Lincoln's Republicans had never supported equal rights for free Negroes. And they would not support American citizenship for what would be a vastly increased free black population if emancipation ever came. What to do with these black aliens? Other than gradual colonization, no one had a practical plan to untie the Gordian knot. Unlike Lincoln, Seward in New York had supported equality for free blacks. "That is his rainbow of hope," Phillips remarked. "It is a noble idea,—equality before the law. . . . Mark it." But now "let us question Mr. Lincoln about it."

With oratorical ventriloquism, Phillips brought a virtual Lincoln onto the Tremont Temple stage.

> "Do you believe . . . that the negro is your political and social equal, or ought to be?"
> "Not a bit of it."
> "Do you believe he should sit on juries?"
> "Never."
> "Do you think he should vote?"
> "Certainly not."
> "Should he be considered a citizen?"
> "I tell you frankly, no."
> "Do you think that, when the Declaration of Independence says, 'All men are created equal,' it intends the political equality of blacks and whites?"
> "No, sir."

Phillips had Lincoln right. Lincoln did not, and never was to, see the light by which abolitionists had for decades been showing the way. His genius was neither for revelation nor for proactive progressivism. It was for prudent response, with the least cost for the best results, to the realities already in place. Slavery existed. He could not change that other than by physical force, by high-risk confrontation when no one and nothing had forced confrontation on him. Phillips accurately assessed the newly elected president. He would do everything he could to keep the peace. If any state should secede, he would offer it what it wanted to return to the Union except the extension of slavery beyond where it already existed. Otherwise, the Southern states could keep their slaves indefinitely.

Lincoln had campaigned and been elected with one firewall: nonextension. That had provided the sectional Republican plurality. Most abolitionists probably voted for Lincoln. Out of the total 1,866,000 votes that produced an Electoral College majority of 180 for the winner, 28 more than needed, no one knows how many abolitionist voters there were. Perhaps less than 100,000 or so. He could have been elected president without a single abolitionist vote. Phillips of course preferred Lincoln to Stephen A. Douglas or the other two candidates. The three together got almost 3,000,000 votes. Together, the two Democrats—Douglas and John C. Breckinridge—had more than enough to have defeated Lincoln if the Democrats had been united. Abolitionists of course had good reason to prefer the Republican. Like Lincoln, they opposed slavery for moral reasons. Some abolitionists believed blacks to be innately inferior to whites. Some also favored colonization. Most, though, unlike Lincoln, favored abolition immediately or at least as soon as possible. About that, they were morally and practically passionate, though opinions differed about the best form of implementation. The newly elected president was not. He wanted nothing to do with abolition and abolitionists. A practical politician, he knew his base and its limitations. But its limitations were his own, not only of politics but of mind-set. An antislavery moralist from Kentucky, Indiana, and Illinois, he favored incremental change, when the country as a whole was prepared for it. In the meantime, he would do all he could to maintain things as they were.

Wendell Phillips expected little from him. With their dramatically differing agendas, it seemed unlikely that he and Lincoln would ever coalesce, at least if matters were in Lincoln's control. Phillips hoped that secession would force total war on the president—then, whatever the president's preference or the country's readiness, universal emancipation. What he feared, though, was that Lincoln, representing the plurality that had elected him, would do everything he could to prevent a war, including accommodation. Most Northerners indeed did hope that the new president could keep the union together. The South should be mollified. Slavery, indeed, bad as it was, was not bad enough to allow the union to become its victim. Two centuries of prosperous commerce between Southern cotton and Northern banking, insurance, shipping, and textiles outweighed slavery's iniquity. Surely a civil war could be avoided but, if war did come, Phillips also feared that Lincoln would do everything he could do to mollify the South before emancipation became inevitable. He would never, Phillips predicted, take the initiative to free the slaves. And who or what could force him? Like Adams, Phillips believed the South would never give up slavery without rivers of blood. "The last ten years of John Quincy Adams' were the frankest of his life," he told his Tremont Temple audience. "In them, he poured out before the people the treason and indignation which formerly he had only written in his diary." Only a slave rebellion or a civil war would end slavery. But if Lincoln were to keep South Carolina in the union by peaceful persuasion, slavery would survive indefinitely.

One month later, on December 3, 1860, the Boston abolitionist community assembled once again in Tremont Temple, this time to commemorate the day, one year before, when the body of John Brown was cut down from the gallows. Phillips had approved of Brown's mission. The newly spilled blood of slave masters seemed a small price to pay for the blood of the lash. Brown's moldering flesh had become, in idea and in illustration, a magical sacrament for his co-revolutionaries. Here was the epitome of commitment, a man willing to kill and be killed, biblical style, in the service of God's justice, for those who believed in this version of God. His attempt to instigate a slave rebellion had failed. What was important to abolitionists was that it had been tried. But since it was a criminal conspiracy, it had made his supporters, a group of six men who had financed the raid, subject to prosecution. One of those six, Lexington's Franklin Sanborn, attending the commemorative Tremont Temple event, was aware that, if his complicity was discovered, the Buchanan administration would have him indicted for treason.

Wary of consequences, Phillips himself had resisted a full association with Brown's violence. He was, though, probably at Tremont Temple on this day, as was his friend Frederick Douglass. They had confided in each other for more than twenty years. Having come close to implicating himself in the illegal raid, Douglass had reason to be nervous. But the Western world's most famous ex-slave, the controversial writer, orator, editor, and antislavery propagandist, was eager to deliver one of his characteristically fiery calls for all black bodies to be as free as his own. The subject for discussion was to be "The Great Question of the Age, 'How Can American Slavery Be Abolished?'"

As Boston's abolitionist community pushed into the theater-like seating arrangement of Tremont Temple, the space quickly became densely crowded, not entirely with abolitionists. The hall, like the nation, was divided between abolitionists and their opponents. Many anti-abolitionist Bostonians, some of them well-dressed members of the Cotton Whig business community, took prominent seats. Anti-abolitionist working-class street and tavern people, identified immediately by dress and tone, crowded the aisles. There were some intemperate Harvard students. Alcohol probably helped loosen tongues. As pro-abolition speakers, including Douglass, rose to the platform, jeers, shouting, and racial obscenities erupted. It was clear that the organizers of the meeting and its featured speakers were not going to be permitted orderly discussion. The policemen assigned to keep the peace had little interest in protecting abolitionists. What had been billed as a memorial meeting turned into a raucous free-for-all.

Voice: Where's the Union?

Sanborn: We come to discuss the subject of American slavery.

Voice: Where's John Brown?

Voice: He's safe.

Another voice: The devil has him.

Voice from the platform: No matter where he may be.

Sanborn: Every man is entitled to express his own opinion.

Cries: No! No! (Three cheers.)

Sanborn: Cannot every man say what he thinks at stated times and in proper places?

Cries: Yes! Yes! (Great noise.) And a few minutes later: Negro voices—We object. It is not right. It is not right.

Mayhem erupted. Speakers were shouted down. "Only Douglass, with his practiced and powerful bass voice, managed to make himself heard for more than a few moments above the din. He reached the podium and, defying the terrible threats of the crowd—Put him out! Down him! Put a rope round his neck!—shouted: This is one of the most impudent, (order! order!) barefaced, (knock him down! sit down!) outrageous attacks on free speech (stop him! you shall hear him!)—I can make myself heard—(great confusion) that I have ever witnessed in Boston or elsewhere. (Applause. Free speech.) I know your masters. (Cries—Treason! treason! Police! police! Put him out! put him out!) I have served the same master that you are serving. (Time! Time!) You are serving the slaveholders." Stomping feet from the anti-abolition gallery imitated boots on the march. A black minister was grabbed by the hair and pulled from the stage. Policemen attempted to either trap or arrest Douglass—it was not clear which. Men in top hats pummeled and were pummeled, people pulled and shoved, collars grabbed, bodies pushed and struck. Men and women shouted racial epithets from the boxes and the pit in a scene of disorder whose major ideological and emotional antagonism was between high- and low-class ruffians and well-dressed white and black abolitionists. It was a race riot of sorts. Orderly tragedy had been reduced to a disorderly historical drama.

When the disorder spread to the nearby streets, the police, unfriendly to all abolitionists and always keen to suppress disorder, secured the Tremont Street and Common area. Douglass and his colleagues rescheduled their meeting to a safer venue. "Boston is a great city," Douglass told his fellow abolitionists a few days later. "Nowhere more than here have the principles of human freedom been expounded. . . . And yet, even here, in Boston, the moral atmosphere is dark and heavy. The principles of human liberty, even if correctly apprehended, find but limited support in this hour of trial. The world moves slowly, and Boston is much like the world. We thought the principle of free speech was an accomplished fact. Here, if nowhere else, we thought the right of the people to assemble and express their opinion was secure. . . . But here we are to-day contending for what we thought was gained years ago. The mortifying and disgraceful fact stares us in the face, that though Faneuil Hall and Bunker Hill Monument stand, freedom of speech is struck down."

Wendell Phillips had made the same point in his coming-out speech in Faneuil Hall in 1837. He had made that constitutional right the keynote of his defense of Elijah Lovejoy. John Quincy Adams had made free speech and petition the grounds of his opposition to the gag rule. The more things changed, the more they remained the same. Now Douglass took up the same high constitutional note. It was the most available and amenable common ground. Still, the controlling issue was not free speech; it was slavery. And once again, as in 1837, the danger to life and limb increasingly came from speech on that subject.

AT HOME in December 1860 in his recently expanded, modest two-story house at Eighth and Jackson in downtown Springfield, Lincoln had to deal with the excitement, exhaustion, and challenge of having just been elected president. Springfield Republicans were at first in a chest-thumping mood, the streets crowded with parades, the air filled with speeches, the roads and railroad station thronged with visitors from near and far, the curious, the aspirational, and the self-interested. The city and its native son had triumphed. Prosperity, material and psychological, had suddenly been or was about to be increased hugely, or so many local people expected. "To-day, and till further notice, Mr. Lincoln will see visitors at the Executive Chamber in the State House, from 10 to 12 a.m., and from 3 1–2 to 5 1–2 p.m., each day," the *Illinois State Journal* had announced in mid-November. These were to be mostly fraternal and public relations sessions: jokes, anecdotes, backslapping, visitors from near and far, job seekers, autograph hunters, and the aggressively curious. Lincoln said almost nothing of anticipatory significance, despite pressure for guidance from friends and enemies around the country. His gut instinct and political savvy told him that he had everything to lose and nothing to gain by saying anything substantive about slavery and the state of the nation in addition to what he had already said.

He probably reread or remembered a private letter he had received six months before from a well-known Ohio congressman, Joshua Giddings. A veteran of more than twenty years of antislavery activism, a colleague of Adams' in the fight against the gag rule, Giddings had for decades been vilified as a radical abolitionist. He was anathema to Democrats and made moderate Whigs uncomfortable. Eager to declare Lincoln guilty by association, Stephen Douglas had repeatedly claimed in 1858 that Lincoln was a close ideological associate of "Father Giddings, the high priest of abolitionism." Lincoln spouted, Douglas asserted, as "radical [an] abolitionism as ever Giddings, Lovejoy or Garrison enunciated." Wendell Phillips and Frederick Douglass also made Stephen Douglas' list of infamy. "Did [Elijah's brother Owen] Lovejoy, or Lloyd Garrison, or Wendell Phillips, or Fred. Douglass" ever take higher abolition grounds than the two-faced Lincoln, who expressed himself differently in Southern and in Northern Illinois?

No one following the 1858 Senate campaign debates believed Lincoln was an abolitionist. But the accusation lent itself to sound bites for partisan advantage, a mid-nineteenth-century version of negative campaigning. Lincoln repeatedly labored to make clear that he deplored abolitionism and opposed civil rights for free Negroes. It was a challenge, though, also to argue that free blacks had the moral and constitutional right to be residents of Illinois. After all, where would one draw the line between residency and civil rights? By conviction and for political expediency, Lincoln had to try. He also made as light of the subject as he could, with humor and evasion. Giddings had always been far to the left of Lincoln on the subject. But by June 1860, convinced that "you are to be elected," Giddings was eager to close ranks with the man likely to be the first president who was an antislavery moralist and who had drawn the line against slavery extension. For abolitionists, this was only marginally better than tokenism, though much better than the electoral alternatives. For Giddings, a veteran of congressional antislavery battles, it was a way forward. And he did not think it presumptuous to weigh in with advice. "I am sure that any suggestions I may make will be respectfully considered."

Anticipating that Lincoln would be pressured between his election and inauguration in March 1861 to elaborate on his views about slavery and secession, Giddings urged him to resist. He invoked the example of the president about whom Lincoln had had almost nothing to say. "I think the administration of John Quincy Adams the wisest and purest on record. . . . After he became a candidate . . . he refused . . . to express any opinion to his most intimate friends until called to act officially. . . . If any question arises as to the detail or manner of carrying out that platform it will be one of such moment that you should reflect deeply upon it before you act[,] and no man has a right to demand of you an opinion until the question shall be practically before you. I refer to this subject from the conviction that enquiries may be propounded touching the question of slavery, as the public mind is most excited in that direction." Giddings also proposed Adams as a model of how to handle Cabinet and patronage appointments. "He used to say he never *condescended* to perform . . . the vexation and responsibility" of "appointing village post masters." The latter was not advice Lincoln could take. Party loyalty and political patronage were inseparable coordinates, keys to sustaining the Republican Party's newly formed base.

But the gist of Giddings' advice focused on the slavery issue. "One class of antislavery men are assailing me for voting for you. I can stand their assaults. I do not wish you to relieve me in any way. I would advise you to give no other answer to any man on that subject further than your intentions to carry out the doctrines of the party as expressed in their platform. Mr. Clay defeated himself and friends in 1844 by attempting to make his opinions acceptable to all. Let me advise you to avoid his example in that respect, and to follow that of Mr Adams."

In effect, keep your mouth shut on this matter for as long as you can. "The exercise of power always brings responsibility and is not to be courted by the prudent. I make these suggestions, not because I think they may not have occurred to you, but because from my past experience and observation, I know that the example of Mr Adams on these points will if followed enable you to enter upon your official duties (if elected) *untrammeled*, and free to act as your judgment and conscience may then dictate." Say nothing to commit yourself beyond the party platform. Keep your options open. In effect, do nothing more to exacerbate the pro-slavery or antislavery factions. Coming from a lifelong abolitionist, it was extraordinary advice. It implies that Giddings, like Adams, expected that some national cataclysm was likely, probably disunion, with or without a civil war. Lincoln continued to believe that disunion would never happen. The South would not secede; that was not in its interest.

Rationality and loyalty would prevail. After all, weren't there more pro-unionists than secessionists in the South?

The view from Springfield was clear about this. The threat of secession was a national danger, but it was exaggerated. It could be accommodated, as long as the South accepted nonextension with the assurance of the perpetuation of slavery where it still existed. Its "eventual extinction" would be so far off as to be more a rhetorical salve than an actual medicinal purge. Slavery would continue to exist as long as the Southern states insisted on it. Senator Lyman Trumbull read from a script Lincoln had written. "When inaugurated," Trumbull assured the South, referring to Lincoln in the third person, "he will be the President of the country and the whole country, and . . . will be as ready to defend and protect the State in which he has not received a solitary vote against any encroachment upon its constitutional rights, as the one in which he has received the largest majority. . . . No encroachments will be made on the reserved rights of any of the States." His administration will have "no more right to meddle with slavery in a State, than it has to interfere with serfdom in Russia. . . . It should be a matter of rejoicing to all true Republicans, that they will now have an opportunity of demonstrating to their political adversaries and to the world, that they are not for interfering with the domestic institutions of any of the States, nor the advocates of negro equality or amalgamation, with which political demagogues have so often charged them. . . . Should any Republican inquire what has been gained by the triumph of Republicanism, I answer, much. We have gained a decision of the people in favor of a Pacific Railroad, a Homestead policy, a judicious tariff, the admission into the Union of Kansas as a free State, a reform in the financial department of the government, and more important than all, the verdict of the people, the source of power, and from whose decision there is no appeal, that the constitution is not a slavery-extending instrument." All the South need do was accept nonextension. In exchange, it had a pledge of noninterference. Was this not fair, reasonable, and constitutionally sound? The South would, sooner than later, Lincoln expected, see the light.

In Lincoln's view, abolitionists were a disruptive minority best stayed away from, Giddings being the exception that proved the rule. Lincoln kept his correspondence with him as private as possible. The *Illinois State Journal* occasionally let names such as Douglass and Garrison seep into its columns, though not regularly and always dismissively. A constant newspaper reader, Lincoln was, as visitors to his temporary office at the Statehouse noticed, often absorbed in the national press. He was well aware of who the prominent abolitionists were and of their views. A few days after Wendell Phillips' secession-baiting speech in Boston about how little he expected from the Lincoln presidency, the *Journal* took notice under the headline "One Northern Sympathiser." Lincoln undoubtedly read the *Journal*'s story. "Wendell Phillips, the ultra-Abolitionist, is out with a speech denunciatory of Mr. Lincoln, Gov. Seward, and the Republican party. Mr. Phillips is one of a very few Northern men who hope to emancipate the slaves by overthrowing the government. The disunionists of the South will get no other 'aid and comfort' at the North." To Lincoln, abolitionists such as Phillips were as threatening to his highest priority, a Union-preserving peaceful solution to the threat of disunion, as were pro-secession fire-eaters such as Alabama's William Yancey.

Lincoln had, for the time being, no role to play other than to watch and wait. He had reason to worry, but he also believed that he had reason to be optimistic. Southerners had been threatening secession for decades, going back at least as far as the Missouri Compromise negotiations in 1819 and the Nullification Crisis in 1832. Why should these be anything more than threats now? After all, as Trumbull, Illinois' antidote to Stephen Douglas, told a huge crowd of Springfield supporters at a bonfire and fireworks celebration in mid-November 1860, the South Carolina fire-eaters were inflaming "the public mind by misrepresenting the objects and purposes of the Republican party, with the hope of precipitating some of the Southern States into a position from which they cannot, without dishonor, afterwards recede, well knowing, if they delay till after the new Administration is inaugurated and tested, it will furnish no cause for their complaints." The slave-owning South had nothing to fear. Its constitutional rights would not be abused, let alone denied. If the South accepted containment, all would be well.

Lincoln did not always and continuously expect Southern compliance. At times, he only hoped for it. Mostly, though, in the winter and into the spring of 1860/1861, he nervously assumed that reason, persuasion, and loyalty to the union would sufficiently motivate the South to remain in the union, or return to it quickly after the maximum pressure of temporary secession had been applied. At the same time and for quite some time, he allowed himself to look into the abyss: the intractability of the slavery problem. The South had a constitutional right to slavery's perpetuation. Northern public opinion had resolved into widespread moral disapproval. Equally, if not more important, free soil ideology and its economic aspirations demanded that the Western territories be reserved for white people only: certainly not for slaves; even free blacks were mostly unwelcome. But the abyss was deeper: the clash between the claim, with the Declaration as its holy text, that "all men are created equal," even if this did not mean that free Negroes had the right to be fully enfranchised citizens, and the fact of slavery. The Declaration and second-class citizenship (or no citizenship at all) were compatible. The Declaration was, though, not compatible with slavery.

And could the nation, Lincoln had asked publicly and prominently in 1858, exist indefinitely half slave and half free? He did not think so. Three years before, he had asked the same question in a private letter to a slave-owning Lexington, Kentucky, judge and politician, a fellow Whig who had orated about "the peaceful extinction of slavery." Lincoln had responded evasively to his own question: "The problem is too mighty for me. May God, in his mercy, superintend the solution." In his candid moments, he acknowledged that he had no faith in "'peaceful extinction'. . . . The condition of the negro slave in America . . . is now as fixed, and hopeless of change for the better, as that of the lost souls of the finally impenitent. The Autocrat of all the Russias will resign his crown, and proclaim his subjects free republicans sooner than will our American masters voluntarily give up their slaves." The problem was not solvable, but it could be postponed, provided that the South accepted nonextension.

As he waited in Springfield to assume the presidency, his public face registered optimism. After all, why should nonextension be so difficult for the South to swallow? Everything else could and would stay the same indefinitely. Clearly, Southern representation in the Senate made antislavery legislation impossible. And the Constitution made any change difficult to enact, the elimination of slavery by amendment almost an impossibility. What was there to worry about? As to the dissolution of the Union, secession had been threatened so many times before, starting with Jefferson's and Madison's "Kentucky and Virginia Resolutions" in 1799, that it had some resemblance to the boy who cried wolf. In 1844, Adams, writing to William Seward, who might have had some anticipation of where he and the country were heading, provided another of his many statements about where he believed the conflict between freedom and slavery would lead. The lust for Texas and the expansion of slavery were pointing the way. The South "is even now lunging us into a desperate war for Slavery, the issue of which can be no other than the dissolution of the Union, and an imperial race of Caesars under the name of Democracy. This is the evil."

Adams was being predictive; Lincoln, rational and optimistic. But the national division had its unmistakable parallel even in Lincoln's own Springfield. His hometown had narrowly split its presidential vote in his favor by only 59 votes. The *Illinois State Journal* had its oppositional counterpart, the *Register*, and its editorials exemplified the extreme polarization. Lincoln soon read in the *Journal* that "dispatches . . . advise us that the movement of the Southern States for a dissolution of the Union is assuming consistency and shape. Mr. Chestnut, of South Carolina, has sent his resignation as U.S. Senator to the Legislature, and a resolution was offered accepting it." A secession convention was scheduled in South Carolina. Other Deep South states were tending in the same direction. On the one hand, it seemed to the ultrarational and prudent Lincoln that secession was an absurdity, so against everyone's interests as to make dissolution of the union a national calamity to be avoided at almost all costs. On the other hand, elements in the South were pushing for it, and pushing hard. Still, it seemed to him that they were a minority, that pro-unionists outnumbered pro-secessionists. And if all that was at issue was nonextension, then the South and North ought to be able to reason together. The good sense of both would recognize that, since the Republicans could not retreat from nonextension but would accommodate the South in most other ways, all talk of secession, other than momentary rhetorical posturing, should be put aside.

Lincoln followed the daily barrage of widely reprinted newspaper dispatches from every area of the country, its wildly beating pulse captured in the diversity of moods and views on every side of the issue. The *Illinois State Journal* recommended to its readers a calming report from Washington's *National Intelligencer.* "During the last thirty years no Presidential election has occurred without the accompaniment of menaces directed against the perpetuity of the Union." This would prove another instance of the same. An angry pro-union border state newspaper excoriated South Carolina as an inveterate troublemaker: "This fountain-head of Tories, nullifiers, rebels, hot heads, fools, and traitors, has become the standard of Southern statesmen." That seemed increasingly the problem. "The truth is, that South Carolina never had a scintilla of wisdom, moderation or conservatism, and has now become completely deranged." South Carolina and its allies did not see it that way at all. The state was preparing to secede. It believed it had excellent cause. The underlying claim was that the Constitution was not a suicide pact. Lincoln's election and nonextension meant that slavery would gradually be brought to an end, sooner or later. The South had not signed on for that in 1787. The end of slavery would mean the death of the South, at least as all living Southerners and their ancestors had known it. That was the same as their own death. And after living with Negroes as slaves for so long, how could Southern whites safely live alongside Negroes if they were free? Though not all Southerners felt this way, most did. Efforts in Congress to forge a compromise failed, one after the other. And President James Buchanan's Cabinet was falling apart.

THE SUFFERING Buchanan was more attuned than Lincoln to the South at its primal level of concern. It was a matter not of intelligence or attention, but of ideology and personality. It was also a matter of sympathy. Lincoln could not quite understand what the South feared, let alone the nature of that fear, how painfully it registered on the South's collective nervous system and how deeply it penetrated into the bloodstream of slave owners. Buchanan could. Much was at risk: on the material level, the entire Southern economy. Without slaves to work the cotton fields, almost every aspect of the Southern economy, every thread of its rural and urban commerce, would collapse; the interwoven fabric of slavery and cotton was so pervasive that almost no aspect of Southern economic survival would be untouched. Yet that was not, as Buchanan recognized, the primary driver of Southerners' alienation.

The last president to be born in the eighteenth century, Buchanan had had a forty-year career in government more noteworthy for the distinguished positions he held than for his accomplishments other than his negotiation, as Polk's secretary of state, of the Oregon boundary treaty with Great Britain in 1846. It was a major accomplishment, though the credit only partly his. The treaty had been long in preparation, fully supported by Whigs and Democrats. Like Adams, Buchanan had started life as a Federalist. Unlike Adams, he turned to the Democrats and Andrew Jackson for career and fortune. A Pennsylvanian who became, as a senator, an ambassador, secretary of state, and then, in 1857, president, the capstone of his career, Buchanan demonstrated decency, modest competence, and a restrained and pacific personality. Liked though not highly regarded, he had no idea that his presidency would turn into a slow-frame nightmare for him and the country. For Lincoln and the Whigs, Buchanan's disaster proved a blessing. It made the Republican Party and made Lincoln president, as Lincoln very well knew when he read in the *Illinois State Journal* Buchanan's last annual State of the Union address.

Between 1855 and 1857, Buchanan handled badly the implementation of the Kansas-Nebraska Act, "bleeding Kansas," popular sovereignty, and the Lecompton Constitution. The result was the opposite of the pacification of the South he had intended. He and fellow Democrat Stephen A. Douglas became bitter enemies. Their party, by the summer of 1860, had split apart. In 1856, Buchanan pledged that he would not run for a second term. By the summer of 1860, a renomination of Buchanan would have been futile anyway. Events had made it impossible, even had Buchanan wanted it. All this was a great gift to Lincoln and the Republicans. Like Lincoln, Buchanan was an antislavery moralist. He also detested abolitionism, which he believed had set back the cause of gradual emancipation by a century. He also had no difficulty living with things as they were. Like Lincoln, he opposed civil rights for free Negroes. A moderate, small-government Democrat who believed that the Constitution severely limited the federal government, he had as his highest priority keeping the country together. The South needed to be ameliorated. With the *Dred Scott* decision happily in place in 1857, he supported the slaveholder's right to retain his property in slaves wherever he went in the United States and its territories. Slaves had always been and still were, by law, property.

Still, as he told Congress and the nation in his State of the Union address on December 6, 1860, things had now come to such a pass that he despaired that common sense, love of nation, and a commitment to mutual tolerance would prevail. "The different sections of the Union are now arrayed against each other, and the time has arrived, so much dreaded by the Father of his Country, when hostile geographical parties have been formed." But secession and a civil war, greater evils than any that currently existed, could be avoided. Actually, "how easy would it be for the American people to settle the slavery question forever and to restore peace and harmony to this distracted country!" Two palliatives, actually solutions, were at hand. "The long-continued and intemperate interference of the Northern people with the question of slavery in the Southern States has at length produced its natural effects." It had to stop. Beginning in 1835, Northern agitators had been directly and indirectly attacking the basis of Southern life. Abolitionists and their allies had caused the problem. "All that is necessary to accomplish the object, and all for which the slave States have ever contended, is to be let alone and permitted to manage their domestic institutions in their own way. As sovereign States, they, and they alone, are responsible before God and the world for the slavery existing among them." How sovereign were they? In Buchanan's view, very sovereign.

And why should these attacks on the Southern way of life drive the South to secession? Free labor versus slave labor? Nonextension? Those were not, Buchanan told Lincoln and the Republicans, as much as one might emphasize them, the deep root causes, the ultimate existential considerations. "The immediate peril arises" not as much from economic considerations as from the fact that "the incessant and violent agitation of the slavery question throughout the North for the last quarter of a century has at length produced its malign influence on the slaves and inspired them with vague notions of freedom. Hence a sense of security no longer exists around the family altar. This feeling of peace at home has given place to apprehensions of servile insurrections. Many a matron throughout the South retires at night in dread of what may befall herself and children before the morning. Should this apprehension of domestic danger, whether real or imaginary, extend and intensify itself until it shall pervade the masses of the Southern people, then disunion will become inevitable. Self-preservation is the first law of nature." From 1835 on, "pictorial handbills and inflammatory appeals" have been "circulated extensively throughout the South of a character to excite the passions of the slaves, and, in the language of General Jackson, 'to stimulate them to insurrection and produce all the horrors of a servile war.'" What were those horrors? Buchanan did not have to list them: murder, rape, miscegenation; black power shedding, drinking, and polluting white blood in the fields, the workroom, and the bedroom; a power structure turned upside down and inside out in the individual body and in the family, in the day-in, day-out social, economic, and physical relationships of Southern life. It was hard for a Southerner to contemplate. It was necessary to resist, to the death.

And to prevent secession, all the North needed to do was mind its own business about slavery. In return, all the South had to do, Buchanan urged, was accept that the Republican president had been elected according to the procedures set out in the Constitution. He was a legitimate president. He deserved, and the law required, that he be given the opportunity to exercise the duties of his office until he proved to be exercising them unconstitutionally. He had pledged to enforce the Fugitive Slave Law. Nonextension was not an imminent practical concern. Probably some compromise, over time, could satisfy both constituencies. The Constitution, Buchanan argued, neither gave the federal government the power to use force to coerce a seceding state to remain in or return to the union, nor gave any state the right to withdraw. So why not keep in place what exists? All the North needed to do would be to prevent antislavery agitation. After all, that was all the South had been asking for since 1835. And all the South needed to do was accept Lincoln as the legitimate president of the entire country until there was some constitutional reason to think otherwise.

In Springfield, as the calendar moved closer to the day of inauguration, Lincoln may have appeared "calm and collected," but he was not. The *Illinois State Journal* had printed the full text of Buchanan's State of the Union message. A few days later, Lincoln read in the *Journal* a devastatingly predictive account of what was to come, reprinted from the *Cincinnati Commercial*, in the Senate's response to Buchanan's plea. "On motion concerning the reference of the President's Message, [Joseph] Lane, of Oregon, made an apology for the dissolution of the Union, saying it must dissolve unless the rights of the South are further guaranteed. [John P.] Hale, of N.H., said the logic of this controversy is war or submission. The minority must submit to the majority. He made no threats, and spoke without having consulted anybody, he spoke for himself only and one little State. 'We must look this matter straight in the face.' [Albert G.] Brown, of Miss. desired to know if Hale presented the issue of war or submission. Hale said it must lead to that. He made no threat. Brown replied sternly: 'We will not submit, and if it is war[,] let it come, and God show the right.' [Alfred] Iverson, of Ga., was quiet at first, but haughty and defiant in the end. Mr. Iverson discarded all shams, saying that the election of Lincoln was no cause for secession; but the South would not be governed by the North, and intended to go out while she had strength, not to wait until she was too weak. Douglas sat scowling in his seat; Southern men looked cool. The Northern men were calm and collected."

An exhausted, depressed Buchanan went home to Wheatland, his Pennsylvania farm near Lancaster. His two indentured servants, formerly his slaves, packed his bags. True to habit and precedent, he had performed his final official duty graciously, the last of a long career, calling on Lincoln and escorting him to the inauguration ceremony on March 5, 1861. He would have agreed with the intention of the new president's prophylactic claim to the South: "We are not enemies but friends." He had been saying that all along. Differences over slavery did not require divorce. Lincoln agreed. Always personable and mostly good-humored, Buchanan had done all he was capable of to persuade the Democratic Party and the white nation to keep the peace. He did not believe that force of arms would solve the problem of slavery or secession. Coercion was unacceptable. But his plea that both sides desist from exacerbation and confrontation—that the South accept Lincoln, that the North resist further antislavery agitation—was rejected by both.

Listening to Lincoln's inaugural address, or reading it soon afterward, he knew, as did Lincoln, that the new president would have to deal with the reality of secession. South Carolina, Georgia, Mississippi, Florida, Alabama, Louisiana, and Texas would not retreat. A strong unionist who, once the inevitable had happened, supported the war, the ex-president was soon distressed to learn that he was being deemed a failed president who ought to have done more to prevent secession. Despite his flaws, it is an unfair criticism. Buchanan did not control events and their timing. He did attempt to supply and reinforce Fort Sumter in January 1861, the use of an unarmed merchant ship signaling to the South that he did not want to start a war. The ship was fired on and driven off anyway. And a plausible argument can be made that whatever he did or didn't do during his presidency, the war would have come. Conditions were in place, including Lincoln's mind-set, that made it inevitable. Southern leaders had decided that the South should and would sustain independence. Could any Republican president have controlled the forces at work that resulted in the refusal of the North to accept an independent Southern confederacy? Not likely. And slavery would still have required redress. By inference, that was the argument Lincoln was to make in his Second Inaugural Address, a month before his death. It was the war that John Quincy Adams had seen no way of avoiding.

WHILE SLAVERY controlled only one-third of the body of the nation, racism animated the national spirit. If there was anything that made slavery an intractable problem, it was this. There were, of course, other things: the Constitution, the Southern and national economies, the social and psychological realities of Southern life, the disinclination of the taxpayer to fund buyouts, and the unwillingness of Americans to have Negroes as fellow citizens, let alone neighbors. This brings the list back to racism. Abolitionists helped raise the consciousness and spread of antislavery moralism, but they had little effect on the widespread conviction that the Negro belonged to an inferior race. Slavery fed and nurtured all of Southern life; it contributed substantially to the economy of the North. And though it had varying gradations, complicated by the reality of free blacks and the mental gymnastics required by the contradiction between "all men are created equal" and slavery, it dominated the psyche and spirit of most Americans. Difficult as it would be to eliminate slavery, there was a more intractable, seemingly irresolvable problem: race.

Lincoln recognized this. Early on, he himself bought into the comfortable co-existence of antislavery moralism and racism in Illinois. That was the world he lived in. It was his mind-set also. That was where he was when he came to maturity as a young man in Illinois. That was where he was when the war started. There is no reason to believe that, at its end, he accepted blacks as equals, though he had begun, pressured by the obvious certainty that America would now be a multiracial nation, to make concessions to the new reality. And he knew, when in 1864 he began tentative efforts at reconstruction, proposing citizenship for a small number of blacks—those who had fought for the Union and the black leadership elite—that he was settling, by necessity, for second best. Colonization, if only it could be made practical, was still preferable.

In the winter of 1860/1861, as seven Southern states and then four more exited the Union, the new president had a number of consequential questions to ponder: whether a state had the right to secede, to revolutionize as he had affirmed in 1848; whether he could tempt or force the seceding states back into the Union; whether his voters would stick with him if he tried either approach; whether the seceding states could be bribed to return short of allowing slavery to be legal in the Western territories, a concession that he could not afford to make; what he could do to prevent additional states from seceding; and, if the newly created Southern Confederacy insisted on its separate sovereignty, under what circumstances he should attempt to coerce it back into the Union. If the Confederacy believed it had a right to take possession of Union property such as forts, what would be an effective response? From one point of view, that would be stealing. After all, federal property belonged to all the nation's taxpayers. And given his commitment to national sovereignty, subject to the provisions of the Constitution, how could he accept what he believed to be an illegal and unconstitutional abrogation of a contractual obligation? This was, in fact, a rebellion, and, as he had said to the House of Representatives in 1848, the majority had a right, in the interest of self-preservation and its own sovereignty, to suppress an illegal attempt by a minority to create an independent sovereignty.

There were three additional complicating factors. There was the moral dimension. The majority (or at least a legitimate plurality) of Americans disapproved of slavery. The rebels favored it. But the moral issues, other than nonextension, could be put on indefinite hold. There was also the political dimension. The Republican Party and its principles probably could not survive if the party did not affirm its legitimacy and its right to rule the nation as a whole. If it turned tail, it might never again elect a president. Then there was the constitutional dimension: Lincoln had been elected, fair and square, by the decision of the ballot box, according to the time-honored constitutional procedures. Did not a commitment to democracy require that his election be honored?

None of these considerations altered the reality of slavery or the racism that animated the spirit of the nation. But slavery was not the primary or even a major consideration in the decisions Lincoln needed to make in 1861. He had no reason to believe that the combined free black and slave populations, if and when emancipation occurred, would be accepted by white Americans as fellow citizens with equal rights, or that, if equality were mandated by law, it would not produce a century or more of vicious hostility. He himself never did and still did not believe a multiracial society desirable, let alone possible. Somehow the entire black population needed to be eliminated, the long-term problem of emancipation made to go away. Colonization was still the answer. Meanwhile, he had pressing life-and-death problems to deal with. As a practical matter, slavery was not one of them, except insofar as the seceding states had withdrawn from the Union in response to his and his party's determination that slavery should exist only where it already existed by constitutional and local sanction. If the South accepted that, there need be no conflict. To Lincoln's mind, his best approach was amelioration, and the main strategical concern was how much carrot and how much stick would be necessary to persuade the states that had seceded to return, and to keep the border states—Delaware, Maryland, Kentucky, and Missouri—from seceding. How much soft inducement and how much iron fist?

NINE

Soft Inducement

Lincoln favored soft inducement. So did his secretary of state, William H. Seward. The powerful senator from New York had, two years before, sent angry tremors rippling through the South, warning that an "irrepressible conflict" loomed. At the Republican convention in Chicago in May 1860, he had been the front-runner. But he had seemed too confrontational to the office-hungry majority. This was their time to elect a president. The more moderate Lincoln seemed more electable, though Southern analysts could see little difference between "irrepressible conflict" and "a house divided against itself cannot stand," Lincoln's most quotable phrase from his 1858 speech to the Illinois Republican Party.

But there was a great deal of difference, and the delegates to the nominating convention knew that. Seward had had good things to say about some abolitionists, he actively opposed the Fugitive Slave Act, and he claimed that there was a "Higher Law than the Constitution." Lincoln had never said anything positive about abolitionists, he favored enforcement of the Fugitive Slave Act, and he did not believe there was a law higher than the Constitution. Illinois spoke through Lincoln; New York, through Seward. The South had grounds on which to call Seward an abolitionist. Factual and fine distinctions, however, were not to the point. All Republicans were black abolitionists.

In May 1860, the Republicans, in their wood-constructed temporary convention hall seemed to some Southerners to have nominated a Negro for vice president and a renegade Southerner for president of the United States. That's how it looked to the editor of the *Charleston Mercury* and his fellow fire-eaters. Maine's swarthy Hannibal Hamlin, the vice-presidential nominee, "is what we call a mulatto," Robert Barnwell Rhett editorialized. "He has black blood in him." And Lincoln? "A renegade Southerner . . . a native Kentuckian." He was also suspiciously dark-skinned. Anyway, all Republicans were abolitionists, intent on depurifying the race; their mission was to insult and degrade the South.

To the surprise of many, Secretary of State–designate Seward became conciliatory between the election and Lincoln's inauguration in March 1861. He seemed no longer to believe in an "irrepressible conflict." His mentor John Quincy Adams had advised him in 1844 that the Southern threat of disunion "should operate as a warning for preparation, but not as a provocation to retaliate." But what to do about the fact that between the election and the inauguration, seven states, led by South Carolina, had seceded, and what to do about the siege of Fort Sumter in Charleston Harbor? Couldn't some compromise be devised? Couldn't something be worked out? After all, wasn't secession being fueled by a small number of hotheads? And wasn't there a great deal of pro-Union feeling throughout the South? And couldn't the issue of slavery expansion be finessed, since almost everyone detested abolition and abolitionists?

Numbers of senators, with Seward's encouragement, tried and failed. Like Seward, Lincoln also misunderstood the South. Its elite despised him and his secretary of state. To the South, Lincoln was a disloyal Kentuckian who fulfilled in caricature and life its projection of what a "Black Republican" should look like. At the same time, Southerners were baffled that a man born in Kentucky could not understand that any relationship between South and North would now have to be between independent equals.

An ameliorative Seward suggested revisions to the text of Lincoln's inaugural address, toning down sternness and consequences. Lincoln accepted most, including his secretary of state's major contribution, a new final paragraph that the president-elect revised into his memorable appeal to "the better angels of our nature." His own fraternal claim to the seceding states that "we are not enemies but friends" expressed his heart and his strategy. For the South, though, there was no going back. Lincoln assumed there was. He had convinced himself that the war could be avoided or aborted. It seemed fairly simple to him and Seward: you keep your slaves where they are, and we will all keep the Union as it has been. The issue is not slavery but union.

President James Buchanan, on March 6, 1861, escorted his successor from his hotel to the Capitol. They first went to the Senate chamber for the swearing in of the vice president, Hannibal Hamlin of Maine, an antislavery moralist less critical of abolitionist activists than Lincoln. "Mr. Buchanan and Mr. Lincoln entered, arm in arm, the former pale, sad, nervous; the latter's face slightly flushed, with compressed lips. For a few minutes, while the oath was administered," they sat next to each other. "Mr. Buchanan sighed audibly," the *New York Times* reporter noticed, "and frequently, but whether from reflection upon the failure of his Administration, I can't say. Mr. Lincoln was grave and impassive as an Indian martyr." On the Capitol portico, when the newly inaugurated president stepped to the lectern, the unfinished dome behind him topped by a crane, sharpshooters surveyed the crowd for potential assassins. His message was more velvet glove than iron fist. Exhausted and depressed, Buchanan dozed, perhaps too tired to notice that Lincoln said in substance much of what he himself had told Congress the previous December. Lincoln said it more cogently and eloquently.

The practical message was the same: Don't attack us, and we won't attack you, though you have taken possession of national property that doesn't belong to you. For the time being, we will make no fuss about that, with the exception of Fort Sumter in Charleston Harbor, which we want to resupply only with provisions, not with armaments. After all, you can't expect us to let the men there go without food and water. Other than that, and that only if we cannot work out some better arrangement, we will not give you cause to act in self-defense. If you are the aggressor, that will be another matter. For the time being we won't make a fuss about the property you have expropriated; we will not provoke you into military action; we will do our best to enforce the Fugitive Slave Act; and we will look to a better, more rational, more patriotic day when our differences will be resolved peacefully.

Lincoln got death threats from those who favored secession. Wendell Phillips, who had bodyguards and carried a gun, got death threats from those who favored union. Intent on offending almost everyone, North and South, Phillips proclaimed repeatedly that if slavery were the price for union, it was too high a price to pay. And Lincoln, it seemed to Phillips, loved union more than he hated slavery. That seemed the cardinal flaw in this wartime president. For much of 1861 and 1862, Lincoln's policy appeared to most abolitionists to have little or nothing to do with ending slavery. And he seemed not to be prosecuting the war energetically or effectively. In fact, Phillips told his large audience at the Grove in Abingdon, Massachusetts, in August 1861, "I believe Mr. Lincoln is conducting this war, at present; with the purpose of saving slavery. That is his present line of policy, so far as trustworthy indications of any policy reach us."

Phillips had reason to think so. The president appeared unwilling to act on what Phillips believed he well knew: "All civil wars are necessarily political wars—they can hardly be anything else. Mr. Lincoln is intentionally waging a political war. He knows as well as we do at this moment, as well as every man this side of a lunatic hospital knows, that, if he wants to save lives and money, the way to end this war is to strike at slavery." But did Lincoln really know this? And if he did, why did he not transform conviction into political and military action?

Furious at Seward for what seemed a betrayal of his previous abolitionist sympathies, Phillips could not be sure whom to blame more,

Seward or Lincoln. Conciliation seemed an evasion of moral responsibility and national destiny. "But you may also ask, if compromise be even a temporary relief, why not make it." He enumerated the reasons why not. "Because it is wrong. 2d. Because it is suicidal. Secession, appeased by compromise, is only emboldened to secede again to-morrow, and thus get larger concessions. The cowardice that yields to threats invites them. 3d. Because it delays emancipation." And, he warned the North, "compromise risks insurrection . . . the worst door at which freedom can enter. Let universal suffrage have free sway, and the ballot supersedes the bullet."

But now that war had come, it should be welcomed, he argued. It should be embraced; it was a positive good because it would end a positive evil. "In my view," he was to tell his audience at the Cooper Union in 1863, "the bloodiest war ever waged is infinitely better than the happiest slavery which ever fattened men into obedience. And yet I love peace. But it is real peace; not peace such as we have had; not peace that meant lynch-law in the Carolinas and mob law in New York; not peace that meant chains around Boston Court-House, a gag on the lips of statesmen, and the slave sobbing himself to sleep in curses. No more such peace for me; no peace that is not born of justice, and does not recognize the rights of every race and every man." Lincoln and Seward, for almost two years of a war that they did not fully embrace and did not seem to want to fight, were a bitter disappointment to Phillips and most abolitionists.

In 1861, Phillips kept Seward clearly in his sights. It was widely assumed that the secretary of state dominated the president. At first Lincoln seemed almost a nonentity. Phillips, though, had not given up hope that he might prove better than he seemed, if only he had the capacity to deal with the administration's two enemies, "Mr. Seward and the South." The secretary of state's "power is large. Already he has swept our Adams [Charles Francis, John Quincy's son] into the vortex, making him offer to sacrifice the whole Republican platform, though, as events have turned, he has sacrificed only his own personal honor. Fifteen years ago, John

Quincy Adams prophesied that the Union would not last twenty years. He little thought that disunion, when it came, would swallow his son's honor in its gulf."

Phillips hit both his major targets, Seward and South Carolina, squarely. The latter stupidly "fancies that there is more chance of saving slavery outside of the Union than inside." The South could never defeat the North, Phillips told his audiences. The "Slave Power" was defined by "the prejudice of race, the omnipotence of money, and the almost irresistible power of aristocracy." It was a feudal world without a middle class. How could it ever defeat the mighty engine of individual and economic initiative that defined the North? So, why not get on with it and fight the inevitable full-scale total war that would make the Union whole again and end slavery forever? Phillips' attack on Seward's efforts at compromise applied equally to Lincoln. Didn't Lincoln share Seward's views? The secretary of state says that the "first object of every human society is safety; I think the first duty of society is justice." And could justice be obtained within a Union that contained slavery?

With the responsibility of governing in a crisis, Lincoln and Seward had decided that the government had no obligation to provide justice to slaves. They were property. The Constitution protected property. It did not protect slaves as human beings. The founding document provided a legal rather than a moral blueprint, and the Declaration's claim that "all men are created equal" was not an absolute. For Lincoln and most white Americans, it depended on one's definition of "equal." Slaves were not. They had only a limited sanctuary under the Declaration's umbrella. And the Constitution, the controlling document, was not about justice and equality. It was a legal contract. The North, at almost every level, had from the start little or no political will to inject morality into economics and politics. Antislavery moralists as different as Jefferson and John Adams could not envision any practical plan for abolishing slavery in any state in which it was a major factor—except for colonization, which remained an unimplemented fantasy. In New England, and over time in Pennsylvania and New York—where farms were small, free labor dominant, and immigrants expanding the working, consuming, and voting population; and where trade, small factories, skilled artisans, shipping, insurance, and banking created a diversified economy—slavery could be eliminated, as long as it cost the taxpayer nothing and the free black population was kept small, with as few rights as possible. The South was a different story.

Much as Lincoln and Seward were antislavery moralists, to make the war about slavery would be, they were convinced, to steer a ship already in dangerous waters directly onto the rocks. Their priority was union. After all, Lincoln had already asserted, repeatedly, that, in Illinois, free blacks were not equal to free whites. And justice for slaves was not a priority for the Lincoln administration; union was. Phillips would not, could not, make that distinction. The Union, with slavery, had no moral basis for continuing to exist. The divisive slavery issue could be resolved, he believed, by absorbing into the national body politic the four million slaves who were to be emancipated. Racism could be eliminated with the creation of an amalgamated race whose prototype was the mulatto. The commingling of bloodlines, especially in the South, had already made the distinction between black and white difficult to determine or sustain. Though not all white abolitionists had a post-racist vision, Phillips had. That vision was anathema to Lincoln. On the one hand, he detested slavery. On the other, like most of his fellow citizens, he wanted to continue to live in an all-white America. He could hardly imagine anything else.

In New York City, on a warm day in May 1863, two months before the Union victory at Gettysburg and the fall of Vicksburg, Wendell Phillips walked up to the same stage at the Cooper Union from which Lincoln, in 1860, had delivered a memorable address. Concluding the speech that had helped propel him to the Republican nomination, Lincoln had proclaimed, "Let us have faith that right makes might, and in that faith, let us, to the end, dare to do our duty as we understand it." But how was "right" to be defined? Lincoln and Phillips were on different pages. The influence of Henry Ward Beecher, the most prominent American clergyman, hovered in the background of both speeches. The Beecher family—from Edward Beecher, Elijah Lovejoy's strong supporter in 1837; to Harriet Beecher, whose antislavery but pro-colonization novel had become a national best seller; to the dynamic Henry at his prominent pulpit in Brooklyn—had established itself as America's first family of Northern antislavery intellectuals. In 1860, Lincoln had been scheduled to speak at Henry Ward Beecher's Pilgrim Church in Brooklyn Heights. Since Beecher's views were incompatible with those of moderate Republicans, influential New York Republicans, eager to promote Lincoln for the national ticket, had at the last minute changed the venue to the Cooper Union. By May 1863, New York had an even greater abolitionist cohort than ever: the war and the January 1, 1863, Emancipation Proclamation had changed the calculus for almost everyone.

The previous Sunday, Henry Ward Beecher had set the stage for Phillips' 1863 address. A consummate showman, Beecher, at the end of his baptismal ceremony before thousands of congregants, had "carried up into the pulpit a little girl about five years of age, of sweet face, light hair, and fair as a lily. Pausing a moment to conquer his emotion, he sent a shiver of horror through the congregation by saying, 'This child was born a slave, and is just redeemed from slavery!' It is impossible to describe the effect of this announcement," the *New York Times* reported the next day. The astounded "spectators held their breath in amazement, and were then melted to tears." The child appeared totally white, an exemplification of the irony Mark Twain later dramatized in *Pudd'nhead Wilson*, the story of a white-skinned black child and a white child, born on the same day in the same household, who were exchanged in the cradle, the black child brought up as white, the white child as black. Who could tell the difference?

The next week, the Cooper Union overflowing with antislavery moralists and abolitionist sympathizers, Phillips took the stage. Should Lincoln, should the Republican administration, Phillips asked, still continue to try to conciliate the South? Shouldn't it clarify its mixed-message policy about how to deal with slaves who fled through the battle lines, mostly in the border states, to what they believed would be freedom? Were they contraband of war? Or should they be returned to their owners, if their owners were pro-Union? The president inched forward on this matter. To the disappointment of many, the Emancipation Proclamation, issued on January 1, 1863, had freed slaves only in the states that had seceded. Congress and some Union officers were pressuring Lincoln to stop trying to mollify the border states.

In a dramatic gesture, Philips then led forward onto the stage, the *Times* reported, "the little white slave-girl baptised by Mr. BEECHER last Sunday." The audience erupted into wild applause. "There is a party for whom I have conciliation and this is its representative. . . . In the veins that beat now in my right hand, run the best blood in Virginia of the white race and the better blood of the black race of the Old Dominion—[applause]—the united race to whom in its virtue belongs, in the future, a country by the toil and the labor of its ancestors redeemed from nature and given to civilization and the Nineteenth Century. [Applause.] For that class I have ever an open door of conciliation—the labor, the toil, the muscle, the virtue, the strength, the democracy of the Southern States. This blood represents them both." The next day, the *Times* published a transcription of Phillips' speech. Phillips hoped for the multiracial America of future centuries. An optimist and a revolutionary, he thought it would work out for the best. The conservative Lincoln, an heir to Calvinistic pessimism, with a darker view of human nature, worried that it would be a disaster.

WHAT TO do in 1861–1862? The president had an ongoing military disaster on his hands: the Union was suffering a series of defeats. Rectification, in the minds of those who worried that the war was being lost or at least unnecessarily extended, resided in three areas in which Lincoln appeared to be laggard: the tenure of his commanding general, George McClellan; the extent of the president's power under the Constitution as a wartime commander in chief; and the shortage of manpower for the military, aggravated by Lincoln's refusal to allow free blacks to enlist. No doubt the war was going badly for the North. An end date for a Union victory seemed to be receding into the indefinite future. Confederate armies and the Southern population were maintaining their will to fight to victory or the bitter end. Divided public and political opinion in the North made the national unity required to win the war worrisomely questionable.

During 1861 and 1862, the search for effective military leadership became a battleground of its own. There was the problem of General George McClellan. He seemed more committed to the parade ground than the battlefield. Constantly overestimating the size of the enemy army, he declined to fight without reinforcements, which he knew to be unavailable. And he was not in the least in sympathy with antislavery views of any sort, including Lincoln's antislavery moralism. His tolerance for slavery and antipathy toward Negroes had a nasty edge: "I confess to a prejudice in favor of my own race, and can't learn to like the odor of either Billy goats or niggers." To Lincoln, McClellan's racism was as irrelevant as Usher Linder's had been. A pro-slavery Democrat, the general disagreed with the administration's refusal to conciliate the South over slavery expansion; he despised Lincoln, whom he thought an uncouth fool, "nothing more than a well-meaning baboon"; and as events developed, he was not averse to becoming president himself in the election of 1864. Many agreed with his conviction that he was more qualified than Lincoln to lead the nation. Like his commander in chief, McClellan recognized that the South's fear of further limitation on the extension of slavery and of an antislavery president who would undermine slavery where it already existed had motivated secession. Unlike Lincoln, he favored conceding to the South slavery's extension and moral legitimacy.

That he was not Lincoln's first choice for commander of the Army of the Potomac did not lessen the reality that McClellan should not have been the choice at all. He was not a man eager to take battlefield initiatives, and this inclination expressed his political and ideological convictions as well as his personality. Usually a good judge of men, Lincoln misjudged McClellan, who was talented at organization but reluctant to do battle, a proponent of the superiority of defensive strategies. Vainglorious and cocksure, he had absolute faith in his superior judgment. Lincoln appears not to have fully vetted McClellan, his personality, his previous record, or his political values. Or perhaps Lincoln knew them well enough but felt he had no better alternative. Hindsight makes vivid McClellan's unsuitability, but there was a lack of foresight. How could Lincoln have imagined that a pro-slavery commander would vigorously prosecute a war against the South? Apparently, McClellan's pro-slavery views hardly mattered because Lincoln, anyway, had no intention of using the military to end slavery. The general and the president shared the view during the war's first two years that the army should respect slaves as private property, to be returned to their owners whenever practical. Eventually Lincoln consented to treating them as contraband, though he was not keen on this, partly because he wanted a consistent policy, mostly because he wanted desperately to placate the border states.

Though McClellan's self-confidence, organizational skills, and spit and polish dazzled some Northern elites, Wendell Phillips had no doubt that he was the wrong man for the job. His pro-slavery convictions were anathema. Lincoln's commitment to McClellan made the president also seem the wrong man for the job. When Winfield Scott, the longtime general in chief, resigned in November 1861, Lincoln elevated McClellan. Scott had doubts, especially when McClellan opposed Scott's grand strategy for defeating the Confederacy, his "Anaconda Plan," which became the template for the Union's eventual success, with a less credible plan of his own. Phillips, though, didn't mince words in a speech he gave in New York and Boston in December 1861. His extreme language was directed at Lincoln as much as at Lincoln's general:

> *McClellan is a traitor [though not literally]but I say this, that if he had been a traitor from the crown of his head to the sole of his foot, he could not have served the South better than he has done. . . . He could not have carried on the war in more exact deference to the politics of that side of the Union. And almost the same thing may be said of Mr. Lincoln,—that if he had been a traitor, he could not have worked better to strengthen one side, and hazard the success of the other. . . . The war can only be ended by annihilating that oligarchy which formed and rules the South and makes the war,—by annihilating a state of society. No social state is really annihilated, except when it is replaced by another. Our present policy neither aims to annihilate that state of things we call "the South," made up of pride, idleness, ignorance, barbarism, theft, and murder, nor to replace it with a substitute. Such an aimless war I call wasteful and murderous.*

Even Phillips recognized that *traitor* was too strong a word. But he had a steely, perceptive, and prophetic argument.

With two successes in minor skirmishes in West Virginia, the relatively unknown McClellan had seemed to Lincoln and Northern public opinion, rattled by defeat at Bull Run, a military savior. With Confederate forces in sight of Washington, McClellan's organizational skills, it was thought, could provide the capital's nervous establishment with a much-needed defense system. But by early 1862, the McClellan problem, including insubordination, needed to be solved. Lincoln procrastinated. Worried that removing McClellan from command would "send ripples of mutiny" through the army, he did not grasp sufficiently or soon enough that insubordination generally leads to more insubordination, failure to more failure. In November 1862, after more than a year had been mostly wasted, he removed McClellan from command.

Over time and at great cost, Lincoln had discovered his mistake. McClellan's failures eventually forced the president to do what he had tried hard to avoid. Few in the Union establishment had cared that McClellan's war would keep slavery intact, protect Southern slave property, and persuade the Confederacy back into the union on modified pro-slavery terms. This was, of course, Lincoln's initial policy also. Circumstances he could not control gradually forced him to change it. Confederate victories in 1861–1862 guaranteed that the war would be long, the casualties huge, the outcome uncertain, and the consequences, short of quick and total victory, damaging to the president and his party. That there seemed to Lincoln no better alternative to McClellan was partly because the cream of the U.S. military, almost all West Point graduates, were Southerners. The non-Southerners were mostly thin milk. The best officers changed their uniforms from blue to gray. That reality underlined Lincoln's predicament regarding military leadership in March and April 1861.

It does not, though, dismiss larger issues about his judgment and vision. When he at first offered command of the Union armies to the Virginian Robert E. Lee, hoping that Lee would remain loyal to the Union, it clearly made no difference that Lee was a slaveholder and a representative of the Southern elite. "We are not enemies but friends." Slavery was not the issue. Though Lee was not an enthusiastic secessionist, Lincoln should not have been surprised that he was more loyal to Virginia than to the Union. That was a given of the Southern state of mind, with some exceptions, few of them in the military. And as the Southern-inflected cream of the Union military committed itself to the Confederacy, it ought to have been clear to Lincoln that he might have a long war ahead of him, that McClellan was not an exemplary choice, that the war would require him to be creative with the Constitution in order to make full use of his war powers, and that slavery could not possibly remain a matter secondary to the conduct of the war. His every virtue and talent acknowledged, Lee was not about to give up his slaves. But until the South made clear that this was war to the death, emancipation was not Lincoln's priority.

That Lincoln hoped to keep Virginia and Lee in the Union is understandable. But it was unrealistically wishful to think that Southern loyalties, even when split, would allow state-proud Southerners to side with Yankee foreigners. Lincoln's, though, was not simply a naive mistake. It expressed his emotional and intellectual conviction. It was a combination of wishful thinking, unrealistic hope, and commitment to a white America. That pro-Union Southerners, with the exception of a fragile majority in the border states, would resolve their dual loyalty in favor of the Union was a delusion with a basis. After all, Lincoln could rationalize, he was still offering the South an all-white America. Why not stay in the Union? It seemed a reasonable expectation to a Kentucky-born resident of Central Illinois. And wasn't Virginia a border state? Actually, Virginia's statewide heart, despite its geographic location, was irrevocably Southern and pro-slavery. Rejecting Lincoln's offer and renouncing his U.S. citizenship did not feel to Lee nearly as much like treason as fighting against the Confederacy would have felt.

While the Southerners' view of Lincoln as a tyrant and the abolitionists' view of him as an ameliorative laggard embody extremes, abolitionists such as Phillips were closer to the reality. Each side, of course, had an axe to grind. The Southern view of Lincoln, as the war began, had its basis in disappointment and anger: why will he not let us alone to go our own way? The basis of the abolitionists' view was similar: Why will he not recognize that the South has forced on us the opportunity to end slavery? That requires total war, not conciliation. And if he will not grab the bull by the horns, we had rather dissolve the Union and have for the first time a slave-free though smaller nation.

In August 1862, Phillips repeated his position and his view of the president: "I never did believe in the capacity of Lincoln, but I do believe in the pride of [Jefferson] Davis, in the vanity of the South, on the desperate determination of those fourteen States; and I believe in a sunny future, because God has driven them mad; and their madness is our safety. They will never consent to anything that the North can grant; and you must whip them, because, unless you do, they will grind you to powder." Lincoln, Phillips correctly predicted, eventually would have no choice but to fight robustly. And to fight a total war against the South, Phillips believed, required enlisting free blacks in the Union army and encouraging enslaved blacks to undermine the Confederate war effort. McClellan, Phillips argued in August 1862, needed to be disposed of. "I do not believe," he told his audience, "that in his heart [Lincoln] trusts McClellan a whit more than I do." But "from fear of the Border States and Northern conservatism he keeps him at the head of the army."

LINCOLN CONSTRAINED himself by his core strategy regarding the Confederacy and the border states. In 1861 and 1862, he thought he could persuade and cajole the South into peace. If that meant leaving slavery in place, he would accept it as the necessary price to pay. And it would be politically viable, if not advantageous. The Republican Party platform had demanded not the end of slavery but only nonextension, and many Northerners would have been willing to compromise even on that. But the Deep South, regardless of internal tensions, was irrevocably committed to independence, much as the Founding Fathers had been in 1776. They were the rebels and revolutionaries the Confederacy took as the model of and sanction for its own rebellion. That the Southern states could be cajoled or bribed back into the Union was obviously nonsense from the start. That the war could be won without black soldiers and emancipation seemed unlikely from early on, especially after the defeats at Bull Run, Manassas, Antietam, and Fredericksburg.

Lincoln's strength was his determination to stay the course. He was, though, committed to an ineffective strategy for close to two years. It took him eighteen months to begin to accept that an end to the war would come only with the total defeat of the South. Months of war might have been saved if he had been more realistic about the South at the start. However difficult it would have been to do the necessary things in 1861, it may have been no more difficult than when he finally came around in 1863. At first, Lincoln, the prudent lawyer with a deep commitment to compromise, the letter of the law, and rational persuasion, was indeed, as Phillips and most abolitionists thought, the wrong man for the job: a well-intentioned but conflicted Midwesterner whose heart was in maintaining the status quo rather than in seizing the opportunity to eradicate slavery, which Phillips rightly believed to be the key to Union victory.

Lincoln's commitment to do everything possible to keep the four proslavery border states—Missouri, Kentucky, Maryland, and Delaware—from joining the Confederacy was an essential part of his core strategy. It required him to make clear that he would not force them to end slavery. This approach, he assumed, would also neutralize those Northerners who opposed the war. If, by mid-1862, he had explained to the North that the quickest way to win the war, with the least cost in money and lives, was to deal a mortal blow to the Southern war effort by making all slaves legally free, would that not have undercut Northern racist opposition to emancipation, especially among antiwar Democrats? Without slave labor, he could have argued, the South could not support its armies in the field and its civilians at home. This would have made clear that it was exclusively a war to save the Union, emancipation a strategy, not an end. But to observers to Lincoln's left, it seemed unmistakable that his conciliatory attempt to shore up the pro-Union forces in the border states would prolong, not shorten, the war. Worse, it was a misjudgment about how best to win. Each of the border states had its own internal civil war to fight, its pro-Union and pro-Confederacy contingents at odds. But even in Missouri, a state crucial in the history of contention over slavery, the pro-Union forces seemed to have the upper hand.

Was there ever a real danger that any of the four border states would become an asset to the Confederacy? None was a cotton state. At worst, they would be secondary battlegrounds, with neither side entirely victorious. At best and more likely, Union sentiment would dominate. Maryland and Delaware could never become significant Confederate assets, let alone Confederate states. Geography and demography were against that. In Kentucky, Union sentiment, even when it was also pro-slavery, was strong, and slavery as a social and economic institution had much less presence and importance than in the Deep South. Union military power and pro-Union sentiment would have kept three of the four border states in the Union even if Lincoln and Congress had abolished slavery there, especially if slave owners were compensated financially, as Lincoln proposed. Missouri was a different matter. It was indeed a battlefield. Geography partly favored its pro-Confederacy contingent—but only partly. And, early on, Union military superiority made it clear that Missouri would not be joining the Confederacy.

Why, then, do so much to placate the pro-slavery element in the border states? It was not necessary, and it kept Lincoln from taking decisive action until 1863 to increase the manpower of the Union army and further destabilize Southern society by communicating to the slave population that their masters would not be their masters much longer. By early 1863, Lincoln, Phillips conceded, had begun to do what had to be done, but hesitantly and within narrow limits. He continued to advocate colonization and compensated emancipation, both of which had all along been nonstarters.

To the admonition of Horace Greeley, the influential editor of the Republican *New-York Tribune,* that it was now necessary to "fight slavery with liberty" and not fight "wolves with the devices of a sheep," Lincoln answered, in August 1862, that his "paramount object in this struggle *is* to save the Union, and is *not* either to save or to destroy slavery." Phillips had gotten Lincoln right. "If I could save the Union without freeing *any* slave I would do it, and if I could save it by freeing *all* the slaves I would do it; and if I could save it by freeing some and leaving others alone I would also do that. What I do about slavery, and the colored race, I do because I believe it helps to save the Union; and what I forbear, I forbear because I do *not* believe it would help to save the Union." Though Lincoln had already written and discussed with his Cabinet in July 1862 a draft version of his "Preliminary Emancipation Proclamation," issued in late September 1862, there is no reason to doubt that he sincerely meant every word he wrote to Greeley. It was not a clever attempt to prepare Northern opinion to accept the Emancipation Proclamation itself. It was one more effort on Lincoln's part to bring the Southern states back into the Union fold.

The Preliminary Emancipation Proclamation invited the seceding states to rejoin the Union, to restore, as Lincoln put it, "the constitutional relation between the United States, and each of the states" in which "that relation is, or may be suspended, or disturbed." That relation included slavery. If the seceding states chose to return, the four million slaves in the South could remain slaves for the time being. The states would receive "pecuniary aid" from Congress, which they could choose to decline. The money would be offered only to states no longer "in rebellion against the United States, and which states, *may* [my italics] then have voluntarily adopted, or thereafter *may* [my italics] voluntarily adopt, immediate, or gradual abolishment of slavery . . . and that the effort to colonize persons of African descent, with their consent, upon this continent, or elsewhere . . . will be continued." It would be used to pay compensation to slave owners and the costs of colonization. But no slave state had to become a free state immediately. "Thereafter" would do. "Gradual abolishment" required no starting or completion date. And the word *may* provided an escape hatch. If a state at issue did not pledge to abolish slavery immediately or had not pledged to abolish slavery at some time in the future, would it still be welcomed back into the Union? Would it be able to restore its representation in Congress and participate in national elections? And would a "slave" still count as three-fifths of a person in congressional and Electoral College representation? It seems so. Given the looseness of the language of Lincoln's offer and the possibility of semi-compliance or evasion, slavery might continue to exist indefinitely.

Its terms, consistent with Lincoln's lifelong approach to the slavery problem, were sincerely offered. If the South had accepted, there would have been no Emancipation Proclamation in January 1863. How would it have been possible for Lincoln, as honorable a man as we have ever had in national politics, to renounce his own offer? And there would have been no more casualties. It was a carrot-and-stick approach. Emancipation would not apply to any states that returned to the Union. It would apply only to states that "shall then be in rebellion." In every state that gave up armed rebellion, and in all if they all should, slavery would remain intact. If all the seceding states returned, there would be no Emancipation Proclamation at all. In effect, in September 1862, Lincoln said to the Confederacy: Accept these comparatively easy terms. If not, then I will raise the stakes to the next level, encouraging slave rebellion by emancipating your slaves and enlisting free blacks into the Union military.

If the South had agreed to Lincoln's offer in September 1862 he would have been pledged to its consequences. It's also likely that he would have lived to serve a full second term. If the Confederacy had accepted Lincoln's proposal, it's unlikely there would have been a Thirteenth, Fourteenth, or Fifteenth Amendment to the Constitution, at least within much if not all of the nineteenth century. The return of Southern congressmen to national government would have prevented that. Moderate Whig and then Republican policies would have been affirmed: no extension of slavery, but the continuation of slavery in the states in which it existed, with the expectation that, over time, with compensation, emancipation would occur, master by master, slave by slave, a variation on traditional individual manumissions. Racial incompatibility between whites and free blacks would be alleviated by gradual colonization. America might no longer have a race problem.

Paradoxically, abolitionists such as Phillips and Garrison welcomed the Preliminary Emancipation Proclamation—but not because they liked the terms. On the contrary, to abolitionists they were abhorrent. But for the first time ever they committed the federal government to the elimination of slavery. A Republican victory in 1860 and Southern secession had made that possible. The war, therefore, was a blessing. Since slavery was a glitch in the machine of economic and moral progress, the nation had to be rebooted, slavery eliminated. Whether Lincoln desired to be its instrument or not, by the very fact of the position he was in, he had no choice, in Phillips' view, but to play the role that the situation had forced on him. Every move the president made, whose purpose was to preserve the Union intact, made emancipation, Phillips realized, an inevitable consequence of the war to save the union. Consequently, by late summer 1862, Phillips and Garrison had become partial Lincoln enthusiasts. The endgame of slavery was well under way—for it seemed a certainty to anyone who had felt the pulse of the Confederacy or who had listened to Southern voices that it would reject the terms of the Preliminary Emancipation Proclamation out of hand.

Would any or all of the four border states, in September 1862, have joined the Confederacy if Lincoln had issued not his Preliminary Emancipation Proclamation but a version of the January 1863 Emancipation Proclamation—or, even better, a comprehensive version that included all slaves, not just those in the rebellious states? They had neither the means nor the will to do so. And by January 1863, it was even more unlikely. If

Lincoln had explained to the North that the war had not been initiated to free the slaves but that, in mid-1862, the quickest way to end it would be to deal a mortal blow to the Southern war effort by making all slaves legally free, would that not have undercut Northern racist opposition to emancipation, even among Democrats? In late summer 1862, when it was already clear that this would not be a short war, he could have argued that the South could not support its armies in the field and its civilians at home without slave labor. Indeed, as more and more slaves learned that they were legally free by federal law, many began to limit their contributions to the Confederate war effort. Those in close proximity to Union army lines liberated themselves. Those fit to serve the Union cause seized the opportunity. Congress, through legislation, had already encouraged this with two Confiscation Acts, one in the summer of 1861, another in the summer of 1862. They defined slaves (with an ironic twist to the long-standing claim that slaves were property) as property to be forfeited if used to support the rebellion or freed by criminal court proceedings if their owners were in rebellion.

Lincoln worried about the effect of the Confiscation Acts on his border state strategy. Though he signed them, he had neither his legal mind nor his moral heart in them. As a conservative lawyer, having begun to worry that the Supreme Court might uphold the Constitution's protection of slavery, he wanted greater assurance of constitutional legality. He also wanted a legally tidier, more structurally comprehensive approach. And he did not want to scare the border states into alienation. Lincoln's penchant for persuasion, prudence, and compromise exemplifies what in this instance was his executive weakness: his lifelong legislator's and lawyer's preference for the middle way. It had served him well and brought him to the presidency. It was sensible for him to fear bold action and its semi-dictatorial potential. But for almost two years he had failed to grasp that the Southern elite were now implacable enemies, that the die had been cast, that bold action was likely to be more in the nation's interest than the slow, slogging alternatives.

Also, misjudging the Southern resistance to what appeared rational and logical to him, he does not seem until very late to have realized that his plan for compensated emancipation could not succeed. In addition, compensated emancipation required colonization, never rational or practical for four million slaves. "Lincoln had long assumed," incorrectly, "that his Kentucky birth, his Border state in-laws, and his long years among the Southerners who had migrated to Southern Indiana and Southern Illinois gave him a special insight into the mind of the Upper South." Actually, he had little experience with the Southern elite, and little capability to understand its values and traditions. It took him two years to accept that the South was determined to fight until the bitter end even when it became increasingly certain that secession would result in what the South had gone to war to prevent.

LINCOLN USED his war powers authority in 1861 and 1862 to suspend habeas corpus (the right of a citizen who is under arrest to have a speedy judicial hearing) in cases of rebellion or invasion. He suspended it in the sensitive Baltimore-Washington area, inhabited by many and infiltrated by some Southern sympathizers, and he later suspended it in order to arrest individuals urging resistance to enlistment or inciting draft riots. The Constitution itself does not use the phrase "war powers," though by the 1840s it had become shorthand for the commander in chief's authority to suspend habeas corpus and use the military to repress rebellion, repel invasion, and act to maintain the peace and protect the security of the nation, subject to court challenge or congressional correction. For "the United States shall guarantee," the federal Constitution states, "to every State in this Union a Republican Form of Government, and shall protect each of them against Invasion; and on Application of the Legislature, or of the Executive (when the Legislature cannot be convened), against domestic violence." Certainly secession was "domestic violence."

Why would Lincoln have used his war powers from the start of the war to suspend habeas corpus but not to emancipate slaves? If he had the power to do one, he had the power to do the other, and any weakening of the slave-based Southern economy would have helped the Union suppress rebellion and domestic violence. The rebellion and the war zone included the entire South. Arguably, it included the entire country. Lincoln's notion of the limited relationship between his power as commander in chief in wartime and the Constitution was noticeably confined to the subject of slavery. There is every reason to believe that the Republican Congress would have been compliant. Lincoln worried, though, about the Supreme Court.

A brilliant logician and capable historian, Lincoln knew well enough the theory of presidential war powers and the historical record. The precedents originated in 1794 with President Washington's suppression of the Whiskey Rebellion, the armed resistance by farmers in Western Pennsylvania to paying distilling taxes. Between 1807 and 1809, President Jefferson and a compliant Congress instituted a form of national martial law to enforce the Embargo Acts. Much of the country, especially New England, refused to obey the acts: how could a commercial, a trading, and a seafaring people keep food on the table if they could not sell or trade with foreign countries as close as Canada and the West Indies and as far away as Europe? Convinced that by depriving England and France of agricultural products he could force them to respect American maritime rights and the freedom of the seas, Jefferson persuaded Congress to pass Embargo Acts, which at their most extensive prevented trade between the United States and all foreign countries. England and France, though, had other sources of produce and lumber. The embargo devastated crucial segments of the American economy. Human nature and necessity asserted themselves. To keep food on the table, to remain economically viable, Americans evaded and broke the laws. By executive order, Jefferson exerted the full power of the federal government to enforce them.

With time of the essence, he did not believe he needed court orders to seize property and arrest suspects. In effect, he suspended due process and other constitutional protections.

To what extent does the Constitution give a president the power to suspend its provisions when he believes peace and security are threatened by domestic violence or external attack? To a considerable extent, depending on the degree to which the president has convinced himself and can, sooner or later, persuade Congress, the Supreme Court, and the country that the situation in which and the degree to which he exercises his power justify the actions he takes. In 1861 and 1862, the answer seemed a no-brainer to those in the abolitionist tradition. The historical precedents were clear. The answer seemed obvious to many, from abolitionist sympathizers to moderate antislavery Republicans: once rebellion was a political and military fact, total emancipation, black Union soldiers, and Union victory were interlocked necessities.

When South Carolina initiated secession, how strong was the country's memory of Jefferson's use of the Constitution's war powers? "Let me remind you," Wendell Phillips told the North in December 1861, "that seventy years' practice has incorporated it as a principle in our constitutional law, that what the necessity of the hour demands, and the continued assent of the people ratifies, is law. . . . I will cite an unquestionable precedent. It was a grave power, in 1807, in time of peace, when Congress abolished commerce; when, by the embargo of Jefferson, no ship could quit New York or Boston, and Congress set no limit to the prohibition. It annihilated commerce. New England asked, 'Is it constitutional?' The Supreme Court said, 'Yes.' New England sat down and starved. Her wharves were worthless, her ships rotted, her merchants beggared. She asked no compensation. The powers of Congress carried bankruptcy from New Haven to Portland; but the Supreme Court said, 'It is legal,' and New England bowed her head." Lincoln may not have read Phillips' speech, but he knew the history and the issue.

In addition, there had been throughout the 1840s debates in Congress about the war powers of the presidency. The national crisis that had been at issue was slavery, as it was to be in 1861–1862. The incendiary events of the 1830s and '40s had produced the lawlessness that Lincoln condemned in his Springfield Lyceum speech in 1838. Much of it had been generated by tension over slavery. Slave insurrections; anti-abolitionist riots; pro-slavery activities against free speech leading to the gag rule; the martyrdom of Elijah Lovejoy; the rise of an active abolitionist movement; the national debates in Congress and in the press in which tempers flared into verbal violence; the Wilmot Proviso (an attempt in Congress to prohibit slavery in the territory acquired from Mexico); the gradual undoing of the Missouri Compromise; the attempts by Presidents Jackson, Tyler, and Polk to extend slavery into new territories and states, climaxing with Polk's spurious use of his power as commander in chief to initiate the pro-slavery Mexican War—the nation, as John Quincy Adams and others warned, was on the verge of civil war.

There would be a mass slave rebellion, Adams predicted. Southern states would then ask Washington to help suppress the insurrection. Massachusetts, though, would not allow its sons to die defending slavery. Or, in an alternative scenario, some Southern states would secede in defiance of the Constitution. Since the long-term cost of allowing the South to go its own way would be more than the cost of a civil war, the North would feel compelled to put down that rebellion. What would be the president's powers if a slave insurrection rose to the level of a national crisis, or if the South attempted to secede? Adams and others had no doubt: the Constitution gave the president the power to suspend the Constitution selectively; the "war powers" provision had the elasticity to allow him as commander in chief to take whatever action he deemed necessary to end the rebellion, including immediate total emancipation.

But theory, Adams knew, could never determine action independent of a specific situation. Washington, Jefferson, and Polk had had theirs.

Lincoln now had his. Disunion threatened the very existence of the nation. In the late 1830s and in the 1840s the implosion had seemed imminent. The Compromise of 1850 had defused the ticking time bomb. But by the late 1850s, the long-delayed explosion seemed about to occur. No one could prevent it. Though it was secession rather than a mass slave insurrection, the impetus was slavery. "The conflict is between *Freedom* and *Slavery*," Adams had written in 1841 to William Seward, then governor of New York, who had asked for his advice. "No sophistry can disguise it. No browbeating can cowardize it. Slavery and Freedom are in the grapples of death." Clearly, there was to be a civil war in America's future. After his years of agonizing about how this had come about, "the conviction forced itself upon my mind," Adams told Seward in 1844, "that it was all traceable to that fatal drop of Prussic acid in the Constitution of the U.S., the human chattel representation. . . . I wonder how it ever could have been consented to by such men as Benjamin Franklin and Roger Sherman." It had led to pro-slavery dominating the Senate, the executive, and the Supreme Court, tainting "the authorities of the Nation. . . . The right of petition, trial by jury, freedom of the press, of speech and of the post-office have fallen and are falling in swift succession before it . . . and leagued with the rapacious passion of national aggrandizement sharpened by the whetstone of the land and stock jobber, it is even now lunging us into a desperate war for Slavery, the issue of which can be no other than the dissolution of the Union."

Nothing had changed by 1861. The South "conspires," Wendell Phillips told his New York and Boston audiences in December, "with the full intent so to mould this government as to keep it what it has been for thirty years, according to John Quincy Adams,—a plot for the extension and perpetuation of slavery." Why was Lincoln holding back?

A constitutional loyalist, Adams had told Congress in April 1842 that he would not support active interference with slavery in the slave states. The Constitution forbade it. But if the slave states should "come to the free States, and say to them, you must help us to keep down our slaves, you must aid us in an insurrection and a civil war, then I say that with that call comes a full and plenary power to this House and to the Senate over the whole subject. It is a war power. I say it is a war power, and when your country is actually in war, *whether it be a war of invasion or a war of insurrection* [my italics], Congress has power to carry on the war, and must carry it on, according to the laws of war; and by the laws of war, an invaded country has all its laws and municipal institutions swept by the board, and martial law takes the place of them. This power in Congress has, perhaps, never been called into exercise under the present Constitution of the United States. But when the laws of war are in force, what, I ask, is one of those laws? It is this: that when a country is invaded, and two hostile armies are set in martial array, the commanders of both armies have power to emancipate all the slaves in the invaded territory."

It is the Congress, Adams affirmed, not the president, that has the "plenary power" to declare war and legislate whatever aspects of the war are in its practical control. But once a war is in progress, the military power supersedes the civil. "I lay this down as the law of nations. I say that military authority takes, for the time, the place of all municipal institutions, and slavery among the rest." And if such a situation arises, who has "the exclusive management of the subject"? The person who is "not only the President of the United States, but the Commander of the Army." He "has power to order the universal emancipation of the slaves."

That power is a double-edged sword, Adams, in 1848, told the venerable Albert Gallatin, Jefferson's secretary of the treasury, who had been Adams' colleague in negotiating the Treaty of Ghent almost thirty-five years before. It was a danger as well as an opportunity, he wrote to Gallatin. The president's war powers, Adams well knew, could be used for aggression as well as self-defense. Both Adams and Gallatin were horrified at the illegality of the Mexican War. A president could initiate, as James Polk did, a preemptive or opportunistic war and, afterward, with the military die already cast, ask or decline to ask for congressional approval. The young Lincoln and the elderly Adams believed that Polk had misused his presidential powers, and had set a horrid precedent. He had created a war. "The most important conclusion from all this, in my mind," Adams emphasized to Gallatin, "is the failure of that provision in the Constitution . . . that the power of declaring war, is given exclusively to Congress. It is now established as an irreversible precedent that the President of the US has but to declare that war exists, with any nation upon earth, by the act of that nation's government, and the war is substantially declared." It was to be an ongoing concern that the nation would find itself debating into the twenty-first century.

Theory aside, Lincoln had an insurrection on his hands. There was no possibility of misinterpretation. Secession was rebellion. At first it was in the hands of James Buchanan, who threw his up in despair. By April 1861, the newly elected president had not only secession to deal with but also a military conflict. He hoped that the rebellious states might see the light of reason and reasonable compromise. The Confederacy, though, had no interest in negotiation.

Could Lincoln have had any real doubt about the scope of his war powers and the appropriateness, even desirability, of using them? From the start, he could have said to the Confederacy: "The Constitution does not give you the right to secede. You claim you have done that. We do not recognize that your claim is valid. You are not an independent nation. You have rebelled against the law of the land. If you challenge the law, do so in the courts and in Congress, through the processes set out in the Constitution. At the moment, you are not an independent nation. You are insurrectionists. You have stolen property that belongs not to you but to the entire American people. You have committed acts of theft and murder. I am asking Congress to pass a law that states that all property used to further such crimes is forfeited—that includes involuntary laborers whom you use to implement and sustain your criminal activities.

In the meantime, since you are in armed rebellion, under my war powers as commander in chief, having taken an oath to uphold and preserve the union, I order the military to confiscate all property that helps the Confederacy sustain its unlawful activity. That includes all slaves. Confiscation means emancipation."

Why, then, promulgate a Preliminary Emancipation Proclamation whose soft terms, if accepted, gave the Confederacy an almost indefinite extension of slavery? And why wait until January 1863 to do what many saw as inevitable? And then, why partial rather than total emancipation? And why hesitate so long to arrange for the enlistment of large numbers of Negro soldiers in the Union army? And why not, at least, on January 1, 1863, take the chance of saying that slavery anyplace in the United States undercuts the moral legitimacy of the Union war effort and declare total emancipation? At the Cooper Union in mid-January 1863, Wendell Phillips, representing antislavery's impatience with partial emancipation, quoted Adams at length. The time, Phillips declared, had at last arrived when antislavery moralism had the legal authority to become antislavery activism. "Military necessity opens the door, but the moment Mr. LINCOLN enters it, there is but one duty under the Constitution, that is, to execute justice betwixt the master and the slave."

As Phillips understood, Lincoln, though his border state policy still held him back, had come very far from his approach in 1861–1862. But self-imposed concern still constrained him. In creating the Emancipation Proclamation, he had acted on his belief that the Constitution gave him the authority to emancipate slaves in the rebellious states. Did it give him, though, he asked, the power to emancipate slaves in the states that were not in rebellion? True, the Republican Congress would most likely be compliant, but would not, at some future date, the Supreme Court exercise its constitutional authority to review the legality of a total Emancipation Proclamation? And what if the Court declared it unconstitutional or even, accepting it as a war measure, ruled that at the end of the war former slaves should be returned to their status as property? And if he included emancipation in states that were not in rebellion, would it not be even more likely for the Court to rule that his war powers did not allow him to do so? There is reason to think, some have argued, that Lincoln took these considerations seriously. "Not even a war-powers proclamation," one of our most distinguished historians of emancipation writes, "could trespass on the civil sovereignty of the law of slavery in the places where there was no war." This is an unduly limited, unrealistic definition of "war": it should be "war zone" or "theater of war," which included the entire South, even the entire country, since every aspect of Southern and Northern life and society contributing to the Southern war effort came within the province of the president's war powers. Anyway, what had Lincoln to fear from the Supreme Court? The only case challenging the president's suspension of habeas corpus that might have come before the Roger Taney Court during the war, the Court declined to hear; the justices found a reason to deny the defendant's appeal. In 1862, Lincoln filled three Supreme Court vacancies. In 1863, he added a tenth judge, and the next year, after Taney's death, he appointed Samuel Chase, his antislavery secretary of the treasury.

Would a partial or even total emancipation act in the winter of 1861/1862 have been appealed to the Supreme Court? Who would have appealed it? Northern Democrats? Not likely. And would they have had standing? Inconceivable. Border state slave owners, who were not in rebellion and were still citizens of the United States? Possibly. Still, it would have been unlikely that the Court would have accepted the appeal. After all, most of the judges were already pro-Lincoln antislavery moralists, and, most important, they would have had the best interests of the Court strongly in mind. There was a war on. The Constitution gave the president immense power in such a circumstance. Lincoln could have been reasonably certain that the Court, whatever the views of individual members, would have, at a minimum, waited until the rebellion was put down, the war concluded. And what then? Put the horse back in the barn? Declare emancipation illegal? Return four million ex-slaves to slavery?

Lincoln may have been "nagged by the fear that the courts and lawyers just might, in the end," as has been suggested, "decide that issuing proclamations of emancipation was not among" the war powers granted by the Constitution. He was, after all, a prudent lawyer, a brooding worrier, a constitutional conservative, and a peacemaker by temperament. His insistence on persuasion, prudence, and compromise rather than on taking risks exemplifies one of his great strengths. And it was sensible for him to fear radical action, especially its semi-dictatorial potential. But for two long years of war he had failed to grasp that the Southern elite was now an implacable enemy, and that boldness might be more in the nation's interest than sluggish alternatives. Radical action meant two things: a defined policy, early on, to implement the enlistment of free blacks and self-liberated or army-liberated slaves into the military; and a comprehensive emancipation proclamation, freeing slaves everywhere rather than only in the states in rebellion.

There was, though, something more than constitutional scruples restraining Lincoln, influencing his judgment, motivating his emancipation proposals, and determining his lifelong commitment to colonization. He was, as he had always been, pessimistic about the practical difficulty, even the impossibility, of ever removing four million former slaves and half a million free blacks from the United States, though, without any more promising alternative, he pushed it as far as reality allowed. Wendell Phillips had predicted, even advocated for, an alternative that Lincoln could not accept. Lincoln deeply feared a multiracial future in which whites would find it difficult, if not impossible, to co-exist with free blacks as equal citizens. It would be, he feared, a future in which a race war, both physical and psychological, would become a permanent feature of American life.

TEN

The Ultimate Gradualists

Hovering in the deep background of Lincoln' concern about America's racial future was that icon of the country's founding, Thomas Jefferson. Like everyone's, Lincoln's Jefferson was selective. Ironically, the immediate pre–Civil War South and the Confederacy were even more selective about Jefferson. After all, of what use could the author of the phrase "all men are created equal" be to a mind-set and an ideology that had now embraced slavery as a positive good and rejected Jefferson's colonization solution? By no stretch of his or his contemporaries' imaginations had Jefferson intended the phrase to include even free Negroes, let alone slaves, but this restriction did not go nearly far enough to satisfy the seceding states. They needed more. Jefferson's mind was not entirely closed about the moral and intellectual capacity of blacks. He was, though, certain that the two races could never live together as equals. Eventually, all blacks should be free, but not in the United States. An antislavery moralist, he had given up early in his public life on the practicality of even minor reconfigurations of slavery in America. He was, especially during crises, such as the Missouri situation in 1819, in low-key despair about the problem. It seemed irresolvable.

Most of the next two generations of Southerners were not at all unhappy about slavery. After 1830, Jefferson had few ideological heirs even in his own state. By the late 1850s, he was useless to the pro-slavery elite. To most Southerners, the problem increasingly was the North, meddling in a God-ordained institution that was none of its business. Lincoln seemed to the South a supreme meddler. That he was considerably less meddlesome than he was regularly accused of being had no traction among the many Southerners utterly disgusted with Northern interference: its attempt to deny their constitutional right to take their property anyplace they chose and its efforts to force unwelcome changes in the racial fabric of their society. That Lincoln favored colonization was not in his favor. He was slow to understand this. Henry Clay and the American Colonization Society were increasingly irrelevant in the South. Most Southerners wanted to keep, not export, their slaves. Lincoln, though, thought there was an opportunity, as did many Northern antislavery moralists, to enlist Jefferson in the Republican ranks. Most abolitionists knew better, especially those who were black. It didn't work, partly because the South was having none of it, mostly because Lincoln provided, in his debates with Douglas in 1858 and on behalf of all moderate Republicans, a qualification of the phrase "all men are created equal" that satisfied neither pro-slavery Southerners nor abolitionists: blacks were equal in regard to having the right not to be slaves, but hardly in any other way.

In this regard, Lincoln was a Jeffersonian at a time when the creators of the Confederacy had cast Jefferson off as outmoded baggage. How much of Jefferson's writings Lincoln had read is unclear. He had read and memorized the Declaration, but that was hardly a guide to Jefferson's thinking on the slavery issue. Its myth that George III rather than Jefferson's own Virginian ancestors was responsible for the existence of slavery in the colonies deflected responsibility away from slavery's ongoing beneficiaries, including Jefferson. Had Lincoln read *Notes on the State of Virginia*, Jefferson's fullest statement about Negroes, slavery, and colonization? Written between 1781 and 1783 and first published in 1785, it was republished in Richmond in 1853 and then included in the twelve-volume 1853–1854 edition of Jefferson's letters and papers. The latter was almost certainly available in Springfield, where Lincoln, from 1854 to 1859, researched and prepared the speeches that helped make him president. It also included Jefferson's *Autobiography*, well-known passages from which Lincoln quoted numbers of times, slightly misquoting *Notes* when he attempted to rebut Douglas' summary of Jefferson's views on slavery. Douglas emphasized what Jefferson believed; Lincoln, Jefferson's antislavery emotion. Jefferson, Lincoln told his audience at Galesburg in 1858, "'trembled for his country when he remembered that God was just.'" But had Lincoln read "Query XVIII" in *Notes*, Jefferson's fullest assertion of Negroes' racial inferiority? Maybe. Anyway, this and other similar quotations from Jefferson's *Autobiography* and *Notes on the State of Virginia* appeared frequently in the public discussion about slavery.

In April 1859, Lincoln, now taken seriously as a presidential possibility, received an invitation to attend a celebration of Jefferson's birthday in Boston. He would have been aware of the irony that Jefferson, who at his death did not emancipate most of his slaves, had become useful to all factions in the North. Each could stress what it chose, interpreting the third president's language as it pleased. Lincoln himself was not interested in parsing the fine points or calling into service an accurate view of Jefferson. Sending his regrets to Boston, he noted how "curious and interesting that those supposed to descend politically from the party opposed to Jefferson, should now be celebrating his birth-day in their own original seat of empire, while those claiming political descent from him have nearly ceased to breathe his name everywhere." In effect, Jefferson was now co-opted as an honorary Republican, an antislavery moralist, useful to the extent that he could help promote the Republican message.

The two original political parties, Lincoln observed, had completely "changed hands as to the principle upon which they were originally supposed to be divided," a point he made again in September in a speech in Columbus, Ohio. It was a politically useful simplification. Once again, he quoted Jefferson's fear for the future of the country. But, he emphasized, the Republicans, unlike their opponents, put human freedom before property ownership. Northern Democrats, deeply vested in their totemic pre-Jackson founder, of course objected to giving up any part of Jefferson to the Republicans. Lincoln, they concluded, was trying to steal for himself and his party some of the reflected glory of the most sacred of the Founders. As the 1860 presidential race got increasingly nasty, the proslavery *Chicago Times and Herald*, the political voice of Stephen Douglas, claimed it had discovered in an 1844 issue of the *Macomb* (Illinois) *Eagle* a speech in which Lincoln repeated the basest slanders against Jefferson. It was an attempt to nullify Lincoln's appropriation of Jefferson for Republican electoral advantage. Lincoln, the Democratic newspaper claimed, actually despised Jefferson.

The accusation that Jefferson had had a slave mistress had been widely circulated since the early 1800s, denied and affirmed by partisans on either side of the divide. "Let us attend to this uncompromising friend of freedom" were Lincoln's purported words in 1844, "whose name is continually invoked against the Whig party. The character of Jefferson was repulsive. Continually puling about liberty, equality, and the degrading curse of slavery, he brought his own children to the hammer, and made money of his debaucheries. Even at his death he did not manumit his numerous offspring, but left them soul and body to degradation and the cart whip. A daughter of this vaunted champion of Democracy was sold some years ago at public auction in New Orleans, and purchased by a society of gentlemen, who wished to testify by her liberation their admiration of the statesman, who 'Dreamt of freedom in a slave's embrace.'" Denouncing the article as a "bold and deliberate forgery," Lincoln included it in its entirety in his rebuttal in the *Illinois State Journal*.

It was an odd way to defend Jefferson. Perhaps Lincoln thought it tactically necessary, though a single phrase conveying the flavor of the forgery might have been sufficient. Lincoln's use of the third person provided some distance and denunciation, as if an independent authority were declaring that "Mr. Lincoln never used any such language in any speech *at any time*. Throughout the whole of his political life, Mr. Lincoln has ever spoken of Mr. Jefferson in the most kindly and respectful manner, holding him up as one of the ablest statesmen of his own or any other age, and constantly referring to him as one of the greatest apostles of freedom and free labor. This is so well known that any attempt, by means of fraud or forgery, to create the contrary impression, can only react upon the desperate politicians who are parties to such disreputable tactics." Still, there may have been many readers of Lincoln's rebuttal who were unaware of the claims about the Jefferson–Sally Hemings relationship. Now they were aware. This probably made no difference in the political wars of 1860, but it exemplifies how both Democrats and Republicans did not hesitate to use almost anything that was to their advantage. Lincoln repeated the allegations only for the purpose of denying that he'd said them. Every and any aspect of Jefferson was in the public and political domain.

WHAT WAS not fully enough in the public and political domain was the most powerful indictment of Jefferson, colonization, and slavery written in the first half of the nineteenth century, the black Bostonian David Walker's *Appeal in Four Articles Together with a Preamble to the Coloured Citizens of the World but in Particular, and Very Expressly, to Those of the United States of America*. Self-published in its final version in 1830, the year of Walker's death, it had only a few readers in the white world. Lincoln was not one of them. It was smuggled into the South, mostly by black sailors, and mostly suppressed. It was death to have a copy in hand or nearby. If Lincoln had read it, he would have been astounded at how effective it was in its crystal-clear style, its concise formulations, its hortatory structure, its modulations of tone, its mastery of English prose, and its distinctive prophetic voice. Ironically, it was, in a limited way, a very Jeffersonian masterpiece by a writer who had read and learned from *Notes on the State of Virginia.* With a difference: Jefferson is often calculating and deceptively calm. Walker's words jump off the page; his combination of concise language and explosively ferocious anger is impressive, a marriage of Jefferson and Jonathan Swift.

A free black from North Carolina, Walker had fled Charleston in the early 1820s, ultimately to make a life for himself in Boston's black community, just off Beacon Hill, within sight of the mansions of Boston's Cotton Whigs. A fervent black Methodist, a Christian enthusiast whose tone and language evoke the prophet Jeremiah, the self-taught Walker was a learned promoter of black equality on every level decades before abolitionism became a prominent movement. In Charleston, he had become a disciple of Richard Allen, the creator and first bishop of the African Methodist Episcopal Church. One of the founders of its Charleston church had been Denmark Vesey, executed in 1822 for his part in a slave rebellion at about the time Walker left Charleston. The church was shut down. "I am one of the oppressed, degraded and wretched sons of Africa," Walker later wrote, "rendered so by the avaricious and unmerciful among the whites. . . . I count my life not dear unto me, but I am ready to be offered at any moment. For what is the use of living, when in fact I am dead."

In Boston, earning his living as the proprietor of a used clothing store, he was, arguably, America's earliest black intellectual. The Boston agent for and a contributor to America's first black newspaper, New York's *Freedom's Journal,* he helped found the Massachusetts General Colored Association, a distant progenitor of the NAACP. It bitterly opposed colonization, slavery, and racism. The four "Articles" of Walker's *Appeal* analyze the past and present reality of the Negro, both free and slave, with a combination of accuracy, knowledge, and literary flair that would have made him, if his book had been widely available, a highly regarded abolitionist contributor to the national dialogue on slavery twenty years later: "Article I: Our Wretchedness in Consequence of Slavery. Article II: Our Wretchedness in Consequence of Ignorance. Article III: Our Wretchedness in Consequence of the Preachers of the Religion of Jesus Christ. Article IV. Our Wretchedness in Consequence of the Colonizing Plan." Walker's appeal is partly to white America, which he feared was incorrigible about race, but mostly to free and enslaved blacks. Aware that few of the former and almost none of the latter could read his words, he had no doubt that white America conspired to keep its black population ignorant and oppressed. It had created a network of customary and conspiratorial realities whose foundation was the conviction that blacks were mentally and morally inferior. Thus Christianity had been perverted by the slave-owning mentality into an anti-Christian conspiracy to keep Southern blacks enslaved and Northern blacks discriminated against; and colonization was an attempt to deprive American Negroes of their inherited nationality, to further enrich slave owners by increasing the value of their slave property, and to secure their way of life by removing black dissidents.

Like Adams, Walker predicts a civil war, though in language even more religious and apocalyptic. "Being a just and holy Being [God] will at one day appear fully in behalf of the oppressed, and arrest the progress of the avaricious oppressors." He will "cause them to rise up one against another, to be split and divided, and to oppress each other, and sometimes open to hostilities with sword in hand." If white America will not see that its oppression of black America is evil, then a just God will assert himself. His instrument will be black courage. For "when I reflect that God is just, and that millions of my wretched brethren would meet death with glory—yea, more, would plunge into the very mouths of cannons and be torn into particles as minute as the atoms which compose the elements of the earth, in preference to a mean submission to the lash of tyrants, I am with streaming eyes, compelled to shrink back into nothingness before my Maker, and exclaim again, Thy will be done, O Lord God Almighty."

If not civil war, then Negro insurrection will end slavery. "This language, perhaps is too harsh for the American's delicate ears. But Oh Americans! Americans!! I warn you . . . to repent and reform, or you are ruined!!! Do you think that our blood is hidden from the Lord, because you can hide it from the rest of the world, by sending out missionaries, and by your charitable deeds to the Greeks, Irish, andc.? Will he not publish your secret crimes on the house top? Even here in Boston, pride and prejudice have got to such a pitch, that in the very houses erected to the Lord, they have built little places for the reception of colored people, where they must sit during meeting, or keep away from the house of God, and the preachers say nothing about it." Worse, "there are not a more wretched, ignorant, miserable, and abject set of beings in all the world, than the blacks in the Southern and Western sections of this country, under tyrants and devils."

Walker's answer: not civil war or insurrection but repentance and reform. "God suffers some to go on until they are ruined forever!!!!! Will it be the case with the whites of the United States of America?—We hope not—we would not wish to see them destroyed notwithstanding, they have and do now treat us more cruel than any people have treated another. . . . O Americans! Americans!! I call God—I call angels—I call men, to witness, that your DESTRUCTION *is at hand*, and will be speedily consummated unless you REPENT." America, Walker believed, was indeed worth saving, but only if its commitment to freedom applied to its black population also.

Not that Walker desired a multiracial future, an amalgamation of the races. Committed to black pride and racial coherence, he mocked the sexually tense claim that blacks wished to marry whites, an inversion of Lincoln's argument twenty-eight years later refuting Stephen Douglas' accusation that he favored miscegenation. "I do not understand," Lincoln was to tell his cheering audience in 1858, "that because I do not want a negro woman for a slave I must necessarily want her for a wife. My understanding is that I can just let her alone. I am now in my fiftieth year, and I certainly never have had a black woman for either a slave or a wife. So it seems to me quite possible for us to get along without making either slaves or wives of negroes." But Lincoln had no argument with laws that prohibited such marriages. "I would wish, candidly," Walker wrote in 1830, "that I would not give a *pinch of snuff* to be married to any white person I ever saw in all the days of my life. And I do say it, that the black man, or man of colour, who will . . . marry a white woman, to be a double slave to her, just because she is *white*, ought to be treated by her as he surely will be . . . as a NIGER!!!!" As long as racism existed, as long as white America used its powers, including Christianity, to oppress blacks, to dehumanize them through slavery or oppression, black-white relations, on every level, would be toxic. Without equality and mutual respect, there could be no love, marital or otherwise.

Walker's heart-wrenching, perfectly chosen word for the psychological and material misery of free and enslaved blacks is *wretchedness*. And, he asks, how did American slavery and racism originate, how were they perpetuated, and how did they compare with slavery and racism in other cultures, past and present? Drawn from his wide reading in biblical and classical texts to show the distinctively cruel nature of American slavery and racism, his effective exposition is in itself a purposeful demonstration of the inherent worthiness of the Negro as a human being, morally and intellectually equal to the white race. It is an object lesson refuting the claim of black inferiority that was, in Walker's view, the foundation of American slavery and racism. His *Appeal* argues that blacks and whites, if they had been or ever could be placed in equal circumstances, are, by nature and God, equal in every respect.

But what made for unequal circumstances? In a powerful Ciceronian denunciation, Walker highlights Jefferson and Henry Clay, two of his premier villains. Jefferson was, for Walker, a man of immense talent who failed the ultimate test, the personal and public fulfillment of the true meaning of his declaration "that all men are created equal." Clay was a gifted politician who could not transcend his personal and political self-interest. Widely worshipped by white America, they were, to Walker, the most troublesome kind of racists. Self-satisfied in their antislavery moralism, they did not act on it except in the most limited ways. Neither in any meaningful way provided for the freedom of his own slaves, let alone advocated national emancipation; both were motivated partly by self-interest and primarily by fear of a race war, a horror to be avoided by racial purification, the voluntary departure of all blacks. The givens of history and genetics, Jefferson and Clay believed, had imposed slavery on nineteenth-century America. The fault, they believed, was not in themselves but in their stars. The only answer was colonization.

For Walker, white men such as Jefferson and Clay tried to justify or collaborated in black subjugation. "Do you believe that Mr. Henry Clay . . . is a friend to the blacks, further, than his personal interest extends? Is it not his greatest object and glory upon earth, to sink us into miseries and wretchedness by making slaves of us, to work his plantation to enrich him and his family?" And has not "Mr. Jefferson declared to the world, that we are inferior to the whites, both in the endowments of our bodies and of minds? It is indeed surprising, that a man of such great learning, combined with such excellent natural parts, should speak so of a set of men in chains." What Jefferson wrote in *Notes on the State of Virginia* "has in truth injured us more, and has been as great a barrier to our emancipation as anything that has ever been advanced against us."

And Jefferson and Clay wreathed their racism with a crown of thorns, their advocacy of colonization. "This country is as much ours," Walker responded, "as it is the whites', whether they will admit it now or not, they will see and believe it by and by. . . . And wo, wo, will be to you if we have to obtain our freedom by fighting. Throw away your fears and prejudices then, and enlighten us and treat us like men, and we will like you more than we do now hate you. You are not astonished at my saying we hate you, for if we are men we cannot but hate you, while you are treating us like dogs, and tell us now no more about colonization, for America is as much our country, as it is yours."

If he had lived a generation later, Walker would have said much the same thing to and about Lincoln, though he would have had to take into account the differences in tone, personality, and material realities. Jefferson's and Clay's solutions to the slavery and race problem had never been tenable. Neither was Lincoln's. His predecessors maintained it mostly as a hope, less as a likelihood, a small start to addressing a seemingly unsolvable problem. Understandably angry and apocalyptic, Walker could hardly credit Jefferson and Clay with anything other than their misdeeds, policies that seemed to him cruel and stupid. As the oppressed underdog, he had less reason to fear race wars than they did, and he would have been equally horrified that, ironically, the multiple deaths he predicted would turn out to be those of many more whites than blacks. But he feared such wars nevertheless, and hoped for the best, hoped for repentance, for reformation, for black-white reconciliation and equality, for a better America, for a "new birth of freedom." Still, he would not have been surprised that it would take seven hundred thousand American deaths, and still not then or now be fully realized.

THOUGH JEFFERSON himself never became a member of the Colonization Society, he set the example, along with Clay, for many antislavery Whigs and Republicans. Eager for the Republican nomination for the presidency, Lincoln reminded his audience in his February 1860 Cooper Union speech that Jefferson himself had shown the way to what Lincoln also hoped would be the eventual solution of the slavery problem. In 1821, in his *Autobiography*, Jefferson made his most concisely powerful statement advocating colonization. Either Lincoln read it in Springfield in the 1853–1854 edition of Jefferson's letters and papers or, orally or in print, his attention was directed to it. He had it on hand when writing the

Cooper Union address. "In the language of Mr. Jefferson, uttered many years ago, 'It is still in our power to direct the process of emancipation, and deportation, peaceably, and in such slow degrees, as that the evil will wear off insensibly; and their places be . . . filled up by free white laborers. If, on the contrary, it is left to force itself on, human nature must shudder at the prospect held up.'" Convinced that gradual emancipation and colonization were viable, he had not moved out from under the influence of Jefferson and Clay as he wrote and refined the Preliminary Emancipation Proclamation.

In August 1862, focusing entirely on his concern about the race problem, present and future, and with the recently composed Preliminary Emancipation Proclamation soon to be on the table for Southern consideration, Lincoln met at the White House with what the *New-York Tribune* called "a Committee of Colored Men." Invited by the president, the Northern clergymen were introduced to him by his commissioner of emigration, a sub-Cabinet appointee Lincoln had assigned the task of working out the nuts and bolts of his colonization policy. In a tender, nonjudgmental voice, Lincoln made his pitch. It would have sounded graciously pragmatic to many Northern whites. It probably seemed insensitively clueless to the free blacks of Baltimore, Philadelphia, New York, and Boston. Both races suffer, Lincoln noted, from their physical proximity to each other. "Your race" is "suffering, in my judgment, the greatest wrong inflicted on any people." But even free blacks are "far removed from being placed on an equality with the white race." The white population doesn't want you here. That, he, emphasized, was an undebatable given. Neither this nor anything else he would say was to be, he made it politely clear, a subject of debate between them.

He had a message for them and their congregations. The reality was indisputable, Lincoln told his guests. Since colonization would improve the lives of most free blacks, "it is better for us both, therefore, to be separated." And those of you who are comfortable enough not to feel the sting of inequality "ought to do something to help those who are not so fortunate as yourselves." The administration, he revealed, was now pursuing Central American opportunities, the details of which would make resettlement feasible. "I want you to let me know whether this can be done or not. This is the practical part of my wish to see you. These are subjects of very great importance. . . . I ask you then to consider seriously not pertaining to yourselves merely, nor for your race, and ours, for the present time, but as one of the things, if successfully managed, for the good of mankind" and for future generations. It should start with the good example of a small number of the free black elite. He was, it was clear, inviting them and their congregants to leave the United States, depicting it as a noble sacrifice to benefit all mankind.

It was an astounding request. It was also a form of moral blackmail. If only you free blacks voluntarily left, you would help me emancipate many slaves, who could then join you in a black country the foundation of which you have laid. If you do not, emancipation is less likely to be successful, as white America will contain four million blacks whom white Americans despise, fear, and want gone. At the end of Lincoln's hour-long presentation, the chairman of the Negro delegation politely responded that "they would hold a consultation and in a short time give an answer." The president said, "Take your full time—no hurry at all." They needed little to no time, so deeply offensive the request had to have been. They did, though, consult with their congregations. The response essentially was "Are you crazy?"

Stuck in a binary trap, Lincoln continued to push colonization. It would be, it seemed to him, either colonization or a multiracial America. For the former, practical obstacles created serious difficulties. What would one do if they simply would not go? It had to be voluntary. And who, other than radicals such as Wendell Phillips, happily anticipated a multiracial America with a huge black population? If Lincoln did not actually shudder at what that might entail, most white Americans did.

And time was running out; the clock was ticking. A year later, in August 1863, Lincoln told a pro-slavery Northerner disgusted with the Emancipation Proclamation that "negroes, like other people, act upon motives. Why should they do anything for us," such as fight for the Union, "if we will do nothing for them. . . . They must be prompted by the strongest motive—even the promise of freedom." Though freedom was not citizenship, Lincoln had started to sense that some concessions would have to be made at the end of the war, especially in the former slave states, until the long-term problem could be solved, if ever. Already in Union hands, Louisiana would be where the experiment began. And colonization was still squarely on the table, though Lincoln had begun to recognize that it had less and less relevance to the new reality the war was creating.

BY THE summer of 1864, much had changed—but not quite enough to liberate Lincoln, a pessimist and worrier by temperament, from the fear that he might not be re-elected in November. Much as the war moved in favor of the Union, it still seemed far from won: the casualties were immense; the Confederacy was stubborn in its insistence that the oppressor would be resisted to the final breath. Perhaps, it hoped, a revivification of the Southern war machine or a collapse of Northern will would result in favorable peace terms. It was also conceivable that Lincoln would not be re-elected.

Many Northerners, led by his opponent in the election, ex-general George McClellan, believed that the best solution to the war and the slavery problem was to let the South keep its slaves. A huge increase in free blacks would be a danger to Southern whites, to Northern workers, to the national economy, and to domestic peace. Perhaps the Emancipation Proclamation could be revoked, some ultra–Peace Democrats speculated. And the North was war weary. How, Lincoln worried, to manage to be re-elected; keep the Union focused on victory; make emancipation irrevocable; and find a way, with minor help from colonization, to start a process that would recognize that most former slaves and free blacks were here to stay, that some limited form of full citizenship would have to be initiated for them, and at the same time bring a deeply racist white majority, especially in the South, to live in peace with those whom they considered inferior? There was indeed much to worry about.

Lincoln was wise, but not always. He was virtuous; but he was a virtuous politician whose highest priority in the summer of 1864 was to get reelected. He feared that if his opponent were to succeed, his war effort and aims would be modified or even abandoned. In the worst-case scenario, the Confederacy would be recognized as an independent nation. That seemed unlikely, since Democrats who wanted peace at almost any price were now a minority within their own party. It was possible, though, that the South would be offered overly generous concessions to facilitate its return to the union. About that, he had reason to be concerned. The Democratic Party platform declared that the war to restore the union had failed; the Constitution had been shredded under the "pretense" of military necessity; states' rights had been disregarded; and it was time to cease hostilities "with a view of an ultimate convention of the States, or other peaceable means, to the end that, at the earliest practicable moment, peace may be restored on the basis of the Federal Union of the States. . . . Resolved, That the aim and object of the Democratic party is to preserve the Federal Union and the rights of the States unimpaired." This was code for concessions to the South.

Ironically, that platform resolution would have had a familiar ring to Lincoln. It had been the main plank of the Republican Party platform in late summer 1860. Only the perpetuation of the Union had been at issue then, with one exception: the nonextension of slavery. The 1864 Democratic platform said nothing about slavery, but the document made clear that everything except disunion would be on the table, including a deal in which slavery, though not expanded, continued to exist, or at least continued to exist in a disguised form.

There was, however, an antislavery firewall. Even if McClellan and a Democratic Congress were to be elected, free soil ideology had by now become sufficiently embedded among Northern Democrats to make it unlikely that any bargain with the Confederacy would allow slavery to be extended geographically. In effect, Lincoln now worried that a Democratic victory would turn back the clock. The compromise would in fact offer the South exactly what Lincoln and the Republican Party had offered it in 1861: if you rejoin the union, you can keep your slaves, as long as you keep them where they already are. Everything else would stay in place, just as it had been. But by the summer of 1864, for Lincoln and the Republicans, there was no going back. The Emancipation Proclamation and Negro soldiers in the Union army had made that a practical and moral impossibility.

Once again Lincoln obsessed about the border states. He no longer feared that they would join the Confederacy, but would they support McClellan? It was possible, he worried, that war-weary electorates in traditional Democratic strongholds in the North might make it difficult for him to obtain an Electoral College majority or might so decrease the Republican majority in Congress that it would no longer be fully committed to the war effort. And could he count on states such as Tennessee, Missouri, Kentucky, Delaware, and Maryland? All had substantial populations that detested him, the Republican Party, and the Emancipation Proclamation. They blamed Lincoln, not Southern slave owners, for a war that had caused so much suffering. With a touch of panic, the president prepared himself for the possibility that he would not be re-elected. History raised a warning sign: there had not been a two-term president since Andrew Jackson. Despite victories at Gettysburg and Vicksburg, as the war continued into 1864 with bitter resistance by the South and high casualties for the Union, Lincoln had to be concerned that his re-election was questionable.

Much as he remained preoccupied with the war, he had also begun to concentrate on how to put Humpty Dumpty back together. The reunionization of two states, Louisiana and Tennessee, became his laboratories for a solution. Unlike laboratories, they were far from germ free. The Confederacy had been driven out of Louisiana early in the war, its world-famous port city a key to Union control of the Mississippi and the defeat of the Confederacy, one of the strangleholds of Winfield Scott's Anaconda Plan to choke the Confederacy to death. Both states had strong pro-slavery elements. Both were deeply racist. Still, they were available for an early experiment in reconstruction. But what would reconstruction mean? How to distinguish between those who had been loyal to the Union and those who had not? Who would govern former slave states? What role would blacks who had been free and those who had been slaves play in governance? To what degree and at what pace should blacks be given civil rights? How could normalcy be restored and what would this new normalcy look like? What kind of rebalance of political, economic, and social power between the white and black populations of these states was possible and with what consequences? Lincoln had only the start of tentative answers to these questions. With his usual prudence and empathy, he hoped to move forward deliberately, cautiously, and with as many Americans behind him as possible. He especially wanted Northern War Democrats, most of whom had not approved of the Emancipation Proclamation and had rejected Negro equality, to become partners in reconstruction. There would be a price to pay for that.

By late spring 1864, Lincoln, thinking about re-election and reconstruction, had a strategy in mind, though he kept it close to his vest. His most pressing concern was re-election. He had one strong card to play: the choice of a running mate. He had probably been, in the months before the nominating convention in May, mulling over his options. The situation and stakes were obvious: if he had as his running mate a War Democrat, especially from a Southern state, it would be both to his electoral advantage and also a signal to the pro-Union forces in the border states and the Confederacy that their views would be represented in his second administration. It would confirm to War Democrats that his would be a unity government. That intention had already resulted, with Lincoln's approval, in the Republican Party's renaming itself the National Union Party in ample time for the Baltimore convention. It was an attempt to prevent a small breakaway radical wing from being effective and to draw as many votes away from McClellan as possible. But there was an obstacle: the sitting vice president. Quietly, mostly by nods and winks, Lincoln and his convention surrogates agreed to dump Hannibal Hamlin.

Who, though, would replace him? Lincoln's favorite pro-Union Southerner was his military governor of Tennessee, Andrew Johnson. Born into the working class, an unabashed racist and eventually a slave owner, a career politician who had become wealthy through buying and selling real estate, Johnson was a states' rights pro-Union Democrat. He had served as Tennessee's prewar civilian governor. The only Southern senator not to resign in early 1861, he had no deep commitment to slavery itself and few objections to it. Blacks simply did not matter. White working-class people did. A Southern populist, he had as the main target of his hostility the white elite, not because they owned slaves but because they lorded it over oppressed white workers. He despised the Southern aristocracy represented by Jefferson Davis. How much Lincoln actually knew about Johnson is unclear.

An honest career politician, a vigorous and effective orator, Hannibal Hamlin had risen through Maine Democratic politics to state office and to the House of Representatives. A native of Maine, he was born in the same year as Lincoln, eleven years before the Missouri Compromise elevated Massachusetts' Northern extension into an independent state. Unlike Lincoln, he was an avid farmer, deeply rooted in the Paris, Maine, community into which he had been born and then the Bangor area in which he established a law practice and political career. A good listener, tactful in his personal and public life, Hamlin was a large, bulky, swarthy, imposingly attractive man, the son of a family that had come to the New World before the middle of the seventeenth century and that had earned a reputation for intelligence, hard work, and civic responsibility. Though stolid and unimaginative, he was considered fair, trustworthy, and sober.

In the winter of 1847/1848, moving from the House of Representatives, where he had sat for four years in the same room with John Quincy Adams, to the Senate, Hamlin probably had heard Lincoln's anti-Mexican War speeches. Both vaguely recalled being in each other's presence. Though on opposite sides of the aisle, Hamlin and Lincoln had one important bond. A Democratic stalwart on every issue except slavery, Hamlin had joined a few of his party colleagues and almost all Northern Whigs in championing the Wilmot Proviso, banning slavery in any territory attained by the Mexican War. It foreshadowed the Compromise of 1850, the political battles about extending slavery, and the Republican Party platform of 1861. Hamlin had believed he could oppose extending slavery and still remain a Democrat.

The Compromise of 1850 shattered his complacency. Having convinced himself that he could best advance his antislavery moralism by remaining within the majority party and not jeopardizing his electability, Hamlin had kept his conscience at bay until 1856, at which point he concluded he had been mistaken. After four years of a pro-slavery Franklin Pierce presidency and then the election of James Buchanan, he could no longer balance his antislavery moralism with his Democratic Party membership. He joined the Republicans. To Democrats, Hamlin was a traitor; to Republicans, a welcome convert, another sign that, if the Democrats continued to divide, the newly formed party might win the presidency in 1860. It also got Hamlin handsomely re-elected to the Senate. Four years later, he was called to Springfield. Lincoln wanted him as his running mate.

A successful political marriage and a balanced national ticket, this pairing had signaled to the Northern states in which the election would be won or lost that all degrees of antislavery moralism could come under the Republican Party umbrella. The only requirement was commitment to nonextension. Hamlin's antislavery views had intensified into a weak form of abolitionism. He acknowledged that the Constitution protected slavery where it already existed. He believed immediate abolition illegal and impractical. Slightly to the left of most moderate Republicans, he was in a slow-paced hurry to continue to discuss practical ways to end slavery. Lincoln, though, had little interest in Hamlin's antislavery convictions. That was not the point. Beyond that, he also had no inclination to make Hamlin an active part of the new administration's policy deliberations. Tradition partly dictated this. Vice presidents, it had been understood since the inception of the office, were to be seen mostly in the Senate and not heard even there except in the case of a tied vote. At best, vice presidents could offer advice privately, if given the opportunity. Lincoln tended to solicit advice from a small number of people, his inner circle of Cabinet members and old colleagues. Hamlin was not one of them.

Also, Lincoln knew that the vice president sided with those in the Republican Party, especially in Congress, who criticized his conduct of the war: too slow, passive, conciliatory, especially in 1861–1862, and too unwilling to commit himself to emancipation and Negro troops. Not that Lincoln rejected Hamlin because of this. He seems hardly to have noticed him, except when custom or politeness required. In public, Hamlin was the good soldier, unquestionably loyal to Lincoln and the party. Like many vice presidents, he felt politically superfluous, irrelevant to the policy-making process. And Lincoln, a consummate politician who accepted that patronage was the lifeblood of power, gave a disappointed Hamlin no opportunity to reward his friends and strengthen his base. Sometimes the vice president wished he were actively back in the Senate, where he had felt useful. Serving as presiding officer of the Senate was tedious and uneventful. When he tried to serve behind the lines in a Massachusetts volunteer unit, official disapproval forced him back to Washington. Although unsympathetic to John Milton's seventeenth-century maxim "that they also serve who only stand and wait," he did his best to serve well by waiting.

Intent on winning the election, Lincoln winked his operatives into dropping Hamlin from the 1864 ticket and selecting Andrew Johnson to be his running mate. It took three ballots. The unsuspecting Hamlin was blindsided, the victim of political maneuvering between pro-Seward and anti-Seward forces and Lincoln's desire for a War Democrat. His virtues were irrelevant. So, too, were Johnson's liabilities. Ex-Whigs such as Lincoln, who had lived through the nasty consequences of John Tyler's accession to the presidency after the death, in 1841, of William Henry Harrison, suspended historical memory in the interest of political expediency. A states' rights Democrat, Johnson was contemptuous of Negroes. A populist, he detested those whom he judged privileged by birth or collusion. Shortsighted and semi-paranoid, he was a stubbornly closed-minded advocate for himself and his particular Southern values. A proponent of an economic and political system in which blacks were subordinate, he was, with his limitations of personality and national vision, an unpromising potential head for the almost exclusively Northern Republican Party.

Did Lincoln and his colleagues in May 1864 care to remember what a disaster "His Accidency," as Adams referred to Tyler, had been, vetoing bills and proposing policies at variance with everything the Whig Party stood for? And had it even been considered that, if Johnson became president, he might not, by personality and ideology, be the right man to preside over the challenges of reconstruction, particularly in regard to civil rights for former slaves and free blacks, and the integration of four million former slaves into a regional and national economy?

There's no record of any such consideration in the executive branch, in Congress, or in the 1864 Republican Party campaign. Lincoln seems not to have given it a first, let alone a second, thought. That seems an especially noteworthy lapse in a president who had for four years been receiving death threats and whose uneasy slumbers frequently brought dreams of his own demise. Of course, no president in good health thinks that he will die in office, but as the most hated man in America, if one includes the South, Lincoln had reason to think carefully about his choice of a running mate. He seems not to have thought beyond the election itself; his highest priority was his expectation that Johnson would enable him to carry the border states. Beyond this, he hoped that reconstruction would be facilitated by the example of a Southerner as vice president.

On Inauguration Day in March 1865, Johnson, apparently drunk, astounded the country by delivering an incoherent, rambling, semi-literate, self-glorifying speech, an embarrassment to everyone there and a national scandal. It was a revelation of character that might have given concern to those who gave thought to Johnson as a potential president. Apparently, no one of consequence did. Moments later, Lincoln delivered the most profound and beautiful inaugural address ever. The contrast was unmistakable.

A few days later, the president defended his choice. "Andy ain't a drunkard," he reportedly said. But a single case of public inebriation or even functional alcoholism was not to the point in a heavy-drinking nation. That alone was not disqualifying for almost anything, and Lincoln, who himself did not drink alcohol at all, had experience with and did find the better side of alcoholics such as Usher Linder. Lincoln, though, could easily have found out much about Johnson's personality, particularly his penchant for irrational stubbornness and arrogant bullying, the qualities of character that isolate a president. And he could have known or at least easily discovered that Johnson was a racist (more like Usher Linder than he) who believed that any black was inferior to all whites; that the blacks in America should remain subordinate always; and that, after emancipation, the substance of slavery could and should exist indefinitely, even if under another name and through other means: oppressive poverty, enforced illiteracy, voter suppression, and then the noose on the lynching tree, the hundred and more years of racial misery that Lincoln feared were in America's future. Johnson did not agree with Lincoln's view that a limited version of Jefferson's famous phrase "all men are created equal" applied to blacks. His long-standing states' rights and extreme racist views made him an unlikely partner for postwar antislavery Union nationalists. Free blacks in the North and South were understandably astounded and horrified at the elevation of Johnson to the vice presidency. The notion that Johnson was a heartbeat away from succeeding a president whose life had been repeatedly threatened terrified people such as Wendell Phillips.

When John Wilkes Booth's bullet killed Lincoln at Ford's Theatre in April 1865, the assassin could not have been fully conscious, if conscious at all, that he had collaborated with his victim in turning the executive branch of the government over to a man who would be closer to his own values than to Lincoln's. In the end, Southern society was to be reconstructed mostly along Johnson's and Usher Linder's lines. Though the blame for that implicates pervasive factors deeper and wider than a single individual, Lincoln's choice of his second running mate was a failure of vision and wisdom. It led to a tone and direction for reconstruction that certainly would have appalled him. It helped put in office a man with none of his own qualities of leadership, a president who was to make America's struggle with racism even worse than it might otherwise have been.

IN HIS Peoria address in October 1854, Lincoln had pleaded for reinstituting the Missouri Compromise, believing that it safeguarded the Union, that it was a successful compromise. Characteristically, he looked for the middle ground, even if that meant the perpetuation of slavery for a century in the states in which it already existed. Consequently, colonization had seemed to him the best long-term solution to the slavery issue, though he knew how difficult it would be to persuade free black Americans to emigrate and how unlikely it would be that taxpayers would agree to pay the immense cost of sending to and resettling four million ex-slaves in Central America or Africa. Much as he felt for slaves as victims, he gave priority to the perpetuation of domestic peace: the indefinite continuation of slavery was more tolerable to him than any advocacy or policy threatening the dissolution of the Union. Was he simply being a practical politician? Or was he being sincere when he proclaimed to his audience in Peoria that he liked the Constitution as it was? Or did he assume there was no point in advocating what he really believed: that, at a minimum, the Constitution should be amended to eliminate the three-fifths provision and, in the best of all possible worlds, amended to abolish slavery, with compensation to slave owners, to be followed by colonization?

The Peoria address started Lincoln on his beleaguered road to the fulfillment of his highest political ambition; to his commitment to keep the Union whole, which led to the "butchering business" of a horrible war; to an assassination that transformed "Father Abraham" into "Saint Abraham"; and to his modern ranking as the most highly regarded president the United States has ever had. Events beyond his control created the circumstances that most presidents fear and perhaps secretly desire: a national crisis by which history and mythmaking elevate him to the equal of those whose faces dominate Mount Rushmore.

Lincoln was to have much that was unforeseen to learn and experience between 1861 and 1865. These were exhausting, embittering, and draining years. Intensified by sadness, his misery became etched in his face; the life that had been draining out of him during his White House years was finally fully drained at Ford's Theatre in April 1865. All the blood that had been shed on the battlefields and from his murdered body became, in the end, a costly transfusion. The union gradually became robust again. A hundred years later, the former slaves came closer to becoming full citizens.

If the Union had accepted peaceful separation, the right of a minority to rebel against a majority that Lincoln had recognized in his speech to Congress in 1848, the cost would have been a diminished country. Although slavery would not have been an issue any longer, racism would, and those many people in the North who supported colonization and an all-white America might have now found colonization decidedly practical: there would have been fewer than two hundred thousand free blacks in the newly configured United States. The possibility that colonization might have helped solve the North's racism problem would have increased. And those free blacks who remained might have been less an irritant or an affront to the Northern conscience, partly because the four million slaves in the Confederacy were not the North's problem anymore. A Union composed only of the Northern states might have moved gradually toward making its free blacks full citizens, but how far and how fast would have varied from state to state. It would have been very slow in Illinois, and Lincoln would not have been inclined to make it faster.

And what would Lincoln have done if the majority sentiment in the North had been to let the South go? Would that not have been the case if, in 1861, the people of the North had had a crystal ball, if they had been able to foresee the carnage and cost of the next four years? If Lincoln had known what price would have to be paid, would even he have been willing to accept separation, with the Confederacy paying for confiscated U.S. property such as forts and post offices? And what if separation had included a treaty agreement that prevented the extension of slavery beyond Texas? It seems likely, given his moderate antislavery moralism, that the existence of slavery in an independent Confederacy would have been a minor consideration, more abhorrent to abolitionists than to moderate Republicans. And it would have been mainly a moral consideration, as it had been for the moderate Whigs and Republicans all along. Lincoln would have been no more of an abolitionist than he had ever been. No doubt there would have been troublesome cross-border incidents and irritants. Abolitionists in the United States would have continued to protest against slavery everywhere. Both countries, though, would have had a strong interest in maintaining peace. Neither the United States of America nor the Confederate States of America would have thought antislavery activity in its best interest. And what would Northern abolitionists, no longer living in a country where slavery existed, have done?

Since the United States did not accept peaceful separation, about seven hundred thousand deaths ensued. But there was a huge benefit to the cost, inherent in the realities and consequences of such a cataclysmic civil war. Abolitionists such as Wendell Phillips and William Lloyd Garrison, a sober cheering squad of religious moralists, believed, as Lincoln was to state in his Second Inaugural Address, that every drop of blood shed in battle was payment for every drop that had been shed by the lash. From the abolitionist point of view, the South in 1861 began the liberation of the United States from a constitutional noose that was choking it to death; the Union and Confederate dead were the price to be paid for the sins of the past. Their bodies liberated the nation from an otherwise insupportable national misery. If the South had not revolutionized, if that minority had not tried to form its own government, would there have been the Thirteenth, Fourteenth, and Fifteenth Amendments to the Constitution? If so, when? It's unlikely that the amendments themselves or their statute law equivalents in individual Southern states ever could have been passed unless the states, in Congress and in their legislatures, had cast their votes for them. Even if the federal government had provided financial compensation, how many slave owners would have agreed? After all, to give up their slaves was to give up an all-pervasive way of life.

Once the South forced a decision on the North, the United States was destined to be a slave-free country, sooner rather than later, though most Northerners, including Lincoln, did not think of it in those terms in 1861. If the North had accepted separation, slavery would have ended in the United States. The slave states would have been gone. By choosing to prevent separation, the North made it likely that there would be one of three results: (1) the North would lose the war and there would be no slavery in the diminished United States; or (2) the North would win the war, a total victory, and slavery would, at some time in the not too distant future, be abolished; or (3), once the war started, a compromise would be effected, of the sort Lincoln proposed in the Preliminary Emancipation Declaration, that would put the nation on the very slow road toward compensated emancipation. At the start of the war, Lincoln hoped for the last. Compromise and gradualism were in his blood. His deep faith in law, reason, and compromise made it especially difficult for him to respond to what seemed stubborn irrationality. Why, he could not help asking, would the South think it to its advantage to leave the union? How could it be better off as an independent nation? And he found it difficult to understand, let alone accept, that the South valued slavery more than it valued keeping faith with the nation that the Founding Fathers had created.

Lincoln's greatness as a wartime president is of a very human kind. He presided over the creation of a new reality that neither he nor anyone could fully embrace, or embrace in a way that would eliminate racial conflict. One of our twenty-first-century dangers is allowing ourselves to be so starry-eyed about Lincoln that we fail to realize that a certain amount of failure is built into the reality every president has to work with. If Lincoln had lived to fulfill his second term, it's unlikely that he could have done much better or better at all than those who came after him, even that he could have done better than the ultraracist Andrew Johnson in harmoniously reconciling North and South and creating a less racist context for the country as a whole. Lincoln today can serve as a reminder that we are no more at fault than he was; that historical givens, which no one individual could or can control or change, have put us where we are; that identity politics and tribalism are built into human nature and into human communities; that we need to face this reality and then look for ways to do better with who and what we are. It has never been and will never be easy.

MYTH AND mythology often serve constructive and aspirational purposes. But they also do harm. The post-assassination Lincoln took on a greatly amplified importance to much of the American public, probably the president most deeply reviled in his lifetime and most highly regarded after his death. The image of Lincoln as the Great Emancipator has contributed to both. It has flattened out our history, especially the history of slavery in America, and allowed many Americans to take refuge under the vast Lincoln umbrella: the Great Emancipator freed the slaves. He did not. He was as much a follower as a leader, a cautious politician who, when he did emancipate the slaves in the Confederacy, in fact freed no slaves at all: they were still slaves under Confederate rule.

From that point of view, the Emancipation Proclamation was a propaganda document to help the Union war effort, though undoubtedly it meant actual emancipation, the end of slavery everywhere, if and when the Union won the war. That was what was so momentous about it. By January 1, 1863, Lincoln knew that this was a necessary war measure, but also that there would be consequences for the white republic and that these would create challenges in the future. And he hesitated and hesitated, and pleaded with the South to help him avoid such a proclamation. But, as he indirectly later acknowledged, abolitionists such as Lovejoy, Phillips, and Douglass laid the groundwork and created the context that pressured him to at last be as bold as he had it in him to be.

During the second half of 1862, as Lincoln put the South on warning that he might proclaim emancipation, did he think back to his cautious reference to Elijah Lovejoy's assassination in his 1838 Springfield Lyceum address? Then he had made it sound as if the major issue was lawlessness: not a word about slavery; not a word about why Lovejoy had been murdered. In later years, he had multiple deaths to think about, the deaths of hundreds of thousands of soldiers. To avoid that, he would, in 1861, have accepted the indefinite existence of slavery. A terrible dilemma. But he had, throughout his life, like most white Americans, valued white lives more than black. This is not a harsh judgment in the context. It is not to Lincoln's discredit. He went, as the war began, step by step, as far as he could go, given who he was and the circumstances as he understood them. He well knew the biblical injunction, "I did not come to bring peace, but a sword." But his sword was to be a killing blade only if killing were forced on him as a last resort. He preferred peace and union at almost any price but one: the extension of slavery into the territories. An antislavery moralist, he had reason to believe that without this one bottom line, slavery would be likely to spread. With that bottom line, he could realistically hope for "eventual extinction." That, which to him seemed enough, made the Republican Party politically viable. The ultimate gradualist, in the last half year of his life, Lincoln began to develop policies for ameliorative reconstruction. Its two pillars were a reasonably quick and gracious reabsorption of the rebellious states into the Union and the slow elevation of a small number of former slaves into citizenship.

Gradualism has its place, but not on all issues, and certainly not always. Perhaps Lincoln is not our best model for the solution of the American race problem today. It is tempting to propose that the abolitionists are, in a line that includes John Quincy Adams, David Walker, Elijah Lovejoy, William Lloyd Garrison, Frederick Douglass, H. Ford Douglas, and Wendell Phillips. But rather than the individual themselves, it is, I think, the overall narrative that can best provide us with guidelines. It is a story with an expanded cast of characters, including John Adams,

Abigail Adams, and Thomas Jefferson; and those of the next generation who struggled with the complications of the institution they inherited: Rufus King, Charles Fenton Mercer, Henry Clay, David Walker, James Buchanan, and Hannibal Hamlin. Of course we treasure Lincoln, but if he is the "Great Emancipator," we must not abstract him from a narrative that gives due attention to the complexities of the man and the situation. We do ourselves a disservice when we self-servingly massage the record. We should have no illusion that Lincoln made a major contribution to solving the race problem. He left us with it. And the reality of racism, as Lincoln had the wisdom to recognize, is only moderately amenable to gradualism in the public sphere. Public policy can make a difference, but not the ultimate one. It is hard to deny, on the evidence of history and experience, that racism is an offshoot of tribalism, of identity politics, of us against them, in every area of human life, for the individual and the group. The pervasive tribal nature of "otherness" is a difficult ground on which to grow togetherness. The individual human heart beats with flawed arrhythmias. Racism perhaps never will be, never can be, totally eradicated.

Lincoln himself needs no vindication. He was always cautious about closing the gap between moral idealism and political reality, between antislavery moralism and antislavery activism. Neither a saint nor a sinner, especially in regard to slavery and what to do about it, he valued union more than he valued a slavery-free Union. He reluctantly reached, in 1863, the conclusion that the preservation of the Union required the help of black soldiers. A deeply moral man, he recognized that black military service made some degree of black citizenship, perhaps limited and phased in gradually, inevitable.

Yet he also anticipated that emancipation, let alone black citizenship, would place bitter, even poisonous fruit on the American table for a long time to come. He was right about that. Most white Americans were to reject integrating blacks and whites into a multiracial society. Slavery and racism would morph into the problem of racism alone. Could anyone else have done better? Could Lincoln have done better? Likely but unknowable. Did he do well enough? Certainly, if the standard is the outcome of the war and his legacy to the country: an extraordinary example of prudent deliberation, thoughtful perseverance, and sensitive decency, the epitome of what we should hope for in a president.

ACKNOWLEDGMENTS

With this book, as with my last two, my major indebtedness is to the digital world, to the computer technology that has revolutionized historical and literary research. I remember the index cards and the steel index card box in which, fifty years ago when I wrote *Thomas Carlyle: A Biography,* I stored my research notes. And the thousands of miles I traveled and the months I spent in faraway archives for my next three biographies. Now the computer on my desk has become the portal to websites that provide access to most of the manuscript archives and book collections of the world. Scholarly writers, especially biographers, have had our writing lives cushioned and extended. Also, the organization of digitalized files makes possible a tidiness and an accessibility that not even a compulsive arranger could have managed before. And my word-processing program has allowed me to write better than I ever could before. Revision is the lifeblood of a good writer. The computer has given me the chance to write and rewrite with less pain.

Complicated legal and cultural problems have arisen in regard to who benefits and who loses (especially institutionally) from this new world of online resources. Not everyone is a winner. Libraries have to redefine themselves and retool, an expensive activity. And the application of this technology to the buying and selling of books creates its own issues. Many independent bookstores have gone out of business. Chain bookstores have had to adapt. And Amazon dominates the book marketplace. This extraordinary company, though, has made its own positive contribution to my life as a writer. In many instances, I need actual physical books. The irony for professional nonfiction writers like myself, who have chosen to live at a distance from research libraries, is that, just as it radically transforms the book marketplace, Amazon also delivers to my door overnight almost all the books I need. For someone who lives in Boothbay, Maine, that is a great asset.

Still, the magic of computers and next-day delivery notwithstanding, there are particular libraries that have been frequent presences in the creation of this book. Nearby, the excellent Bowdoin College Library and its ever-helpful staff; at greater distances and mostly online, the Massachusetts Historical Society, the Library of Congress, and the Gilder-Lehrman Institute. There are numbers of people, some connected with institutions, others not, who have been of particular help. Douglas Wilson has kindly shared with me his expertise about Jefferson and Lincoln. At the Massachusetts Historical Society, Emily Ross has provided a much-needed scan of a Charles Francis Adams diary entry, and Dan Hinchen offered helpful guidance in regard to Adams and Elijah Lovejoy. Bill and Jane Ann Moore, the foremost experts on Lovejoy's life and writings and co-directors of the Lovejoy Society at Princeton, Illinois, have generously helped with source material and guidance. Penny White at the Albert and Shirley Small Special Collections Library at the University of Virginia has helped with a scan of a letter from Charles Fenton Mercer to John Hartwell Cocke.

The image archives that have permitted me to reproduce items in their collections are separately acknowledged, but the people who have helped facilitate this warrant acknowledgment: Erin Beasely, the National Portrait Gallery; Joshua Blay, the Philadelphia History Museum at the Atwater Kent; Jaime Bourassa, the Missouri History Museum; Caroline Keinath, the Adams National Historical Park, National Park Service; Bruce Kirby, the Library of Congress; Ellen Sandberg, the Granger Collection; Tatyana Shinn, the State Historical Society of Missouri; and Patricia H. Svoboda, the National Portrait Gallery.

My apologies to those who have been rewarded for their curiosity about what I was writing with mini-lectures when a sentence or two would have been appropriate. And my thanks to those who didn't let on that writers are better read than heard. To four friends, special thanks: to Peter Felsenthal for his photographic expertise; to Susan Hirschman for her warm interest and hospitality; to Charles Molesworth, who kindly read the manuscript and from whom I have borrowed his phrase about Elijah Lovejoy: "an immortal ghostly shadow"; and to Moreen Halmo for empathetic support on a wide range of concerns. The first reader, Rhoda Weyr, provided helpful editing; the second, Georges Borchardt, my longtime agent, has the great talent of being both magically concise and helpfully precise. My excellent technician, Mike Gudroe, has kept my computers alive and well. At HarperCollins, my thanks to my editor, Jonathan Jao, whose commitment to the book has been expressed throughout in word and deed; and to the associate editor Sofia Groopman, who has kept me informed and well chaperoned through the production process. HarperCollins has given the book the advantage of an excellent copyeditor, Jenna Dolan, an excellent proofreader, Susan Gamer, and a superlative production editorial department, led by John Jusino. My thanks for the blessing of three estimable children, Julia, Noah, and Benjamin, who amid the demands of their own lives find moments in which to be interested and encouraging.

Fred Kaplan
Boothbay, January 2017

NOTES

Abbreviations

AA Abigail Adams

AFC *Adams Family Correspondence*. Ed. L. H. Butterfield, Margaret A. Hogan, C. James Taylor, et al. Vols. 1–11. Cambridge, Mass.: Harvard University Press, 1963–2013.

APM Adams Papers Microfilms

CW *The Collected Works of Abraham Lincoln*. Ed. Roy P. Basler. New Brunswick, N.J.: Rutgers University Press, 1953; 1974.

DCFA *Diaries of Charles Francis Adams*. Ed. Aida DiPace Donald and David Donald. 6 vols. Cambridge, Mass.: Harvard University Press, 1964–1974.

DJQA *The Diaries of John Quincy Adams*. Massachusetts Historical Society. *Memoirs of John Quincy Adams*. Ed. Charles Francis Adams. 12 vols. Philadelphia: J. B. Lippincott and Co., 1875.

DWA David Walker. *David Walker's Appeal to the Coloured Citizens of the World*. Ed. Peter P. Hinks. University Park: Pennsylvania State University Press, 2000.

EB Edward Beecher. *Narratives of the Riots at Alton in Connection with the Death of Rev. Elijah P. Lovejoy*. New York: John S. Taylor, 1838. Reprint, New York: Haskell, 1970.

EPLM *Memoir of the Rev. Elijah P. Lovejoy; Who Was Murdered in Defence of the Liberty of the Press. At Alton, Illinois, Nov. 7, 1837. By Joseph C. and*

Owen Lovejoy. With an Introduction by John Quincy Adams. New York: John S. Taylor, 1838.

HI — *Herndon's Informants: Letters, Interviews, and Statements About Abraham Lincoln*. Ed. Rodney O. Davis and Douglas L. Wilson. Urbana and Chicago: University of Illinois Press, 1988.

ISJ — *Illinois State Journal*

JA — John Adams

JQA — John Quincy Adams

UFL — Usher F. Linder. *Reminiscences of the Early Bench and Bar of Illinois*. Chicago, 1879.

WJQA — *Writings of John Quincy Adams*. Ed. Worthington Ford. New York, 1913.

WP — Wendell Phillips. *Speeches, Lectures, and Letters*. Boston: Lee and Shepherd, 1872.

Preface

xi *"Shelley plain"*: Robert Browning, "Memorabilia," in *Men and Women* (London: Chapman & Hall, 1855).

xvii *"Three hundred thousand"*: Gary W. Gallagher, *The Confederate War* (Cambridge, Mass.: Harvard University Press, 1997), p. 168; Eric Foner, *Reconstruction: America's Unfinished Revolution, 1863–1877* (New York: Harper and Row, 1968); David W. Blight, *Race and Reunion: The Civil War in American Memory* (Cambridge, Mass.: Harvard University Press, 2001).

Chapter 1: A Continual Torment

1 *"Sale of Slaves"*: *DJQA* 9, 417. 10/23/1837. See Alison T. Mann, *Slavery Exacts an Impossible Price: John Quincy Adams and the Dorcas Allen Case, Washington, D.C.*, diss., University of New Hampshire, Durham, 2010.

1 *"I asked"*: *DJQA* 9, 417. 10/23/1837.

2 *"HORRIBLE BARBARITY"*: *Alexandria Gazette*, 8/24/1837.

4 *"long conversations"*: *DJQA* 9, 365. 9/1/1837.

4 *Quincy and Boston*: See Charles Francis Adams, *History of Braintree, Massachusetts (1639–1708); The North Precinct of Braintree (1708–1792); The Town of Quincy (1792–1889)* (Cambridge, Mass.: Riverside Press, 1891).

4 *"a mulatto boy"*: *DJQA* 5, 191. 10/22/1830.

5 *"about a negro woman"*: *DJQA* 6, 278. 4/3/1824.

6 *"It is a case"*: DJQA 9, 418. 10/23/1847.

6 *no slavery, no Union*: See David Waldstreicher, *Slavery's Constitution: From Revolution to Ratification* (New York: Hill and Wang, 2009).

6 *"the prohibition"*: DJQA 9, 418. 10/23/1847.

6 *"that there was"*: Ibid.

6 *"weeping and wailing"*: DJQA 9, 421. 10/28/1837.

8 *"to his word"*: DJQA 9, 425. 9/2/1837.

8 *"Here, then"*: Ibid.

8 *"The evidence"*: Ibid.

9 *the Methodist Church*: See Donald G. Mathews, *Slavery and Methodism: A Chapter in American Morality, 1780–1845* (Princeton, N.J.: Princeton University Press, 1965).

9 *"It is very doubtful"*: DJQA 9, 424. 10/31/1837.

9 *"came again about"*: DJQA 9, 427. 11/9/1837.

9 *"I told him"*: DJQA 9, 428. 11/13/1837.

10 *"the legality of"*: Ibid.

10 *"But he does not know"*: *Speech of John Quincy Adams . . . upon the Right of the People, Men and Women, to Petition; on the Freedom of Speech and of Debate in the House of Representatives of the United States on the Resolutions of Seven Legislatures, and the Petitions of More Than One Hundred Thousand Petitioners Relating to the Annexation of Texas to This Union, Delivered in the House of Representatives from the 16th of June to the 7th of July, 1838* (Washington, D.C.: Gales and Seaton, 1838).

11 *"I am well aware"*: Ibid.

12 *"delicious dishes"*: CW 1, 262. 9/27/1841.

12 *"the best cure"*: Ibid.

12 *"about his life"*: 5/4/1887, in James Speed, *Address of Hon. James Speed* (Louisville, Ky.: J.P. Morton and Company, 1888); David Herbert Donald, *"We Are Lincoln Men": Abraham Lincoln and His Friends* (New York: Simon and Schuster, 2003); Jennifer Cole, "'For the Sake of the Songs of the Men Made Free': James Speed and the Emancipationists' Dilemma in Nineteenth-Century Kentucky," *Ohio Valley History* 4, no. 4 (Winter 2004): 27–48; Bryan S. Bush, *Lincoln and the Speeds* (Morely, Mo.: Acclaim Press, 2008).

12 *"Cheapside Auction Block"*: See J. Winston Coleman Jr., "Lexington's

Slave Dealers and the Southern Trade," *Filson Club Quarterly* 12, no. 1 (January 1938); Ivan E. McDougle, *Slavery in Kentucky, 1792–1865*, diss. Clark University, Worcester, Mass., 1918.

12 *"saw Negroes Chained"*: *HI*, 457.

13 *"chained six"*: *CW* 1, 261. 9/27/1841.

14 *"some traders tried"*: Robert H. Gudmestad, *A Troublesome Commerce: The Transformation of the Interstate Slave Trade* (Baton Rouge: Louisiana State University Press, 2003), p. 46.

15 *"I hate to see"*: *CW* 2, 321. 8/24/1855.

15 *"You may remember"*: Ibid.

15 *"the better angels"*: *CW* 4, 272. 3/4/1861.

16 *"name was early"*: *Congressional Globe*, 2/13/1847.

17 *Henry Clay*: For the standard and the latest look at Clay, see, respectively, Robert Rimini, *Henry Clay, Statesman for the Union* (New York: W.W. Norton, 1993); and David S. Heidler and Jeanne T. Heidler, *Henry Clay: The Essential American* (New York: Random House, 2010).

17 *"We had political"*: *HI*, p. 114.

17 *"say from 1820"*: Ibid.

17 *"let ould acquaintance"*: Ibid., p. 216.

18 *"he was a warm"*: Ibid., pp. 101–102.

19 *"Your subscriber"*: *CW* 1, 38. 11/3/1835.

20 *"a conscious pride"*: *SJ*, 4/19/1832.

21 *"readers to the discussion"*: Ibid.

21 *"who were on the frontier"*: *SJ*, 5/3/1832.

22 *"To avoid the crowded scene"*: *SJ*, 3/3/1833.

22 *"Should a conflict"*: *SJ*, 3/16/1833.

23 *"we are not enemies"*: *CW* 4, 272. 3/4/1861.

23 *"the most remarkable man"*: *SJ*, 10/31/1835.

24 *"We shall not be"*: Ibid.

26 *"Resolved, That"*: *SJ*, 1/16/1836. See Arthur C. Cole, *The Constitutional Debates of 1847* (Springfield: Illinois State Historical Library, 1919); Leon F. Litwack, *North of Slavery: The Negro in the Free States, 1790–1860* (Chicago: University of Chicago Press, 1961); Eugene H. Berwanger, *The Frontier Against Slavery: Western Anti-Negro Prejudice and the Slavery Extension Controversy* (Urbana: University of Illinois Press, 1967); James Simeone,

Democracy and Slavery in Frontier Illinois: The Bottomland Republic (DeKalb: Northern Illinois University Press, 2000); John Craig Hammond, *Slavery, Freedom, and Expansion in the Early American West* (Charlottesville: University of Virginia Press, 2007); Darrel Dexter, *Bondage in Egypt: Slavery in Southern Illinois* (Cape Girardeau, Mo.: Center for Regional History, 2011); Christopher P. Lehman, *Slavery in the Upper Mississippi Valley, 1787–1865* (Jefferson, N.C.: McFarland, 2011); Jerome B. Meites, "The 1847 Illinois Constitutional Convention and Persons of Color," *Journal of the Illinois State Historical Society* 108, no. 3–4 (Fall/Winter 2015): 266–295.

Chapter 2: The First American Martyr

27 *Elijah Parish Lovejoy*: *EPLM*; EB; William S. Lincoln, *Alton Trials* (New York: John F. Trow, 1838); Henry Tanner, *The Martyrdom of Lovejoy* (Chicago: Fergus Printing, 1881); Merton L. Dillon, *Elijah P. Lovejoy, Abolitionist Editor* (Urbana: University of Illinois Press, 1961); Paul Simon, *Freedom's Champion, Elijah Lovejoy* (Carbondale: Southern Illinois University Press, 1994); Louis S. Gerteis, *Civil War St. Louis* (Louisville: University Press of Kentucky, 2001), pp. 7–29; Michael Kent Curtis, "The 1837 Killing of Elijah Lovejoy by an Anti-Abolition Mob: Free Speech, Mobs, Republican Government, and the Privileges of American Citizens," *UCLA Law Review* (1997): 1109–1184.

30 *"religion, morality"*: Dillon, *Elijah P. Lovejoy*, p. 30.

31 *"They are impatiently"*: *EPLM*, p. 66.

31 *"we believe"*: Dillon, *Elijah P. Lovejoy*, p. 41.

31 *"a slanderer"*: Ibid., p. 40.

33 *"something must be done"*: *EPLM*, p. 128.

34 *"I have never, knowingly"*: Ibid., p. 141; *St. Louis Observer*, 11/5/1835; Dillon, *Elijah P. Lovejoy*, pp. 69–70.

35 *"I can make no compromise"*: *EPLM*, p. 142.

35 *"the long nights"*: Dillon, *Elijah P. Lovejoy*, p. 65.

36 *"immediate and unconditional"*: *EPLM*, p. 123.

36 *"the public mind"*: Ibid., p. 159.

36 *"I have sworn"*: Ibid., p. 141.

36 *"Nothing could have been"*: Ibid., p. 168.

36 *"we are getting"*: Ibid., p. 159.
37 *"Our creed is"*: Ford Risley, *Abolition and the Press* (Chicago: Northwestern University Press, 2008), p. 70.
37 *"a rabble of boys"*: *EPLM*, p. 175.
38 *"cruel and unusual . . . but not this way"*: Ibid., pp. 168–179; Elijah P. Lovejoy, "Awful Murder and Savage Barbarity," *St. Louis Observer*, 4/30/1836; Tanner, *The Martyrdom of Lovejoy*, pp. 74–85; see Neil Schmitz, "Murdered McIntosh, Murdered Lovejoy: Abraham Lincoln and the Problem of Jacksonian Address," *Arizona Quarterly: A Journal of American Literature, Culture, and Theory* 44, no. 3 (1988): 15–39.
39 *"has kindled up"*: *EPLM*, p. 182.
40 *"The duty of Christians"*: Tanner, *The Martyrdom of Lovejoy*, pp. 45–48, 99.
40 *"Let every freeman"*: *EPLM*, p. 213.
41 *"ANTI-ABOLITION MEETING"*: Ibid., p. 217.
41 *"the arid dissemination"*: Ibid.
41 *"That we, as citizens"*: Ibid., p. 219.
42 *"I am in your hands"*: Tanner, *The Martyrdom of Lovejoy*, p. 124.
42 *"quiet and gentlemanly"*: Ibid., p. 129.
43 *Lincoln's in Coles*: See Charles H. Coleman, *Abraham Lincoln and Coles County, Illinois* (New Brunswick, N.J.: Scarecrow Press, 1955).
45 *"How would you"*: "Mayor's Office, City of Alton. Nov. 8th. 1837. To the Public," *Alton Spectator*, repr. *SJ*, 11/18/1837.
45 *"As they emerged"*: Tanner, *The Martyrdom of Lovejoy*, pp. 150–151.

Chapter 3: A Difficult Year

46 *"The perpetuation"*: *CW* 1, 109. 1/27/1838.
47 *"winter of starving"*: Wayne M. Wendland, "A History of Weather Observations in Illinois," *Transactions of the Illinois State Academy of Science* 83, no. 1 and 2 (1990): 47.
48 "THE CLOSING YEAR": *SJ*, 1/27/1838.
49 *"the increasing disregard"*: *CW* 1, 109. 1/27/1838.
50 *"Awful Murder"*: Tanner, *The Martyrdom of Lovejoy*, p. 74.
50 *"We must stand"*: *EPLM*, p. 173.
50 *Mayor John Krum's*: *SJ*, 11/18/1837.
51 *"wild and furious passions"*: See Leonard L. Richards, *"Gentlemen of*

Property and Standing": Anti-Abolition Mobs in Jacksonian America (New York: Oxford University Press, 1970); David Grimsted, *American Mobbing, 1828–1861: Toward Civil War* (New York: Oxford University Press, 1998).

52 *"being politic"*: *CW* 1, 115.

53 *"With this ring"*: Henry C. Friend, "Abraham Lincoln and a Missing Promissory Note," *American Bar Association Journal* 54 (September 1968): 863.

53 *"that as citizens"*: *SJ*, 10/23/1837.

54 *"is likely to check"*: Ibid.

55 *"assorting, filing"*: *DJQA* 9, 479. 1/28/1838.

57 *Cotton Whigs*: Among the many informative books on the economics of the cotton industry in the North and South, two recent studies stand out: Sven Beckert, *Empire of Cotton: A Global History* (New York: Penguin Random House, 2014); and Edward E. Baptist, *The Half Has Never Been Told* (New York: Basic Books, 2014).

57 *"I sternly rejoice"*: Ralph Waldo Emerson, *Selected Journals, 1820–1842* (New York: Library of America, 2010), p. 571.

59 *"The rich and fashionable"*: *The Works of William Ellery Channing* (Boston: American Unitarian Association, 1900), p. 748.

60 *"Freedom of speech"*: See *Memoir of William Ellery Channing* (Boston: Crosby and Nichols, 1851), vol. 3, pp. 211 and 199–217.

60 *"A spirit of lawlessness"*: William Ellery Channing, *A Letter to the Hon. Henry Clay on the Annexation of Texas to the United States* (Boston: James Munroe and Company, 1837).

60 *"Suppose . . . emerge from slavery"*: James Trecothick Austin, *Remarks on Dr. Channing's Slavery, by a Citizen of Massachusetts*, 3rd ed. (Boston: Russell, Shattuck and Co., and John H. Eastburn, 1836).

62 *"The speech of"*: *Boston Daily Evening Transcript*, 12/12/1837.

63 *"the youngest son:"* *DJQA* 8, 406. 8/31/1831.

63 *a lifelong commitment*: See James Brewer Stewart, *Wendell Phillips, Liberty's Hero* (Baton Rouge: Louisiana State University Press, 1986).

64 *"As much as thought"*: Wendell Phillips, *"The Murder of Lovejoy"*: *Speeches, Lectures, and Letters* (Boston: Lee and Shepherd, 1872), p. 9.

65 *the "first American martyr"*: JQA, "Introduction," in *EPLM*, p. 12.

66 *"Could the* People": John E. Lovejoy/JQA, 1/12/1837. APM.

67 *"I hope and believe"*: JQA/John E. Lovejoy, 4/13/1837. APM.

68 *"this Lovejoy"*: *DJQA* 9, 432. 11/22/1837.

68 *"One of the leading"*: Ibid.

69 *"I never saw"*: *SJ*, 12/14/1837.

69 *"In the House"*: Ibid.

69 "COLOURED CITIZENS": *EPLM*, p. 319.

70 *"was very glad"*: Owen Lovejoy/John Lovejoy, 2/26/1838, Owen Lovejoy Papers, Clements Library, University of Michigan.

70 *"introduced to"*: Sarah Moody Lovejoy/Sibyl Lovejoy, 2/27/1838.

70 *"It is done"*: Owen Lovejoy/Betsy Lovejoy, 3/22/1838.

71–73 *"The absolute despotisms . . . OF THE SLAVE"*: JQA, "Introduction," in *EPLM*, pp. 9–12.

74 *"Friend Lemen"*: Willard C. MacNaul, *The Relations of Thomas Jefferson and James Lemen in the Exclusion of Slavery from Illinois and the Northwest Territory with Related Documents 1781–1818* (Chicago: University of Chicago Press, 1915), pp. 50–51.

Chapter 4: A Field of Blood

76 *In the early 1780s*: See Everett Somerville Brown, *The Constitutional History of the Louisiana Purchase, 1803–1812* (Berkeley: University of California Press, 1920); George Henry Moore, *Notes on the History of Slavery in Massachusetts* (New York: Appleton, 1924); Lorenzo Johnston Greene, *The Negro in Colonial New England* (New York: Atheneum, 1968); Joanne Pope Melish, *Disowning Slavery: Gradual Emancipation and "Race" in New England, 1780–1960* (Ithaca, N.Y.: Cornell University Press, 1998); Robert E. Desrochers Jr., "Slave-for-Sale Advertisements and Slavery in Massachusetts, 1704–1781," *William and Mary Quarterly* 59, no. 3 (July 2002); Jed Handelsman Shugerman, "The Louisiana Purchase and South Carolina's Reopening of the Slave Trade," *Journal of the Early Republic* 22, no. 2 (2002): 263–290; Thomas Fleming, *The Louisiana Purchase* (Hoboken, N.J.: John Wiley and Sons, 2003); George William Van Cleve, *A Slaveholder's Union: Slavery, Politics, and the Constitution in the Early American Republic* (Chicago: University of Chicago Press, 2010); Sanford Levinson and Bartholomew H. Sparrow, *The Louisiana Purchase and American Expansion, 1803–1898* (Lanham, Md.: Rowman and Littlefield, 2005).

76 *"man stealer"*: Theophilus Parsons, *Memoir of Theophilus Parsons, Chief Justice of the Supreme Judicial Court of Massachusetts, with Notices of Some of His Contemporaries, by His Son* (Boston: Ticknor and Fields, 1859), p. 16.

76 *"all men are born"*: Constitution of Massachusetts, 1780.

76 *"slaves into his sitting-room"*: Parsons, *Memoir of Theophilus Parsons*, p. 2.

76 *"of pure African descent"*: Ibid., p. 17.

77 *"It was not merely"*: Ibid., p. 18.

78 *"the ex-deacon"*: Ibid., p. 17.

80 *"I give unto"*: Reverend William Smith, 9/30/1783. *AFC* 5, 247.

81 *"I gave them"*: AA/JA, 2/11/1784. *AFC* 5, 303.

81 *"I have determined"*: Ibid.

82 *"keeps [your house] in nice order"*: Mary Smith Cranch/AA, 8/7/1784. AFC 5, 420.

82 *"How does Pheby"*: AA/Mary Smith Cranch, 9/11/1785. *AFC* 6, 359.

82 *"Abdy and Phebe"*: Mary Smith Cranch/AA, 11/26/1786. *AFC* 7, 400.

83 *"I had rather"*: AA/Mary Smith Cranch, 3/12/1791. *AFC* 9, 201.

83 *"I have been much"*: AA/JA, 2/13/1797. *AFC* 11, 561–562.

83–84 *"heard no objection . . . the subject"*: Ibid.

85 *"the Rights of Britons"*: Entry of 1/2/1766, in John Adams, *Diary and Autobiography of John Adams*, ed. L. H. Butterfield (Cambridge: Harvard University Press, 1966), vol. 1, p. 285.

85 *"I wish most sincerely"*: AA/JA, 9/22/1774. AFC 1, 162.

87 *"If it is debated"*: 7/30/1776, in Adams, *Diary and Autobiography of John Adams*, vol. 2, p. 246.

87 *"the Manners of Maryland"*: 2/23/1777, ibid., vol. 2, p. 261.

88 *"Having had a full"*: AA/JA, 5/23/1794. *AFC* 10, 188, 54–55.

88–89 *"the practice of slavery . . . common Sort"*: JA/George Churchman and Jacob Lindley, 1/24/1801, Gilder Lehrman Collection, GLC0092, www.gilderlehrman.org.

89 *"and terrifyed him"*: JS/AA, 7/7/1774. *AFC* 1, 131.

90 *"his Estate"*: Ibid., 132–134n1.

91 *"Mrs. King"*: Robert Ernst, *Rufus King, American Federalist* (Chapel Hill: University of North Carolina Press, 1968), p. 11.

91 *"I am engaged"*: JA/AA, 7/7/1774. *AFC* 1, 131; JA's minutes for his 1773 brief on behalf of King are in APM reel 185.

92 *"These private Mobs"*: Ibid.
93 *"I feel myself"*: *DJQA*, 4/2/1803.
94 *"real and haughty"*: AA/JA, 5/10/1794. *AFC* 10, 169.
95 *"whether it will ever"*: JQA/Rufus King, 7/8/1803, APM.
98 *"the great fish"*: AA/Cotton Tufts, 12/18/1791. *AFC* 9, 247.
101 *"that a dissolution"*: JQA/Charles Adams, 6/9/1796. *AFC* 11, 311.
101 *"all my hopes"*: Ibid.
102 *"much as I must"*: Ibid.
103 *"If the negro keepers"*: JQA/William Vans Murray, 8/14/1798, *WJQA* 2, 349–350.
103 *"attempt to arm"*: JQA/William Vans Murray, 3/30/1799. *WJQA* 2, 398–400.
103 *"an appeal to arms"*: Ibid.
103 *"between the Ancient"*: Ibid.
104 *"to avoid the supposition"*: JQA/Thomas Boylston Adams, 12/30/1800. *WJQA* 2, 490–491.
104 *"to dissolve the Union"*: JQA/William Vans Murray, 4/7/1801. *WJQA* 2, 527.
104 *"if this bill passes"*: Brown, *The Constitutional History of the Louisiana Purchase, 1803–1812*, pp. 183–186.
104 *"There is a darkness"*: AA/Thomas Boylston Adams, 2/28/1802. APM.
105 *"Two centuries have"*: JQA, *An Oration, Delivered at Plymouth, December 22, 1802, at the Anniversary of the First Landing of Our Ancestors* (Boston: Russell and Cutler, 1802).
106 *Haiti*: See Henry Adams, *History of the United States of America During the Administrations of Thomas* Jefferson (New York: Charles Scribner's Sons, 1890); Tom Matthewson, "Jefferson and the Non-Recognition of Haiti," *Proceedings of the American Philosophical Society* 40, no. 1 (March 1996); Don F. Fehrenbacher, *The Slaveholding Republic: An Account of the United States Government's Relations to Slavery* (New York: Oxford University Press, 2001), pp. 11–118; Laurent Dubois, *Avengers of the New World: The Story of the Haitian Revolution* (Cambridge, Mass.: Harvard University Press, 2004); Gordon S. Brown, *Toussaint's Clause: The Founding Fathers and the Haitian Revolution* (Jackson: University Press of Missouri, 2005); Edward Bartlett Rugemer, *The Problem of Emancipation:*

The Caribbean Roots of the American Civil War (Baton Rouge: Louisiana State University Press, 2008); Susan Buck-Morss, *Hegel, Haiti, and Universal History* (Pittsburgh, Pa.: University of Pittsburgh Press, 2009); Matthew J. Clavin, *Toussaint Louverture and the American Civil War: The Promise and Peril of a Second Haitian Revolution* (Philadelphia: University of Pennsylvania Press, 2010); Philip K. Abbott, "United States–Haitian Relations from 1791 to 1810: How Slavery and Commerce Shaped American Foreign Policy," *Small Wars Journals* (May 2011); Gerald Horne, *Confronting Black Jacobins: The United States, the Haitian Revolution, and the Origins of the Dominican Republic* (New York: Monthly Review Press, 2015); Ronald Angelo Johnson, *Diplomacy in Black and White: John Adams, Toussaint Louverture, and Their Atlantic World Alliance* (Athens: University of Georgia Press, 2014); Marlene L. Daut, *Tropics of Haiti: Race and the Literary Revolution in the Atlantic World, 1789–1865* (Liverpool: Liverpool University Press, 2015); Phillipe Girard, *Toussaint Louverture: A Revolutionary Life* (New York: Basic Books, 2016).

109 *"I knew as well"*: Brown, *The Constitutional History of the Louisiana Purchase, 1803–1812*, p. 31.

110 *"consistently with"*: Ibid., pp. 30–31.

111 *"The real reason"*: *DJQA* 1, 293. 1/31/1804; Brown, *The Constitutional History of the Louisiana Purchase, 1803–1812*, p. 120.

111 *"a field of blood"*: *Columbian Centinel*, 7/2/1803. See George William Van Cleve, *A Slaveholder's Union: Slavery, Politics, and the Constitution in the Early American Republic* (Chicago: University of Chicago Press, 2010).

112 *direct taxes*: See Robin L. Einhorn, *American Taxation, American Slavery* (Chicago: University of Chicago Press, 2006).

112 *"Every planter"*: Publius Valerius [John Quincy Adams], "Serious Reflections, Addressed to the Citizens of Massachusetts," *Repertory*, no. 4, 11/2/1804.

113 *It soon changed its mind*: See Jed Handelsman Shugerman, "The Louisiana Purchase and South Carolina's Reopening of the Slave Trade," *Journal of the Early Republic* 22 (Summer 2002): 263–290.

113 *"The natives"*: *Columbian Centinel*, July 2, 1803.

114 *"It is forming"*: Brown, *The Constitutional History of the Louisiana Purchase, 1803–1812*, pp. 233–234.

Chapter 5: The Distant Goal

118 *"Slavery, unhappily"*: Rufus King, Senate speech, 2/11 and 2/14/1820. See Robert Ernst, *Rufus King, American Federalist* (Chapel Hill: University of North Carolina Press, 1968), pp. 369–375. For the full text, https://www.gilderlehrman.org/history-by-era/slavery-and-anti-slavery/resources/founding-father-missouri-compromise-1819.

120 *"Freedom and slavery"*: Rufus King, Senate speech, 2/11 and 2/14/1820.

120 *"exceedingly valuable"*: *CW* 3, 550. 9/6/1860.

120 *the "son of* the *Rufus King"*: *CW* 6, 149. 3/25/1863.

120 *"His manner is dignified"*: *DJQA* 4, 522. 2/11/1820.

121 *"I heard him"*: *DJQA* 4, 533. 2/20/1820.

121 *"With the exception"*: *DJQA* 4, 502. 1/16/1820.

121 *"more upon"*: *DJQA* 4, 528–533. 2/20/1820.

121 *"A dissolution"*: Ibid.

122 *"the North and East"*: *DJQA* 5, 53. 1/31/1820.

122 *"I believed it now"*: Ibid., 53–54.

124 *"that a coupling"*: James Madison/James Monroe, 2/10/1820. James Monroe Papers, Series 1, General Correspondence, Reel 19, Library of Congress, Washington, D.C.

124 *"It would be better"*: James Monroe, 2/13/1820.

124 *"to proscribe slavery"*: *DJQA* 4, 528–531. 2/23/1820.

124 *"by a vote of ninety"*: *DJQA* 5, 3. 3/1/1820.

125 *"King is ready"*: Thomas Jefferson/James Monroe, 3/31/1820. James Monroe Papers, Series 1, General Correspondence, 1758–1839, Reel 7, Library of Congress, Washington, D.C.

125 *"is one of the men"*: *DJQA* 5, 38. 3/25/1820.

125 *"be permitted in Missouri"*: Rufus King, Senate speech, 2/14/1820.

126 *"The discussion of this"*: *DJQA* 5, 3–15. 3/1/1820.

126 *"Missouri question"*: Ibid., 12.

126 *"And so it is"*: Ibid., 3–15.

126 *"I consider myself"*: Rufus King/John Alsop King, 3/4/1820, in *The Life and Correspondence of Rufus King*, ed. Charles R. King, vol. 6 (1816–1827) (New York: G.P. Putnam's Sons, 1900), p. 289.

127 *"It shall be . . . the duty"*: Missouri State Constitution (1820), Article 3, Section 26.

127 *"The Citizens of each State"*: Constitution of the United States, Article 4, Section 2.

127 *"Full Faith and Credit"*: Ibid., Section 1.

128 *"Missouri question"*: DJQA 5, 3–15. 3/1/1820.

128 *"The article in"*: DJQA 5, 208–211. 11/29/1820.

129 *"Upon the Missouri question"*: DJQA 5, 206–207. 11/25/1820.

130 *"So polluted are"*: DJQA 5, 3–15, 3/1/1820

130 *"perverts human reason"*: Ibid.

130 *"since the Missouri debate"*: DJQA 5, 67–69. 4/13/1820.

133 *"Often for amusement"*: HI, p. 43.

137 *"through my whole life"*: JA/Robert J. Evans, 6/8/1819. APM.

142 *"at the head of"*: AA/JA, 2/10/1795. AFC 11, p. 23.

142 *"slaves guilty"*: Thomas Jefferson/Rufus King, 7/13/1802, Founders Online, foundersarchives.gov.

143 *"The course of things"*: Ibid.

143 *"Can the people"*: Fehrenbacher, *The Slaveholding Republic*, p. 116.

144 *"pause in their mad"*: Henry Clay, "On Abolition Petitions," U.S. Senate, 12/7/1839 (Boston: James Munroe and Company, 1839).

145 *"all the opponents"*: CW 1, 146. 2/27/1839.

147 *"proclaim to the world"*: Michael Burlingame, *Abraham Lincoln: A Life* (Baltimore, Md.: Johns Hopkins University Press, 2008), vol. 1, 148.

148 *"Slavery is undoubtedly"*: Henry Clay/John Switzer, n.d., 1831, Gilder Lehrman Institute. Digital History, ID 323, http://www.digitalhistory.uh.edu/disp_textbook.cfm?smtID=3&psid=323.

148 *"It can only be justified"*: Ibid.

148 *"Congress has no power"*: Ibid.

151 *"The first are those"*: Ibid.

152 *"I am, Mr. President"*: Ibid.

Chapter 6: The African Mirage

153 *"a consummate hypocrite"*: Douglas R. Egerton, *Charles Fenton Mercer and the Trials of National Conservatism* (Jackson: University Press of Mississippi, 1989), pp. 105–106; Lacy K. Ford, *Deliver Us from Evil: The Slavery Question in the Old South* (New York: Oxford University Press, 2009), pp. 70–73.

153 *Philip Doddridge*: See W. T. Willey, *A Sketch of the Life of Philip Doddridge* (Morgantown, W. Va.: Morgan and Hoffman, 1875).

159 *American Colonization Society*: See P. J. Staudenraus, *The African Colonization Movement, 1816–1865* (New York: Columbia University Press, 1961); Douglas R. Egerton, "Averting a Crisis: The Proslavery Critique of the American Colonization Society," *Civil War History* 43, no. 2 (June 1977): 142–156; Douglas R. Egerton, "'Its Origin Is Not a Little Curious': A New Look at the American Colonization Society," *Journal of the Early Republic* 5 (Winter 1985): 463–480; Michael Vorenberg, "Abraham Lincoln and the Politics of Black Colonization," *Journal of the Abraham Lincoln Association* 14 (Summer 1993): 22–45; Phillip Shaw Paludan, "Lincoln and Colonization: Policy of Propaganda," *Journal of the Abraham Lincoln Association* 25 (Summer 2004): 23–37; Eric Burin, *Slavery and the Peculiar Solution: A History of the American Colonization Society* (Gainesville: University Press of Florida, 2005); Phillip W. Magness and Sebastian N. Page, *Colonization After Emancipation: Lincoln and the Movement for Black Resettlement* (Columbia: University of Missouri Press, 2011).

160 *"on the coast of Africa"*: Thomas Jefferson/Dr. Thomas Humphreys, 2/5/1817, in *The Works of Thomas Jefferson, Federal Edition*, ed. Paul Leicester Ford (New York: G.P. Putnam's Sons, 1904–1905), vol. 12.

161 *"No symptoms"*: Ibid.

164 *"Sale of African Slaves"*: See www.archives.gov/files/atlanta/finding-aids/african-slave-trade.pdf and www.archives.gov/research/african-americans/slavery-records-civil.html.

164 *"make such regulations"*: Egerton, *Charles Fenton Mercer*, pp. 164–169; Charles Fenton Mercer, *An Address to the American Colonization Society at Their 36th Annual Meeting in the City of Washington on the 18th of January 1853* (Geneva: F. Ramboz and Co., 1854); Eric Burin, "The Slave Trade Act of 1819: A New Look at Colonization and the Politics of Slavery," *American Nineteenth Century History* 13, no. 1 (2012): 1–14.

165 *"a territory on the coast"*: DJQA 4, 291–292. 3/12/1819.

165 *"I thought it impossible"*: Ibid.

165 *"This project"*: Ibid.

166 *"been recommended"*: Ibid.

167 *"it was soon settled"*: Ibid.

167 *"bitterly repented"*: *DJQA* 4, 364. 4/29/1819.

167 *"their project of expurgating"*: Ibid.

167 *"that the mass of colored people"*: Ibid.

168 *"ready to make a Colony"*: *DJQA* 4, 475–477. 12/10/1819.

168 *"indefatigable in their efforts"*: Ibid.

168 *"objected that there"*: Ibid.

168 *"a land so beautiful"*: *SJ*, 3/15/1832.

169 *"Colonize the blacks"*: WP, p. 546.

169 *"Tax us today"*: Drew Gilpin Faust, *James Henry Hammond and the Old South: A Design for Mastery* (Baton Rouge: Louisiana State University Press, 1982), pp. 147–148.

169 *"I freely gave"*: *DJQA* 9, 11/30/1837. APM, 437.

170 *"the purpose of the Society"*: Henry Clay, 1/20/1827, *Speech of the Hon. Henry Clay, Before the American Colonization Society: in the Hall of the House of Representatives, January 20, 1827: with an Appendix, Containing the Documents Therein Referred To* (Washington, D.C., 1827).

171 *"There is a moral fitness"*: Ibid.

172 *"us in the free states"*: *CW* 1, 349. 10/3/1845.

174 *"It is the victory"*: *DJQA* 12, 103. 11/8/1844.

175 *"violent riot"*: William S. Lincoln, *Alton Trials* (New York: John F. Trow, 1838), p. 77.

175 *"to teach rebellion"*: Ibid.

177 *"plain, common horse sense"*: John M. Palmer, *The Bench and Bar of Illinois: Historical and Reminiscent* (Chicago: Lewis Publishing Company, 1899), p. 33.

177 *"vain, but just enough"*: Ibid., p. 181.

177 *Linder and Lincoln . . . in each other's company*: Daniel W. Stowell, "Usher the Influence?" *Journal of the Abraham Lincoln Association* 33, no. 2 (Summer 2012): 64–68.

178 Robert Matson: See Charles R. McKirdy, *Lincoln Apostate: The Matson Slave Case* (Jacksonville: University of Mississippi Press, 2011).

181 *"It is considered"*: *CW* 1, 395. 6/24/1847.

182 *Judge David Davis*: William D. Bader and Frank J. Williams, "David Davis: Lawyer, Judge, and Politician in the Age of Lincoln," *Roger Williams University Law Review* 14, no. 2 (2009): 163–214.

182 *the free Negro issue*: See Arthur C. Cole, *The Constitutional Debates of 1847* (Springfield: Illinois State Historical Library, 1919); Leon F. Litwack, *North of Slavery: The Negro in the Free States, 1790–1860* (Chicago: University of Chicago Press, 1961); Eugene H. Berwanger, *The Frontier Against Slavery: Western Anti-Negro Prejudice and the Slavery Extension Controversy* (Urbana: University of Illinois Press, 1967); James Oliver Horton and Lois E. Horton, *In Hope of Liberty: Culture, Community, and Protest Among Northern Free Blacks, 1700–1860* (New York: Oxford University Press, 1997); James Simeone, *Democracy and Slavery in Frontier Illinois* (Carbondale: Southern Illinois University Press, 2000); Richard E. Hart, *Lincoln's Springfield: The Early African American Population of Springfield, Illinois (1818–1861)* (Springfield, Ill.: Spring Creek Series, 2008); Darrel Dexter, *Bondage in Egypt* (Cape Girardeau, M.O., 2011); Christopher P. Lehman, *Slavery in the Upper Mississippi Valley, 1787–1865* (Jefferson, N.C.: McFarland, 2011); Paul Finkelman, *Slavery and the Founders: Race and Liberty in the Age of Jefferson*, 3rd ed., chap. 3: "Evading the Ordinance: The Persistence of Bondage in Indiana and Illinois" (Armonk, N.Y.: M. Sharpe, 2014); Jerome B. Meites, "The 1847 Illinois Constitutional Convention and Persons of Color," *Journal of the Illinois State Historical Society* 108, nos. 3–4 (Fall/Winter 2015): 266–295.

182 *"full faith and credit"*: Constitution of the United States, Article 4, Section 1.

183 *"Illinois the only"*: Burlingame, *Abraham Lincoln: A Life*, vol. 1, 104.

184 *Orlando B. Ficklin*: See "Orlando Bell Ficklin and Usher Ferguson Linder," in Coleman, *Abraham Lincoln and Coles County, Illinois*, pp. 112–124; McKirdy, *Lincoln Apostate*, pp. 104–111.

185 *"believed his client"*: Charles S. Zane, "Lincoln as I Knew Him," *Sunset, the Pacific Monthly* 29 (October 1912): 433.

186 *"The hall and every avenue"*: *Niles' National Register*, 1/29/1848.

186 *"Calls were . . . made"*: Ibid.

188 *"I have brought"*: *Speech of Henry Clay, at the Lexington [Ky.] Mass Meeting, 13th November, 1847; Together with the Resolutions Adopted on That Occasion* (New York: G.F. Nesbitt, 1847), p. 3.

189 *"Among the resolutions"*: Ibid., p. 10.

190 "Resolved": Ibid., p. 11.

191 *"We live here"*: Frederick Douglass, "Colonization," *North Star,* 1/26/1849.

192 *"There is too much"*: Rimini, *Henry Clay, Statesman for the Union,* p. 697.

193 *"Go on, then, gentlemen"*: *Niles' National Register,* 1/29/1848.

195 *"The procession"*: *Illinois Daily Journal,* 7/9/1852.

195 *"teaches that in this country"*: *CW* 2, 124. 7/6/1852.

195 *"By some judicious"*: Ibid.,129.

196 *"He ever was"*: Ibid., 130.

197 *"from a speech"*: Ibid., 131.

198 *"is a moral fitness"*: Ibid., 132.

Chapter 7: The Constitutional Rag

199 *"elegant and happily"*: *DCFA,* 3/12/1848. APM; *Salem Gazette,* 3/14/1848, p. 3.

200 *"to the Adams mansion"*: *Salem Gazette,* 3/14/1848, p. 3.

200 *"visible through a glass"*: Lynn Hudson Parsons, "The 'Splendid Pageant': Observations on the Death of John Quincy Adams," *New England Quarterly* 53, no. 4 (December 1980): 464–482.

200 *"a splendid pageant"*: James K. Polk, *Diary* (Chicago, A.C. McClurg & Co., 1910), p. 363.

201 *"the coffin . . . covered"*: George Cochrane Henderson, *The National Capitol: Its Architecture, Art, and History* (New York: J.F. Taylor and Company, 1902), p. 227.

201 *"At our first meeting"*: *CW* 1, 475. 6/1/1848.

203 *"It is with much pleasure"*: Joseph Wheelan, *Mr. Adams's Last Crusade: John Quincy Adams's Extraordinary Post-Presidential Life in Congress* (New York: Public Affairs, 2009), p. 245.

203 *"Any people anywhere"*: *CW* 1, 438. 1/12/1848.

204 *"not to go by"*: Ibid., 439.

205 *antislavery activist*: The literature on abolitionism and abolitionists is large and rich. The reader's best resource can be found in the Google listings under the search phrase "bibliographies of abolition and abolitionists." Among the many bibliographies, the most useful are www .digitalhistory.uh.edu/teachers/modules/slavery/topics.html; www .abolition.nypl.org/essays/abolition/13/; www. americanabolitionist

.liberalarts.iupui.edu/signif.html; www.history.ac.uk/ihr/Focus/Slavery/books.html; and www.americanabolitionists.com/bibliography.html.

205 *Theodore Weld*: See Benjamin O. Thomas, *Theodore Weld: Crusader for Freedom* (New Brunswick, N.J.: Rutgers University Press, 1950).

209 *"the heaviest calamity"*: *DJQA* 12, 173. 2/28/1845.

210 *"The Constitution is"*: Ibid., 171.

210 *"sinking from his seat"*: *Journal of the House of Representatives of the United States, 1847–1848*, 2/21/1846.

210 *"gallantry and military skill"*: Ibid.

212 *Shakespearean*: See Michael Anderegg, *Lincoln and Shakespeare* (Lawrence: University Press of Kansas, 2015); Fred Kaplan, *Lincoln: The Biography of a Writer* (New York: HarperCollins, 2008), pp. 124–125, 346–349; and Fred Kaplan, *John Quincy Adams: American Visionary* (New York: HarperCollins, 2014), pp. 316–318, 480–482.

214 *"I have no prejudice"*: *CW* 2, 255. 10/16/1854.

215 *"I surely will not blame"*: Ibid.

216 *"While I was at"*: *CW* 3, 145. 9/18/1858.

216 *"I say upon this occasion"*: Ibid., 146.

217 *"As God made us separate"*: *CW* 2, 498. 6/10/1858.

217 *"ought to be the chief"*: *Diary of John Quincy Adams* (Cambridge, Mass.: Harvard University Press, 1981), vol. 2, pp. 84–86.

219 *"contraband"*: See James Oakes, *Freedom National: The Destruction of Slavery in the United States, 1861–1865* (New York: W.W. Norton, 2013).

219 *"The Character of Desdemona"*: JQA, "The Character of Desdemona." *New England Magazine*, December 1835, repr. in James Hackett, *Notes, Criticism, and Correspondence upon Shakespeare's Plays and Actors* (New York: Carleton, 1863).

220 *"It is to me"*: JA/AA, 3/15/1796. *AFC* 11, 216–217.

221 *"I was last Evening"*: AA/William Stephens Smith, 9/18/1785. *AFC* 11, 216–217.

223 *if "the color of Othello"*: JQA/George Parkman, 12/31/1835. APM.

226 *"You know" he assured him, that "I mean"*: *CW* 1, 453. 2/20/1848.

227 *"Friend Linder"*: Ibid., 457.

228 *"Ten Reasons Why"*: *SJ*, 10/3/1848.

228 *Free Soil Party's candidate*: See Jonathan H. Earle, *Jacksonian Antislavery*

and the Politics of Free Soil, 1824–1854 (Chapel Hill: University of North Carolina Press, 2004).

229 *"I desire," he wrote in 1874, "in these"*: UFL, p. 51.

230 Dred Scott *decision*: See Don E. Fehrenbacher, *The Dred Scott Case: Its Significance in American Law and Politics* (New York: Oxford University Press, 1978); and Austin Allen, *Origins of the Dred Scott Case: Jacksonian Jurisprudence and the Supreme Court, 1837–1857* (Athens: University of Georgia Press, 2006). Three engaging books and one article discuss *Dred Scott* in regard to the nature of constitutions as compromises: Sanford Levinson, *Constitutional Faith* (Princeton, N.J.: Princeton University Press, 1988); Mark A. Graber, *Dred Scott and the Problem of Constitutional Evil* (New York: Cambridge University Press, 2006); Louise Weinberg, "Dred Scott and the Crisis of 1860," *Chicago-Kent Law Review* 82 (December 2006): 97–139; Justin Buckley Dyer, *Natural Law and the Antislavery Constitutional Tradition* (New York: Cambridge University Press, 2012).

232 *"would be in bed"*: UFL, p. 79.

232 *"Some very honest"*: Ibid.

233 *Douglas' popular sovereignty*: See Earle, *Jacksonian Antislavery and the Politics of Free Soil*, pp. 141–142, for evidence that it was Senator Louis Cass, not Douglas, who, in 1848, introduced the phrase and the concept.

234 *"visited our friend Douglas"*: UFL, p. 321.

235 *"We began to feel"*: Ibid.

236 *"I had not been"*: Ibid., p. 325.

236 *"I had no intercourse"*: Ibid., p. 322.

236 *"We tried every expedient"*: Ibid.

237 *William Seward*: For JQA's influence on Seward, see Walter Stahr, *Seward, Lincoln's Indispensable Man* (New York: Simon and Schuster, 2012); and Kaplan, *John Quincy Adams: American Visionary.*

238 *"Your son Dan"*: CW 7, 94. 12/26/1863.

238 *"to gratify . . . the father"*: Coleman, *Abraham Lincoln and Coles County, Illinois*, p. 122.

238 *"utter abhorrence of Abolitionists"*: UFL p. 223.

238 *"a vigorous prosecution"*: Ibid.

239 *"The hotel where we stopped"*: Ibid., pp. 329–330.

Chapter 8: The Ameliorative President

240 *"very quietly"*: *Illinois State Journal*, 7/5/1860.

240 *"He promises very well"*: *CW* 4, 82. 7/4/1860.

240 *"They then marched"*: *Illinois State Journal*, 7/5/1860.

241 *"electric cord"*: *CW* 2, 500. 7/10/1858.

241 *"the same old serpent"*: Ibid.

242 *"That the history"*: *The American Presidency Platforms: Republican Party Platform of 1860*, www.presidency.ucsb.edu/html.

244 *H. Ford Douglas*: See Robert L. Harris, "H. Ford Douglas: Afro-American Antislavery Emigrationist," *Journal of Negro History* 63, no. 3 (July 1977): 217–234; see Matthew Norman, "The Other Lincoln-Douglas Debate: The Race Issue in a Comparative Context," *Journal of the Abraham Lincoln Association* 31, no. 1 (2010): 1–21.

245 *"We, the Republican party"*: Lyman Trumbull, *Illinois State Journal*, 11/21/1860.

245 *"'the preservation'"*: H. Ford Douglas, "Speech at Framingham, July 4, 1860," *Liberator*, July 13. 1860.

245 *"I care nothing about"*: Ibid.

246 *"I know Abraham Lincoln"*: Ibid.

246 *"extreme gratification"*: *CW* 4, p. 184.

247 *"What can I say"*: Douglas, "Speech at Framingham, July 4, 1860."

247 *"What an army"*: Ibid.

249 *"not an abolitionist"*: *WP*, p. 294.

251 *"a menstruous rag"*: *DJQA* 12, 171. 2/19/1845.

251 *"the Slave-hound of Illinois"*: William Phillips, *Liberator*, 6/22/1860, p. 99; *HI*, p. 704.

251 *"is a party of one idea"*: *WP*, p. 302.

252 *"That is his rainbow"*: Ibid.

252 *"Do you believe"*: Ibid.

254 *"The last ten years"*: Ibid., p. 309.

255 *"the Great Question"*: Adam Goodheart, "Silencing the Fanatics," *New York Times*, 12/2/2010.

256 *"Voice: Where's the Union"*: Ibid.

256 *"Only Douglass"*: Ibid.

257 *"Boston is a great city"*: Ibid.

258 *"To-day, and till further notice"*: *Illinois State Journal*, 11/13/1860.

258 *"Father Giddings"*: *CW* 3,105;175. 9/18/1858.

259 *"I am sure"*: Joshua Giddings/AL, 6/19/1860, Abraham Lincoln Papers at the Library of Congress, transcribed and annotated by the Lincoln Studies Center, Knox College, Galesburg, Ill.

259 *"I think the administration"*: Joshua Giddings/AL, 6/19/1860.

260 *"One class of antislavery men"*: Ibid.

261 *"When inaugurated"*: Lyman Trumbull, *Illinois State Journal*, 11/21/1860.

262 *"One Northern Sympathiser"*: Ibid.

263 *"the peaceful extinction"*: *CW* 2, 318. 8/15/1855.

264 *"is even now lunging"*: JQA/William Seward, 5/10/1844. APM.

264 *"dispatches . . . advise us"*: *Illinois State Journal*, 12/10/1860.

265 *"During the last"*: *Illinois State Journal*, 12/4/1860.

265 *"This fountain-head of Tories"*: Ibid.

266 *The suffering Buchanan*: See Philip Klein, *President James Buchanan: A Biography* (University Park: Pennsylvania State University Press, 1962); Jean H. Baker, *James Buchanan* (New York: Henry Holt and Company, 2004); Norman, "The Other Lincoln-Douglas Debate. The Race Issue in a Comparative Context."

268 *"The different sections"*: James Buchanan, 4th Annual Message to Congress, 12/3/1860, American Presidency Project, www. presidency .ucsb.edu.html.

268 *"The immediate peril"*: Ibid.

270 *appeared "calm and collected"*: *Illinois State Journal*, 12/10/1860.

270 *"On motion concerning"*: Ibid.

270 *"We are not enemies"*: *CW* 4, 271. 3/4/1861.

Chapter 9: Soft Inducement

275 *"irrepressible conflict"*: Speech of William Henry Seward, 10/25/1858 (New York, Republican Executive Congressional Committee, 1860).

275 *"a house divided"*: *CW* 2, 461. 12/28/1857.

277 *not slavery but union*: See Charles B. Dew, *Apostles of Disunion: Southern Secession Commissioners and the Causes of the Civil War* (Charlottesville: University of Virginia Press, 2001), for a definitive demonstration of

Lincoln's misunderstanding of the South. John Ashworth's brief "What the North Got Wrong," *New York Times*, 2/21/2012, provides a variant on the multiple misunderstandings on both sides. His *Slavery, Capitalism, and Politics in the Antebellum Republic*, vol. 1: *Commerce and Compromise, 1820–1850* (Cambridge, U.K.: Cambridge University Press, 1995), and vol. 2: *The Coming of the Civil War, 1850–1861* (2007), develop this theme and others in an impressive rethinking from a light Marxist perspective of the larger subject.

277 *"Mr. Buchanan and Mr. Lincoln"*: *New York Times*, 3/5/1861.

278 *"I believe Mr. Lincoln"*: WP, p. 448.

278 *"All civil wars"*: Ibid.

279 *"But you may also"*: Ibid., pp. 382–383.

279 *"In my view"*: Ibid., p. 419.

279 *"Mr. Seward and the South"*: Ibid., p. 354.

280 *"Slave Power"*: See David Brion Davis, *The Slave Power Conspiracy and the Paranoid Style* (Baton Rouge: Louisiana State University Press, 1969); Leonard L. Richards, *The Slave Power: The Free North and Southern Domination* (Baton Rouge: Louisiana State University Press, 2000).

280 *the "first object"*: WP, p. 346.

281 *"Let us have faith"*: *CW* 3, 550. 2/27/1860.

282 *"carried up into"*: *New York Times*, 5/11/1863. See Miriam Foreman-Brunell and Leslie Paris, *The Girls' History and Culture Reader: The Nineteenth Century* (Urbana: University of Illinois Press, 2010), p. 134; Mary Niall Mitchell, *Raising Freedom's Child: Black Children and Visions of the Future After Slavery* (New York: NYU Press, 2010), p. 84.

283 *"the little white slave-girl"*: *New York Times*, 5/11/1863; see William Page Johnson, II, "A Sad Story of Redemption," *Fare Facs Gazette: The Newsletter of Historic Fairfax City* 12, no. 1 (Winter 2015): 4–17; Catherine S. Lawrence, *Autobiography* (Albany, N.Y.: J.B. Lyon, 1896); Mary Niall Mitchell, "Rosebloom and Pure White, or So It Seemed," *American Quarterly* (2002): 369–408; and Mary Niall Mitchell, "The Young White Faces of Slavery," *New York Times*, 1/30/2014.

284 *"I confess"*: Stephen W. Sears, *George McClellan: The Young Napoleon* (New York: Da Capo Press, 1988), p. 116.

286 "Anaconda Plan": James Oakes, *The Scorpion's Sting: Antislavery and the Coming of the Civil War* (New York: W.W. Norton, 2014).

286 *"McClellan is a traitor"*: WP, p. 450.

286–287 *"send ripples of mutiny"*: Allen C. Guelzo, *Lincoln's Emancipation Proclamation: The End of Slavery in America* (New York: Simon and Schuster, 2005), p. 111.

289 *"I never did believe"*: WP, p. 455.

289 *"from fear of the Border States"*: Ibid., p. 460.

292 *"fight slavery with liberty"*: Horace Greeley/AL, 8/19/1862; "The Prayer of the Twenty Millions," *New-York Tribune*, 8/20/1862.

292 *"paramount object"*: *CW* 5, 388. 8/22/1862.

292 *"the constitutional relation"*: Ibid., 434, 436.

296 *"Lincoln had long assumed"*: Guelzo, *Lincoln's Emancipation Proclamation*, p. 102.

296 *"the United States shall"*: Constitution of the United States, Article 4, Section 4.

298 *"Let me remind you"*: WP, p. 437.

300 *"The conflict is between"*: JQA/William Henry Seward, 4/16/1841. APM.

300 *"with the full intent"*: WP, pp. 426–427.

300–301 *"come to the free States"*: JQA, 9/14/1842, *Mr. Adams's Speech, on War with Great Britain, with the Speeches of Mesrs. Wise & Ingersoll, to Which It Is a Reply* (Boston: J.H. Eastburn, 1842).

302 *"The most important"*: JQA/Albert Gallatin, 12/26/1848. APM.

303 *"Military necessity"*: Wendell Phillips, "The State of the Country," Cooper Institute, New York, 1/21/1863 and 5/11/1863; *New York Times*, 5/12/1862, rev. text in WP, pp. 525–562, titled "State of the Union."

304 *"Not even a war-powers"*: Guelzo, *Lincoln's Emancipation Proclamation*, p. 173.

305 *"nagged by the fear"*: Ibid., p. 228.

Chapter 10: The Ultimate Gradualists

307 "Notes on the State": See Douglas L. Wilson, "The Evolution of Jefferson's *Notes on the States of Virginia*," *Virginia Magazine of History and Biography* 112, no. 2 (2004): 98–133.

308 *"curious and interesting"*: CW 3, 376. 4/6/1859.

308 *"changed hands"*: Ibid.

309 *"Let us attend"*: CW 4, 113n1; *Chicago Times and Herald*, 9/4/1860.

310 *"Mr. Lincoln never"*: CW 4, 113n1.

311 *A free black*: See Donald M. Jacobs, ed., *Courage and Conscience: Black and White Abolitionists in Boston* (Bloomington: Indiana University Press, 1993); Peter P. Hinks, *To Awaken My Afflicted Brethren: David Walker and the Problem of Antebellum Slave Resistance* (University Park: Pennsylvania State University Press, 1997).

311 *"I am one"*: *DWA*, pp. 74–75.

312 *"Being a just"*: Ibid., pp. 5, 30.

313 *"This language, perhaps"*: Ibid., pp. 42–43.

313 *"I do not understand"*: CW 3, p. 146. 9/18/1858.

314 *"I would wish"*: *DWA*, p. 11.

314 wretchedness: Ibid., p. 9.

315 *"Do you believe"*: Ibid., p. 52.

315 *"Mr. Jefferson declared"*: Ibid., p. 12.

317 *"In the language"*: CW 3, 542. 2/27/1860.

317 *"Your race"*: CW 5, 371–372. 8/14/1862.

317 *"it is better for us"*: Ibid., 371.

318 *"they would hold"*: Ibid., 375.

319 *"negroes, like other people"*: CW 7, 500. 8/17/1864.

320 *"with a view"*: 1864 Democratic Party platform, 8/29/1864, Presidency.ucsb.edu.185.

322 *Louisiana and Tennessee*: See Louis P. Masur, *Lincoln's Last Speech* (New York: Oxford University Press, 2015).

323 *Hannibal Hamlin*: See Charles E. Hamlin, *The Life and Times of Hannibal Hamlin* (Cambridge: Riverside Press, 1899); H. Draper Hunt, *Hannibal Hamlin of Maine, Lincoln's First Vice-President* (Syracuse, N.Y.: Syracuse University Press, 1969).

326 *"His Accidency"*: *DJQA* 10, 463–464. 4/16/1841.

327 *"Andy ain't"*: Hans L. Trefousse, *Andrew Johnson: A Biography* (New York: W.W. Norton, 1989), p. 191; Annette Gordon-Reed, *Andrew Johnson* (New York: Henry Holt and Company, 2011), pp. 82–87.

329 *"butchering business"*: CW 7, 112. 1/7/1864.

333 *the Great Emancipator*: See Charles H. Wesley, "Lincoln's Plan for Colonizing the Emancipated Negroes," *Journal of Negro History* 4, no. 1 (January 1919): 8; Earnest Sevier Cox, "Lincoln's Negro Policy," *Barnes Review* (Washington, D.C.), 1938; Richard N. Current, *The Lincoln Nobody Knows* (New York: Hill and Wang, 1958); Benjamin Quarles, *Lincoln and the Negro* (New York: Oxford University Press, 1962); James M. McPherson, *The Struggle for Equality: Abolitionists and the Negro in the Civil War and Reconstruction* (Princeton, N.J.: Princeton University Press, 1964); Winthrop D. Jordan, *White over Black: American Attitudes Toward the Negro, 1550–1812* (Chapel Hill: University of North Carolina Press, 1968); George M. Fredrickson, "A Man but Not a Brother: Abraham Lincoln and Racial Equality," *Journal of Southern History* 41 (1975): 39–58; Don E. Fehrenbacher, "Only His Stepchildren: Lincoln and the Negro," *Civil War History* 20, no. 4 (December 1974): 95–112; Robert Morgan, "The 'Great Emancipator' and the Issue of Race: Abraham Lincoln's Program of Black Resettlement," *Journal of Historical Review* 13, no. 5 (September–October 1993): 4–25; Lerone Bennett Jr., *Forced into Glory: Abraham Lincoln's White Dream* (Chicago: Johnson Publishing Company, 2000); Allen C. Guelzo, "How Abraham Lincoln Lost the Black Vote: Lincoln and Emancipation in the African American Mind," *Journal of the Abraham Lincoln Association* 25, no. 1 (Winter 2004): 1–22; Michael Lind, *What Lincoln Believed: The Values and Convictions of America's Greatest President* (New York: Anchor Books, 2006); Phillip Shaw Paludan, "Lincoln and Negro Slavery: I Haven't Got Time for the Pain," *Journal of the Abraham Lincoln Association* 27, no. 2 (2006): 1–23; Brian R. Dirck, ed., *Lincoln Emancipated: The President and the Politics of Race* (DeKalb: Northern Illinois University Press, 2007); Thomas L. Krannawitter, *Vindicating Lincoln: Defending the Politics of Our Greatest President* (Lanham, Md.: Rowman and Littlefield, 2008); George M. Fredrickson, *Big Enough to Be Inconsistent: Abraham Lincoln Confronts Slavery and Race* (Cambridge, Mass.: Harvard University Press, 2008); *Lincoln on Race and Slavery*, ed. Henry Louis Gates Jr. (Princeton, N.J.: Princeton University Press, 2009); Michael Burkhimer, review of George M. Fredrickson, *Big Enough to Be Inconsistent: Abraham Lincoln Confronts Slavery and Race*, in *Journal of the Abraham Lincoln Association* 30, no. 2 (2009): 86–93; Paul

D. Escott, *"What Shall We Do with the Negro?" Lincoln, White Racism, and Civil War America* (Charlottesville: University of Virginia Press, 2009); Eric Foner, *The Fiery Trial: Abraham Lincoln and American Slavery* (New York: W.W. Norton, 2010); Brain R. Dirck, *Abraham Lincoln and White America* (Lawrence: University Press of Kansas, 2012); Richard Striner, *Lincoln and Race* (Carbondale: Southern Illinois University Press, 2012); Stephen Kantrowitz, *More Than Freedom: Fighting for Black Citizenship in a White Republic, 1829–1889* (New York: Penguin, 2013); Allen C. Guelzo, review of Phillip W. Magness and Sebastian N. Page, *Colonization After Emancipation: Lincoln and the Movement for Black Resettlement*, in *Journal of the Abraham Lincoln Association* 34, no. 1 (Winter 2013): 78–87; John M. Barr, "Holding Up a Flawed Mirror to the American Soul: Abraham Lincoln in the Writings of Lerone Bennett Jr.," in *Loathing Lincoln: An American Tradition from the Civil War to the Present* (Baton Rouge: Louisiana State University Press, 2014); Allen C. Guelzo, *Redeeming the Great Emancipator* (Cambridge, Mass.: Harvard University Press, 2016).

333 *laid the groundwork*: See James Oakes, *The Radical and the Republican: Frederick Douglass, Abraham Lincoln, and the Triumph of Antislavery Politics* (New York: W.W. Norton, 2008).

INDEX

ABOUT THE AUTHOR

FRED KAPLAN is Distinguished Professor Emeritus of English at Queens College and the Graduate Center of the City University of New York. His books include *Lincoln: The Biography of a Writer,* which was a finalist for the Lincoln Prize; *John Quincy Adams: American Visionary*; and *Thomas Carlyle,* which was a finalist for the National Book Critics Circle Award and the Pulitzer Prize. He is the author of biographies of Charles Dickens, Henry James, Mark Twain, and Gore Vidal. He lives in Boothbay, Maine.

ALSO BY FRED KAPLAN

JOHN QUINCY ADAMS
American Visionary

Available in Paperback and eBook

Fred Kaplan brings into focus the dramatic life of John Quincy Adams and persuasively demonstrates how Adams' inspiring, progressive vision helped shape the course of America. Kaplan examines Adams' myriad sides: the public and private man, the statesman and writer, the wise thinker and passionate advocate, the leading abolitionist and fervent federalist who believed strongly in both individual liberty and the government's role as an engine of progress and prosperity. This sweeping biography makes clear that Adams' leadership, both in and out of the White House, is as much about twenty-first century America as it is about Adams' own time.

"There is much to praise in this extensively researched book. . . . Kaplan is a master historian and biographer." —Carol Berkin, *The Washington Post*

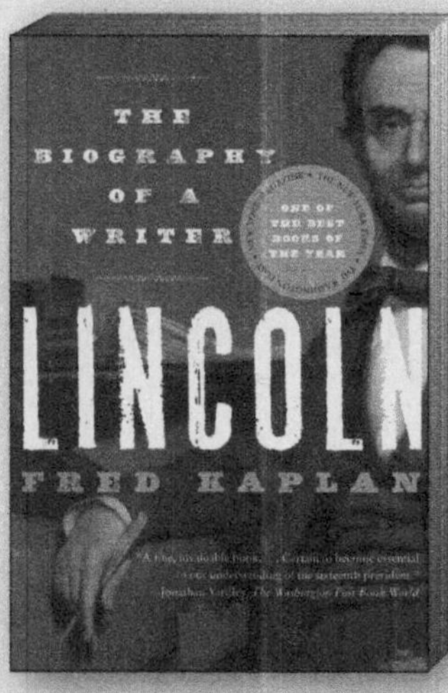

LINCOLN
The Biography of a Writer

Available in Paperback and eBook

For Abraham Lincoln, whether he was composing love letters, speeches, or legal arguments, words mattered. In *Lincoln*, Fred Kaplan explores the life of America's sixteenth president through his use of language both as a vehicle to express complex ideas and feelings and as an instrument of persuasion and empowerment. This unique account of Lincoln's life and career highlights the shortcomings of the modern presidency, reminding us, through Lincoln's legacy and appreciation for language, that the careful and honest use of words is a necessity for successful democracy. Illuminating and engrossing, *Lincoln* brilliantly chronicles Abraham Lincoln's genius with language.

"Fascinating. . . . Persuasive [and] highly perceptive."
—Michiko Kakutani, *The New York Times*